CAMPAIGN FOR PRESIDENT

The Managers Look at '92

CAMPAIGN FOR PRESIDENT

The Managers Look at '92

Edited by

Charles T. Royer
Director, The Institute of Politics
John F. Kennedy School of Government
Harvard University

Hollis Publishing Company

95 Runnells Bridge Road • Hollis, New Hampshire

CONTENTS

THE PARTICIPANTS

Jill Abramson
Reporter
The Wall Street Journal

Elizabeth Arnold
National Political
Correspondent
National Public Radio

Paul Begala
Senior Strategic Consultant
Clinton/Gore Campaign

Charles Black
Consultant
Bush/Quayle Campaign

Ken Bode
Political Analyst
Cable News Network

Richard Bond
Chairman
Republican National Committee

David Broder
Associate Editor and National
Political Correspondent
The Washington Post

Ronald Brown
Chairman
Democratic National
Committee

Bay Buchanan
Campaign Manager
Buchanan for President

Daniel Butler
Northeast Field Coordinator
Brown for President

David Carney
Director of Political Affairs and
National Field Director
Bush/Quayle Campaign

James Carville
Strategic Consultant,
Clinton/Gore Campaign

Tad Devine
Campaign Manager
Kerrey for President

E. J. Dionne
Staff Writer
The Washington Post

Edward Fouhy
Executive Producer
Commission on Presidential
Debates

Mark Gearan
Chief of Staff to Al Gore
Clinton/Gore Campaign

Paul Goldman
Campaign Manager
Wilder for President

Stanley Greenberg
Polling Consultant
Clinton/Gore Campaign

Frank Greer
Media Consultant
Clinton/Gore Campaign

Sharon Holman
Press Secretary
Perot '92 Campaign

Dennis Kanin
Campaign Manager
Tsongas for President

Elizabeth Kolbert
Reporter
The New York Times

William Kristol
Chief of Staff
Office of the Vice President

Thomas Luce
Chairman
Perot Petition Committee

Mary Matalin
Political Director
Bush/Quayle Campaign

Clayton Mulford
General Counsel
Perot Petition Committee and
Perot '92 Campaign

Martin Nolan
Associate Editor
The Boston Globe

Thaleia Tsongas Schlesinger
Consultant
Tsongas for President

William Schneider
Political Analyst
Cable Network News

William Shore
Consultant
Kerrey for President

David Shribman
Political Reporter
The Wall Street Journal

Susan Spencer
White House Correspondent
CBS News

Fred Steeper
Polling Consultant,
Bush/Quayle Campaign

George Stephanopoulos
Communications Director
Clinton/Gore Campaign

Orson Swindle
National Executive Director
United We Stand America

Lorraine Voles
Press Secretary
Harkin for President

David Wilhelm
Campaign Manager
Clinton/Gore Campaign

Betsey Wright
Deputy Campaign Chair
Clinton/Gore Campaign

THE OBSERVERS

Albert Carnesale
Dean
Kennedy School of Government

Francis Bator
Lucius Littauer Professor of
Political Economy
Kennedy School of Government

Margaret Carlson
Deputy Bureau Chief
Washington Bureau
Time

Richard Cavanaugh
Executive Dean
Kennedy School of Government

Charles Campion
Partner
Dewey Square Group

Hale Champion
Pforzheimer Lecturer
in Public Policy
Kennedy School of Government

James Connor
CNN "Special Assignment"

Thomas D'Amore
Managing Director
Bigler/Crossroads

Honorable Rosa DeLauro
U.S. Representative
House of Representatives

Ann Devroy
Staff Reporter
The Washington Post

David Ellwood
Academic Dean
Kennedy School of Government

Elizabeth Eisenstat
Former SAC Member
Harvard University

Daniel Fenn
Teaching Programs/Executive
Programs
Kennedy School of Government

Howard Fineman
Chief Political Reporter
Newsweek

Kate Fruscher
Senior
Harvard College
National Student Coordinator
Clinton/Gore Campaign

Jack Germond
Syndicated Columnist
Baltimore Evening Sun

Joseph Goode
Analyst
Greenberg-Lake

J. Joseph Grandmaison
Former Chair
New Hampshire Democratic
Party

Tony Halmos
Associate Director of Public
Affairs
Hill & Knowlton, Ltd.

Robert J. Healy
Associate Editor
The Boston Globe

Ellen Hume
Senior Fellow & Adjunct
Lecturer
Joan Shorenstein Barone
Center on Press, Politics &
Public Policy
Kennedy School of Government

Maxine Isaacs
Former Institute of Politics
Fellow
Fall 1987

Edward Jesser
President
Jesser & Associates

Marvin Kalb
Edward R. Murrow Professor
of Press & Public Policy &
Director of Joan Shorenstein
Barone Center on the Press,
Politics & Public Policy
Kennedy School of Government

William Kanteres
President
Kanteres Real Estate

Xandra Kayden
Visiting Scholar, Center for
Politics & Policy
Claremont Graduate School

James King
State Director
Office of U.S. Senator John
Kerry

William Kovach
Curator of Nieman Fellowships
Nieman Foundation

Frank Li
Visiting Scholar
Institute of Governmental
Studies
University of California/
Berkeley

Marty Linsky
Chief Secretary to the Governor
Commonwealth of
Massachusetts

Dotty Lynch
Political Editor
CBS News

Erin Martin
CNN "Special Assignments"

John Mashek
Reporter
The Boston Globe

Tom Matthews
Fellow
Institute of Politics, fall 1992

Patricia McGovern
Fellow
Institute of Politics, fall 1992

David McNeeley
Political Editor
*The Austin American-
Statesman*

William Nelson
Fellow
Institute of Politics, fall 1992

Richard Neustadt
Douglas Dillon Professor of
Government Emeritus
Kennedy School of Government

R. Marc Nuttle
Attorney at Law

Thomas Oliphant
Columnist
The Boston Globe

Rod Petrey
President
Governor LeRoy Collins
Center for Public Policy

Barbara Pieper
Fellow
Institute of Politics, fall 1992

Martin Plissner
Political Editor
CBS News

Victoria Radd
Attorney at Law
Williams & Connolly

Alan Rosenthal
Fellow,
Program in Ethics and the
Professions
Kennedy School of
Government

John Sasso
President
Advanced Strategies

John Shattuck
Vice President for Government
Community and Public Affairs
Office of the President
Harvard University

Mike Shea
President
Shea & Associates

Allison Silver
The Los Angeles Times

Carole Simpson
Senior News Correspondent
ABC News

Edward Sims
Chairman
Democratic Party of Georgia

Lisa Smith
Senior Producer
KCTS-TV, Seattle

Robin Toner
National Political
Correspondent
The New York Times

Kenneth Walker
Fellow
Institute of Politics, Fall 1992

Linda Wertheimer
National Public Radio

Michael Whouley
Field Director
Clinton/Gore Campaign

Thomas Winship
Chairman, Center for Foreign
Journalists

Peter Zimmerman
Associate Dean for Teaching
Programs Adjunct Lecturer in
Public Policy
Kennedy School of Government

INTRODUCTION

Every four years since 1972, on the first weekend in December, the principal players and decision makers of the campaign for President of the United States have gathered at Harvard's Institute of Politics to reflect on the campaign and to write this book.

It is very much an insider's book, written as spoken by the insiders of the political parties, the campaigns and the media organizations who cover them. It is a unique book in American politics; basically a verbatim transcript of spirited, off-the-record discussions among players fresh from the contest, moderated by veteran political reporters and analysts. The words, reorganized and edited only slightly, describe in intense and personal terms the strategies and methods of the biggest political campaign of them all.

In 1972, a young Gary Hart, representing George McGovern, sat across the campaign strategists' table from a young Jeb Magruder, spokesman for President Richard Nixon, while political reporter David Broder probed for information.

In 1992, David Broder was back leading a discussion aimed at learning from this campaign lessons which might improve future campaigns and campaign coverage.

One purpose of this book is historical record. Oral history. But mostly it is about the key actors in one political campaign and what they said they did. And what they did in the unique political year 1992 is well worth reading about, learning from, and, if you're a true political junkie, enjoying.

It was the year of Ross Perot, who got in, got out, got in again, confounded the press and the political pros, turned on disenchanted and alienated Republicans, Democrats and Independents, and won almost 20 percent of the popular vote, a record for a third party candidate.

It was a year in which those expected to run opted out, frozen in place by the nearly unprecedented popularity of George Bush, whose 89 percent approval ratings in the polls following the Gulf War made him look virtually unbeatable to nearly everyone except Paul Tsongas. Tsongas' campaign manager described him as the most improbable candidate who ran, "another Greek from Massachusetts with a perceived charisma deficit," who felt America was in economic decline and decided to do something about it.

It was a year that gave new meaning to the phrase "plummeting in the polls," as the President saw his post–Desert Storm approval numbers drop more than 40 points in the last six months of 1991.

And it was a year in which an honest-to-goodness substantive campaign issue was found lurking behind those falling poll numbers; an issue that energized the candidates and went into history as a hand-lettered sign over Clinton strategist James Carville's desk: "It's the Economy, Stupid."

While an unusual campaign year, 1992 did not disappoint those who expect the media always to be controversial high-profile players. Candidates Clinton, Brown, and especially Perot cut new political trails around sometimes frustrated reporters and institutions to take their appeals directly to the people through talk shows and "infomercials." The mainstream press found itself uncomfortably in league with the supermarket tabloids chasing the Gennifer Flowers-Bill Clinton allegations, producing some of the most heated give and take of the conference.

As in past presidential campaign years, the conference ran from Thursday evening, December 3, through Saturday afternoon, December 5. All sessions except for the Friday evening discussion and dinner at the Harvard Faculty Club were held at the John F. Kennedy School.

In a large room overlooking John F. Kennedy Park and the Charles River, 38 participants sat around a table surrounded by 58 observers from the campaigns and media and a number of Institute and Kennedy School faculty, staff and students while court reporters transcribed the then off-the-record proceedings.

The conference opened with representatives from the nine campaigns sharing their early thinking and overall strategy. Friday dealt with both party primaries, with Friday night given over to a discussion of the Ross Perot candidacy. Saturday's sessions covered the conventions, the general election campaign, including the debates, and concluded with some thoughts on what this campaign offered as lessons for 1996.

As always, this conference and this record of the 1992 presidential campaign would not have been possible were it not for the significant gift of time from the participants and observers. Their extraordinary candor makes not only for fascinating reading, but also provides real insight into the stuff of which political campaigns are made: the people who manage them.

The people who manage this conference—the staff and students of the Institute of Politics and of the Kennedy School of Government— must also be acknowledged and thanked. One veteran of several of these conferences said, "This clearly is the best organized of them all. The preparation and background materials, the organization, the facilities, all have been first-rate."

Special thanks to the first-rate staff at the Institute, especially Cathy McLaughlin, Heather Campion, Jo-Anne Wilburn and their organizing committee which included the Kennedy School's "Mr. Politics," Nick Mitropoulos, Steve Singer, and John Ellis, who, along with Roy Wetzel produced the campaign timeline. For their help during the conference, thanks to IOP staffers Nate Gemitti and Kristine Zaleskas, and graduate student Katherine Simshauser. Our gratitude to Victor Burg for reading and editing, to Florence Chien and Sue Wood for editing and word processing, and to Mary Maguire and Fred Lyford at Hollis Publishing.

Charles Royer
January, 1994

CHAPTER ONE

FIRST NIGHT: CAMPAIGN STRATEGIES

"We thought we had a great financial base, the 14,000 Greek contributors to the Dukakis campaign. We were sure that having taken a bite of the apple once, they would be hungry for more. We just did not take into account massive Hellenic burnout."

— Dennis Kanin, Campaign Manager,
Tsongas for President

The Campaign Managers meeting opened on the evening of December 3, 1992, in the Institute of Politics at Harvard University's John F. Kennedy School of Government with Martin Nolan serving as moderator. Nolan, associate editor of the *Boston Globe* and former chief of that newspaper's Washington bureau, had also led the initial session of the Institute of Politics' Campaign Decision Makers conference following the 1988 presidential election.

The Discussion

Marty Nolan: We were thinking of inviting to this conference the spokesmen for all the people who thought about running for president, but didn't. It's very cold in Fenway Park in December which is about the only place we could have had it.

This was a very unusual year. You're going to hear from spokespersons for each of the campaigns and for one campaign's early phase, because it had two phases. We try every time to organize things by having somebody from each campaign answer the question that every politician finds hard to answer: Why are you running? What is this campaign all about?

The next two days will be all about tactics; what happened then, in Iowa, in New Hampshire. And because we have so many people, we have asked them to do it in five minutes or so.

The first Democratic candidate was former Senator Paul Tsongas of Massachusetts. And to represent him is his old pal, law partner, and former chief of staff when he was a congressman and a senator, Dennis Kanin.

Overview of the conference room

Paul Tsongas

Dennis Kanin: About the only thing they can say about me was that I was the campaign manager for the most improbable candidate who ran, first to enter the race, the one who was in the primary season the longest, and the one who was last to be taken seriously. If you think that's an overstatement, 14 weeks before New Hampshire, the Hotline poll of the 50 great experts around the country, many of whom I'm sure are sitting here, rated Tsongas sixth out of six in terms of the likely Democratic nominee. So, why did he do it?

Well, aside from the gonad factor, [laughter], he did it because he felt America was in an economic decline. I'm sure you've all heard this, because the next generation, future generations, were being saddled with enormous debt, because George Bush, and not just George Bush but the Democrats as well, seemed paralyzed and unable to do anything about it. And he also did it because we thought George Bush could be taken. He had been leaving himself incredibly vulnerable on the great looming issue of the '92 cycle, the economy. We thought he could be taken because, unlike Ronald Reagan, he had no real reservoir of deep affection and support in the country, and he didn't do anything to build one up. If you can go *to* 91 percent overnight, you can also plummet *from* 91 percent overnight.

So much for George Bush, but what about our guy? We had a few weaknesses. I think most of you are aware of them: Greek, Massachusetts...out of office for seven years, no name recognition, unusual speech pattern, a perceived charisma deficit, [laughter], which I think ultimately was to his advantage.

So, in light of all this, how did we intend to win the Democratic nomination? Well, first of all, we felt we had a very compelling message, and it was particularly compelling because it came from the mind, experience, and hand of Paul Tsongas himself. That fact, that he committed it to paper in the book that drove everybody crazy during the debates, gave him great authority to talk about the issue that people cared most about in 1991 and 1992 — the economy.

Second, our theory was that 1992 would pick up where 1984 left off, that it would be a continuation of the great battle for the soul of the Democratic party, between the traditional coalition, Mondale-ites — and then Chuck Robb and the new-direction, new-ideas wing with Gary Hart. We thought Paul was in a particularly good position to claim the mantle of the Gary Hart reign in most respects. [Laughter] And we obviously also hoped it would be a different ending.

Third, we thought there was a great advantage in getting in early. We felt that would give us a chance to make our case without getting our head handed to us, a chance to overcome some of the weaknesses we had.

Fourth, the debates. We thought the debates would be our secret weapon, that we would surprise people, that we would prove that Paul Tsongas was no Bruce Babbitt, that we would exceed expectations. And I think that turned out to be the case in the early debates.

Fifth, Paul Tsongas had an inspirational story to tell. We felt that story of courage, of overcoming odds, would be a metaphor for America's own situation, and what America could do.

Sixth, we thought we had a great financial base, the 14,000 Greek contributors to the Dukakis campaign. We were sure that having taken a bite of the apple once, they would be hungry for more. We just did not take into account massive Hellenic burnout. [Laughter]

Seventh, eighth, and ninth, New Hampshire, New Hampshire, New Hampshire. We felt we had real regional advantages in that Paul lived five miles from the New Hampshire border and that it would be easy to move our organization from Lowell, Massachusetts, to New Hampshire. That Paul and Niki Tsongas could travel the state without much problem. The fact that New Hampshire was a major outlet for Boston media.

All of those reasons, we believed, gave us a real advantage. We knew the dangers of being a neighbor. Ed Muskie had learned that in '72. I had learned it running Ted Kennedy's New Hampshire campaign in 1980. But unlike Ed Muskie and Ted Kennedy, we didn't have anything to lose. So we took the downside along with the upside.

The dilemma we faced in New Hampshire was that we knew we could not win New Hampshire just as a regional candidate. You had to prove national credibility and national viability. How we did that without money is something that I'll talk about tomorrow in terms of tactics.

The other thing I'll talk about tomorrow is that in 1991 we did have a state-by-state plan for what happened after New Hampshire, long before Paul announced. But we had to change it about once every two weeks because during 1991, the calendar kept changing — some of you may remember the March California primary. And the candidates kept changing, some of you may remember the six candidates who were going to run in 1992, Rockefeller, Cuomo, Jackson, Gephardt, Gore, and, who's the other one? Bentsen. The six who didn't. So I'll also talk about what our state-by-state strategy was as we got to the end of the year. And I'll also talk tomorrow about my favorite theme, which was the impact of the fact that the press basically dismissed us throughout 1991 in our long-term campaign. Thank you very much.

Marty Nolan, Bay Buchanan

Marty Nolan: The next campaign got under way in September, and it was historic in its own right. Douglas L. Wilder, governor of the Commonwealth of Virginia, is represented here by the man who served as his campaign manager and also as the chairman of the Virginia State Democratic Party, Paul Goldman.

Doug Wilder

Paul Goldman: My friend, Dotty Lynch, tells me that I have to tell the truth. [Laughter] I told her I was a lawyer, and she said, "Well, 'try' to tell the truth." So I'll start with the truth. I bet that the Governor wouldn't get into the race, and then I bet that he wouldn't get out. I don't want to speak for anybody, I'm not going to put any words or any ideas into the Governor's mouth, but I think that I can explain the genesis of it.

I think that there were three forces you had to deal with to run for President. First, there were the real forces, the economy, and other things which are happening, that really determine it. And we thought that the forces were on our side. The deficit would be an issue, we had a record on that; not raising taxes, balancing the budget, and still getting very high rankings in education. We could point to the fact that he had been involved, not just as governor, but as lieutenant governor for 16 years, and had been in a leadership role.

The next was the campaign itself, the forces in the campaign: you have debates, you have things that come up. Iowa did not appear to be a factor because Senator Harkin had it. If New Hampshire was won by a neighbor [Tsongas], that wouldn't necessarily be a factor. That left you the South.

And what struck us was that Super Tuesday had been understated because of what happened in 1988. But, obviously, Super Tuesday would be important; we would have a national base, a real chance. So, the strategy on that point was to get through Super Tuesday and go on to New York, hopefully as one of the three candidates. That was the way we thought the campaign would work out.

And, also it seemed — at least it seemed to me — that the regional force in politics was on our side; that if Cuomo had run, perhaps he would have had a regional argument in the East and in the Midwest. It has always struck me, as a Northerner down South, how the East doesn't react as a region. The South feels very strongly about itself as a region. And if you look at it historically, since World War II, if you look at who the South voted for, they tended to be Southerners. But the North and the Midwest don't have that sense of being left out as much, so that if Tsongas or someone could make the case in the Northeast and do something in the Midwest, that would probably limit us perhaps to a Southern area and a few other areas. But, that not being the case, we thought we could get into the top three and then decide.

If nobody could break through, we felt that, obviously, Clinton had the best chance in putting the Gore and Jackson thing together. With Super Tuesday the way it was, if that happened, we would win fairly easily. But we were the one possibility to change that because the other candidates didn't have much experience in the South and in building the kind of coalition that they would need.

So, it seemed that, tactically, there was an opening there. And when you look at the polling, we were in fairly good shape in some of the Southern states, and with Iowa off the map because of Harkin, and New Hampshire off the map because of Tsongas, well, then, hey, everybody's going down South and we maybe can win our primary. And in the South you can do it without a lot of money. We were running to win, which is why I mentioned the real forces, because I thought we could beat Bush. Historically, by the way, no incumbent in this century has had the kind of fiscal problems that this incumbent had and been able to win. The fact of the matter is, governors have beaten them all the time because governors are the only ones that can make the case: "They're not from Washington." We had some good candidates from the Senate and former Senate, but it was our thinking that they didn't have a chance this time. It just wasn't going to be in the cards for them.

The third force, and I think the one that I've learned to respect more, is the press, because they are a force in the campaign. They say they're not. But they do create forces in politics that the real events aren't creating.

I think, if you look at it in terms of how the strategy developed, you had the 1990 budget deal, you then moved into other economic stuff. And so the Governor had our Committee for Fiscal Responsibility testing the waters in late March, on taxes, on financial issues, the issues that seemed to be real, and also on race relations, partially as a result of David Duke's showing,* which we thought would play. We didn't know we'd have an L.A. riot, but we knew racial tensions would be a big issue. Things looked fairly good in March, and then we ran into the problem with the Governor being bugged** and that's when it started turning against us.

What had gotten us into the race was the tactical sense that real events were on our side and that we could win the campaign. I wish Pat Caddell was here because we talked about it in September when we first thought Governor Clinton would be the competition. We thought that Governor Wilder had the best chance of making it hard for him to pull away from the field. And that was the strategy. The Governor decided not to run, so it never really got tested, but that's what was in our minds at the time. Thank you.

Editor's Note: Duke, former Grand Wizard of the Ku Klux Klan, won 39 percent of the vote in the Louisiana gubernatorial runoff against Edwin Edwards. In December 1991, he announced he would enter the contest for the Republican presidential nomination.

**Editor's Note:* In March 1991 Wilder claimed that Senator Robb had in his possession an illegal tape of Wilder's cellular phone conversations, made in 1986. In July Robb announced the resignations of three of his top aides because of their involvement in recording those conversations.

Marty Nolan: A lot of things begin in the great state of Iowa, the nation's corn crib. You're going to love Lorraine Voles. She has worked for Senator Tom Harkin. She worked for the Dukakis campaign in 1988 in Iowa. And she understands, as Senator Harkin does, the rules of the House and Senate. She'll yield back the balance of her time. She promises that she won't speak any longer than her candidate was in the race. [Laughter]

Tom Harkin

Lorraine Voles: Thank you. With all the journalists in the room, I do feel the need to make a little news and that is that we actually did have a strategy. Tom started talking about the 1992 presidential race minutes after he was elected to the Senate in 1990. He did it in kind of an obscure way, just talked about getting involved, in a general way, in the election, having a role in message development and things like that. And naïve people, like myself, didn't realize that the wheels were churning. And then, soon after the Gulf War, he started talking about himself as a candidate. To be very honest about it, as a staff, we were caught very unaware, and a lot of us weren't thrilled about it, having done two, three, in some cases four, presidentials. We weren't really up for it.

I think what motivated him was that, during his '90 race, he raised over $6 million, which is a lot for a Senate campaign in Iowa. He traveled a lot of this country, and he concluded that George Bush was vulnerable. Democrats thought they were robbed in '88, and Tom believed he had a rallying cry. It was part of the strategy, too, early on when we were testing the waters, which we did from January until September. I still don't know if this was a good thing or a bad thing, but we put him in his kind of crowds, large labor groups, Democratic meetings, and he got a very favorable response, he got great press and, in a way, it was delusionary.

I think he did offer a lot to Democrats. He tried to make people feel good about *being* Democrats. He didn't run away from the term "liberal," he sought to redefine it, and that was his whole shtick, which you've all heard a million times: "If by 'liberal' you mean someone who looks ahead and not behind." And it was successful at that point.

As I said, he was very negative on George Bush early on, which was a blessing to me because he didn't attack any of the other candidates. But he was very positive about the country, and about what he had done. I think that was because he thought Bush was so vulnerable, for several reasons. One, the talk that President Bush really couldn't relate to people on a one-to-one basis. He thought the President was really going wrong spending so much time on foreign policy. All the people around Bush were singing different songs, they weren't on the same message.

So, you can see from all this where our problems might come from. He had a lot to say about George Bush, but not a lot to say about other things later on. We did have a strategy, which we called the catapult strategy. Tom would win Iowa, and we did. Tom would do well in New Hampshire, we could win in New Hampshire, and then, as California moved up, we would catapult from winning those two states to winning California, then Michigan and Illinois. But the basic part was that we just needed to survive Super Tuesday.

Now, whether this was right or wrong, Tom feels some vindication in that strategy because he really felt that Clinton and Gore won the race basically without winning the South. He always carried around with him that Tom Wicker article about where the ducks are. It outlined a strategy for a Democrat winning without winning the South. No one really paid attention to Tom when he was saying that. He was using a general election strategy for the primaries.

We did accomplish some of our early goals as a campaign, which were (1) that Tom be taken seriously as a candidate; (2) that he establish himself in New Hampshire, which up until November he did; and (3) that he shore up his base in Iowa and among labor, and raise money, which he did for a while.

So, Tom believed during the whole primary season — that short little primary season that *we* were in — in serendipity, and he used to think that things happen for a reason. He got in for a reason, so he feels vindicated because of his Southern strategy and because of seeing the vulnerability of George Bush. That was our strategy and it was good while it lasted.

Marty Nolan: If Senator Harkin represented the old-time religion of the Democratic party, his neighbor from Nebraska, Senator Bob Kerrey, was supposed to represent New Age thinking or whatever. Everybody liked Bob Kerrey, but nobody quite knew why he was running or, indeed, who was running the campaign. Tad Devine has a lot of experience. He hunted delegates for Mondale in '84 and Dukakis in '88, and he was the man brought in to do what he could, and on January 2, right?

Bob Kerrey

Tad Devine: Thank you for pointing out that I arrived on January 2. I thought we had agreed to say that I arrived the day after New Hampshire. [Laughter] After I was told I had five to ten minutes to sum up the Kerrey campaign, someone said, "How are you going to fill up all that time?" I thought I would do it by speaking briefly about three things: one is the early problems that we had; second is what we tried to do in New Hampshire and, I think, did successfully in South Dakota; and, third, the reason why this all didn't succeed, at least my perspective on it.

I think early on there were three major problems that the campaign encountered. I can't talk a lot about the decision to enter. As Marty said, I wasn't there, but in that early period after the announcement, between then and the end of the year, I think three things in particular occurred.

The first was high expectations. This was a glamorous candidate who was being measured against an image, which in many ways was larger than life. And he appeared to get out of the box quickly. He raised $200,000 in Lincoln, Nebraska, on the day of his announcement — something that's never happened before — and was actually ahead in a Time Warner poll, published in early October, 21 percent, nationally. But these larger-than-life expectations and this image were perhaps unattainable. It simply was something that he couldn't easily reach, especially in the time period when he was working the kinks out of his campaign. He needed the spring and the summer, and they weren't available to him.

The second problem of the campaign in the early days from the candidate's viewpoint, I think, was a lack of a national perspective. In the early period, 1991, Senator Kerrey hadn't developed the comprehensive yet concise answers on a broad range of issues that you must have in presidential politics if you're going to be accepted as credible by the press and the political community. And he was uncomfortable with the repetitious style of the presidential campaign and some of the nuances, especially of the New Hampshire primary.

Third, and most important, there was a series of bad stories in 1991. The first had to do with the joke on C-SPAN.* I'd tell it to you, but I really don't know what it was. This was a candidate on the defensive. The second problem that arose in mid-December was the story about child labor law violations from his restaurants. It sounded like we were abusing children or something. It sounded pretty bad. Third, and most significant, were stories published at the end of December about a lack of health care coverage for employees in his restaurants. I certainly didn't appreciate, until about a month later, the impact that this had, especially with the electorate in New Hampshire. For a campaign that was trying to make health care a central issue, it was particularly devastating.

These factors led to additional organizational and financial sick calls. Our money began to dry up. Come December through January, the key

---

Editor's Note: At a New Hampshire political event, Kerrey, unaware of the open mike, told Clinton a joke involving lesbians. He later apologized.

fundraising people were particularly frustrated by the campaign's apparent lack of progress. The organization, especially outside of the state campaigns in New Hampshire and South Dakota, just didn't seem to be functioning. There was a lack of strategy, especially in respect to paid media. And in the midst of these problems, Governor Clinton was clearly emerging as the front runner in the race.

The emergence of Governor Clinton and the Kerrey campaign's numerous problems led to the decision to change management. I met with Senator Kerrey on December 18 in New York. He asked me to come in, but I didn't really become the campaign manager until New Year's Day. And during that whole period there was a lot of back and forth about exactly the scope of my responsibility and role. And that wasn't fun.

During that period, from early December to early January, effectively the Kerrey campaign wasn't being managed. This hiatus of leadership was occurring precisely at the point in time when we were taking some of our biggest hits, the child labor hit, the health care hit.

When I got there, I felt I needed to act immediately with three main tasks: The first was the media. The answer to that was: "Go to Doak and Shrum [political consultants]." I thought it would help to have good credibility with the press, with fund-raising, and with the political community. The second was to get a better handle on the money. The third was to develop a more coherent strategy.

Two days after I arrived, Doak and Shrum went to Portsmouth, New Hampshire to talk with Senator Kerrey for the first time about what we wanted to do on television in New Hampshire. Out of that discussion some issues and themes emerged: health care, certainly, where he had a detailed plan; trade, on which he had spoken forcefully in the past; and a bit of biography and background. We felt intense pressure to get on television; we filmed and were ready to pull the trigger any day then — this was early January. We decided on a dual track of trade and health care as the key issues of the campaign, and we launched our first generation of media with an ad about trade, a hockey ad, and a health care ad. They're still talking about the hockey ad. Johnny Apple [R.W. Apple, Jr., of *The New York Times*] did a "Week In Review" piece on Sunday, in which he talked about the hockey ad. The President was returning from Japan, an ill-fated trip. The ad, while it was received well at first, was later criticized, first by our opponents, then by the pundits, and, finally, by the campaign itself.

I just want to say that I respectfully have to disagree with that assessment. I believe that the hockey ad brought us back from the dead. We were really on the verge of collapse. When the ad came out, for the first time in the campaign our opponents began to respond to us. We were out with the trade issue. The Tsongas campaign did a very good ad saying: "Don't blame Japan, the problem is here." We were out with health care. The Clinton campaign showed a very good ad about a young boy who had open heart surgery and the family couldn't afford health insurance. At least we were beginning to drive something, which I think is really what you're supposed to do in a campaign.

Our failure lay not in the hockey ad, which was a convenient scapegoat for a lot of people, but in our inability to advance the argument to another generation, and our failure to deal with the very effective counter punches that our opponents made when we put those messages on the table.

We didn't connect trade to jobs effectively. We didn't talk about Senator Kerrey's commitment to a broader economic renewal. And we didn't aggressively attempt to distinguish his health care plan from his opponents' proposals.

In the end, we lost in part because of the early problems I talked about, the organizational problems. We were blocked by Governor Clinton's emergence, first by his domination of the media at a time when we were just starting and later by the problems of the campaign. The scandals of his campaign made it difficult for us, I think, to break through in terms of free media coverage.

Finally, I think we were caught in what I call "the Catch-22 salience." With all the tracking polls in New Hampshire, we simply couldn't get into play. I think it was epitomized by a guy in a focus group in early February, who liked Kerrey, said good things about Kerrey. The leader of the group said, "Well, you like him, why won't you vote for him?" He said, "Well, I can't vote for him; he's not going to win." So we were depressed in that respect.

By the end of February, I think we were really running a good campaign. And, as proof of that, I would submit the case of South Dakota where our media was together; where we had a good initial wave of media introducing the candidate and talking aggressively about health care, moving to a strong comparative near the end, and to an electability message in the final weekend, where we won 40 percent of the vote in a contested contest. Senator Kerrey was functioning very well, from hopping onto a horse, to working on an Indian reservation, to climbing Mount Rushmore. He was very much at home. It felt a lot like four years ago when we left Iowa with Governor Dukakis. We left Iowa and we landed in New Hampshire. It just felt a lot better to be there.

And I thought the paid media, in particular, was effective. But we were broke. If you look at the FEC [Federal Elections Commission] report at the end of January in 1991, you would see that our campaign had $114,000 cash in hand and $361,000 of debt. We were insolvent. The others were not. And that, I think, as much as anything else, led to the end of our campaign.

I would like to conclude by saying, after we got out of South Dakota, we had a tough decision to make. Would we aggressively take on the candidate who in our mind was the front runner, Governor Clinton? We decided to do that. We felt, if we didn't make a case against him, having absolutely no money — we were a million dollars in debt the day after South Dakota — we would not be able to drive any message, we couldn't have any paid media. We knew, unless we attacked, we wouldn't get coverage from the press. And that's the reality of presidential politics. We tried to make a case against him, a tough case on the draft. We felt, if we didn't make it, Bush would make it later on. And you might as well make it now.

So, we did it. It didn't work, we didn't knock him off his horse, and after the results of the March 3 primaries and caucuses came in, it became clear to us that we needed to pull the plug. We came back and withdrew the next day. Senator Kerrey's withdrawal statement was probably one of the finest speeches that he made during the campaign. We had a very compelling case for fundamental change, which genuinely connected with the people who were there and, I think, the people who saw it.

In the end, I guess it was too little, too late. I do believe, though, that Senator Kerrey really understood the intense desire for real, even radical change that existed and moved the electorate this year. We had a very powerful message and he would have been elected if everybody was ready to listen. And, unfortunately, he had a campaign that was not a very good helper. Thank you.

Marty Nolan: Now, September of 1991 began. There were four Democrats in the race, and they were all long shots. And so was the next candidate to announce, who was the little known governor of Orval Faubus' state, by the name of Bill Clinton. The acronym FOB now has new meaning, [Friend of Bill], and one of the foremost FOBs is also a pollster speaking for Bill Clinton, Stan Greenberg.

Bill Clinton

Stan Greenberg: I'm happy to be here to represent what has turned out to be a fairly motley crew that lived in a war room in Little Rock, Arkansas, for almost six months. Also, for those who were worried the flame has been dampened, another flame has been lit — we have devoted the entire transition to promoting the star of George Stephanopoulos.

I'm not going to talk about New Hampshire. I was asked to talk about the strategic thinking that went on in the early phase of the Clinton campaign. And, I should tell you that the place to start on this is Bill Clinton's head. This is not flattery to the president-elect. It is the reality, for those who managed his campaign, that the starting point was a candidate who had layers and layers of friends and that he had, over the years, drawing on different intellectual traditions and advisors, constantly worked through his ideas about governance and his political career.

He had spent the year prior to running for president touring the country speaking on behalf of the DLC.* If you go back and read the Cleveland DLC speech, which preceded handlers and any of us who were ultimately involved in that campaign, you'll discover how much of this race was thought through by Bill Clinton before it ever began. This was a campaign that evolved out of Bill Clinton's head.

Stan Greenberg, James Carville, David Wilhelm, George Stephanopoulos

He had a vision about a changing America. It was rooted in his try for Congress in 1974 when he ran on a rural-populist platform. It was rooted in the progressive traditions that he experienced going back to Oxford and Yale Law and McGovern days. He has lived the civil rights movement and the struggle that the South had with race relations, which is still part of his consciousness, as it was in the course of the

Editor's Note: The Democratic Leadership Council was formed in 1985 by several prominent Democrats who believed the party needed to move toward the center if it was to capture middle-class voters. Bill Clinton served as chairman of the group in 1991.

campaign. He learned from his loss in the 1980 governor's race. He recognized the arrogance and elitism of the Democratic party and what that said to middle-class voters, something I think he understood earlier than most of the party leadership. It goes back to his years as governor, as an activist governor in a low tax state. And it goes back to the DLC and the focus on reinventing government and coming to terms with populist values. I'm talking about what it means to be a new kind of Democrat.

All of that was going on in Bill Clinton's head, before there was a campaign. I can tell you that the early meetings on the campaign did not center on figuring out a message or strategy. We dealt very quickly with the question of winnability. By July, the polls, some of which were done by the Democratic National Committee and some done jointly with Fred Steeper suggested that George Bush was beatable, and that question was put aside very early.

We did not spend a lot of time focusing on primary opponents. We thought that was basically an unknown. There was some consideration of whether we would stay in if Al Gore ran but there was very little time spent thinking about what the field of candidates would be and what that would mean.

We spent a lot of the time talking about Governor Clinton's pledge not to run for president, to finish out his term. This was something that he was obsessed with; he toured the state and spent an enormous amount of time on it, I think more time on that subject than any other.

In September, we did some initial research in New Hampshire. Interpretations of the results of that research led us into this race. We concluded that the normal assumption that the New Hampshire primary electorate is liberal and that a moderate candidate would not face good prospects was wrong-headed. But, more importantly, voters didn't care about ideology; they did not respond to anything we tested about "a new kind of Democrat"; they did not want to hear about it. There was only one thing they wanted to hear about, just what James Carville made us all remember, *the economy.* This shaped our thinking, as much as anything. In this race, the bread-and-butter issues were all New Hampshire voters wanted to hear about.

We tested and we thought and talked about personal responsibility and such messages. The New Covenant,* I can tell you, was not something New Hampshire voters spent a lot of time thinking about.

Editor's Note: In announcing his candidacy (October 3, 1991), Bill Clinton said, "We need a new covenant to rebuild America." The New Covenant became the theme of his acceptance speech (Madison Square Garden, July 16) — a "solemn agreement between the people and their government, based not simply on what each of us can take but on what all of us must give to our nation."

The third thing we learned was how serious voters were about this election. This election mattered to them; it was important to their lives. And New Hampshire proved it, with a very high turnout. They said to us, in that early research, that they wanted a plan, they wanted specifics, you know, don't go off on tangents. We want to know what you're going to do to change America and get this economy moving. And the seriousness of the voters in New Hampshire was very important to our whole strategy, which centered on our economic plan. There were other things that distracted us later on, but we began to very clearly focus on an economic plan.

In mid-September we had a meeting of the FOBs, broadly defined. It was a fairly extraordinary, bizarre meeting, but it showed Bill Clinton's friends on display. You'll see them, I'm sure, on January 20, but they were on display early on in September. I'm actually surprised that not more of that meeting became public. We talked through how to run; we talked about personal issues. There was a major debate over whether to run very self-consciously as a moderate Southerner, build a base, win big in the base, and then build from there. The dominant faction, however, wanted a middle-class populist candidacy, both in economic terms and value terms.

We believed that we could contest New Hampshire. We hoped to be stuck somewhere back in third place through most of the process, and then make a run on it, for a respectable showing, but we didn't have to win New Hampshire at that point. I know some assumed we were going to win; there were some who thought we wouldn't do very well there at all.

There was a strong aversion to running as a Southern candidate. Gore's experience was very much in our heads — the belief that running as a self-conscious Southern candidate diminished the importance of winning on Super Tuesday; that it was important to run as a national candidate and win elsewhere so that winning on Super Tuesday would become part of a national victory, not become a measure of one's regionality.

The Georgetown speech, I believe, was a very important part of defining this candidacy. It was an idea that Al From [President of the DLC] and Will Marshall [Director, Progressive Policy Institute, DLC] brought to the campaign — to give three major speeches early on. We decided to make it an integrated whole under the rubric of the New Covenant, to do them all at Georgetown, and to do them fast. Because we decided that our advantage in the primary was the fact that we knew why we were running and we believed the others didn't, that we had thought about government, about America's identity, and about democracy in a changing world. That thoughtfulness was a strategic advantage for us at this time, given the seriousness of voters and the seriousness of the problems facing the country.

So, we began with the New Covenant speeches which introduced the concepts of opportunity and responsibility, middle-class populism, welfare reform, and national service. Then Clinton went on to deliver an economic plan and a defense speech and a speech about democracy, all done in the fall. The fact that we had announced in early October and that we gave all those speeches from November into early December, was fairly extraordinary, but it created, I think, a fascination with Clinton's candidacy among the press and the attentive public. Our votes initially came from the best educated and the most liberal Democrats because I think Bill Clinton was seen as the most thoughtful candidate.

As I listened to the other presentations, it struck me that what was important about our strategy was that it had a pre-New Hampshire phase. New Hampshire is obviously very important, and we're going to talk about it tomorrow. But a major part of our campaign is what happened *before* New Hampshire. From the beginning, we were running a national, general election campaign. We decided that the best strategy for winning the Democratic nomination was being a candidate who could capture America and not necessarily a candidate who could win specific primaries.

So we were obviously influenced by what we learned in the research in New Hampshire, but if you look at what we were thinking about, we were focused on the long term. If I think about why it is we ultimately won this election, there isn't a lot that's very different from what we said in the fall and what Bill Clinton said a year prior to that. We focused on the national election. I think that's a good reason why we ultimately won.

Early in January we went to New Hampshire with a TV spot about our economic plan. We talked about middle-class populism and we talked about our plan. We jumped 13 points in a week. The combination of the Cuomo withdrawal and our initial media made us the front runner in New Hampshire. That primary was not, in any sense, the race any of us designed. At least for a period, it looked like nothing that any of us could have imagined, but ultimately, I believe, the race was run the way we set out to do it. The rest is history. James [Carville] came on, got cleaned up, scrambled, and survived.

Marty Nolan: The Bush/Quayle campaign had several political people, spokespeople. One of them, I think, starred as a Midwest coordinator four years ago for the Bush/Quayle campaign. And if you don't recognize her, you don't own a television set. Mary Matalin.

George Bush

Mary Matalin: I did want to say something to the media, something that's been particularly annoying me about the media, since the election, that I want to get off my chest. I want to report that the President is carrying on. I had lunch with him this week, and he is beginning to have a softening of his heart about you guys chastising him. To those of you who have sent him notes, particularly about his mom, he was very touched, and for that we thank you. And we would like to say, we hope that there is no lasting offense from the campaign. Some of the things that he said, you have to admit, were pretty funny — all his supporters sticking you in the back with those little flags. You really did what you had to do, largely professionally, and we had to do what we had to do, meaning assault your character. Speaking of character assassination, to our Clintonese friends, as a gesture of good will before the inauguration, we're turning over Virginia Kelley's passport files. You really did an excellent job, focusing more, and we were particularly proud that you were able to implement all the ideas, tactics, and strategies that you stole from us. We are not masochists. We have not had a fun year. But we come here with no bitterness and no defensiveness and bring congratulations for our opponents, and we come to have civil discussion and to leave more informed. And there will be no philandering, pot-smoking, draft-dodging bimbo. [Laughter]

We're going to spend the whole time talking about strategies. Actually, Dave Carney and I had our own kind of internal strategy that was akin to the primal-scream strategy. Whenever our big strategy failed us, we would resort to our tested and true duck strategy. This is a true story, I'm not making it up. In the general election, I got reassigned to travel full time, and Carney got reassigned to do my old job full time, which I really wasn't doing because I had too many compulsive-obsessive fax attacks. I'm on a plane one day when the White House operator rings in and Carney says, "You've got to stop the President from talking to that chicken. It's on CNN." I'm *not* going to tell him to stop talking to the chicken; he likes the chicken, he looks for the chicken. He then says, "You're not doing your job. You can not have the President of the United States talking to an overgrown chicken."

I *am* doing my job. Right now I'm pasting two covers of the "Agenda for America" speech back to back and upside down so no matter which way he holds it up, the camera will get it right side up. So, Carney and I have devised our own strategy for the chicken-man, to which I think, "Great, that's worth a five-point bounce!" The next morning Carney calls and he says: "We've got a problem." I said, "Oh, something new and different on the Bush campaign." He says, "No, this is serious. [Bob] Teeter just called from Baker's office and they want ducks."

Excuse me, they want ducks? I've got 200 chickens going to Madison, Wisconsin, for Clinton's rally and they want ducks? I said, "They want ducks, you've got chickens, what's behind this?" He says, "No, I'm serious. What am I going to do?" I said: "Well, even if you can get the ducks, what do you do with the chickens?" He said, "Just let them go." I said, "Are you kidding? Clinton will have the ASPCA marching on Washington about violence toward chickens."

You get 100,000 young Republicans with duck calls, you send the 200 chickens, you do your duck calls, you hold up the phone, and Teeter will never know the difference. To this day, Bob Teeter and Jim Baker are patting themselves on the back for fixing the chicken-man problem. Near the end of the campaign, whenever we were particularly racked with a problem with Teeter, we would simply duck call.

All right, strategy. That's a good story because this year was nothing if not wacky, and that was not an unrepresentative day on the campaign. But we actually did have a strategy. It was complicated and sophisticated. It was very simple. It was long-lived, and it actually was laid out, sketched out, with some definition at Camp David in August of 1991, and we did repeatedly try to come back to it. And we're happy to dwell on a lot of reasons and maybe mistakes we made that we couldn't dwell on then. Because I'm quite sure our gracious opponents are not going to want to dwell on that, are they?

Contrary to conventional wisdom at the time, we did not ever plan or think that we were going to run on the laurels of the Persian Gulf War. We knew that this election was going to be on the economy and domestic affairs, but we thought it was quite legitimate to launch from our foreign policy achievements. We wanted to make the connection that the leadership required for foreign policy achievements is transferable to domestic problems, and make the case that foreign policy successes abroad meant economic prosperity at home. Through foreign policy achievements, new democracies, new markets, expanded trade, expanded exports, you get jobs, jobs, jobs in America.

There was a legitimate and quite good argument to make about exports: we are the world's number one exporter, which is obviously crucial to growth in our economy. This strategy was based on three assumptions: (1) that there was an electorate awareness of our domestic policies and some of our past achievements; (2) that the President would get credit for foreign policy achievements, and (3) there would be an economic recovery.

Even before we got out of the box, some of these assumptions were undercut by problems endemic to the institution of the presidency and endemic maybe to an incumbent, but exacerbated, I think, in our case. The first one, which undercut electorate awareness of a domestic agenda, domestic accomplishments, was — and I now speak for myself, I don't want to incriminate anyone by my comments here — that there was a structure devised at the White House that was not as effective as it could have been in communicating. Again, the political communications apparatus. They consistently, in the three years preceding the campaign, separated government and politics. You just cannot do that. As you've all been reading, Clinton is going out of his way to make sure that there is a connection between government and politics. We, or they — we're all one entity — did not do that. That did not necessarily help the political environment.

So, one of the most striking pieces of data to me — which I carried around for a long time because I just couldn't believe it — was when we kicked loose the domestic policy accomplishments of the Bush administration: ADA [Americans with Disabilities Act], The Civil Rights Act, the Clean Air Act, Surface Transportation Act, on and on, our numbers moved 14 points. That was great news. The bad news was, nobody knew we had done them, and no one believed that we had done them. That is not something that a campaign can easily overcome.

I also think, and this is my personal opinion, that even before we launched, we had a hole punched in our assumption of foreign policy excellence by, frankly, Governor Sununu blowing the Japan trip.* That, in conjunction with going into the first of the year with the worst right track-wrong track, the worst job-approval rating, and an economic environment which some of the others have alluded to, was not a propitious beginning. Another assumption was undercut by the perception that the economy could not recover. It was particularly and uniquely a bad recession for us because it hit white-collar workers; it hit segments of our constituencies that hadn't been hit before. It hit key states like California. Take California out of the mix and you have a long haul ahead. And finally, even with all of that, with the wind in our face, we assumed that we could right ourselves between the State of the Union and the end of the Democratic primaries. Presuming what we perceived as a relatively weak field, they would be killing each other for the next three months, and we assumed that we could right ourselves from that period.

Still another factor that persisted was unanticipated negative events. The very first devastating blow was our own primary, which got us off our message and helped lay the groundwork for the Democrats to just come back in and pick up after the primaries were over. Quickly following on the heels of the primary, we had the problem with Ross Perot being in and he was also reinforcing our negatives. Then, right after that, we had the L.A. riots. Then we had Perot getting out, which

---

Editor's Note: See Campaign Calendar Highlights for Jan. 8, 1992.

catapulted Governor Clinton from a third-place free fall going into the convention and into first place coming out.

Then, of course, we had our own convention, which we'll discuss this weekend. And then, you know, on and on it went. It was a snakebite kind of year ending with the Lawrence Walsh memo* on the Friday preceding election day. So, we're not a campaign without flaws, and I think you'll have to admit that we recovered some. But external forces that you cannot anticipate in laying your strategy prevented us from staying on our message.

We will talk at this conference about some of the good things that we did, but I think that our predominant conclusion is one that has already been mentioned by most of the Democrats, that no incumbent has ever won with negatives in the right track-wrong track, job approval, and the economic environment. Charles Black will talk more about some of those economic factors this weekend. I think that if we could have done 300 things differently, we could have done 300 things better — maybe three would have made the difference. Presidential elections are about peace and prosperity and having largely achieved peace, there's even more focus on the prosperity, which was not our best issue.

As a concluding point, something that I think was sort of cosmically against us, is something Lee Atwater said in '88. He thought our biggest enemy was history, the rhythms of history, in that there is a cyclical and reliable compulsion by the electorate to just want change. And the Clinton campaign, starting with the candidate, understood that from the beginning; never forgot it; never got off of it. In their worst days, they always came back to that.

Again, for an extraordinary campaign, we applaud you and we now look forward to you-all fulfilling those promises, except for raising our taxes.

Marty Nolan: There were several unusual campaigns this year and one that was very unusual — I refer to the third, but perhaps not final, campaign of Edmund G. Brown, Junior, a/k/a Jerry. Pat Caddell, of course, is somewhere in the ozone. I talked to Pat about his role in the Brown campaign yesterday, and I said, "Your title, exactly what? Informal advisor?" He said, "Well, that's a little too specific." That post-linear lingo never went over big. So, we have a real hero here, a student, a mid-career student at the Kennedy School. Give a 1-800 welcome to Dan Butler.

Editor's Note: In late October 1991, press attention focused on an excerpt from notes written in 1986 by then-Defense Secretary Caspar Weinberger indicating that then Vice President Bush was aware of and supported the Reagan administration's arms-for-hostages strategy. Bush has always claimed that he was "out of the loop" on Iran-Contra. Weinberger was indicted and then pardoned by Bush.

Jerry Brown

Dan Butler: Thank you. I just found out that Pat Caddell couldn't make it here — about thirty minutes before the dinner — so I didn't come terribly well prepared, but that should come as no surprise to anybody who watched the Brown campaign. And I wish I had known ahead of time. I would have gone home and dressed appropriately, I apologize for that. I would have worn my turtleneck. [Laughter]

I'm glad that the topic tonight was on strategy. I think I can talk a little bit about that. I worked as deputy campaign coordinator for the Northeast. I directed the Connecticut primary campaign, and I was Governor Brown's driver when he was up in New England. So, I did hear a few tidbits and snatches of strategy. I'm glad we're not talking about organization because I think [Brown advisor] Jacques Barzaghi said it best, "Our organization transcends understanding."

As far as our strategy goes, I think it's fair to summarize it and say that we did run a very unconventional, some would say revolutionary or innovative or creative, campaign. I would say it was cheap. Especially up here in New England. We did not have very much in the way of resources.

Governor Brown ran this race because he wanted to emphasize quite a few things, and I think he made his point. First, campaign finance reform. He did innovate in that he, as a presidential candidate, refused to accept any campaign contributions in excess of $100, and that surprised a lot of people. It also surprised a lot of people that we survived financially all the way to the convention. The 1-800 number, 1-800-426-1112, was an innovation that was adopted by other campaigns, as you saw during the close of the presidential season.

We did almost no TV advertising, at least during the early phases of the campaign. What we did do was a 30-minute infomercial which you might have caught if you were up at 3:00 in the morning watching Channel 84. We really didn't have much money. We were running a mean, lean, low-to-the-ground campaign.

Governor Brown also innovated the use of talk radio. The other candidates, particularly Mr. Perot, got credit for doing talk shows, but actually Chris Black [political writer, *Boston Globe*] was here in Boston for Jerry Brown's first visit in September, I think it was, or when the Governor was on the Jerry Williams show, WRKO, which is well listened to here in the Boston metropolitan area. I tried to talk the Governor out of doing Jerry Williams, but he insisted, and it turned out to be a brilliant stroke. He made frequent appearances not just on Jerry Williams but on a lot of talk shows. And for a lean, mean, low-to-the-ground campaign, that was a very cheap way to get the message out.

The Brown campaign was very grassroots, there's no question about it. This campaign was run on the backs of amateurs, but very, very devoted and dedicated amateurs.

Those of you in the press who covered it probably saw the messianic fervor of the Brownies, or the Brown Democrats. They were amateurs — something that Governor Brown insisted on. In fact, a small group of people in New Hampshire gathered around him one day and insisted that he bring in some pros to help us because they didn't feel we were up to the task, and he refused. He wanted us to learn from our mistakes, and he wanted us to get better. He was insistent that the campaign be run by average Americans without experience, who weren't paid.

And that reminds me, he also tapped into voter discontent. That was, obviously, one of his foremost thoughts. He knew that the electorate was discontented, and he also believed that George Bush could be beaten.

We ran and organized early in the caucus states. We thought we had an advantage as a grassroots campaign in those states. And we did well in Maine and Vermont. I think Governor Brown was confident that the Perot phenomenon would coalesce around him, that a grassroots following would sweep him into the White House. I think that Governor Brown actually spoke over the heads of most voters whereas Mr. Perot very effectively, in a very folksy fashion, spoke to the voters in language they could understand. I think the message was very similar, almost identical in many cases, but Mr. Perot did a much more effective job of communicating it to the voters.

Our campaign strategy obviously evolved. Probably the biggest turning point in the campaign was when Senator Tsongas dropped out in Connecticut during the heat of the primary battle. The campaign immediately changed gears. Governor Brown spent a lot more time there than originally planned and we spent a bit more money than we had planned. I think we surprised Governor Clinton's team with how well we did and how quickly we captured some of Paul Tsongas's votes. We anticipated that the Connecticut victory would be a big boost, a catapult if you would, as Lorraine suggested. I was in the Navy for ten years before I joined Governor Brown's campaign. When I think of a catapult, I think of jets taking off and going skyward. In this case, we went in the drink.

New York was make it or break it for us and for Governor Clinton and his team and, quite frankly, they beat us. They did a much better job in New York than we did. The things that hurt us there, I think, were strategic errors. One of the biggest strategic errors was that Governor Brown named his vice-presidential choice [Jesse Jackson] early. That was innovative and it was unprecedented, but it definitely hurt in New York. I don't remember the exact figures, but I think 91 percent of the Jewish vote went for either Governor Clinton or for Paul Tsongas; we only got 9 percent of the vote there.

Also, Mayor Koch hurt. He was endorsing Senator Tsongas as a good protest candidate. And protest was a large part of Governor Brown's appeal. He was a vehicle for protest more than anything else. So that hurt.

Another strategic error we made in the campaign was advocating a flat tax. The unadulterated flat tax was very effectively attacked by Citizens for Tax Justice and by the Clinton campaign; their TV ads were very effective and that, I think, spelled the end of the Brown campaign. From there, it was all downhill.

A lot of people talk about strategy all the way to the convention, and I will talk about that very briefly because I think some people had hard feelings about the way Governor Brown operated at the convention, the way his supporters operated. He did have a motive. He wanted to influence the platform, he wanted to foster an open debate.

In summary, I think the Brown campaign strategy stands out as unconventional and innovative. We surprised many of the pundits with the way we were able to carry on a sustained campaign. We were the only other challenger to Governor Clinton that did survive all the way to the convention. And I think Governor Brown was a good sparring partner for Governor Clinton in the primary season. He did inject debate and controversy into the campaign. I think he heightened interest among the electorate and in the long run, I think people will decide that Governor Brown actually did help the Democratic party win in November.

Marty Nolan: Our next speaker has had a lifelong commitment to her candidate, and has learned patience and determination as one can only do in a large Irish family. I introduce Bay Buchanan.

Pat Buchanan

Bay Buchanan: It was last Thanksgiving that I was discussing running with Pat privately and I asked, "Do you think you're going to get into this thing or not? It's getting a little late." It was already about 12 or 13 weeks before New Hampshire when we were discussing it seriously and ten weeks before New Hampshire that he announced.

He took a leave from CNN saying he wanted to talk about two things that happened which had turned him around to looking into this, the "quota bill" right on top of the Thornburgh defeat [by Democrat Harris Wofford in Pennsylvania]. These told us, one, that the President was continuing to move in a direction that we thought was wrong, and, two, that the President was very vulnerable.

So he started looking at it, and I was getting phone calls from the press, "Is he going to do it?" "Is he not going to do it?" And Pat said, "Look, Bay, I'll make some phone calls. I've got to talk to people at CNN and other places. Put the word out that it's serious, but don't commit." So, I called my good friend Ralph Hallow [writer, *Washington Times*] and he said this would be a good place to move this story. And I said: "Well, you know, I'm coming back, to look for space, just in case, and I'm doing this and we're doing that, and nobody knows he's serious." "Bay, that's not good enough." I said: "Well, Ralph, he's very serious. We made a firm decision. Okay, off the record, Ralph, it's a go." The headlines the next day, "It's a Go." [Laughter]

Anyway, we were in the race at that stage. There were a number of reasons why we were going to run, the least of which is that we wanted to win. There were some fleeting moments when we actually thought we might win, but that certainly wasn't the main reason we got in. However, we wouldn't have gotten into it if we didn't think there was any chance.

The other three reasons, I think, can be summarized: First, we felt very strongly that the President was the heir to the Reagan legacy, that he had taken the country in a certain direction, and it was assumed it was the direction the conservatives would have taken. Pat thought that we needed a spokesperson to represent conservatives, to say this *isn't* the direction we think is in the best interest of conservatives, and so bring back alive a conservative movement with a real spokesperson out there. Second was eminent domain. David Duke, who had been made a national figure, was speaking about some of those issues that we thought were ours legitimately. He was being made the ultimate spokesperson for conservatives, a development which was going to do incredible damage to the conservative movement. But, as I told Pat, when you face off with David Duke, if you lose, even Kinsley [co-host on "Crossfire"] will not take you back. If we're going to take this on, we've got to finish him off, which was one of the goals. The third was to actually move the President, force him to keep to the issues that we felt were right and proper for the Reagan legacy.

And so we did get into the race. The strategy was simpler than some of the ones you've heard this evening. The strategy was New Hampshire. We recognized that it was important for the press to perceive our results in that primary as a victory. If we did not succeed at that, we were gone, it was over. And so we put our entire focus there. We thought, if we do well in New Hampshire, we would move over to South Dakota, and maybe be able to bring in the same numbers, then go into South Carolina where we would be able to beat Duke and go strong in Georgia. But we recognized an enormous wall — Super Tuesday. That wall was thick, heavy concrete, and we knew the only way we were going to get through it was to have terrific momentum by

March 10. The forces were against us. The President, of course, had organizations in every state, he had money, and he had the ability to get national attention.

So we looked at two things in New Hampshire. First, Pat was going to have to be something other than a talking head. He was going to have to turn himself into a serious candidate. He had to do retail politics, go up to New Hampshire and work it, and work it, and work it. He initially thought maybe he could do everything from television because he was so successful there, but we felt we had to do both in New Hampshire. Pat spent ten weeks virtually working the entire state, meeting as many people as he could. And at the same time, we had some advantages. Pat *was* a sound bite. You guys love sound bites, it saved him a lot of work. [Laughter]

The free media would help compensate for the fact that we were up against the President with all his money and ability to get media. We recognized from the very beginning that going up against the President of the United States would also give us free media, because nobody likes a fight better than the press. We had to maximize Pat's ability to get free press and at the same time he had to knock on every door so people in New Hampshire would realize he was very serious about this effort.

We did that rather successfully. He didn't have any trouble getting the press. We really had hoped and expected to be ignored by the Bush campaign early on and we were in the early days. In fact, we had hoped it was going to last a couple more weeks but a poll came out and showed us stronger than we were, to be quite honest, and all the press came in and gave us incredible attention.

Then we weren't able to get on the ballot in South Dakota. That's still in dispute as to exactly what happened. The establishment in South Dakota kept us locked out, which I think hurt us; 30 percent went to "Undecided." We were able to do well in South Carolina. We had an organization in Georgia but we had everything in the world open fire on us, which of course was expected.

One other point is money. In New Hampshire, the game plan was to keep as tight an operation as you can, pay for Pat's travel and the good New Hampshire organization, and hoard every other penny. Maintain a very small national staff. We thought we would get a couple weeks of media and we would be lucky in New Hampshire. We did a direct mail piece. Pat, of course, came to the campaign table with 15,000 newsletter names, and that was it. We mailed that in early December and raised half a million dollars in three weeks. The money came in so fast and so heavy that in three weeks we stopped casting. We just bought every list we could get our hands on and dumped it in the mail. By February 1 we raised nearly $2 million. We qualified for matching funds in three weeks, which is unheard of. We knew that we wouldn't have time to put on high donor events. In fact, we couldn't pull Pat out of New Hampshire to go to them, it got to be so tight.

We knew that the grassroots support was there from the money. We were able to match, not beat, the President's spending in New Hampshire. Again, the time wasn't there to raise the kind of money and build the organization in the states. We always recognized that organization was going to be a weak spot. We did well in New Hampshire and we tied in Georgia, but we hadn't picked up the back stage, so we knew that Super Tuesday was going to be the end of that stage. We had made a commitment from the very beginning to stay in. It was a commitment to people who had talked to Pat saying, "If we go out on this limb and get behind you, we don't want you dropping out after New Hampshire — you're going to still be out there!" We made that commitment and kept it. We stayed in through California for that reason and for one other reason — because we were having a great time.

Marty Nolan: The last campaign that got under way got under way twice, and Charley Royer says it, it's *Home Alone I* and *Home Alone II*. [Laughter]

Anyway, in politics it takes weeks, months, years to establish that threshold of credibility. But on the night of February 20, in one hour on "Larry King," Ross Perot sprang from the brow of Job or Larry King. And in the Ross Perot petition drive, if we call it that, heavily involved was Tom Luce who is a former candidate for governor of Texas, and more important than that, a former Fellow here at the Institute of Politics. Tom Luce.

Ross Perot I

Tom Luce: Thanks very much, Marty. I appreciate the opportunity, I guess, to be here. I'm actually going to talk tomorrow night, so I thought what I would do tonight is simply review each of the other candidates who have already spoken and point out similarities and some slight differences between Ross Perot and the other candidates.

I'd start with Dennis Kanin's comments about Paul Tsongas and challenge. Dennis said his candidate was the most improbable candidate in the presidential race. I would submit that Ross Perot might really qualify for that, Dennis.

With respect to Doug Wilder and Paul Goldman's remarks that he bet against Wilder getting in and getting out, well, I bet against Perot getting in, getting out, and getting in.

With respect to the Harkin campaign, Lorraine Voles bragged that they actually had a strategy. I deny that we ever had a strategy.

Dan Butler, who did such a great job on Brown's campaign, said he learned the Brown strategy by driving. I never was allowed to drive with Perot, so I never knew what the strategy was.

With respect to Clinton, Stan Greenberg talked about how Bill Clinton had plotted his presidential campaign since he was six. Perot plotted his for about six hours on the night of February 20.

With respect to the Kerrey campaign, Tad Devine revealed that they had a lack of management during some portion of the Kerrey campaign. I would submit we had him topped in that regard as well.

Now, with respect to the Bush/Quayle campaign, and Mary Matalin's comments. I can't help but reflect upon the fact of how her candidate referred to Ross Perot occasionally as a "kook." When I hear her talk about chickens and ducks, bozos and ozones, I feel a little bit better. I would like Mary to deliver, also to us, the passport files. I've always wanted to know what was in them.

And, I guess last but not least, with respect to the Buchanan campaign and Bay's remarks that she had a candidate who was a walking sound bite, well, I had one who was a walking sound bite who denied that he knew what a sound bite was.

All in all, I think it was a rather remarkable year for the Perot campaign. I actually joined the effort around the first of April, and I would say, therefore, we didn't have to worry about New Hampshire, nor did we have to worry about Iowa and a whole lot of other things. We did have a lot to worry about — it was like being dropped into the Super Bowl in the fourth quarter and we were still trying to put on our uniforms. We didn't do a very good job of ever getting on our uniforms.

In closing, I would also say with respect to Jerry Brown, he *wanted* his team to make mistakes. That was not exactly what Perot wanted me to do. [Laughter] But Perot, like Brown, didn't want to bring in the pros. So, again, we have something in common with the Brown campaign.

All in all, I stand before you tonight as a man who has, over the last two years, been trounced by Clayton Williams, you remember him. And I was also the campaign manager for a portion, a very small portion, of what turned out, in hindsight, to be a rather improbable campaign, a campaign that really did impact not only the political calendar in 1992 but, I would submit, will impact the political calendar in 1996 even more profoundly. I want to debate that issue a little over the next couple of days.

Marty Nolan: Now for phase two. From the great State of Hawaii, the Aloha State, as they would say at a convention that Ross Perot never had, Orson Swindle.

Ross Perot II

Orson Swindle: I seriously considered trying to do my part of this on "The Larry King Show" or "Crossfire" but I couldn't work out the details. I envy all you guys who could fill out the whole page.

It's interesting, being the underdog, that it's always the best position to work from. But I thought at some point during the 30-day campaign that we were reaching a certain point of recognition and promise. I was invited to be on CNN with two of my favorite people, John Sununu and Michael Kinsley, and Charlie Black was there. We got to know each other intimately through the television screen. I felt I had really made it, and I got up there and I was going to be actually live sitting in front of these prominent pundits of the political scene, and lo and behold, they put me in another room behind the wall and let these other guys talk. You know, some people just never get any respect. It taught me a lot about TV.

It was an interesting thing to pick up on what Tom Luce said. I personally feel that politics in this country probably has changed forever because of Ross Perot's involvement. I think that's basically a good thing. I would contend and predict, if it hasn't changed, we've got major problems down the road.

But in a less serious sense, Tom stole my line. I bet that Ross would never get out and then bet he'd never get back in. In fact, when I was asked to join the effort — I'm a friend of Ross's from my having been a POW — when I came home, I got to know him because of an experience 19 years ago. I was asked on July 3 to resign my job and take a position in the campaign, and because I love the man so much, and I believe in what he was saying, I said "Right on." But first I had to have assurance that we're in this thing for the duration. I got it. Two weeks later he withdrew, and I'm standing there wondering what in the hell has happened. But that's when I introduced the theme song of the campaign, "Crazy." If I could sing like Patsy Cline, I'd sing it for you right now.

It's been interesting. I'm sort of following Tom's pattern here of commenting on what other people have said. We didn't have much in the way of money problems, as I recall. [Laughter]

Our campaign was not 15 months long, in fact, I think it was twice that many days. I think it was 31 or 32 days or something like that — short and sweet.

Contrary to what Tom said, we did have a strategy. Ross is writing his memoirs. I hope I know what that strategy is sometime in the next year, and I'll share it with you next time. He didn't tell me either.

We enjoyed what has to be considered an extraordinary roller coaster ride. I've heard several people talking about grassroots. I got into a little bit of a debate with John Anderson over what he accomplished [in 1980] in getting on the ballot in all 50 states. He seemed to resent that we did it, and he claimed that he did it, and I said, "Well, we'll just compare performances after a while." Contrary to what some would say, this was truly a grassroots movement, driven by one man's appeal to the common person in this country, which is what I think is basically the guts of this country.

Contrary to what Mr. Brown dictated, Ross told us — and a few of us were paid — we damn well better not make mistakes. I echo what Tom said. But in all seriousness, there was an enormous movement of people out there that got involved in this thing. I'm a Reagan conservative. I worked for eight years with President Reagan, and five or six brief months for President Bush, and I thought we had a lot of emotion back in the 1981 campaign. But I've never seen anything quite like what I saw involved in this grassroots movement around the country as I talked to hundreds, if not thousands, of people.

The extraordinary thing about it to me was the fact that here I was, a Reagan conservative, sitting down having serious dialogue with McGovern Democrats. Having been a prisoner of war, I don't have the kindest regard for Senator McGovern, at least for his philosophy. He's a fine man, but I really take exception. But I thought it extraordinary that people from such diverse backgrounds, politically and socially, could come together in a common cause.

And there were people involved who were totally turned off by the political process, who had not voted in years — staunch, lifelong Democrats, staunch, lifelong Republicans, business people, unemployed people, all different races. And they were all concerned about where the country was and where it was going.

We all took great pride in the remarkable feats of our military in Desert Storm, but we were all concerned that there seemed to be very little interest in domestic affairs on the part of the Bush administration.

Nineteen-plus million is an extraordinary statement. I was fascinated with the polls. I personally felt that this thing had a lot of potential. I said 15 million votes is not impossible and I kept reading the political experts and the statisticians. The polls were saying Perot's 14 percent was going to drop to 9 but that was not right. You guys make a living being accurate, and you are accurate. I would like, as part of the discussion this weekend to ask, why the distortion? Purely a quirk?

I felt like we were working with a snowball on the bottom side of a slope, pushing it up a hill, and I felt that the top of the hill was 20 percent. If we could ever get to 20 percent, and God knows I never thought we could do it, it would pick up momentum and we would become real, could easily come in second. We could overcome the statement by President Bush to Perot people, "Don't waste your vote on Ross Perot, he can't win." I happen to like President Bush. I think he's a fine man.

But I was appalled that the President of the United States of America would suggest that voting one's convictions would be wrong. This country was founded by people, the underdogs, standing up for what they believe in. That's what we're all about.

I look forward to what we're about to do this weekend. I'm sure I'll learn a lot from all of you. And it was fun. Bay, I agree with you, *it was a kick.*

CHAPTER TWO

THE DEMOCRATIC PRIMARIES

"Brown couldn't pay us and Tsongas couldn't stand us."

— James Carville, Strategic Consultant, Clinton/Gore
Campaign, on why he and Paul Begala joined the
Clinton campaign

William Schneider, a political scientist and writer who covered the election for CNN, moderated the session and Elizabeth Kolbert, *New York Times* political reporter, served as questioner.

The Discussion

Bill Schneider: We're looking for two different things in this session, I believe. On the most immediate level, we want to talk about revelations: "Now it can be told." For instance, the real story about Ross Perot's withdrawal from the race in July; we have information on how the Republicans planned to disrupt his daughter's wedding. According to our sources, the Republicans gathered an army of computer nerds who broke into the secret computer codes of the Dallas Neiman-Marcus store and secretly changed his daughter's silver pattern. When Ross Perot learned that his daughter would have to go through life with mismatched silver, he was horrified and immediately got out of the race. We'll need to have comments on that from both the Bush people and the Perot people later.

We also want to talk about some of the big picture items in the election. This morning's issue is the Democratic primaries. We'll be investigating the strategy behind the primaries from the candidates' perspectives, but we also want to look at the big picture in terms of what the primaries did. They are not only designed to choose a candidate, but also to find a theme or a message. The Democrats this year, as in most recent years, were the opposition party. For the opposition, the problem is always to figure out two things — what do the people want that they're not getting from the incumbent and how do you sell it to them?

Over the last 12 years, the Democrats have tried again and again to figure out what the market was looking for. They tried fairness in 1984. It was a great theme for the 1982 recession when Reaganomics had not worked. Unfortunately, when the economy was booming, it was difficult to sell fairness. When the economy is doing well, middle-class voters believe that the system is fine and if people aren't making it, there must be something wrong with them. When the economy is stumbling, however, middle-class voters believe that there's nothing wrong with them, there must be something wrong with the system. By 1984, the Democrats' timing was wrong.

Charley Royer, Bill Schneider, Betsy Kolbert

It was wrong again in 1988 when the Democrats nominated a candidate whose chosen theme was competence. It was a very good theme coming out of the Iran-Contra affair, when there was a president in the White House who didn't know what was going on in the White House basement, but it was kind of hard to place the charge of incompetence against George Bush, who had held every top job in Washington.

I don't think there's any great mystery about the theme for 1992. The Democrats discovered it early on and then they almost got trumped by the theme — change. They talked about change incessantly. It was in virtually every sentence of every speech at the Democratic convention. They almost got trumped because Ross Perot was a candidate who offered a much more fundamental and dramatic kind of change for voters who were desperate to change the system.

Some of the remarks last night suggested that the candidates who did well in these primaries, the candidates who seem to make an immediate impression on the voters, went one step beyond the change theme. They offered something that Americans were not getting from George Bush, or at least believed they weren't getting.

In order to get anywhere in this year's election, you had to have an economic plan. Paul Tsongas was the first to figure that out. He published his *Call to Economic Arms,* hawked it on television, and won the New Hampshire primary. Clinton put together his plan very quickly, waved it around, came in second in New Hampshire. When the press started asking Ross Perot to explain the details of his plan, he decided he'd better get one, too. He took a leave of absence from the campaign, published his plan, and, presto, he was all set to resume the race.

Eventually, George Bush got the idea. He came up with his agenda for American renewal in mid-September. He came up with a plan which — I think I agree with Mary — was an interesting one. It talked about reviving the American economy through international trade. The problem is, Americans expected the plan on January 29 in the State of the Union speech in Washington. They got it on September 10 in Detroit. No one paid a lot of attention to it, unfortunately for the Bush campaign, because it did little to dispel the impression that the real plan was to muddle through. I think Bush was the no-plan man, and he got clobbered for it.

The Invisible Primary

"From the beginning, we were running a national, general election campaign. We decided that the best strategy for winning the Democratic nomination was being a candidate who could capture America and not necessarily a candidate who could win specific primaries."

— Stan Greenberg, Polling Consultant,
Clinton/Gore Campaign

This morning we're going to start with what I think was the first primary of the 1992 campaign season. Sidney Blumenthal's article in the

January *New Republic* referred to it as the "Invisible Primary." Before a single vote was cast, there was a growing consensus in the political community and the press, a consensus that was quickly picked up, interestingly, by the voters of New Hampshire, that Bill Clinton was the man to watch. It seemed to come out of the Florida straw vote in December and the dramatic and impressive speech that Bill Clinton delivered to the Democratic state chairs at their meeting in Chicago. Somehow in this entire process, everything seemed to get started with a growing consensus in the political community on who was important, who was the one to watch. And sometime in January, Bill Clinton began to move into the front-runner position in New Hampshire, again, before a single vote was cast.

I'll turn to Betsy Kolbert, of the *New York Times,* who will be our questioner for this morning's session, to raise some questions about these very early stages of the Democratic primary process.

Betsy Kolbert: I want to ask the first question of Stan Greenberg, who suggested last night that you all had gone into the New Hampshire primary not expecting to win, in fact, hoping to do a respectable third. I wanted to ask when this consensus Bill Schneider talked about started to emerge. Was it when Governor Clinton was on the cover of *Time* magazine? [Jan. 27, 1992] How did that change your strategy? How much did it help you in terms of raising money? How much did it hurt you, perhaps, in terms of really raising expectations?

Stan Greenberg: I should say that we enjoyed it when that emerged, but there was a lot of ambivalence about being in the front-runner position going into New Hampshire. I think both David Wilhelm and Frank Greer ought to speak to this. Our assumption was not that we'd end up third. We presumed that Tsongas and Kerrey would hold the lead well into the primary and, in fact, the spotlight would not be on us for most of the primary and that we would emerge late and win late, if we were to win. But in any case, we were already well set to move on to subsequent primaries.

You're right to call attention to the Chicago speech which followed the New Covenant speech. That was when the networks began to talk about Bill Clinton as a front runner. And then *Time* magazine — we enjoyed that glow, and I would say when we put on the first week of media, we were stunned by the degree of movement that we got within one week. It moved us into the lead position.

At that point, and I may turn to others who may recall more specifically, events took over. Before we could develop a strategy for holding onto that lead, there were day-to-day events that we had to survive. And I think that dictated the strategy, though I don't know whether Frank wants to speak to it.

Frank Greer: As Bill Schneider said, this was a year where voters were very cynical and very alienated and tired of politics as usual. I think they wanted more than just vague promises. They wanted some real substance, and the three Georgetown speeches laid the foundation because I think they revealed a candidate who'd really thought about the problems of the country and had a plan and a program and a rationale for his candidacy.

It was in Chicago that a lot of skeptical political leaders in the Democratic party, across the spectrum, all of a sudden were impressed by Bill Clinton, including Karen Marchioro [Chair, Washington State Democratic party], who I think was probably the most skeptical and one of the most liberal leaders. Clinton appeared to transcend the ideological concerns of a lot of people in the Democratic party.

But, Elizabeth, one thing I would say is, when we went on the air in New Hampshire, despite the front-runner status that had been given to us by the media, we were still in fourth place and sitting at about the mid-teens, at about 15 percent. So we had to build up and really earn our votes. By the way, also, the Florida straw poll was just partially an organizational effort that I think was supreme and excellent. Bill Clinton worked this poll and Florida very hard and showed his strength there as a kind of grassroots candidate.

Bill Schneider: I note that according to our time line provided by the Institute, on Wednesday, January 15, the New Hampshire poll indicated that Bill Clinton was already in the lead in New Hampshire. This was shortly before the troubles began. But he did establish an early lead, I think based in large part on the positive press coverage.

David Wilhelm: I would just add one thing from a tactical point of view. You asked the question how money responded to our emergence. I think one of the big reasons for our emergence was a feeling among many party professionals and media people that we had an edge in fundraising, and that didn't happen by accident. We made maybe one of the toughest single strategic calls in December and early November. It was a decision to stay out of New Hampshire, by and large — which drove our New Hampshire supporters absolutely crazy — in order to do 20 fundraisers in the first 16 days of December.

That was not an easy decision to make at the time. We raised, I think it was, $2 million in the month of December, which sounds like peanuts now, but back then it was a huge amount of money. We raised $1 million on December 16 at a Little Rock fundraiser. That, combined with the performance in the Florida straw poll, which was far from a foregone conclusion, would give us a solid base. When we were doing our own internal polling of the Florida delegates going into that weekend, we had only a 10-point lead over Harkin. That could have been a devastating defeat for us, but I think, largely because of the work of Bill Clinton that weekend, we did very well.

So you had the Clinton speech, you had the Florida straw poll, and you had the Clinton campaign emerging as the strongest at fund-raising coming out of the month of December.

Bill Schneider: Let me ask you a question about the Chicago speech. Was there a deliberate strategy to play it to the press? Was there a calculation that you wanted to make a certain impression in this speech because you know that the press was there or did it just sort of happen? How much was this the result of real planning?

Stan Greenberg: One of the things that happened with the New Covenant speech, is that Bill Clinton, by that point, had a very crisp delivery. It was not new. But when the candidates were all there on stage at one time, it became evident that Bill Clinton was the only one who had a coherent view of how to run for this office. I don't think that we specifically understood that this speech would have this kind of network coverage.

Frank Greer: We expected good coverage and we encouraged that. But part of the synergy of this was, as Stan said, that it was the first time everybody was on the stage together. But, also it was a challenge to see if we could impress and influence a whole spectrum of Democratic party leadership, which was the other audience there. Whether or not we could go beyond "he's too conservative; he's a Southern governor; he's really not going to be able to go up against a Tom Harkin or a Bob Kerrey for the mainstream." That was really the challenge there, as well as the press coverage.

Betsy Kolbert: I wanted to ask Lorraine Voles and Tad Devine and Dennis Kanin how the sense that Clinton was emerging as a front runner, even before the polls started to move, affected your money raising strategy? Lorraine?

Lorraine Voles: Can I ask a question about the Chicago speech?

Betsy Kolbert: Sure.

Lorraine Voles: At that time, if I recall correctly, all the other candidates went on one night, and Governor Clinton went on the next morning. Isn't that correct?

David Wilhelm: There were a couple of candidates that went the next morning.

Lorraine Voles: Fine. Okay. I thought it was separated.

David Wilhelm: It was Kerrey and Clinton the next morning.

Lorraine Voles: We saw that as a real turning point in the campaign, too, for you guys. I remember Senator Harkin thinking that you did something really smart that we didn't do, which wouldn't be the first time that happened. You worked those state chairs and you worked the people in the crowd so that afterward everyone was talking about that speech. Now, was that a false impression on his part? Was there a concerted kind of political effort there?

David Wilhelm: Well, yes.

Frank Greer: We worked the state chairs very, very hard.

David Wilhelm: We were all over that room definitely, and we also had some friends in Chicago. So they kind of just turned up. [Laughter] Which helped the dynamic of the room, I think, but ...

Lorraine Voles: And that affects media coverage.

David Wilhelm: Right, but I really think you can put a few people in the room, and you can work state party chairs and you can do all that, but if you don't deliver the goods, then there's not going to be any excitement, there's not going to be any energy.

Lorraine Voles: Obviously.

David Wilhelm: And I think that the excitement and the energy in the room was genuine, even though I do think we worked it well.

Frank Greer: I think one of the major strategic errors that the Kerrey campaign, and the other unsuccessful campaigns, made was not to realize in advance the likelihood that Clinton would emerge as the front runner and, therefore, the possibility of setting off different dynamics in the race. We basically had five or six people who were all running just kind of flat out to get to the front of the pack. In my only other experience, in 1984, Gary Hart had set himself up as the dark horse candidate who was going to run a guerrilla campaign and so forth.

In the Kerrey campaign, for example, there had never been any discussion of that because we hadn't anticipated the likelihood, particularly after Cuomo announced that he wasn't going to run, that Clinton would become such a solid front runner. In retrospect, there are some reasons I think we should have been able to anticipate it, that it really could have created a different dynamic.

Charley Royer: What was the date of the Chicago speech?[*]

David Wilhelm: It was like November 22, something like that.

Charley Royer: If that's not the time, I want to make sure we get ...

---

[*]*Editor's Note:* The date of the Chicago speech was November 23, 1991.

David Wilhelm: Late November. I think it was the first week of December.

Lorraine Voles: Yes, the first week of …

James Carville: No. It was in November.

David Wilhelm: It was late November.

James Carville: Before I went to work. I went to work on December 1. It was like the day I'd already decided on.

Stan Greenberg: It was the week before Thanksgiving.

David Wilhelm, Lorraine Voles, Bill Shore

James Carville: It was right in there, I think, but I can't remember …

Dennis Kanin: Well, I have to go back because the context for us was totally different than the context for the Clinton campaign or the Kerrey campaign. Just to remind people, going into 1992 there were two tiers of candidates that, basically, had been set up by the press. Kerrey, Harkin, and Clinton were in the first tier. And the second tier, which was the unelectable tier, was Tsongas, Wilder, and Brown.

We had a situation in 1991 where we were, basically, written off as a serious candidate from the very beginning by the press, perhaps based on rational judgment at the time. But the fact of the matter is, a projection was made that Tsongas had absolutely no chance to win, that his ideas were respectable, that he was contributing to the Democratic debate and all of that, but that he could not win.

The result was, we couldn't raise money, and Paul spent a lot of time trying to do it. In 1991 we raised about $19,000 a week, which is a pitiful amount. That's what people raise in congressional races. It was not for lack of trying, but people made the rational choice not to throw their money away on a candidate who could not win. So by the end of 1991, after ten months in the race, we had raised a million dollars. After three months in the race, Clinton had raised about $3 million, Harkin had raised about $3 million, and Kerrey had raised between two and two-and-a-half, I believe.

So we were playing with a whole different deck of cards when we went into 1992. Stan Greenberg mentioned last night, planning a general election strategy from the beginning of the Clinton campaign. We also had a general election strategy. We just didn't have any money to implement it, and so, ultimately, we were left with a New Hampshire strategy.

The dilemma for us, as I said last night, was how to convince people in New Hampshire that Paul Tsongas was a national candidate, because as long as they thought he was a regional candidate, we had no chance. What we did was to make a virtue out of necessity. We decided to use events in New Hampshire to impress the national press and generate some national publicity so, in turn, we could convince people in New Hampshire that we were a national candidate. That wasn't easy, but we did it.

Specifically, the first turning point for us in New Hampshire was the November 2 Democratic State Convention where we had a big show, pulled in everybody we knew from Massachusetts, made it look like we had taken over the state convention. And we did get a fair amount of coverage and recognition in the press that Tsongas had, if nothing else, a strong organization there.

Perhaps more significant was the night before. We had contacted Chris Spirou, who's the chairman of the New Hampshire Democratic Party, a few weeks earlier and suggested to him that it was a shame that New Hampshire, which had the first primary in the nation, would not have the first debate. That would be the AFL-CIO debate in Detroit, which we were not looking forward to. So Spirou quickly pulled together a debate for us with Clinton and Wilder, totally for the national press. We were trying to show that Paul Tsongas was in the same class as Bill Clinton, that he belonged in that first tier.

We generated some press, and it started to have an impact in New Hampshire. Then we had some intuition about a *Boston Globe* poll that would be coming out in December, so we borrowed against our meager matching funds almost everything we had and threw on television, at saturation levels, our first ad. It was the swim ad that Paul Tsongas had conceived in the summer and that Mike Shea, who's sitting over there, Fred Woods, and Fred Faust had produced.

Bill Schneider: If you haven't seen the ad, it's still playing. [Laughter]

Dennis Kanin: Yes. It's actually been on TV a lot in the last week. But the result was, when the *Globe* poll came out, it was Tsongas 15, Cuomo 15, and I don't remember what the numbers were for the others. I think Kerrey was third and Clinton right behind him, but I'm not sure. Anyway, that gave us a little boost. We had a very incremental program here. We were doing it step by step, trying to build one thing on another, and it was all kind of an illusion.

The next turning point for us was January 19 because that was the day that we finally got a subheadline in the *New York Times* — I'm talking about the front page in the *New York Times.*[*] We hadn't been on the front page before, and the significant thing is what the subheadline was about: "Only Tsongas is calling for tough action on the economy or tough decisions"...and that really was the theme of our campaign. We had achieved something there because, in our first ads in January, we were trying to draw some distinctions between Tsongas and the other candidates.

The night of January 19, there was a debate — I believe it was in Durham, New Hampshire — that according to the *Concord Monitor* poll late that week, 43 percent of New Hampshire voters watched. In that debate, Tsongas very successfully set himself apart, as different from the rest of the group. And at that point, we moved up within five points of Clinton, who had been about 20 points ahead of us only a week-and-a-half earlier. Then a few days later, Gennifer Flowers occurred.

Bill Schneider: Well, we'll get to that shortly. Are there any other campaigns that want to comment? We are still at the stage of the invisible primary.

The very visible Democratic Chairman.

Ron Brown: We looked at 1988, and there were something like 70 joint appearances by candidates during the primaries in so-called debates. We decided that that was not a very healthy way to move through the primary season. So I went to see every candidate and asked if they would agree to participate only in party-sanctioned debates. Then we went to the networks to see if the networks would broadcast them nationally, which would give some incentive for everybody to show up, with the hope that the candidates would refuse all invitations to everybody else's debates. Well, the first break was this AFL-CIO invitation, which we tried to stop, tried to ask them to cancel, and finally negotiated a format where it would be more like a joint appearance than a debate.

---

[*] *Editor's Note:* The subheadline read: "Except for Tsongas, Candidates Are Avoiding Remedies That Might Antagonize Voters."

Ron Brown

Although we did a lot better this time in limiting the number of debates and, therefore, giving more national focus to our candidates, we really didn't pull off the objective, which was to limit it to six or seven or eight nationally televised debates that everybody would participate in. I forget what the total number was. A lot better than 1988, but it was — I think it was maybe 15 or so.

Bill Schneider: James Carville.

James Carville: I think there's a big point here we're missing. When Harris Wofford won [the Senate race over Dick Thornburgh in Pennsylvania], the intensity of the spotlight increased because people said, wait a minute, one of these guys might win. Okay? And so the stage cast, the press, and everything else, just the whole illumination factor of the race, went up.

Paul and I probably had a rare chance during that period in November. We were talking to Kerrey and we talked to Senator Harkin and talked to Clinton; Brown couldn't pay us and Tsongas couldn't stand us so … [Laughter]

Bill Schneider: That's a very good observation.

James Carville: But it was clear in November that they had thought about it longer, so under a normal set of circumstances — well, gee, after Christmas, you know, is when they really start thinking about New Hampshire, which was a rational strategic position to be in at that time.

When Wofford won, everybody started covering the campaigns more. Contributors were paying more attention, and to some extent voters were paying closer attention. Just that Clinton started earlier or thought about it more.

You know, you hear David and Stan and Frank and Ron, the whole infrastructure was already in place down there in Little Rock when this occurred. I think that was a big factor in the invisible primary, and Tsongas was probably strategically more ready at that point, also. He published his recycled paper plan or whatever it was on. That, I think, had a big impact on this December kind of primary that we had.

Bill Schneider: Dave Wilhelm.

David Wilhelm: One other point in this invisible primary period. We worked very hard, very early, to pick up the support of African-American leaders around the country. We did that with some success, and we certainly laid the groundwork for future endorsements during this period. I think that effort, combined with Governor Wilder's withdrawal from the race, is generally overlooked. It set up Super Tuesday for us in a major way, that it would always be our firewall. Governor Wilder was really the only candidate that would have competed with us for the votes of African-Americans on Super Tuesday. The early work that we did getting the support of people like Congressmen Lewis and Jefferson and Bobby Rush and Danny Davis in Chicago and Mike Espy, combined with Governor Wilder's withdrawal, was very important.

James Carville: Huge. That is the first thing I said in the campaign when I went to work. I said, you can cut this thing any way you want to cut it but unless you have Southern blacks in there, you can't figure this thing. There is no way we can get the nomination without a substantial black vote in the South. And to this day, no one could do arithmetic to show how Clinton got the nomination without substantial black votes.

Stan Greenberg: And we were doing polling and research among black voters in the South early in the New Hampshire primary, well before Wilder pulled out, to make sure that that was a possibility.

James Carville: When he got out, that was as big to us as Cuomo getting out, I think. There was a huge sigh of relief in the Clinton camp at that event.

Bill Schneider: You're suggesting that his decision to run in the first place was a critical factor in your campaign, too, because you wouldn't have felt the need to work nearly as hard to sew up that kind of support if you didn't feel that …

Stan Greenberg: And it froze African-American leaders' willingness to support us.

James Carville: But that was strategic gospel in the Clinton campaign: there was no way to win without black support.

Waiting for Cuomo

*"I think there were three tiers in 1991. The
first tier was Mario Cuomo all by himself."*

— Tad Devine, Manager, Kerrey for President

Betsy Kolbert: Well, that sort of leads us to the next question, which is, did you all have strategies for if Governor Cuomo ran and if he didn't? As this went on did you find yourselves in a position that you might not have wanted to take, had you known that he wasn't going to run? And, also, were there people who actually weren't going to run, were going to drop out, if Mario Cuomo got in the race? I open this up. Who wants to take it up first?

Bill Schneider: We are on December 20, 1991. Mario Cuomo decides he's not going to run for president, blaming the Republicans, blaming Ron Brown, blaming lots of people for the premature decision not to run. How did this affect the campaign and your own strategies?

Stan Greenberg: There was a very — I don't want to say heated — but one of the stronger discussions in the campaign. It was whether we wanted Cuomo in the race or not. Let me say that when he decided not to run, there was a universal sigh of relief, even from those people with bravado who said that they wanted him in. But there were some, including myself, who wanted him in and wanted the definition that his presence would have given. Indeed, there was one speech that we geared up to give in New Hampshire prior to that decision, to begin to draw the contrast with Cuomo. The only one not on board for that was Bill Clinton, but we all had a terrific speech for him to give.

Paul Begala: We were going to go after and kind of pop him, maybe not by name, maybe by name, but the Governor just decided at the end of it, I'd just as soon not whack somebody who's not running against me.

Tad Devine: Dennis said before there were two tiers in this '91 period. I would amplify that a little bit. I think there were three tiers in '91. The first tier was Mario Cuomo all by himself. He received more coverage on network television than any other candidate running for President who had announced. The second tier, I agree, was Kerrey-Harkin-Clinton, and then there was a third tier as well. When I met with Senator Kerrey right about that time, a couple of days before, I said that I thought this whole thing was about 40,000 people in New Hampshire and that, basically, was the nomination. I think that's true. They wound up voting for Bill Clinton, 41,000 I think it was, but that, essentially, was our strategy, that we were going to New Hampshire.

Paul Begala, Frank Greer, Stan Greenberg

We would have preferred to go to Iowa, and I think if we had the resources, you know, we would have preferred to start the thing off there because it would have been more of a home turf. But once Cuomo got out, and in light of where we were resource-wise, we just focused on New Hampshire. His [Cuomo's] presence, and all the time he was taking hurt Kerrey in terms of coverage. Clinton's emergence as a clear front-runner also hurt because Kerrey was being measured against very high expectations, and it depressed our fundraising pretty substantially as well. Dennis said it was too bad Tsongas never got on the front page of the *New York Times*. Well, unfortunately for us, we were getting on the front page all the time. The stories were not that good. So I think once Cuomo got out, we just focused on New Hampshire and were determined to make that the battleground.

Betsy Kolbert: Lorraine, obviously, Harkin was very strongly affected.

Lorraine Voles: Yes, we were. We were very strongly affected. Unfortunately, we didn't know what to do with it, once it happened. We used to talk about it all the time — what if he's in, what if he's out, and then he was out and what did we do? We didn't do much. Which is illustrative of the problem with our campaign, which was that we didn't have the firepower that we needed, the political professionals, in our camp.

That was kind of the divide in the campaign, who to bring on when. This was such a critical time for us because at the same time we were trying to decide who our media consultant would be. We really lost a two-week period in December because a lot of us were under the assumption that we were going to be working with Squier-Eskew.*

Their people met with Tom and our campaign management, and this went back and forth. But it all fell apart and they weren't going to do it. This is after the contract is written and many of us think that all we're waiting for is the signature.

So we're sitting there in the middle of December with no ads, no media consultant, Cuomo out of the race and not really knowing what to do. So we went on vacation. We're still on vacation. [Laughter]

Paul Begala: That's a very important point. When Cuomo got out, in terms of the media spotlight, the question became who was ready to dance in the spotlight? All the rest of us, I think, were probably ready to play off Cuomo, each of us in our own way, in much the way others tried to play off Gary Hart in '88, or Gary Hart did off Mondale in '84, or Carter did off everybody in '76. It was a sort of time-honored strategy to win the nomination by positioning yourself as the outsider, insurgent. But when that was gone, when that eclipse passed, and the spotlight was on you, the only people who were ready to dance were Bill Clinton and Paul Tsongas, because they had done the intellectual heavy lifting before political people were around. Before the press was focusing on any of this, they were focusing on the issues and their ideas mattered.

Lorraine Voles: And we, in contrast, what we thought was, oh, God, we can get some money out of New York now. The thinking was that simple.

David Wilhelm: We did have a strategy through Illinois in the context of a race with Cuomo. I think we always thought that even then we would have a pretty good day on March 10, on Super Tuesday, that we would need to marshal our resources to ensure that it happened. Then we had an infrastructure in Illinois so we kind of rolled the dice there. Cuomo would have been expected to do very well, surprisingly so, in the city of Chicago and then really surprise people in the suburbs and downstate. Who knows what would have happened from there? But we did have kind of a thought-through scenario through Illinois.

Dennis Kanin: We had convinced ourselves that we wanted Cuomo in the race. We had this construct that was a repeat of the Hart-Mondale kind of situation, and Cuomo was the perfect antagonist, he was our Mondale, but it didn't seem to be working out. With Harkin fading, we thought Cuomo would be the perfect replacement, considering our New Hampshire base. We figured we had at least 15 percent, perhaps 20 percent, of a vote in New Hampshire, ultimately, and Cuomo was

---

Editor's Note: Political Consultants Bob Squier and Carter Eskew.

clearly going to be in the same range, at least. That would knock any other candidate out of the running, as the two of us moved up.

All I can say is, like Stan Greenberg, the day Cuomo announced he wasn't running, the huge whoop that went out from our entire campaign staff told us that not all these people wanted Cuomo in that race after all. So I guess there was a little ambivalence on our part.

Bill Schneider: Is there anyone from the Brown campaign here? No. I want to give Paul Goldman a chance to talk about the Wilder campaign.

Paul Goldman: It seemed to me the South snookered the rest of the country, just that it took four years for people to realize it. The election in '92 with Cuomo dropping out was set up by the Southern primary. The fascinating thing to me since, obviously, I have a Southern accent but it's Southern New York, is that the rest of the country didn't react. After 1988, the Southern primary didn't work. If it had, I think you would have seen changes in 1992 scheduling. But the Southern primary was considered a failure because of the results of 1988, so nobody gave it another thought. What happened was with Cuomo getting out, as Mr. Begala was saying, everything changed. Playing off the big heavyweight, trying to be the insurgent, that changed. The 20 years of history and people saying it's like a third party. It's like running in a three-way race, how do you do it? No one had the experience. So that stops that.

It just seems to me that Cuomo dropping out set up the Southern primary, and then when you had the DLC candidate able to get the Jackson vote, it pretty well ended the situation because you come up with 60, 70 percent victories, and then you've got the delegate count problem. The media starts playing look at the delegates, and everybody can't possibly win, so it always seemed to me that, as Jim said, the black vote in the South was going to be the key. You had to be able to compete for that or you couldn't possibly win. When Cuomo dropped out, I was convinced that that would determine it. But when they let the DLC get the Jackson vote, you don't have to be a Harvard scholar to figure out there ain't a lot left.

Bill Schneider: Well, the guy who was on the spot on this in many ways was Joe Grandmaison.* I want to ask Joe if he wants to make a comment as a New Hampshirite who was very much involved in the Cuomo in or out effort.

Joe Grandmaison: I'd like to remind the Clinton people of the Cuomo week, thank you very much.

Editor's Note: Joe Grandmaison, Democratic political consultant, was an observer at the conference.

The first week of December or so, John Marino [Chair, New York State Democratic Party] called to get a reaction as to how Cuomo's candidacy would play in New Hampshire. What was somewhat amazing, during this entire three-week period, was that it was quite obvious that Marino, party chair, Cuomo's political lieutenant, was as uncertain as everyone else was as to what his prospective candidate might or might not do. We had preliminary discussions relative to the difficulty of somebody of Cuomo's stature, skills, oratorical skills, doing retail campaigning, which we believed was necessary in New Hampshire.

In those discussions, I remember outlining the fact that what you saw was what I felt was occurring in the state, that Clinton had brought with him the experience of Arkansas, an ability to communicate with handfuls of people to build a base. And I was uncertain, given the time period, how well Cuomo could, if so inclined, begin to talk with six or eight, 10 or 20 people, rather than the hordes he deals with in a major metropolitan state. Other than that, there were perhaps 80 to 100 people who had indicated an interest in being involved in his candidacy.

The week that ended with the December 20 Cuomo press conference began with a need to handle the picky little detail of how one files for office in New Hampshire; I remember being asked if I could get the application form discreetly. I thought that relatively unlikely. [Laughter]

There's a provision in the law that if you file on the last day, you must do so in person. We attempted to get a ruling from the Attorney General, not easy in New Hampshire, as to whether that was specifically for people who were state candidates as opposed to a presidential primary situation. They're still working on that ruling.

On Thursday, they flew in a young aide who had with him the documents signed by Cuomo to file on his behalf. Keep in mind, the decision would have had to be made on Thursday, unless on the Friday, he was actually willing to fly up himself. They sent advance people in on Thursday night. The form lay dormant. We did nothing with it actually because at three o'clock that afternoon, no decision had been made.

We had a preliminary schedule for Friday, and we stood by the pay phone at the Ramada Inn waiting, waiting and waiting. I think about three o'clock he made the final announcement. And about two-thirty, we had received a call from Marino saying, "I hate to tell you this, but ..." and by that candor, I mean, your excitement is somehow lost. You can only spend so many hours at the pay phone at the Ramada Inn and still be excited. And at that point in time, they just notified us that he had decided it was a no-go. Maybe the best story of it, I'm told, was the reaction of his wife who was somewhat aware of his nature to procrastinate. When told on the Thursday that she would be needed on the Friday to travel to New Hampshire with them, she explained that she was going to be working with their daughter and an interior decorator and "just tell Mario that when he decides, send a helicopter for me then." [Laughter]

Bill Schneider: I must remind you that Mario Cuomo was asked recently how he would respond if the President invited him to serve on the Supreme Court. He said, "My answer would be so swift that you would say I was the most decisive man in American politics." When a reporter said, "What would your answer be?" He said, "I have no idea."

Ron Brown: Bill, it seemed to me that everybody was second tier in December. All the talk was, the heavyweights aren't in. The first team isn't on the playing field, and as long as Cuomo hovered above everything with the chance that he might come in, there was still that talk. Once he decided not to get in, you could focus on the field. From among these people is going to come the Democratic nominee for President.

So it changed people's perspective in evaluating these candidates. Coupled with what Paul Begala said about the political realities that flowed from that, it really was a very important turning point in the campaign.

Just to correct the historical record—although my friend Governor Cuomo, in his press conference, made it sound like he had just gotten off the telephone with me and I had just bludgeoned him into staying out of the race, I hadn't talked with him for three months. He knew clearly what my position was, that I thought he had to either make up his mind to get in or get out, and do it quickly. I had really not talked to him, and I listened to that press conference rather incredulously when he called my name about eight times, as if we had just talked. I wish John Marino was here to speak for him, but at any rate, I wanted to make clear that there had been no recent conversations with Governor Cuomo.

James Carville: The Chairman was trying to get him in, remember the thing in Pebble Beach, and Jay Rockefeller called and said he was very disappointed. Ron Brown's position was always, anybody who wanted to run, get in, but if you're not in, you're not running. I've got to say, he was very faithful to that. But this was in August, I remember, when Rockefeller called you to tell you he was not going to run, and he was very disappointed.

Bill Schneider: We're talking about the New Hampshire primary. I think in some ways we have a reversal of the conventional wisdom which says that in New Hampshire you work the state very hard. It's a state with a lot of retail politics, as Joe said. It's on-the-ground politics. Someone emerges as the winner in New Hampshire, gets a lot of national press coverage, picture on the cover of the national news magazines, on the network news that night, and becomes a national front runner.

In many ways this year was different. You had a reversal of that wisdom: there was an invisible primary in the national press which seemed to spill over into the New Hampshire campaign, providing a national press consensus on who the front runner was, who the candidates to watch were. And that seemed to have a visible and palpable effect on the New Hampshire campaign. I think James Carville made an important point that this might have been a product of the perceived importance of the Democratic race after the Harris Wofford victory in Pennsylvania; that suddenly, with the Democrats having a real chance to win, it became an instant national story. In any case, that conventional wisdom about a national candidate growing out of New Hampshire retail politics may have been reversed this year.

I want to pass on to Friday, January 17, on which our timeline indicates newspapers report that Clinton had affairs. This had to do with the lawsuit by Larry Nichols, the beginning of the great Gennifer Flowers episode, followed by the television debate with Cokie Roberts on January 19. I'll ask Betsy to pose some questions relating to that particular long episode in the New Hampshire primary.

Paul Begala: Well, for the record, before that, there was one other thing that Goldman reminded me of. Georgia moved its primary date right about this time. That's damned important and thank you, Zell Miller [Governor of Georgia]. Were you all tracking that? Were you working it? We were working it like crazy. We happened to have the Governor, the Lieutenant Governor, the Speaker for us so that helped. Very important to us to move that primary.

Ken Bode: Well, why did the Governor move the primary?

Paul Begala: To put Georgia in the spotlight, make sure that they got the kind of attention from national candidates and potential Presidents that folks in that wonderful Peach State deserve, and so that America would get good government. [Laughter]

Bill Schneider: Was there any intervention or campaign on your part? Did your campaign discuss this with Governor Miller?

Ed Sims [Chair, Georgia Democratic Party]:   That began, in all honesty, a year, year-and-a-half, before the campaign; Governor Miller asked us to do a study of the party and what the impact of being a part of Super Tuesday was. The result was less candidate attention and less money spent, fewer ads in Georgia. It was clearly the result of both Texas and Florida dominating Super Tuesday.

So, in an effort to get some attention in Georgia well before anyone knew who the candidates were going to be, we proposed a change be made. One of the key elements was approval of the Justice Department because of the federal laws which require approval of any change in the laws relating to elections. Is Charlie Black here? Anyway, we understood that that could be blocked at the Justice Department at any time.

Mary Matalin: No, we would never do that. Let's just say we knew it was a question.

Ed Sims: So in advance, we talked to some of the people at the Republican party and said if you want to block this, tell us now and we won't even attempt to change it, and we received a nonbinding informal indication that the change would be allowed to go forward.

Ken Bode: In 1988 South Carolina had its primary early as well. It was a way to get South Carolina attention, but it was also a very, very important element in the Bush strategy going into Super Tuesday. In 1992, you were trying to get Georgia some attention. To what extent were you also consciously, with Sam Nunn and Zell Miller, helping Bill Clinton?

Ed Sims: The genesis of the idea of moving Super Tuesday had occurred well before Clinton was backed openly by Miller or Nunn.

Ken Bode: I'm not sure I'm getting an answer to my question.

Ron Brown: Just for context purposes and related to a comment that James made, the fact that we established a principle a couple of years ago that having an early nominee was very important is the piece that we've missed in this discussion. The reason we were pushing people in the summer of 1991 to get in or say they're not going to get in, was because all the press was claiming nobody wants to run for this nomination. It's worthless. George Bush is at 70 percent or 80 percent. You don't even have a nominee. You might as well wait for '96 and forget about '92. So that was a part of that drive, coupled with the Mario factor, which would have kept us from having an early nominee, if we had had candidates of the potential power and force of Mario Cuomo still hovering. In January and February, it would have delayed coming to closure, so it was all a part of trying to come to closure to get an early nominee so that we could start focusing on the general election campaign.

David Wilhelm: I just want to add to that. From a money management point of view, there were 27 primaries and caucuses by March 17, and this was really a front-loaded process and put a premium on things happening early. The other factor was proportional representation in the way delegates were selected. It made it impossible for a latecomer, a late entrant into the race, to really have any notion that he or she would actually win. At best, that person could only be a spoiler.

James Carville: That was, of all of the press things, the stupidest. This idea that somebody was going to get in after Illinois and win the thing. In fact, [the late] Tully [Paul Tully, strategic consultant, Clinton campaign] explained to me that proportional representation, at about a third of the way through the process, kicks in and works enormously to the front runner's benefit. You don't even have to win these final primaries and it was actually put in after Carter lost the last six primaries in 1976 to Frank Church or whoever got in late there.

Ken Bode: That was Jerry Brown.

James Carville: Jerry Brown, okay, but that was the dumbest idea, and it got widespread circulation in the press that somebody was going to get in and capture the nomination. Numerically, it was impossible.

Dennis Kanin: Somebody could get in and block, but somebody could not get in and win. You could block someone from winning the nomination through proportional representation.

Bill Schneider: The primaries are a killing field. The whole point is to get rid of dead candidates and get them off the field. To my mind, proportional representation is a way of keeping dead candidates alive. It seems to me you have proportional representation so someone who is dead can continue to run and get votes and make trouble.

Dennis Kanin: No.

James Carville: That's an opposite effect.

Bill Schneider: No?

Dennis Kanin: I don't think it works that way.

Bill Schneider: You don't think it works that way?

James Carville: No. I think it works the other way.

Dennis Kanin: It doesn't work that way because you need a majority of the delegates at the convention. If Tsongas had stayed in the race, it would have been Tsongas, Brown, and Clinton. Even if Clinton had won every single primary after Illinois, he would have only about 40 percent of the votes because of proportional representation. He would have been stopped from getting a first ballot victory.

James Carville: But the system doesn't work like that, Dennis. What happens is, we don't have to win. Once you have a 500-delegate margin, even if you lose a primary, you're still adding to get to the 2,145 or whatever the number is.

Dennis Kanin: But you're not adding 50 percent. You're only adding...

David Wilhelm: But the rationale of a candidate who continues is to be a spoiler, and it's hard to raise money running that way, it's hard to have an organization, and it's a bad message.

Ron Brown: This discussion indicates the exact reason why I didn't let us have this debate in the Democratic party. It's the same debate we've been having for four election cycles, fighting over the rules, fighting over whether we ought to have winner-take-all or proportional representation, very disruptive to focusing on winning elections. We didn't have it, and I think it served us well.

Bill Schneider: The Republicans don't have proportional representation. Mary, would you have preferred that or not?

Mary Matalin: No. We liked it just the way it was, but can I go back, this is just curiosity for me, to what Chairman Sims was saying? Because part of this game is psyching the other side out, and we had very early identified Clinton as the guy. The rest of you are all thinking that might not have been the case, but we saw this as a very Atwateresque move when the Georgia primary thing was moved as South Carolina's had been. We went to desperate ends to get that not to happen, short of calling the Department of Justice, but we were trying to leave you with the impression that we would block it at Justice. I'm curious to know why and how the communication came back to you via the Republicans that it was okay to move this primary. We saw that as a very pivotal advantage for Governor Clinton and one we desperately did not want to happen.

Ed Sims: Well, the first discussion of moving the primary truly took place, James and Paul, what, a year, a year and...

James Carville: Yes. We talked about that even in the nineties, during the nineties.

Ed Sims: 1990.

James Carville: It's a cycle.

Mary Matalin: You guys got Governor Miller to do that like [snaps fingers].

Frank Greer: It was for Governor Clinton, it was in our great interest to move the primary.

James Carville: And that discussion had started way before we went to work with Clinton.

David Wilhelm: The people in the Georgia House created Super Tuesday.

James Carville: We had a problem. We worked for Ed Sims and Zell Miller, too, so we felt it was in Zell's interest as well as in Clinton's interest.

Mary Matalin: That was just a curiosity. This is about a total communication breakdown. I don't know what Republican told you that we wanted it moved but we absolutely did not, so let the record show that.

James Carville: We are starting to drag a lot of fake hands out of the basement here, right?

Mary Matalin: And winner-take-all, obviously, it serves the incumbent. So, of course, we preferred that and thought it was okay in the states where we had proportional representation.

Feeding Frenzy I. Gennifer Flowers

"I know about affairs. Gennifer Flowers
did not have an affair with Bill Clinton."

— Betsey Wright, Deputy Campaign Chair,
Clinton/Gore Campaign

Bill Schneider: Well, despite all these delaying tactics, we will talk about the Gennifer Flowers episode, and I call on Betsy to raise some issues with respect to that.

Betsy Kolbert: The first question is, I guess, an obvious one, and that is that the campaign seemed emotionally unprepared for the Gennifer Flowers feeding frenzy that occurred. Yet all the way back in September, we in the press, and I assume all of you, had every reason to believe that something like this was going to happen. What I want to ask whoever over there who wants to take it up is, "How candidly did you all discuss this and why wasn't the campaign better prepared?"

Stan Greenberg: Frank, why don't you take that?

James Carville: I didn't come aboard until December 1. I don't know of any way that you could be emotionally prepared for something like that. I was in Boston. We came up here to do something for Metzenbaum's outfit, the Coalition for Democratic Values. I was traveling with the candidate, and there was a media feeding frenzy. I feared for my life and actually was picked up and carried for like four feet. I had absolutely no control over it. People were screaming, and a radio guy was crawling over me with the microphone, screaming about Gennifer Flowers.

Certainly, we had heard about all that but maybe Bill Kristol could talk to this, the only thing that was big, or as big, was the Quayle thing right after the Republican convention in 1988. But in that period of time, I had never seen a feeding frenzy like this one, and, no, I wasn't any way, shape, or form emotionally prepared for it.

Betsey Wright: I hadn't come on the campaign officially at that point. Bill was driving around the state doing the meetings about whether he could break his vow not to run for president. There were times when I would drive him between the towns, and we discussed the draft and the women, the general as well as the specific. We were very mindful that part of the generational difference of a Clinton candidacy was that someone who was good-looking and had gone to college in the sixties during Vietnam and marijuana would have to expect some focus in that direction.

Then he had specific problems and began dealing with what I refer to as the Sperling breakfast strategy,* which acknowledged affairs and then opened him up for anybody to claim to have been one of them by saying that he wasn't going to discuss it.

Obviously, Gennifer was not specifically discussed but, what do you call them, gold diggers were. The last time I had trouble remembering the word gold diggers, I came up with bimbo eruptions. We knew that some of that was going to happen, and I would play through with Bill the questions as if Chelsea had heard something on the news. They were brutal sessions, and we were trying to deal with this before he had made the decision to run.

So a lot of the emotional preparation that Bill and Hillary and Chelsea went through was around this stuff. When the Gennifer thing hit, I made numerous attempts to get in contact with people in the campaign. I felt that in addition to the strategy about how Bill and Hillary would deal with it publicly, there had to be a simultaneous strategy for discrediting Gennifer in her previous associations with Clinton, and I was the person who knew those.

I was the person who had refused to help her get jobs in the past. I was the person who had returned the phone calls she was always making to Bill. I was the person who knew that in '87, when she thought he was going to run, she moved back to Little Rock to set up this kind of thing.

I couldn't get any of those guys on the phone. So, the whole thing about her pattern in his life got left out in the frenzy because we in the Clinton family were in as much a frenzy as the press was, and it was all focused on how to deal with Bill in it and we've never had this particular conversation before. I had similar kinds of conversations with Bill on the draft stuff that summer driving between Pine Bluff and Warren and so on.

Bill Schneider: Frank?

Editor's Note: For many years Godfrey Sperling, a Washington columnist, has given regular breakfasts that bring reporters together with a guest. Bill Clinton was a guest in 1992.

Frank Greer: Just to add to what Betsey was offering, let me give a little bit of a historical perspective. First of all, Gennifer Flowers' name did not surface in New Hampshire for the first time in Bill Clinton's political life. It came up in the gubernatorial campaign in 1990.

Betsey Wright: Oh, we had been dealing with her since 1984, Frank.

Frank Greer: Absolutely. But all I'm saying is in the world of political press coverage of Bill Clinton, the first story that was picked up from the tabloids was not a Gennifer Flowers story. It was a story about an accusation by Larry Nichols, who had been fired from state government for making 430 calls to the Contras because he thought that he could be a part of Ollie North's network. He had a grudge against Bill Clinton, had decided during the gubernatorial race, as a threat to try to get his job back, to make some wild accusations about a number of people that he speculated had had a relationship with Bill Clinton. The press in Arkansas, to their credit, in that gubernatorial campaign, never printed a word of it. They looked into it. The AP, the *Democrat* [the *Arkansas Democrat-Gazette* newspaper] is not our best friend in Arkansas. None of those folks gave it any credibility. They said this is off the wall, and they spent a long time ...

Betsey Wright: But not without tremendous work behind the scenes with every single one of them about both Larry and lists.

Frank Greer: Absolutely. Okay? So one of the things is we thought that, at least, the press who knew him best had gone through this rumor before, and we had the hope, I believe, that nobody would give it much credibility. It appeared in the *New York Post*. I never will forget that first Thursday night. It was coming out on Monday, and we got word of it. We were in Boston, as a matter of fact, filming, and in New Hampshire. But it was still our hope — and we referred a lot of the national reporters to the Arkansas press corps — that the mainstream media was not going to give this a lot of credibility.

The fact of the matter is, in terms of going back to the Sperling breakfast and the discussions within the campaign, and with Bill and Hillary, I think this campaign was prepared. This is my one point I want to make. Given the history of this kind of story and feeding frenzy in American politics, because of the strength of character of Bill Clinton and Hillary, we handled it pretty damn well. I would say that if it was not handled well, it may have been on the other side of it, in terms of the way it was covered, not on the campaign side. The one thing I want to point out, and Greenberg can comment on this, we had, after two or three weeks of media and campaigning in New Hampshire, moved into first place. Our numbers did not significantly drop through two weeks of the tabloids and then the mainstream press picking up the tabloid accusations all the way through. As a matter of fact, in our focus groups, people said they admired Bill Clinton and Hillary, for both "60 Minutes" and for the way he stood up to the feeding frenzy, for the way he handled it with good grace and style and courage and was not afraid to face the press. If anything, I think he was strengthened by that, and our numbers were not collapsing.

Dennis Kanin: Can I just say that I agree completely? We got exactly the same kind of results, and as a matter of fact, our polls, two days before the Gennifer Flowers thing broke, that's the second Thursday, showed us five points' difference, Clinton ahead of Tsongas. Within a couple of weeks, you were 15 points ahead of us, after the Gennifer Flowers incident. And it was only the draft ...

Frank Greer: Stop there. [Laughter]

Dennis Kanin: That's the stuff that hurt.

Stan Greenberg: But that's an important point that will be evident when we talk about the poll numbers. We were much better prepared to deal with the Gennifer Flowers question, and we had talked this thing through, much better prepared on that issue than we were on the draft.

Paul Begala: January 27, the Monday after the Thursday when the story first hit, all three networks led with the Gennifer Flowers story. That was the day the following things happened: Yeltsin disappeared from the Kremlin. No one knew where he was. Macy's, America's largest retailer, declared bankruptcy. The President of the United States interrupted the printing of his budget in mid-printing because of a health care dispute. The Supreme Court, for the first time in American history, limited the scope of the Voting Rights Act, and Middle East peace talks convened anew in Moscow.

It was a big news day. Yet all three networks led with a failed lounge lizard who held a press conference at the Waldorf-Astoria. And one network carried it live. No, we weren't ready for that.

James Carville: There was no strategic dissent in the Clinton campaign that I know of from the governor, from Mrs. Clinton, or anybody else. We wanted to get out there as fast as we could and in the biggest way we could. There's a phrase we had in the campaign. The first word is cluster, the second word is a naughty word that rhymes with truck. We knew from the minute it hit that the media was going crazy. The feeding frenzy was there from the minute the story hit. You could tell that's all the reporters wanted to talk about. Am I right on that so far, Frank?

Frank Greer: Absolutely. There was absolutely no disagreement. There was a logistical problem, and especially because we also thought that Bill and Hillary should deal with this together, and she was in Atlanta, and he was in a blizzard in New Hampshire. Unfortunately, there was also an ABC reporter traveling with him. And so he had given the first indication they might try to do "Nightline." But it was not going to be physically possible to do it so that's how that all got started. We then searched immediately, with George Stephanopoulos, for the next best forum, and "60 Minutes" seemed to be the best opportunity to deal with this issue.

Stan Greenberg: First it was newspapers.

Frank Greer: We had a problem with CNN because I think the ...

James Carville: We stiffed them.

Frank Greer: Yes.

James Carville: I mean, that's what happened. They were mad, and they got us back again, again, and again.

Frank Greer: For weeks and weeks.

James Carville: We said we were going on "Newsmaker Sunday" and "60 Minutes" called. We said more people watch "60 Minutes" than "Newsmaker Sunday." That's just a fact, and they were not amused, and not amused for a long, long time after that.

Frank Greer: They had also canceled Mario Cuomo for that "Newsmaker Sunday" in order to put Bill Clinton on.

Carole Simpson: May I ask a question as an ABC observer?

Frank Greer: Yes.

Carole Simpson: ABC's impression was that you went for the bigger numbers. "Prime Time Live" wanted you on. Right? You had the next opportunity with "Prime Time Live," and you refused that and went for "60 Minutes."

James Carville: It was on Thursday it broke, "60 Minutes" was on Sunday. We were going to try to get to "Nightline." We couldn't, and yes, we wanted as big an audience as we could get. It was Super Bowl Sunday and they said they would give us the time right after the Super Bowl.

Frank Greer: James, you may not remember this. One other thing that most people didn't notice is that we had an execution in Arkansas on Friday. We did not think it would be appropriate for us to be on Friday night television talking about Gennifer Flowers.

James Carville: We couldn't do that, that's right. I do remember that now.

Elizabeth Arnold: So you were stunned by the feeding frenzy, but what was the plan? What was the plan when you went on "60 Minutes," Frank?

James Carville: To get it out in front.

Frank Greer: And, basically, going back to the same strategy and message of the Sperling breakfast, for them to admit that they're not perfect, but that they do have a marriage and a relationship, and that they also have a commitment to each other that we think will withstand the test of public opinion. And I think they did it very effectively.

Stan Greenberg: But the goal was to take it on.

Betsey Wright: Also between live versus taped.

Stan Greenberg: Take it on in as big a way as possible so that no one could ever say through the rest of this campaign that we did not confront the issue.

Paul Begala: We made a mistake in that we gave them an hour and 45 minutes. What we should have done is give them 15 minutes, if they were going to air 15 minutes, just live to tape.

Frank Greer: Period.

Paul Begala: We should have done live to tape, but we let "60 Minutes" edit that. And the best, most powerful parts of that interview wound up on the cutting room floor.

Tad Devine: Just from the perspective of another campaign, looking at this thing. First of all, our research was showing that this was not affecting Clinton. I agree with what Dennis said, that in some of the focus groups, responses were actually very favorable to what we did. But this is sort of like Cuomo hovering in '91, this was taking up a lot of space, a lot of coverage, and it was very difficult for someone like Kerrey to get in the mix.

We had to become part of that story, and, you know, we didn't want to become part of that story. We faced this same issue later when we made a decision to get into the draft story. It was the same kind of pervasive overwhelming coverage. Either you're in or you're out, and we were out.

Betsy Kolbert: And was that a very clear decision, we don't want to get, or was that really ...

Tad Devine: Yes. I mean, to the point of going into the campaign headquarters with this. There was a tabloid on the front desk, and I suppressed it. I said, you know, we're not talking about this, we are out of it, we're completely out of it. It was also built on a belief that if this was going to be a harmful story, we weren't going to get mixed up in the second wave of us pushing it around. We wanted it to have its own legs and we weren't going to get mixed up.

Bill Shore: I think it was also clear, as Frank said, that if Clinton survived the story, he was going to be very tough. It was a story that was either going to kill him or was going to make him very strong, which is what happened.

Ken Bode: There's a certain depth of feeling at the Clinton campaign that the national press seems to have engaged in something unseemly here, and I just want to make a comment or two about the responsibility of Arkansas press versus the national press. We were directed by a lot of you guys to go talk to Arkansas journalists. You may think that they gave Bill Clinton a cleaner bill of health on this issue than they actually did when we talked to them down there. They restrained themselves in the last gubernatorial election, but remember Larry Nichols' lawsuit, which was filed in Federal Court in the summer of 1991.

The Federal Court files in Arkansas was not the only place that the lawsuit turned up. A lot of us had that lawsuit in our own research files very quickly after Larry Nichols filed it. He listed a whole group of names. All of us understood that Larry Nichols was an enemy of Bill Clinton. All of us understood that these were unsubstantiated facts. There were a lot of networks, a lot of newspapers that sent a lot of reporters down from Little Rock to look into these matters.

Nobody published a thing about this for a long period of time until Jerry Nachman at the *New York Post* got hold of the lawsuit. And this may indicate some of the sorts of conflicts when you work for something that's protected by the First Amendment. Jerry Nachman said, "What is going on? This is a completely libel-free lawsuit. It's a Federal Court document and any newspaper in the country can publish the contents and never be sued for libel. The very fact that nobody is publishing anything about this amounts to a giant press conspiracy to suppress this as something that's making its way through the courts." Nachman said, "I won't be part of that," and he put it in the *New York Post,* and that's where it all began. It wasn't a sleazy tabloid that began all this, Paul.

Frank Greer: That was a lawsuit that had been dismissed at the state level and had been reintroduced. Several national publications had already interviewed Larry Nichols and a number of other people involved in that, and if you will remember, a week after Larry Nichols' story appeared in the *New York Post,* he said, "It wasn't true. I made it up, I was just trying to get back at Bill Clinton; there was no basis to those rumors that I put in that lawsuit." He withdrew the lawsuit a week later. You didn't see a hell of a lot about that, and major national publications admitted that Larry Nichols had, in September of that year, said that he made this whole thing up. If they knew that, why didn't they publish it when the first story came out in the *New York Post?* Because they wanted to make this a big sleazy story.

James Carville: And let some media defenders justify to me that three networks on the night of the Gennifer Flowers thing led with tapes that were not verified and further found to be selectively edited in 12 different places.

Frank Greer: Or let a network that carried her press conference live defend itself.

James Carville: Live.

Ken Bode: You know, Bill Clinton verified the tapes for everybody.

James Carville: No, he didn't verify.

Ken Bode: Yes, he did. He called Mario Cuomo and apologized for what was on the tapes.

James Carville: All he said was it was his voice. I can take a question and splice a different response in. I can say, is your name Ken Bode, and you say yes, and I say, did you kill Stan Greenberg and you say no, and I can take the yes you said to Ken Bode and put it on there. [Anthony] Pellicano [expert in tape recording] said that the tapes tended to verify that. I could go on and on. I'm not going to go on and on about this. There is no justification.

Paul Begala: Jackson and WCBS in Los Angeles and the *L.A. Times,* those are the only three I could find that did analyze the tapes, but this was after the fact.

Ken Bode: At CNN, we analyzed the tapes, and long after a call to Cuomo, our verification came in so we played the press conference, but not the tapes on CNN.

Carole Simpson: There was so much agony over whether we should go with that stuff or not, and the decision was finally made because Clinton had to respond to it on the campaign trail. They decided it was justified. His message was lost because he was being asked repeatedly about the tabloid story, and that was what led ABC to say, hey, that becomes a legitimate story now because he is being hounded by it.

James Carville: I'm sure all you news people were just saying, "Oh, we just hate this story. We have got to do it because everybody else is doing it, but we just hate this." I think that Gennifer Flowers had the most positive impact on press coverage of anybody in the cycle. You know, because after '88, it's like a bunch of drunks. You know, you all go off to Columbia [University] and say, we swear, we're not going to do it again, we're not going to do it, we promise, we promise, we're going to dry out. And then she comes up, puts a jug of whiskey on the bar, and everybody gets drunk. Then they got this terrible hangover. I just don't want to feel that bad again. The way a lot of people covered it was, "We're not really covering Gennifer Flowers. We're just covering the way the press is covering Gennifer Flowers."

Ken Bode: The special on "Nightline"...

James Carville: Yes. "It's not like that. You've got to understand, James. We think this is a sleazy story. There's no place in mainstream journalism." Then I think the *Washington Post* had their media reporter cover how the media was covering it. I mean, you know, the media ...

Ann Devroy: Let the *Washington Post* speak for one minute here.

James Carville: Okay.

Ann Devroy: I know you're totally outraged about this.

James Carville: There are a lot of other people here who feel the same way.

Ann Devroy: I noticed there were plenty of Democrats, certainly not you, at all levels calling the *Washington Post* and asking why aren't you doing the Jennifer Fitzgerald story.*

Mary Matalin: Thank you, Ann.

Ann Devroy: Certainly, I would not accuse anybody in this room of that, but I got at least a hundred phone calls ...

James Carville: Well, I'll tell you, my best moment in the campaign is when they said, the White House said, I was pushing the Jennifer Fitzgerald story. And Andrea Mitchell [NBC News White House correspondent] says I've talked to her every day, and she never said a word to me about that.

Ann Devroy: We certainly got unbelievable amounts of encouragement to pursue that subject, including Hillary Clinton talking about it in a magazine.

Marty Plissner: This Sunday appearance by Hillary denying it to an audience three times the size of any that heard Gennifer the following day, took place three days after it was in the *Star*. It was the first reference to it on CBS. It was in the process of having it denied twice by Clinton and by both Clintons.

Editor's Note: Allegations of an affair were first explored in Bush's 1980 presidential bid by reporter Ann Devroy. Allegations resurfaced in the 1988 election, and in the July 1992 issue of *Spy* magazine the woman was named as long-time aide, Jennifer Fitzgerald. The story was "angrily denied" by the White House.

James Carville: Therefore, you had to play *unverified* tapes.

Stan Greenberg: Let's not forget that this story was taken into the mainstream press by Cokie Roberts in the debate in New Hampshire when she asked Bill Clinton in a tactical way, "How can you be sure it's not going to hurt you in the future?" But the fact is, it was a proactive effort by segments of the press to make this a story.

Bill Schneider: Well, you know, the press is now being widely excoriated for not pursuing stories about senators about whom rumors have been circulating for years and years about womanizing and sexual harassment, and the idea is, why does it take so long for these to surface?

In the case of Governor Clinton, unlike the case of President Bush, here was someone [Gennifer Flowers] who had a press conference at the Waldorf-Astoria and played some purportedly accurate tapes. We didn't broadcast those tapes. If Jennifer Fitzgerald had gone to the Waldorf-Astoria and had a press conference, my guess is we would have covered it and there would have been a story. So there was a real discrepancy between those two stories, in that respect.

Mary Matalin: You did cover it. A footnote in that stupid book* and your network did it. Mary Tillotson [CNN correspondent] asked George Bush at a press conference on Bosnia, if I'm not mistaken. So I hate to take up on their side, but the dean of political snoopery, Ann Devroy, tried to get this Fitzgerald thing done for ten months and she couldn't. It's been going on for a hundred years and it's a footnote by a dead guy, and it gets into you guys pushing it all around. What is this?

Ann Devroy: We're not accusing, in fact, we totally exempt every single person here about every call.

Mary Matalin: Brooks Jackson [CNN correspondent] said on the air that the Democrats had said to him that they'd been in contact with the Clinton campaign. That really isn't my point. My larger point is ...

James Carville: Let me tell you something. All of us talk a lot to reporters in this room. Forget the *off-the-record* thing. Have I called any of you about any of this crap, or people here?

Editor's Note: A footnote in *The Power House: Robert Keith Gray and the Selling of Access and Influence in Washington,* by Susan B. Trento, quoted Louis Fields, an ambassador to the nuclear disarmament talks in Geneva who died in 1986, as saying that he had arranged for President Bush and Jennifer Fitzgerald to have adjoining hotel rooms during an official visit Mr. Bush made to the talks in 1984. An aide to Vice President Bush at the time and, in 1992, working at the State Department's Protocol Office, Ms. Fitzgerald routinely traveled with the Vice President as part of her official responsibilities.

Paul Begala: Why don't we make that a rule from now on? If someone calls on something sleazy like that, they waive the privilege. No more confidentiality. So if I place a call to Ann Devroy and say, hey, I've got a rumor about X and Y doing Z ...

James Carville: Well wait a minute, what is considered sleazy? I ain't waiving nothing but the flag. [Laughter]

Marty Plissner: Bill, did you say that CNN did not broadcast the Gennifer Flowers tapes?

Bill Schneider: We broadcast the press conference. We did not play the audio tapes. We blanked out the tapes themselves because they had not been verified.

Ken Bode: You guys think that the press enjoys this story but I want to tell you, you're not exactly accurate about that. I think maybe each time this happens, all of us learn a little bit more about a responsible way to cover this thing the next time it happens, hopefully. But when there's a fairly substantial charge made about a politician who's running for President of the United States or serving as President of the United States, that he has or has had a mistress on the public payroll, that is going to be a story. It's going to be covered. I think it's a legitimate issue.

Frank Greer: That is a total mischaracterization of what this story was.

Ken Bode: Frank, it's what drove the stories, that Gennifer had a job on the Arkansas ...

James Carville: That is not what drove the story.

Ken Bode: It is certainly. You guys are mistaken if you think that inside journalism we did not talk about others. Why do you think all the rest of the names were not mentioned? How many bimbo eruptions were there, Betsey?

James Carville: If you, the networks, did the right thing by playing unverified, edited tapes.

Ken Bode: Jim, what you're trying to do is to get this red herring back in here again.

James Carville: I'm trying to ask a question.

Ken Bode: Gennifer had a job on the payroll. That's what drove the story.

Bill Schneider: Gentlemen, I give the floor to Betsey Wright.

Frank Greer: That was not a part of the story.

Ken Bode: It was, of course, a part of the story.

Bill Schneider: Betsey Wright.

Betsey Wright: It was part of the rationalization and justification for the story, Ken. Because she did have a job on the government payroll, which was some stupid person's idea, and she claimed she had had an affair. I know about affairs. Gennifer Flowers did not have an affair with Bill Clinton. But you all allowed those two things to be put together as if they were there. She was lying, and her lie got credibility, and part of what gave her credibility was pointing to the fact that she had a state job. James is exactly right that after this calmed down, the legitimate mainstream press was so cautious and gun shy that it would double check everything.

It made my life of swimming in sleaze a lot easier because I could say, you know, the next one that you all are going to get is on such and such, and they'd say, well, are you telling the rest, and I'd say yes. As long as somebody was going to do a surprise on it and the groundwork was there, the caution and responsibility was enormous because you all felt bad about what you did with Gennifer Flowers.

Betsy Kolbert: Can you tell us though why Bill Clinton never just said flat out, I never had an affair with Gennifer Flowers?

James Carville: He did.

Frank Greer: He did.

James Carville: He certainly did. He said it any number of times. He did.

Betsey Wright: Now, what he said, James, was ... Let's not do a slick Willie here.

Ken Bode: What did he say, Betsey?

Bill Schneider: "A draft I didn't dodge and a woman I didn't sleep with," was the quote that I recall.

Betsey Wright: And he said she was lying.

James Carville: He said she was lying.

Betsey Wright: And she was, and she has been lying since she was three years old.

James Carville: You're not dealing with Mother Teresa here.

Frank Greer: Let me mention one thing which I actually thought was a fairly good standard, and in this campaign it was completely destroyed, blown out of the water. In the book *Feeding Frenzy,* Larry Sabato said, "The old standard used to be before you go with something

this damaging, this devastating, you're to have two sources that can verify it."

Bill and I talked about this in terms of the standard change this year
— make any accusation, say anything, no substantiation, and, it becomes a legitimate story. If there was some way to go back to the fact
that you needed to have at least two sources or some ability to verify a
charge or an accusation, the journalistic community and the political
community would be a hell of a lot better off.

Bill Schneider: Let me observe as someone who was watching the
polls very carefully throughout the campaign that there was a certain
lack of credibility. I think what contributed to it on the part of the voters
were two things. One is that the initial accusation appeared in *The Star.*
The very fact that it appeared in the tabloid, which a lot of voters are
familiar with, gave the story a kind of incredible aura because voters
tended to be familiar with the kinds of stories printed in the tabloids.

Second of all, a point that has not been mentioned, but I think that
was critical in raising questions about Gennifer Flowers' credibility, was
the widely known fact, widely discussed, that she was paid for the story.
That fact raised questions, the tapes notwithstanding, about her credibility and her motivations. That element should not be ignored.

Betsey Wright, Dennis Kanin, Thaleia Schlesinger

Betsey Wright: The difficult thing on the follow-up on that, Bill, I
think, is my residual frustration about the process, and some day I'm
going to get it really clear what should have happened. But I tried for a
long time, knowing that Gennifer would be back, to get a major story

done about her, raising the question of credibility, which should have been done in the beginning. Nobody would do it unless I would produce the Republican connections, and, as far as I was concerned, the Republican connections were not the key story.

I had them. I had her phone calls with Ron Fuller and Sheffield Nelson* and their phone calls moments afterwards. I had the Republican connection, but that wasn't the issue. She was lying. She was paid, and nobody will do the life story of Gennifer Flowers. Now, the stupid *Penthouse* thing finally worked in a little bit of stuff, but nobody wanted it there, nobody would go do the story of her, once it calmed down. They only would do it if I could prove the Republican role.

Tom Luce: As one of the few people in this room who had not been on the national scene in a presidential race, what staggered me was the enormous amount of time the press devoted to checking out these kinds of stories, all of this garbage. Regardless of where it comes from, whether it comes from the Democrats or Republicans, the *Star* or whatever, how quickly everybody gets absorbed in running it down as opposed to finding out what happened to the S & L's or Somalia or whatever. That's what's staggering to people who've never observed it before. And I think it's something that ought to be talked about in terms of what it does to the distortion of the process.

Howard Fineman: I just had a question. Since Mary said that it was quite obvious to her and all the other Republicans early on that Bill Clinton was going to be the man, what did you know and when did you know it about Gennifer Flowers and the other bimbos.

Mary Matalin: When we were at the [Republican National] Committee, by virtue of having the apparatus and a lot of stuff early, we decided, at the outset of our opposition research project, that we weren't going to touch any of that stuff, and we didn't. Lord knows, from then throughout, certainly after bimbo eruptions, it came over the transom endlessly, and we just threw it out. It didn't matter that we knew about it because there wasn't anything we were going to do with it. But I will say at that time, that in the invisible primary period, at least — I only bring this up because it's so hypocritical, it bothers me — the press and reporters and columnists were calling around every kind of story and rumor and innuendo, and then, after the fact, came back and said that they were hearing all these stories from the Bush campaign, from

---

* *Editor's Note:* Ron Fuller is a former Arkansas Republican state representative; Sheffield Nelson ran unsuccessfully against Clinton for governor in 1990, and is co-chair of the Arkansas GOP.

Republican officials, from the Republican community. That's simply not the case. We were hearing it from them. I'm not trying to act holier than thou or as Mother Teresa, as James says, but we had no intention ever to use that stuff. George Bush was unequivocal about this, did not like the Big A question in '88, and it was just off the table.

Howard Fineman: But as Betsey was saying, there was a history of Republican efforts in the state.

Mary Matalin: We are not as attached. You're thinking of this big monolithic Soviet Union or something. These state parties frequently act in their own interest. Sheffield Nelson — Betsey, I swear to God — Sheffield Nelson is not our agent down there. He would try to work with us but we don't want him getting involved in that kind of stuff.

Betsey Wright: Mary, let's get a little honest. You didn't have to. One of the things that the Gennifer Flowers story spurred was an enormous amount of money on the streets to people to lie and to take disconnected things and try to make them facts. The tabloid part of this world, both print and TV, put money on the street. You didn't have to worry about it. I swam in it every day. There was a market that everybody could legitimately claim wasn't a part of the news world and they didn't have to deal with. It had a profound impact on the electorate and in the kind of defense mechanisms that we had to put together to try to keep these things out. Because it wasn't just the fear that you all would pick up a story from another tabloid program again.

It was that the American people are now so confused about the information they get from tabloids versus news, and whether it's all just part of the information gathering process. What bimbo eruptions was all about was money on the streets to pay people to lie. And Mary Matalin has at much at stake in stopping it as I do, and Bill Clinton and George Bush did. And some day, she's going to help me on it because something has to happen to stop it.

Two days before the election, we were still in a battle with one of the tabloid TV people who find all of these very vulnerable people for unbelievable stories. This one involved a stepsister of Bill's that none of us even knew he had. One thing about having a mother who's been married four times is that you just have an extended family that keeps showing up. His stepsister had, two weeks earlier, been released from a Texas prison where she had served seven years on armed bank robbery, and she was a very mentally unstable woman. I learned that one morning she got up and the kitchen curtains fell down, her husband's ottoman fell apart, and the light bulb burned out in the bedroom, and so she got a gun and took her 14-year-old kid and went and robbed two banks. That's how she dealt with a bad stress day. [Laughter]

She got her sentence commuted because, like her father, who was one of Bill's stepfathers, she had severe diabetes, was legally blind, and was about to get into major medical expenses. How the hell Sheffield Nelson and "Inside Edition" found this woman we didn't even know existed, I will never understand, but they found her.

She very soon became convinced that Bill Clinton and his mother were responsible for the deaths of both of her parents. Well, she was broke, and days before the election, they're staking this person out. Something's wrong with this process.

Ken Bode: You know, it's interesting that you say this. You may think that there's a closer connection between those of us who work for television networks that have news divisions, but I don't think Carole Simpson at ABC or Marty Plissner at CBS, certainly, I and Bill Schneider at CNN, we don't run into these people walking around the streets of Little Rock with cash.

Betsey Wright: But you have to, because the people do. Something has to happen.

Ken Bode: You're actually telling a lot of journalists here things that we probably didn't know about.

Betsey Wright: Of course you don't know. I'm hoping to spend the next year of my life working on getting the folks that buy the tabloid programs and the news people together, just to have a discussion about what the impact of this is on the electorate.

Ken Bode: It's a good idea.

Betsey Wright: It's got to happen because it's a meat cleaver over everybody's head.

Ken Bode: You know, the people sitting over there laugh because we don't know about this, but Tom Luce says, oh, you guys spend too much time tracking down rumors. I don't want to spend more of my time tracking down tabloid TV rumors as well. I think it's a serious problem. I think it's one that we ought to address as professionals, you know, perhaps not at this conference, but at a future conference about this because it's an important issue.

Bill Schneider: There's an important observation here about the process which Betsey brings up. The experience of the Gennifer Flowers story is very different from the experience that Gary Hart and Joe Biden had in 1988. In my view, Bill Clinton himself and your campaign figured out a way to beat this story. I think one of the ways you did it, aside from "60 Minutes," was to confront the story directly, to wade directly back into the campaign, try to bypass the press by going directly to the voters of New Hampshire. You placed a bet. The bet was that if you met openly in town halls with the voters of New Hampshire and just answered their questions, they were not going to ask questions about Gennifer Flowers. They were going to ask questions about the economy and jobs and your economic plan. Now, that was a risky situation because you could have been asked questions about tabloid journalism and Gennifer Flowers. But the risk you took was to have the candidate not try to look evasive and hide from the press, but to say I'm going to answer questions from the voters.

I think Ross Perot tried to do the same thing later when he was being pinned down by the press. There is a lesson here, that one of the ways you can bypass or get around the feeding frenzy — it's risky and it might not work — is to take the campaign directly to the people and see if that was what they were interested in and let them try to form an alternative agenda to the press. Do you agree with that?

James Carville: After we taped "60 Minutes" in Boston, we flew back up to Portsmouth, New Hampshire. A woman, who did not identify herself as a reporter, asked about it. The crowd booed her down. If they had known that she had been a reporter, I would have feared for her safety. They'd have ripped her apart.

Stan Greenberg: We learned our strategy here from Bill Clinton and the voters. Bill Clinton's instinct was, "I've got nothing to hide here, I'm going to wade in and talk about this." What we didn't understand — until we saw it visually and then in focus groups, when so many people responded to it — was that Bill Clinton is someone who's comfortable with himself. We self-consciously didn't go in back doors. We self-consciously subjected ourselves to this because Bill Clinton's self-confidence was a central part of the strategy. We also understood that the voters were doing our work for us. If anyone brought Gennifer Flowers up, even in a focus group context, he or she would be booed out of the group. People just did not want this discussion. They hated this issue, and, in fact, the issue, I think, interacted and worked for us. It got mixed up with the draft. Both the draft and the Flowers issue created an environment where people would ask that the campaign focus on real issues.

Betsey Wright: What Stan just said is that the strategy was the cradle that allowed Bill to do what came naturally and instinctively from who he was, and not surviving it was never an option.

Feeding Frenzy II. The Draft

"Sunday night, we verified the meltdown and Greenberg accurately said: 'We got trouble in River City.'"

— James Carville, Strategic Consultant,
Clinton/Gore Campaign

Bill Schneider: Let me take the agenda to the next point. We talked about the fact that the press might have, should have, could have learned some lessons about this at the next opportunity for a feeding frenzy. That came on February 6, which was when the *Wall Street Journal* reported a story regarding the Clinton draft record, and I'll turn to Betsy to begin to explore this second stage of the unfolding New Hampshire drama.

Betsy Kolbert: Accounts that have subsequently come out suggest, and Stan's been pretty open about this, I think, that your initial focus group led you to misread the initial reaction to the draft. I think the Governor was sick that week and he went home, and the numbers really started to drop. Once again, how extensively had this possibility been discussed, that the draft was going to come up? How, when, were you going to deal with it? Also, shouldn't you have known in a gut sense that coming right after Gennifer Flowers, the draft thing was really going to take a toll?

Stan Greenberg: Well, we had, early on, discussed all the possible negatives that could befall the candidacy, and the draft was among them. I have to say that if there was a mistake, it was in our *initial* sense of the draft issue. I'm going back to the summer. Bill Clinton was confident that we could handle it, that there wasn't anything there. He had already addressed it, and saw it as a not very complicated story. So the draft piece in the *Journal,* at the outset, was not seen as debilitating. But there was a big difference when the issue broke in New Hampshire because it immediately followed the Gennifer Flowers story. And, unlike Gennifer Flowers, it began in the *Wall Street Journal,* so it was considered a legitimate story from the outset. I think James will talk to this. We, in fact, handled the draft issue, for a variety of reasons, differently from the way we handled Gennifer Flowers. We left New Hampshire. I think it would have had an impact in any case because of the accumulation of facts and because it seemed to be a legitimate public discussion about the candidate. We were not intensively on top of the draft issue in the same way we were intensively on top of the Gennifer Flowers issue.

Frank Greer: Just a little more history on this. It was one of the first things, and really, in the spring of '91, that Bill raised with Stan and me. It was also a generational candidate running against the hero of the Gulf War. And Clinton's position was, "I didn't serve, I basically got a high lottery number. This has been brought up in my gubernatorial campaign time and time again and the people at the draft board, the people involved with the ROTC, have always backed up my version of the events in this case and I imagine that will happen again."

We went through it extensively, even in the spring, and there was no expectation on anybody's part that any of the stories, in terms of the Republican draft board members or Colonel Holmes* or anything else, was going to change, and that's the way we walked into the situation in New Hampshire on that first day when it broke in the *Wall Street Journal.*

James Carville: Well, we made some big mistakes there. Big mistake number one was that we weren't prepared for the story. Betsey had to come back; she can talk about it. The biggest mistake, I think was that I just didn't insist, let's get a suite at the Ritz-Carlton in Boston and just stay in the news mix in New Hampshire, not get out of the news mix no matter what happens.

There was just a lot of resistance to the idea. He and Hillary really wanted to go home. He hadn't seen Chelsea.

Paul Begala: He was really very, very sick. Thursday, the fifth, Clinton was speaking at Concord High School. The next day, there was a big picture in the *New York Times*. His fever was so high, he was sweating profusely, and the cut line on the picture was: "Do you think they'll vote for a dead guy?" We cancelled the rest of the day and the speech at Dartmouth for that night.

James Carville: Then the story hits on a Thursday in the *Wall Street Journal*. We go back. We collapse on Sunday night big time. Then, you know, the phone call.

Paul Begala: This is very different because it's the *Wall Street Journal* and not the *Star*, and the *Journal* handled it responsibly. The only nit I had to pick, and we talked to Jeffrey Birnbaum [writer for the *Wall Street Journal*] and Al Hunt about this ad nauseam, was that the *Journal* should have told its readers that Colonel Holmes, for the first time in 13 years or 15 years, changed his story. For all of Clinton's public life, Colonel Eugene Holmes had been asked about this and had always said Clinton did nothing wrong. We were unprepared for him to change his story and we did not handle it that well.

Editor's Note: Colonel Holmes, an Army Reserve Officers Training Corps recruiter, was the recipient of Bill Clinton's 1969 letter on the draft. See Appendix for text.

David Wilhelm: From a campaign management view, the thing that we did worst early on was research on ourselves.

James Carville: Terrible.

David Wilhelm: We didn't have any. Betsey wasn't there. We were all from different parts of the country. We had virtually no institutional history or memory, and when these stories kept coming out, we were not prepared the way we should have been. If we were to do one thing over again, I think it would be that we would have much better research done ourselves and we would have devoted a lot more resources to doing that.

James Carville: When Paul and I came on board, we were just appalled. In the Wofford race, I mean, we knew way more about Wofford than Thornburgh ever thought about.

Bill Schneider: I want to pass this issue to the other campaigns because it seemed to me that the draft issue had a much more profound effect on the New Hampshire race, on the polls, on what was happening out there, than the Gennifer Flowers story did. Tad Devine suggested earlier that the candidates perceived that and decided that, unlike Gennifer Flowers, the draft issue was an issue that Kerrey, Harkin, and others might have been interested in. So I want to ask the Kerrey, Harkin, Tsongas people what kind of opportunities or problems this particular story, unlike Gennifer Flowers, presented to your campaign.

Tad Devine: Well, I saw it as representing real opportunity [for the Kerrey campaign] and with it were real problems. It was difficult for us to deal with for a number of reasons. I picked up Mike McCurry [Communications Director, Kerrey campaign] at Logan Airport that morning, and he handed me the *Wall Street Journal* and said, you know, we've got a real story here. By the time we reached the candidate, he had already made a public statement about it. His statement, his first initial statement, was, as I recall, that it should not be an issue. Now, this is very complicated, obviously. You know, Vietnam — arguably the most important episode in his life — changed him in many ways.

We arrived on the scene. We were having a hard time breaking through. We were stuck. We were moving nowhere for a couple of weeks. At this point in time, I thought we had pretty good media going. The campaign was working. I saw it as the first opportunity for us to get in the mix. Kerrey had the standing to deal with it, obviously, from his own background, and we desperately needed to get into the free media mix somehow, but his own personal feelings, which were very, very strong, complicated it. When we got the second wave, which was what Governor Clinton had said about the incident, I think Senator Kerrey then said that Clinton's explanation did not have the ring of truth to it.

But it wasn't until a couple of weeks later that he was really willing to get into it and make it an issue. He saw it then in much broader terms as an issue which reached the potential electability of Clinton in the context of the general election. Then he was willing to engage it frontally.

Bill Shore: When the issue became the veracity of Clinton's explanation about it all, he was more comfortable. As Tad was saying, he had, I think, really deep personal ambivalence that had nothing to do with politics, really about what Clinton did with the draft and whether that should be an issue against him.

Kerrey had a lot of friends who did not serve, and he understood why, and he was sympathetic to them, and he just really felt uncomfortable introducing that into politics, and he knew with his posture as a Medal of Honor winner and all that, it would take on a special significance, and that ambivalence really remained all the way through Georgia. We went back and forth on this a number of times.

Bill Schneider: Lorraine, did you have a comment?

Lorraine Voles: Yes. We had a bit of that ambivalence, too. For us, at that time, Tom's [Harkin] negatives were so high that any kind of attack gave a lot of us real problems. We didn't want them [the Clinton campaign] on the attack. We wanted desperately to be in the mix, but the only way we were ever getting in the mix was when we were attacking someone. So we didn't really want Tom to go after him. We had our own vulnerabilities on Vietnam, so it was a difficult situation for us, but, then, as so often happened on our campaign, maybe reflecting a lack of discipline, we couldn't help ourselves.

Tom came out with something like, hey, look, if he wanted to serve, he would have served, not really understanding the implication of what he perceived as a real casual remark in the context of the New Hampshire primary and one candidate saying this about another.

Stan Greenberg: It actually helped us begin to get out of that story and to build back toward the comeback. The initial reaction to it was, oh, God, more of the same, and part of our overall thinking, and I think allowing him to leave, was that perhaps the public would deal with this issue as it had dealt with Gennifer Flowers. That turned out to be wrong.

The two things that were different, were the *Wall Street Journal* — mainstream press — and the *Boston Globe* poll reporting that Clinton was dropping, which CNN picked up throughout the weekend. The public was hearing, unlike in the Gennifer Flowers case, that their neighbors were taking this story seriously and pulling off this guy. When Kerrey and Harkin got into the story, we began to pick up that this was a political story, whereas before it had been a press story.

It was being pushed by politicians so that now we could say, this is part of the same ploy, using issues that are not central to people's lives to affect this election. So we were actually quite happy to see the other candidates either choose to or get drawn into the story.

Dennis Kanin: I think it was more than that though. Let me just say, in terms of the Tsongas campaign, we never had any discussion about whether we'd bring it up because it was very clear from the top, Paul would not allow any discussion of it. As a matter of fact, he had me send out an order to all our campaign workers in New Hampshire that they were not to discuss with the press — either the issue of the draft or Gennifer Flowers or anything related to it.

Bill Schneider: Now, wait a minute. The draft, Gennifer Flowers, these are two very different stories.

Elizabeth Arnold: He commented on Kerrey and Harkin commenting on it.

Dennis Kanin: He was asked about what they were saying, and he was critical.

Elizabeth Arnold: So he wasn't getting into the mix.

Dennis Kanin: No, no. I know it sounds naive and some of us thought it was naive, but he thought he had this bond with Bill Clinton. I'm not sure it was reciprocal, but for him, it was kind of a personal bond that he felt he had developed, and he just would not get into personal issues. But I do think what happened was not so much Harkin and Kerrey discussing it, but the draft letter. When that was released, it took a lot of the steam out of the draft issue because it brought out a lot of the ambivalence that voters felt about Vietnam and the war. It was a strong personal statement for people that resonated with their own feelings.

Tad Devine: I just want to say we actually had a focus group scheduled that night, February 6. That's why I was heading up to New Hampshire. Mike Donilon did it. We put the draft issue right on the table the night the story broke, and we got nothing back from the focus group at all. But then in the tracking, once we got to the weekend when all this stuff started breaking, that's when we got free fall for Clinton and that's when we started tracking it too.

James Carville: Sunday night, we verified the meltdown and Greenberg accurately said: "We got trouble in River City." Monday, Paul, you and George stayed up all night working on statements.

Paul Begala: And radio spots and wrote a "Mad as Hell" speech, a "Fight like Hell" speech.

James Carville: We flew up on, I think it was, Harry's [Thomason] plane, and I said, look, man, your life, all of our lives, have been training for this week. We've got to have the best week that anybody has ever had running for office. I mean, everything we do has to be perfect. And of course, we step out, and we have the disastrous press conference in front of that house where Bill and Hillary are standing by themselves. Mark Halperin and Jim Wooten [ABC News correspondents] are there and they hand us the letter [to Colonel Holmes] and, of course, Stephanopoulos says, "That's it! We're out of the race."

Paul Begala: It's sort of a generational thing, and George and Dee Dee [Myers] and I are all of 31. We were in the second grade when Bill Clinton wrote that letter. George and I looked at the letter, and the first thing we saw was the first thing a lot of reporters saw. It's a "thank you for saving me from the draft."

Bill Schneider: Which was also on the front page of the *New York Times.*

James Carville: Seven stories in one day.

Paul Begala: Yes. James and Hillary and the Governor had completely different reactions at the same instant, which expresses all the ambivalence that people felt. The only thing I cared about back then was whether the Mets were going to win the World Series. I was a second grade kid. But the people who went through it had a lot more understanding for how voters were going to process it.

Bill Schneider: Tuesday, February 18 — Lorraine?

Lorraine Voles: I didn't mention this earlier. The one fear we did have was that if Tom attacked the Governor, it would help Senator Kerrey more than it would ever help the Harkin campaign.

Bill Schneider: Let's go to the day of the New Hampshire primary, Tuesday, February 18. Once the draft story hit, Bill Clinton started dropping; Paul Tsongas started moving up. The results came in, I remind you, Tsongas 33 percent, Clinton 25, Kerrey 11, Harkin 10, Brown 8. Two stories got widely reported the night of the New Hampshire primary. One, Bill Clinton came on television shortly after 9:00 P.M. and announced "New Hampshire tonight has made Bill Clinton's comeback."

Second, the Pat Buchanan story in the Republican primary where it was widely and inaccurately reported that he virtually beat George Bush. Betsy, let's talk about the coverage and the impact of the New Hampshire primary. Lorraine, did you want to make a comment?

Lorraine Voles: Did I miss it? Did we already have the discussion of the Iowa caucus? [Laughter]

Betsy Kolbert: Why didn't the Harkin campaign succeed in making more of the Iowa caucuses?

Lorraine Voles: That is a very good question. We won the Iowa caucus with 73 percent of the vote, which was pretty incredible. Expectations were mostly at 60 percent, but, because of that, we pulled out of New Hampshire for that critical weekend beforehand. We had to spend a lot of money in Iowa because we couldn't be embarrassed in Iowa, and we weren't, but we got absolutely nothing for the experience. There would have been a lot of damage done, had he lost or had he not met or beat expectations, but we got zip coverage. You can't force people to cover what they perceive as a non-event. But it was the high point of our campaign so I just wanted to make sure we got a little bit of it in here.

Bill Schneider: Thank you. Dennis, a footnote to the Iowa footnote.

Dennis Kanin: Quick footnote. Kerrey was running around New Hampshire attacking Tsongas as a regional candidate which, of course, was our greatest vulnerability among New Hampshire voters, so we were very concerned about it. We sent ten organizers into Iowa quietly about a week before the caucuses because the one thing we did not want to do was come in last in Iowa, and we thought that was a real possibility. We actually came in second. It was 4 percent or 4.5 percent, but Kerrey came in fourth. This ended any reference to Tsongas as a regional candidate in New Hampshire, and one thing I'm curious about is why Kerrey didn't try to do better in Iowa.

Bill Shore: Well, we wanted to in the worst way, and that's what we did. We had no money, and we just decided that we really couldn't pull it off.

Bill Schneider: I apologize for ignoring the Iowa caucuses. There seems to be a tradition of that this year. Frank, did you want to make a comment?

Frank Greer: This is not the point I wanted to make, but I should say that my friend David Wilhelm was really intrigued by going in there. We kept holding him back from Iowa.

Paul Begala: Until we saw Stan's polling, which confirmed how strong Harkin was.

Bill Schneider: Yes, and I assume Kerrey had some indication that Harkin just wasn't going to be beaten in Iowa.

Frank Greer: Before you get to election day, I just want to mention one thing. Beyond the initial response, the meltdown, I think the other thing was the way Bill Clinton handled that week-and-a-half leading up to the primary from the draft story on and we haven't mentioned that. He agreed to go on "Nightline" with the letter. That was a gutsy thing to do. James and I agreed, having come out of that same era, that the letter was the Governor's best friend. We also did two rather unique things. David said we'll do whatever it takes to build our numbers back up and turn the tide and get back into this game.

We decided to buy two 30-minute blocks of time on Thursday and Friday night. In the first we used a group of undecided voters, who were recruited by an independent research firm and one of the things that "town meeting" demonstrated was that the voters of New Hampshire were not interested in the same thing — the feeding frenzy — that the press was interested in. As a matter of fact, we got a little bit of criticism from the national press corps that they weren't asking questions about Gennifer Flowers and the draft.

The next night we did a call-in program, also with a live audience, and I was worried sick because we'd gone through about 20 minutes of this program taking unscreened telephone calls and we still had not gotten questions from real voters in New Hampshire about the draft or Gennifer Flowers. Finally, we got one question, "Do you feel comfortable serving as Commander in Chief since you didn't serve in the military yourself?" It wasn't a real tough question on the draft, but I said, thank the Lord, at least the national press corps will believe that we didn't rig this thing.

We went through two 30-minute programs talking with real voters, and they wanted to know about health care and jobs and about education, college education for their kids. Those were the issues they were concerned about.

Dennis Kanin: The other thing Bill Clinton did was, for the last seven days in the New Hampshire primary, he was everywhere, around the clock.

Frank Greer: Taking questions at every event. We had a microphone at every event.

Dennis Kanin: And I've got to tell you something. Paul Tsongas was not everywhere because the Tuesday before the primary, he visited a wood chip factory and got a wood chip in his eye, came down with conjunctivitis, his eyes were all puffed up, and he had gunk in them. Sometimes he'd go out and do one appearance with glasses. On the Wednesday before the primary, he did no appearances, and, of course, that got the press starting to ask about his health, his stamina, all of those questions. The conjunctivitis ruined our last week, and it hurt us during the debate as well.

David Wilhelm: The Clinton campaign did one other little thing the last weekend, which wasn't that little, maybe. We handed out 25,000 to 30,000 videotapes door to door, the same thing that we did before the Florida straw poll. It was extraordinary. I don't think it's ever been done on that level before, and I thought it was pretty useful and just another way of Bill Clinton being in everybody's face the last week.

Frank Greer: But the willingness to cut through news coverage and go directly to voters, willing to take their questions — I think it revolutionized presidential politics. I don't think it will ever go back to the way it was; it began the whole dynamic change. Voters said we want to be a part of this process, and we don't want it all through the filter. We want to be able to relate to Bill Clinton; we want a direct exchange between us and the candidates.

Dennis Kanin: Don't you think all the candidates were doing that?

Lorraine Voles: Don't you think there was a real willingness on their part? I always felt it was something to do with a willingness to go into debt.

Dennis Kanin: Oh, we went into debt.

Lorraine Voles: I mean, we went into debt, too, but there was a point, this was how far in debt we would go, and that's really what stopped us from doing that.

David Wilhelm: We didn't go into debt, and even during the worst times of the campaign, we had Southern governors doing these fundraisers. In the middle of Gennifer Flowers, didn't we have the biggest New York fundraiser that gave us the wherewithal to avoid some of the harsh trade-offs that you guys had to face.

James Carville: It would be hard to overestimate Rahm [Emanuel]'s contribution to the campaign.

Betsey Wright: Well, the new standard for who's the most deserving of Inaugural tickets is, "I endorsed him in the middle of the mess in New Hampshire between the draft and Gennifer Flowers." [Laughter]

Bill Schneider: There is an important message here, which I think will go through our discussion, the unusual degree to which the voters set the agenda of this campaign. I think in Governor Clinton's case, there was some confidence that he felt comfortable with that. It provided, at least for this campaign, an answer to how to deal with feeding frenzies. Take your message directly to the voters, avoid the press, and let the voters ask the questions and, in the end, the voters will trump the press.

The only question that I would raise is, Was that true specifically of this year in New Hampshire and in other states where you had angry voters, who had very deep personal concerns about their economic future and their economic security? Or is this generally true, that it's a useful strategy for dealing with a feeding frenzy? This will come up again and again because it came up with Bush's attempt to criticize Clinton on the general election and, also, in Ross Perot's efforts to avoid some of the negative press coverage that he was getting.

"The Comeback Kid" —
Election Day in New Hampshire

"Well, I probably should since we won it."

— Dennis Kanin, Campaign Manager, Tsongas for
President, on being asked to comment on New Hampshire

Bill Schneider: I want to turn now, finally, to the New Hampshire primary, the night of the primary, February 18. The results have already been announced. Then an interesting twist. The news coverage seems to dwell on Bill Clinton as the "Comeback Kid" and, also, the proposed or presumed Buchanan upset. I'll turn to Betsy to talk about that.

Betsy Kolbert: The first question I want to ask is, once again, to the Clinton people, and that is "How much thought had gone into managing that story that night?" You came out very quickly, I think even before most of the results were in, and who were you pointing to? Paul? Go ahead. Shoot.

Paul Begala: Joe Grandmaison's the one that really pushed so hard to go down there, and, again, it all reflected the Governor's own inclination which is always to be more aggressive, always to get out there, not sit and wait and react. It was Joe's idea to go down early and perhaps proclaim ourselves the winner for having survived it. That was more important than who wrote the phrase "Comeback Kid."

James Carville: Paul wrote the phrase "Comeback Kid." They have notes from that night and everything else. I had already gone to Georgia so I can't take credit.

Stan Greenberg: There was an enormous amount of strategizing about the result in New Hampshire.

Betsy Kolbert: What was your biggest fear? I mean, were you concerned that people were going to say, well, this is a really disappointing second?

Joe Grandmaison: No. I think what had happened is that Clinton, in the final week in New Hampshire, proved to voters there that he had the "character" to be President. I can remember a speech on the Wednesday night in Dover. It was one of the most incredible speeches, and some of you were probably there. He was absolutely spectacular, and his actions followed through on the strength that he exhibited. There was every reason to believe that he would win back half of what he had lost, which is just about what he did. On a Saturday night in Nashua,

1,200 people filled the gymnasium at Fairgrounds Junior High School. Nobody expected that. He kept asking questions: Well, what does this mean? There was just some magic going on in terms of the people from the very beginning wanting to hear him out.

I think you've got to go back to the beginning and realize that the scenario in New Hampshire, the feel, the dynamics, were clearly established by George Bush for both sides of the political aisle. The resentment was that the New Hampshire economy was falling apart. Five of our seven major banks had failed. Home values had decreased 30 percent in two years. They wanted real answers. They didn't care about all this political horseshit that was going on. They just didn't.

The recommendation to go out early had everything to do with his success. If you have the ability to frame how the coverage is going to be taken, the starting point of it, you obviously have a great advantage.

The feeling was very genuine on our part as far as a strategy and we really felt vindicated. Mickey Kantor went into the inside of the campaign, to the inner circle, and convinced several people, and if you read *Newsweek* correctly, the person that was also very convinced by that strategy was Hillary Clinton.

Bill Schneider: The Tsongas campaign, do you want to make a comment about the New Hampshire primary result and how much good it did you?

Dennis Kanin: Well, I probably should since we won it. [Laughter]

Bill Schneider: Are you going to let them dominate the interpretation?

Dennis Kanin: No. I think the amazing thing that happened in New Hampshire for me was that Paul Tsongas won New Hampshire, considering that we were outspent by Clinton, not just by Clinton, but by Kerrey and Harkin, by ratios of three to one and two to one. And I think that the reason we did well was partly because of the problems that Clinton had with the draft, and partly because of Paul Tsongas' message: You need to make hard choices to deal with our economic problems.

Part of that was in response to the Kerrey ads. They gave us a great opening with the net ad we talked about last night, the hockey ad. We came back with "Japan bashing won't open this factory." Now, that is not your typical approach to the Democratic electorate. We also were critical, as you know, of the middle-class tax cut. That's not your typical approach to a Democratic electorate. What we were saying was, this is one person who'll be honest with you, who'll give it to you straight and I think I know that it worked in New Hampshire. Despite the tremendous disadvantage we had in terms of money, despite the fact that we had been dismissed all through '91 by the press and despite the last horrible week that we had on the trail, Tsongas managed to win.

Now, I think that night we made a terrible mistake, and it wasn't that it wasn't discussed. You know the old story about Lincoln and the Cabinet. Well, the Cabinet cast 12 votes and Lincoln cast one, and that one vote carried. Anyway, there was a decision to hold off on coming down to claim victory, and I think it was a mistake. However, it wasn't that big a mistake because in the next two weeks, the primaries that went through March 3, the primaries and caucuses, Bill Clinton won one of those primaries or caucuses in Georgia, in his home region, and Tsongas won five of them. So I don't think the "Comeback Kid" had that profound an effect. I think it was a useful phrase, however.

Bill Schneider: In the next stage of the campaign, there was an intensive period with a series of debates in the Maryland and Colorado primaries. I think Betsy wanted to pursue a question relating to those debates.

Betsy Kolbert: There was a 24-hour or 36-hour period, I guess, where Maryland, Colorado, and Georgia all held debates. You guys all flew from one state to the other, and I was wondering if there was anything that anyone wanted to talk about, about what you were trying to achieve in those debates.

James Carville: I want to talk about the *Atlanta Constitution* editorial board that had already decided to endorse Tsongas and kept calling me to see if Clinton could talk to them for an hour-and-a-half while we held up and missed an event in Prince Georges County, Maryland. We had to sit there and listen to them slobber all over everything, knowing full well they'd written the endorsement. That's one thing. Made me look like a damned fool. Other than that I don't have an opinion on them.

Dennis Kanin: Let me just say something in terms of strategy. For us, there was a major question in our camp about whether to even contest Georgia. What we were facing was March 10. We knew Super Tuesday was going to be a major, major problem, and we came out of New Hampshire feeling that we thought we'd win Maryland. We also thought that we'd do well in some of the caucus states because caucuses often vote for issue-oriented candidates. You can really get the activists worked up, and generally the polls were showing at that point that Tsongas was leading in terms of being able to handle the economy. Clinton was leading in qualities like leadership. So we thought we'd do well in Washington State, but the question was: Would that all matter when we got to March 10?

So we made two decisions about which we didn't have much choice. Both turned out to be unfortunate. First was to contest in South Dakota.

We figured we just came out of New Hampshire, we've got momentum. Maybe this will do something for us in South Dakota. We didn't count on the gas tax and Bob Kerrey's very effective negative ads in South Dakota and Paul's transparent unfamiliarity with agricultural issues.

Bill Schneider: That's a Massachusetts Greek liberal.

Dennis Kanin: He knew not to say Belgian endive, but that's as far as it went. Anyway, we survived South Dakota. We still went on and won Maryland the next week, and we won Washington State, and we won Utah, but we had contested Georgia.

The reason we contested Georgia is we had polls that showed Clinton at 43 and Tsongas at 25, and we figured if we can keep Clinton down below expectations, that would give us some kind of momentum going in to Florida. Florida was the one state we thought we could take on Super Tuesday other than Massachusetts, Rhode Island, and Delaware. Anyway, we went in to Georgia, and Zell Miller and some of the other political leaders in the state really did a job on Tsongas. They sent the message to Georgians that this is not our kind of guy. The Lieutenant Governor said: "Tsongas isn't Greek for 'bubba,' " and that sent a message.

Paul Begala: Did you know what the context of that was though?

Dennis Kanin: Yes, I know. The Lieutenant Governor said his name was French for "bubba."

James Carville: His name is Pierre, and so his campaign said don't worry, Pierre is French for "bubba."

Dennis Kanin: Well, actually, there was a big debate about that. Paul wanted to have a very strong response to that statement, and we held him back from it because we understood there was that context. Zell Miller was a lot tougher than that, but what it came down to in the end is Paul Tsongas was another Greek liberal from Massachusetts and Bill Clinton's a Southerner and this was Bill Clinton's home base. Our polling showed that that ultimately was the decisive factor.

James Carville: Let me give you a couple of points here. The first thing is, you got to give a lot of credit to David and the people that early on lined up. Remember, you weren't going anywhere in this deal without the blacks, without the black vote in the South. That was strategic assumption number one. It was the first thing that they recognized, the first thing I said when I came aboard. On the afternoon of New Hampshire, the exit polls said we were going second, and I said, yeah, I'm going down to Atlanta now, that's it, you know. We were playing tough. Zell came out the next day, and we were lining people up and we were shooting every tenth one that didn't fall in the line, at that time in terms of getting the vote. This was our turf, and we knew we were going to be there. And I'll say this, not just because he's my friend and client, but I think if you had to pick the single best political supporter we have, no one would say there was any better than Zell. He was there at every point that we needed him.

So the Governor and I go to Houston, and, of course, I was in a George Stephanopoulos depression, and I said, man, we're bleeding out there. He said, no, man, we're hemorrhaging everywhere. We said, we are going to lose, and then the exit polls came in and I do think that the Georgia primary was the thing that really ...

Stan Greenberg: We ought to put Betsy's question in the context of the three primaries because we were scared of that day. We thought a Tsongas win in Maryland was almost certain. We thought Clinton would be adversely affected by a Maryland defeat, a weak performance in Georgia, a Tsongas win in Colorado, and a Tsongas win in Washington State, which would have given him a coast-to-coast sweep.

Because we wanted to prevent a Tsongas sweep prior to going into Super Tuesday, we devoted our resources to two things: winning Georgia with an impressive number because that in itself would have been sufficient, and making sure that Tsongas did not win in Colorado. Which is why in the debate strategy in Colorado, we went to the nuclear question, and why our media in Colorado shifted to the nuclear question. Even though we doubted that Bill Clinton would be the beneficiary of that issue, we thought Jerry Brown would be, and that Tsongas would be hurt by it.

What we don't understand is why Kerrey went to Georgia and not to Colorado. Because we did think there were possibilities for Kerrey in a messy race in Colorado. If there was any place where it looked like a Kerrey candidacy might emerge, it was Colorado.

Betsy Kolbert: Also, wasn't that the moment of the soft peanut?[*]

Tad Devine: Yes. We went to Georgia partly out of a lack of information. The day after the South Dakota primary, we're a million dollars in debt. We've got no more polling. So we're just driving blind. We're reading what's in the newspapers. We can't go on TV. We've got 60,000 bucks.

James Carville: You could have called us, we would have told you. [Laughter]

---

[*]*Editor's Note:* At a news conference in Atlanta, Bob Kerrey predicted that if Bill Clinton were nominated, his avoidance of the draft would be an issue in the general election: "I think he's going to get opened up like a soft peanut in November of 1992."

Tad Devine: We decided that we had to try and shake this thing up as much as possible. So I went to Georgia and I went to Colorado because Kerrey was there. We had our 60 grand. We had two ads. One, which never aired, was a pretty nasty draft ad. The gist of it was Bill Clinton's call for national service, but he never showed himself, you know, blah, blah, blah. The second ad was a comparative on the environment which said Tsongas and Clinton were polluters. We had 60 grand so we said, well, let's fire it into Colorado because maybe we can buy a little bit of air time there. There's no way we could get up — we were hoping for some money to come in after South Dakota. Pledges came in, but money did not.

Since there was no way we could really get into the mix we said let's go to Georgia, just try to shake the thing up as much as possible, put a big hit on Clinton, and then retreat to Colorado and campaign there. We thought if we went down South and put a big hit on him, maybe we could get him to stumble, maybe we could get him off-track.

We had the national press corps looking at us for one day after we won South Dakota. We thought maybe this would be a big, big hit and we could knock him over, then stay below the radar screen for a couple of weeks, grab some delegates, and come back later and really make it a race. It was an assumption made a lot out of ignorance because we just didn't have any polling at all.

Dennis Kanin: Actually, I think the Kerrey ad is what killed us in Colorado more than any single thing, and the fact that the big issue in Colorado at that point was the Rocky Flats nuclear dump.

Frank Greer: Well, we were also on the air in Colorado going after you on nuclear power. But it's Georgia, that day was the first time that we really drew a direct contrast with any other campaign, and we drew it with Tsongas, and we did it on populist issues. We used his quote that he would be the best friend Wall Street ever had. We went after him on the gas tax, and trickle-down economics versus "Bill Clinton wants to put people first." And we drew the contrast that we wanted the best in training and education, etc. But it was a direct populist contrast which would also reaffirm our African American base in the South. And in Colorado, the only twist on it was that we went after you on nuclear power.

Dennis Kanin: By the way, just for the record, since there's going to be a record here, Tsongas's quote, which was back in March or April of 1991 was, if you do such and such — this was a speech to some business people — "I'll be the best friend Wall Street ever had."

Bill Schneider: We haven't heard from the Brown campaign. I see Dan Butler is here. Let me remind you of the context of this story so far. Until Georgia, on March 3, I think it was, Bill Clinton had not won a single primary. He ended up not winning any primary or caucus in New England. Brown or Tsongas won every New England state. Someone mentioned regionalism earlier last night. Regionalism is not only in the South. On March 3, Clinton won Georgia, his first primary win, his first state win. Tsongas won Maryland. Brown won Colorado and he ended up being the candidate who went the distance.

Dan, you were strategist in the New England region. I don't know if you had anything to do with the Colorado race. I wonder if you wanted to make a comment about the Brown campaign at this stage.

Dan Butler: Yes. I'll make a few comments. To correct the record, we did win in Maine.

Bill Schneider: You did. Okay.

Dennis Kanin: Not that night, not the night of the first caucuses. Only after the county caucuses and we got out of the race, but anyway, go ahead.

Dan Butler: Yes. What actually happened was Paul Tsongas won that first night, but we sent volunteers …

Dennis Kanin: By 20 votes. It was close. It was very close.

Dan Butler: We sent volunteers all over Maine in what we called the "hamlet strategy," and we tried to scare up Democrats just by talking to people in the hardware stores or the pharmacies. We'd get three or four Democrats together. They'd organize a caucus and they'd vote for Jerry Brown, and that's how we ended up winning the Maine caucus.

Bill Schneider: Well, let me just pursue that a second. I think it was just before the Maine caucuses that Governor Brown indicated that he would ask Jesse Jackson to be his running mate, and my recollection is that there was some kind of a Jackson-oriented organization in Maine.

Dan Butler: I think the biggest factor is the person who was organizing Maine, John Michael, a very effective state representative. Early on, he put together a terrific field organization. He was actually organizing for the caucuses several months ahead of time, signing people up, organizing them in their local communities, and that was really the biggest factor.

Governor Brown also spent a lot of time there. He bounced back and forth between New Hampshire and Maine quite a bit, spent a lot more time there than any other candidate. His nephew was going to college up there and was a very effective organizer, and I think those are the factors that came together.

Thaleia Schlesinger: Because Brown had run in Maine before, he was the most familiar candidate. I was up in Maine a lot. There was a Grateful Dead concert reunion and they just came out. [Laughter]

Super Tuesday

"We weren't losing the delegate race, and we were demonstrating an ability to compete everywhere, and we were ready to come out of Super Tuesday."

— David Wilhelm, Campaign Manager,
Clinton/Gore Campaign

Bill Schneider: After Jerry Brown won the Colorado primary, someone noticed that Jerry Brown did very well in states that had a lot of mountains. In mountainous states with remote regions, people seem to come out and vote for Jerry Brown.

The perception on March 3 was that this was going to be a regional race. You had Tsongas doing well in New England and the Northeast. Clinton was the Southern candidate. Brown was the Western candidate because he had won Colorado, and the conventional wisdom became, there's nothing but regional candidates here, no national candidate coming out of this.

Frank Greer: Bill Clinton and David Wilhelm realized the danger posed by that, and that is why months before, they had begun putting Illinois together.

David Wilhelm: Yes. And although we were losing, we weren't losing by much. I mean, we were close in Colorado and close in Maryland and close in New Hampshire. We weren't losing the delegate race, and we were demonstrating an ability to compete everywhere, and we were ready to come out of Super Tuesday.

Bill Schneider: Tsongas made an effort to break out of this regional pack by taking on Bill Clinton in Florida. Florida turned out to be the critical contest on Super Tuesday. And Betsy, I think, wanted to pursue the Florida primary campaign, which was the critical race on Super Tuesday.

Frank Greer: Bill, the one thing I would say, by the way, in Georgia, the Tsongas campaign spent as much in terms of paid media as the Clinton campaign. I think you were making a serious run in Georgia as well, right?

Dennis Kanin: Yes, we did make a serious run in Georgia. We were concerned that Georgia would set the stage for Super Tuesday, and it did. For us, Georgia was the critical primary.

Bill Schneider: But Florida looked like a good bet because it had a non-Southern profile.

Dennis Kanin: After Georgia, it didn't look like such a great bet. We had no choice but to go into Florida. We had Super Tuesday. We were going to win Massachusetts and Rhode Island. We had a bit of a fight in Delaware, but nobody was going to pay attention to that and so we had no choice but to fight it out in Florida.

Betsy Kolbert: Why didn't you concede the South, even Florida, and move into the Midwest? It probably wouldn't have worked anyway, but in retrospect, Florida was a pretty bad idea.

Dennis Kanin: In retrospect, of course, Florida was a bad idea. In retrospect everywhere we lost was a bad idea.

Betsy Kolbert: Why did you feel you had to make a stand in Florida?

Dennis Kanin: It goes back to the fact that we had always thought about this race in terms of general election. We felt, unlike Tom Harkin, that we had to do something in the South. We were looking ahead to November. We had always thought that to win the race, we had to take some of the border states of the South like Tennessee and Arkansas and Georgia and Kentucky, and we planned to have a Southern vice presidential candidate to help us do that, a Sam Nunn or an Al Gore or somebody like that, despite Paul's comments. We felt we had to prove that Paul was a national candidate, and even if it meant losing Florida and some other Southern states, we had to show that we had some support in the South. Not only that, but we could not cede all those delegates that were available on Super Tuesday to Bill Clinton. We had to pick up some through proportional representation, which we did. In Florida, we got about 75 delegates to Clinton's 150.

Bill Schneider: Did you think the Clinton campaign against you in Florida was unfair?

Dennis Kanin: I think our perception at the time was that the ads and some of what was happening on the campaign trail were unfair.

Stan Greenberg: We shouldn't focus on those last ads because they are part of a process that began with Georgia, indeed South Carolina. Georgia was important, not just because of the regional division of the country, but also because of the trust question. Many Georgians liked Bill Clinton — he was from their area. But there was also some ambivalence — the trust question that came out of the primary process. When Georgia went so overwhelmingly for Bill Clinton, it said to Southerners that people like you, who are also ambivalent, had resolved their feelings in favor of Bill Clinton.

It was very evident in South Carolina. We were running as a moderate candidate stressing welfare reform. South Carolina was pretty much on its own. You had Harkin visibly with Jesse Jackson — he was on the air with Jesse in South Carolina. We won South Carolina very big, and I believe combined with Georgia set the stage for Florida. Our polling showed after Georgia that we went way ahead in Florida, immediately after Georgia. In the end, it didn't happen because of last-minute ads or what happened in the condominiums.

For some reason, nobody else, none of the newspapers, polled in Florida. The *New York Times* released a poll that had been done prior to Georgia. There were no public polls during the primary. So the perception was that this was a close contest. It was *not* a close contest and, therefore, we called a lot of attention to Florida as the testing ground for a disciplined campaign. James ought to talk to that. Because the words "people first" were introduced in the media in Georgia — the concept of a very sharply drawn contrast between a Bill Clinton, who wanted to put government behind people, against a Paul Tsongas, whose theme was trickle-down economics.

We came back again and again to that contrast on Super Tuesday and in Florida, and that's where we really developed the first disciplined message, which could have a broader impact because it was a national, not a regional message.

Frank Greer: One other thing. Even though the press suggested that we ran against Paul Tsongas on the issue of Social Security cuts, in terms of paid media, we never did because we found in Stan's polling that the gas tax proposed by Paul Tsongas was *more* unpopular with senior citizens, so we could focus on that issue in our advertising.

Dennis Kanin: Whoa, we had a response ad on Social Security. We wouldn't have had that if you didn't have an ad that covered four points including Social Security. "Paul Tsongas wants to cut Social Security for the elderly." Mike Shea can attest ...

James Carville: It was Medicare.

Dennis Kanin: Fine. Medicare.

Stan Greenberg: There is a difference.

Dennis Kanin: Yes, but Bill Clinton in New Hampshire had said that he thought he had to look at cuts in Medicare benefits for the wealthier citizens. That's why we thought it was unfair. Let's not relive Florida.

There are a number of reasons why we lost Florida. First, after Georgia, we couldn't even fight it out in northern Florida. I think you're right. Northern Florida is a Southern state. That issue was resolved in Georgia. That's why I'd say Georgia was the pivotal primary for us. Second, state organization was behind Clinton. That happened in many of the primaries. Third, I think the attacks you staged were effective. Fourth, Bill Clinton, and I think this explains why he succeeded, is a tireless and effective campaigner, and he was very effective in Florida.

Bill Schneider: Did Pander Bear[*] backfire or work in any way for you?

Dennis Kanin: I'm not sure that it was helpful.

Paul Begala: I don't want to let the Medicare thing go. Our principal position had been that if you made more than $125,000 a year, your Medicare ought to be subject to taxation. Tsongas later, after we attacked him in Florida, adopted that position. In his book, he posed the question, Would the Congress pass cuts in Medicare that would be 1 percent below the consumer price index?

Dennis Kanin: Politically, it will not pass. Even for those above a certain income level. Would the Congress support a policy? This is a question, by the way.

Stan Greenberg: Well, the whole book is that way.

Dennis Kanin: No, it isn't. This book was not all questions. Would the Congress support a policy of reducing the yearly increase in entitlements by 1 percent below the cost of living? It's not a great deal, but it would establish a policy of economic response that politically will not pass even for those above a certain income level. He was asked about it in New Hampshire. He was very clear. For people above $125,000, exactly the same figure ...

Betsy Kolbert: He wanted to reduce the cost of living increase.

Dennis Kanin: The ad didn't make any distinction. The ad said cuts for the elderly.

Frank Greer: He said below cost.

Dennis Kanin: Tsongas favors cuts for the elderly.

Frank Greer: Let me ask another question. Why did you go into Texas and spend so much money there?

Dennis Kanin: Well, we had to go to Texas for one reason, to get into the debate. So we spent a day in Texas.

James Carville: Oh, that fiasco. Oh, yeah.

Dennis Kanin: The other reason was, again, delegate numbers.

---

[*] *Editor's Note:* Tsongas frequently used the term "Pander Bear" to characterize Clinton as a candidate who promised anything to get votes.

Frank Greer: But you were spending a good bit of money in Texas.

Dennis Kanin: We didn't spend a lot. We put some money in initially, and then we pulled it out. We pulled out of Texas and basically put our money into Florida. We spent, like, $120,000 in Texas. It was not a lot of money for Texas.

James Carville: An important point here. Georgia was basically an organizational win. We had the political infrastructure of the state, maybe intimidated, but in Florida was the first time that we really developed a sort of a message vis-à-vis Tsongas. We drove it home, and that carried us into Michigan and Illinois. We took the Florida message and the contrast and went to Michigan and Illinois with that.

Again, I can't overestimate what the black vote in the South meant for us, and that was the foreign thing to Tsongas. Somebody said Tsongas got 3 percent of the black vote in South Carolina, and I said: "How'd he do that?"

Bill Schneider: Let me pursue that point because it's an interesting one. One of the things we nutty pollsters noticed in New Hampshire, which has very few blacks, is that the race between Tsongas and Clinton had taken on a very powerful class dimension. What we found in New Hampshire, as well as in the South and elsewhere, a phenomenon that persisted throughout the entire primary campaign, was that the wealthier and better-educated the voters, the more likely they were to vote for Tsongas.

The poorer, the less well-educated the voters, the more likely they were to vote for Clinton. Now, this, I perceived, was not the vote Clinton initially thought he was going to go after as a new kind of Democrat. The message you honed in Florida was a message that was really forced on you by the nature of the vote you were getting. It became a sort of Walter Mondale against Gary Hart campaign. It began to take on that sort of shape. You were defending the traditional Democratic message because Paul Tsongas became the candidate that I thought Bill Clinton wanted to become at the outset of the campaign.

Stan Greenberg: No. First of all, from the beginning, we knew we were running bottom up, that we were going to win with a black-white bottom-up coalition. We couldn't do it in New Hampshire, which has a very highly educated electorate. But as a strategy overall for the South and as a strategy for the industrial Midwest, we knew we were building bottom up. I remember the debates in the campaign. Bill Clinton wanted to win everybody. There was not a voter in America that Bill Clinton did not want to win. It bothered him when the *Atlanta Constitution* didn't endorse him. It bothered him when the best-educated voters were not voting for him, but as a strategic question of the campaign, we knew our strategy was bottom up and had to be black and white.

I remember a very explicit debate in Florida over the question of how we run, whether we try to compete with Tsongas for those better-educated voters or whether we continue to run bottom up. When you looked at where the votes were, you still had about two-thirds of the voters who were non-college graduates in the Florida primary, and it was those numbers that were persuasive. That was a coalition we wanted, though we would just as soon have taken it all the way up and taken every voter.

James Carville: You guys ran a good campaign. I'm serious. In many ways, it was one of the more remarkable campaigns. I've been in this political party for a long time, and this party is not going to nominate somebody that favors a gas tax and an across-the-board capital-gains tax. That's just the nature of the Democratic party. New Democrat, old Democrat, today's Democrat, tomorrow's or yesterday's. Tsongas expressed ideas out of pure conviction, but that's just not the nature of the electorate that decides on the Democratic nominee for President.

Dennis Kanin: I think there's something to that.

James Carville: Yes.

Dennis Kanin: Tom Oliphant, I think, put it that we were building a college, with great facilities and great professors and all that. The only problem, according to Tom, was we weren't letting anybody in. We had a gas tax for the farmers. We had nuclear power for the environmentalists. We had no middle-class tax cut for the middle class, and we were ecumenical.

But Paul said what he did out of conviction, and I do think, just to follow up on what Bill Schneider said, that in Florida, it did become the Hart versus Mondale construct. Unfortunately, we were at the short end of the stick.

Bill Schneider: Mondale won, remember.

Dennis Kanin: Mondale won. He didn't win in Florida, but he did win.

Bill Schneider: Mondale won in the nation.

Stan Greenberg: Let me deal with this point because it has to do with the character of the Democratic party. When Bill Clinton thought about running for president, he was thinking about an independent electorate that he wanted to win over, one that did not traditionally vote Democratic. Many of those were better-educated voters, but within the Democratic electorate, the best-educated voters were the elite liberal segments of the party which he was running against.

So there was a tension between the Bill Clinton who had a plan, who was smart, and the Bill Clinton who was running for the middle-class values that had been neglected by the Democratic party. That tension played itself out in this question of whether we competed for better-educated voters.

Frank Greer: Reagan Democrats were downscale voters, too. The people that we had lost for the last ten years were the people who were more blue collar, more downscale, and you had to win them back as well, in terms of winning in the general election.

James Carville: Basics count. We've got to re-emphasize that because I think we're missing the point here. The basics are, and particularly in the Southern primary, you have to have the right vote, and it is not an appealing message to have a gas tax, the nuclear power thing, and across-the-board capital gains.

Bill Schneider: Howard Fineman wanted to ask, I think, about Jesse Jackson.

Howard Fineman: Yes. I was just going to ask James, what did you figure Jesse was going to do or not do? How did he fit or not fit into your equation?

James Carville: This idea that people in Washington have that Jesse Jackson is "the black vote" in the United States, that is only in Washington. He's a very forceful person. He's got a large following, and maybe Paul might want to speak to this. I suspect that you all instinctively knew the same thing, too, and so people would say, well, Jesse is not for you, Jesse said this.

We had a huge, well-developed, well-worked-out plan in Georgia, and as we moved through the South, in Mississippi. We had plenty of people who had been around for a long time:

John Lewis, Mike Espy, Calvin Smart, Jasper Williams are pretty formidable politicians on their home turf.

Bill Schneider: If you weren't worried about Jesse Jackson, why did Bill Clinton react so violently to the incorrect statement about Jesse's endorsement of Tom Harkin?

James Carville: Wait a minute. I didn't say he wasn't worried about it, Bill. I'm just saying when the national media covers the black vote, they cover Jesse Jackson.

Howard Fineman: I was going to ask you that question. What did you think Jesse Jackson was going to do, or did you care?

James Carville: Sure, we cared.

David Wilhelm: Reverend Jackson wasn't on the ballot so that's a big difference from 1988; there was open competition, so we just went for it. We worked for the African-American vote. The thing that caused Bill Clinton to react the way he did was that up until that point, Reverend

Jackson had made it clear to all of us that he was staying out of the race. Thus, there could be free and open competition for African-American voters. So when Clinton perceived or was told by a reporter that Reverend Jackson had endorsed Tom Harkin, that certainly would have changed the dynamics from a free and open competition to something different.

Howard Fineman: Given this great structure of other black leadership outside of Washington, for those of us based in Washington, that we don't know about ...

James Carville: That's true. You don't know about it.

Howard Fineman: Do you think that there was any percentage in taking Jesse Jackson on more directly? In other words, that it wouldn't be a problem to have Jackson endorse someone else.

James Carville: No, because the black voters in the South want the President to do a lot of things. Clinton had campaigned for the black vote all his political life. It still does count in this business, it really does matter that a candidate running for president has political skills.

Bill Schneider: Let me ask Paul Goldman if he wants to make a comment on this issue.

Paul Goldman: Southern populism Clinton understood. Easterners don't understand it, and populism has never done well in the East.

Next, liberals, whatever that means, totally lost their connection because liberals forgot that without the support of blacks, there is no liberalism. There isn't any. Eventually, the few that will be left will come to that conclusion, will then be able to rebuild it. Southern populism has the ability. It's some sort of a middle-class populism that Stan was talking about, and that's what they were aiming for.

Yes, it is true that Clinton, at some point, had the ability to go either way. If Doug Wilder stayed in the race, then, sure, they would have had a different strategic imperative. The beauty of it when Wilder got out, Bill Clinton knew how to keep his DLC base and add to it the other base, and, unfortunately, everyone else was shut off from that.

This experience helped. Another thing that Dennis [the Tsongas campaign] was up against was regionalism.

We don't like to talk about it, but the regional advantage in this is tremendous in the South. Look, every Southern state that you've got to try to compete in costs money. You don't find any small Southern states. North Carolina's almost as big as New Jersey. Virginia's two electoral votes short of New Jersey. I've nothing against Maine and Vermont, but, you know, you carry Atlanta and that's equal to New England.

So my point is, this is what you're up against as you try to go to the South, and I think that's Frank's point. If you want to show you're a

Southern candidate, and Dukakis traps you into that because he was able to carry Texas and Florida in a fluke, you run in Florida and Texas and it costs you a fortune. You would have been better off to take all that money and try Illinois, which is where the Tsongas campaign saw their firewall.

Someone would break out of the regional situation. It was either going to be Illinois or New York, but I think you did a great job. You just didn't have the money and you just couldn't find a Southern primary that was winnable.

The Midwest and East

"He said he did not want to be a spoiler. He had concluded he couldn't win the nomination and that's why Tsongas dropped out."

— Dennis Kanin, Campaign Manager,
Tsongas for President

Bill Schneider: I wanted to get to two other critical primary stages, Illinois and Michigan on March 17 and then April 7 or thereabouts, the Connecticut and New York primaries. Illinois and Michigan were important, as Paul indicated, because they were the first real test on neutral ground, and everybody reported it that way. Neither Tsongas nor Brown nor Clinton had particularly strong roots in the Midwest, and I'll turn to Betsy now to pursue the climax of the campaign on March 17 in the Midwestern primaries.

Betsy Kolbert: I guess this question goes to the Brown campaign. I don't know how much you were out there in the Midwest, but in Michigan, Jerry Brown got on his UAW jacket and made a lot of news. A lot of people thought that was pandering at its best. Can you talk to us about what the Brown campaign hoped to achieve out there?

Dan Butler: Yes. I can talk a little bit. I didn't go to Michigan or Illinois. I stayed in New England, but we were planning to try and court the labor vote, obviously, as much as we could. We were planning ahead for Connecticut and New York. And we felt that we could win the labor vote.

I don't know if you would call it pandering that Jerry wore the UAW jacket. He wore a lot of different things in the campaign that were unconventional, but that was the strategy in the heartland. We felt that we could inherit the Harkin labor vote.

Bill Schneider: Do you want to put a question to Clinton or Tsongas on that?

Betsy Kolbert: I'd like to go to right after the primaries when Paul Tsongas dropped out of the race.

Dennis Kanin: Before you do that, let me talk about Illinois a minute. In Illinois, we felt we had to get back on the message that we had gotten off in Florida, and we worked very hard at doing that. During the week of Illinois, for some reason, and I don't really understand why, our polling information didn't provide the answer.

Clinton was starting to lose some of his momentum in Illinois. I know that by the weekend before the primary, our polls were showing us closing in on Clinton in Illinois to the point where the Saturday/Sunday polling had us ten points behind and eight points behind among likely voters.

In the St. Patrick's Day parade, Tsongas got wild cheers and did far better than Clinton did, and we just started to get the feeling that this thing was turning around. I don't know if it's true or not, but that's certainly what our polling showed. Then came the debate on Sunday night, which I think was critical. The final turning point was when Brown attacked Hillary Clinton at the end of the debate, and Clinton effectively stood up for Hillary. More important, it dominated the last several minutes of the debate. Paul was kind of off there somewhere and not part of the battle.

I know that those of us who were in the room thought, these guys look like they're going at each other, and [Tsongas] is the only one that, you know, looks responsible and presidential.

My wife had a different reaction. She said, "I'm sick about it." I asked why. She said, "People like a guy who stands up for his wife." And all day on Monday, all the news programs and CNN had this every 15 minutes, Clinton standing up for Hillary. We were gone. We had disappeared entirely on Monday, and I think that sealed our fate. We probably would have lost Illinois anyway. I don't think we could have closed it enough, but we would have shown that we had a certain amount of momentum going in our direction if we had come within ten points.

David Wilhelm: Illinois, Michigan, we never showed that kind of fluctuation in the polling. It was always strong. We always had about a 20 to 25 percentage point lead, and there are several reasons for that. We were extraordinarily strong downstate in Illinois where, again, there's that Southern cultural affinity. We won Madison and St. Clair counties, which are in the St. Louis media market, by margins of six and seven to one over you guys. When you do Illinois, it's important that you do well downstate, central and southern Illinois. The other thing is that it's a state that doesn't need to relearn the lessons of trickle-down economics, the loss of manufacturing jobs, and so on. That week may have been our best week of the primary in terms of sending the message about rebuilding the economy and the message that Bill Clinton was a unifying figure on the national scene. Maybe I'm naive about that kind of thing, but I really think that we had an extraordinarily strong message in Illinois.

Ultimately, we did win an overwhelming vote in the African-American community. We did very well among ethnic voters, and we did well downstate. What was your question?

Betsy Kolbert: I was going to ask to what extent you also had concluded what James was saying, that the [Tsongas] message just couldn't carry a Democratic primary. Also, could you could talk about the issue of Paul's health, how much that did hang over you.

Dennis Kanin: Health was not an issue at that point. At that point he was fine and his status as explained earlier remained the same. But money was a major factor. It wasn't just being in debt. It was also lacking capacity to raise a lot of money at that point, so it was money from two angles. It wasn't because we concluded that his message could not carry the Democratic primary. Actually, the South was out of the way. The major coming battles were in the Northeast: Connecticut, New York, and Pennsylvania. We definitely felt we could win in Connecticut and New York. But Paul had concluded he could not win the nomination even if he won in Connecticut and New York. He would face Bill Clinton all the way to the end, Jerry Brown would probably stay in the race to the end and what would happen is some other candidate would become the nominee of a deadlocked convention. He said he did not want to be a spoiler. He had concluded he couldn't win the nomination and that's why he dropped out.

Bill Schneider: Stan?

Stan Greenberg: Let me make a point about Michigan and Illinois. They were overshadowed by what happened in Connecticut, but we can miss the larger point because it relates to why we ultimately won this election. In Florida, we developed a very clear definition on a populist contrast between Tsongas and Clinton. We were on TV in Illinois with that very hard-hitting spot.

As we were finishing Illinois and Michigan, we had Robert Kennedy in mind as an example of the last Democrat who had united ethnic voters and black voters together in the same party, and we very consciously, in Michigan, went to Macomb County and then to a Detroit church to deliver the same message about unifying this party. In Chicago we went very visibly to white ethnic and black events to deliver a general election message about a Democratic party that, based on common values, can have a very broad base. As we were moving toward winning these primaries, we were elevating ourselves to a position that would enable us to compete in November.

Paul Begala: And the fact that [Clinton] went to Flint, Michigan, to the birthplace of the UAW, and reiterated his support for free trade in a primary when Jerry Brown was wearing the UAW jacket and Tsongas was pushing the theme that Clinton's a liar, he's a pander bear, he'll say anything. To go that forcefully to that powerful a group in that state and that primary, I think said a lot to the rest of the country, which was beginning to clue in to the race.

Bill Schneider: With Tsongas out of the race, when Brown became the principal contender, I think you put together a brilliant populist strategy including white ethnics and blacks. But you continued throughout to show weakness among suburban voters.

Stan Greenberg: Democrats.

Bill Schneider: Did that bother you as a sign for the general election?

Stan Greenberg: No, because I view those as the McCarthy voters of an earlier era, hooked on the kind of Democratic liberalism that we think sinks Democrats. Those are not the same suburban voters that you run for in the general election.

Bill Schneider: Okay. Let's go to New York, which, in many ways, was the wrap up of the campaign, not California. It was Clinton versus Brown, but also Clinton versus the press. Betsy's with the *New York Times*. She's covered New York so I leave it up to her.

Betsy Kolbert: One of the things I wanted to ask someone was, when did you see defeat coming in Connecticut? Then you get to New York, and there's this tremendous press coverage, not very favorable, and Governor Clinton makes his famous "didn't inhale" remark. I'm wondering what kind of a toll that took?

David Wilhelm: We blew Connecticut. We had a plan through Illinois, and then we, like, forgot.

Stan Greenberg: The record should show that the last election that Bill Clinton perhaps would have lost in his entire life was in my home state.

Frank Greer: We like to blame it on Greenberg because we said he was responsible for Connecticut.

Stan Greenberg: Well, we made a decision. We came out of Illinois. I remember this debate very vividly. The campaign centralized at various points. It centralized in New Hampshire. It centralized in New York, and it centralized in Chicago, and we had discussions at that point. The Governor was desperate to go back to Arkansas and rest. We made a decision that Tsongas winning Connecticut would not resurrect his candidacy. It would be seen to be New England, just an extension of his earlier victories, and we could withstand not winning in Connecticut. So the Governor went home. What we didn't factor into this was that Tsongas would pull out of the race in mid-week, redefining the race. We were not there. Brown was in the state at the time that Tsongas pulled out. We didn't have a campaign in Connecticut. We had poll numbers saying we were in trouble. We weren't surprised by it, but we couldn't really put together a campaign in a couple days.

David Wilhelm: We were not ready. We didn't have a plan. The Tsongas withdrawal threw us for a loop.

Bill Schneider: Since Jerry Brown won the Connecticut primary, Dan, do you have a few words to say about Connecticut and what happened thereafter?

Dan Butler: Let me say, Connecticut was important to the Brown campaign and to the Brown phenomenon. I thought I would talk about, just briefly, lessons learned from that campaign, for anybody that is ever considering running a Brown-style, grassroots, nationwide, unconventional, innovative campaign. I saw this in New Hampshire and Massachusetts and then again down in Connecticut. Grassroots campaigns tend to sprout competing organizations. I know that's news to a lot of you, but in the case of Connecticut, we had two competing organizations.

One was based in Bridgeport, the other in Farmington, just outside Hartford, both very capable and well organized. They were competing for the attention of the national campaign, the Santa Monica office, competing for Jerry Brown's presence, competing to make the schedule and drive the strategy in Connecticut, and they had two completely different strategies.

I was asked to go down there to reconcile those two camps, bring them together, mediate, and come up with a consolidated strategy, which I did just about two weeks before the campaign. The only way I was able to do that, aside from just being a good negotiator and a mediator and a nice guy, was that I held the purse strings. It was the first time in the campaign that I saw the power of the purse. As soon as those two camps saw that I could write the checks to buy the signs or pay for the buttons or rent a van, they immediately came together in one organization. Then we developed a coordinated strategy on the first day. For a neophyte like myself that was a valuable lesson.

Obviously, Jerry Brown went into Connecticut intending to come in second, until Paul Tsongas withdrew from the race. At that time, we smelled victory. We knew that the Clinton campaign chose not to emphasize the Connecticut campaign. So we thought we actually had a legitimate chance to win it. We poured a lot of resources — manpower and volunteers — into Connecticut. We brought a lot of our most successful organizers from Vermont, Maine, Massachusetts, and New Hampshire down to Connecticut, and they lived in volunteers' homes all over the state. Basically, we augmented the Connecticut organization with experienced people from the previous primaries. The New Hampshire primary — although we were barely a blip on the radar screen in New Hampshire — was a very valuable training and recruiting ground for later primaries and that's how we used it.

We wanted to show in Connecticut, after Senator Tsongas dropped out, that we could win in a head-to-head battle with Governor Clinton, and we wanted to lay the groundwork for New York and Wisconsin. We knew that if we could begin to bring unions on board in Connecticut — we very assiduously cultivated Phil Wheeler, the head of the UAW in Connecticut and New York — we might start a domino effect. We thought if we could win in Connecticut and if we could get the unions to jump on board the Governor Brown bandwagon, we might have a very big impact on the Wisconsin primary, in particular. We did get the UAW to sign on thanks to a secret weapon there, a fellow by the name of Danny Perez. If anybody ever goes again to Connecticut to campaign, you should immediately seek out Danny Perez. He's a scrappy union organizer for the ILGWU who immediately transformed our strategy the minute we recruited him into the campaign.

We specifically sought him out because, when I got there a couple of weeks before the primary, the Brown organization was white and green. There were almost no minorities involved. The white organizers and workers were primarily environment-oriented. That was their agenda. It was obvious to me that we had no coalition. We were very narrowly focused, and we needed to bring in the minorities. Danny Perez was able to do that for us. He immediately brought in Mayor Perry of Hartford, [Connecticut State Representative] Juan Figueroa, and Ed Vargas, another prominent minority representative. So we were able to capitalize on the timing of Paul Tsongas's withdrawal.

What stopped the big move for us after coming out of Connecticut was Tom Harkin. Harkin's move to Clinton took the wind out of our sails in places like Wisconsin. I don't think we were able to come up with a counter to that.

The flat tax, obviously, is the big issue that was seriously contested in New York, and we lost on that. Then naming a vice-presidential choice early — particularly a potentially controversial vice-presidential choice [Jesse Jackson] — hurt us badly as well. So that's what happened. The Connecticut campaign was our big boost, but we blew it leaving Connecticut.

Bill Schneider: Let's move on to New York now. Does anyone from the Clinton campaign want to talk about their plan for New York?

Stan Greenberg: Yes. We had a plan that centered on keeping Jerry Brown from having momentum out of the Connecticut win. We had poll data that said that the race was even in New York immediately after Connecticut. The press did not have that, and they didn't take us seriously when we expressed worry about Brown's momentum. We decided to devote the entire first week, after Connecticut, to the flat tax [Brown's proposal]. As we were disciplined in our focus on "people first" in Florida, we would talk about nothing but the flat tax out of the box in order to block any momentum for Brown. The one thing we did believe is that raising taxes on working people was not going to be a winning message in a Democratic primary. We did a press conference in front of H & R Block the day after the Connecticut primary. We went on the air with flat tax. We debated flat tax. We did everything to try to stop Brown from getting any momentum and that worked.

David Wilhelm: We had to get people to take Jerry Brown seriously as a candidate because as long as he was just a protest vote, he was going to be okay. But once he was taken seriously, we had to engage the flat tax issue. We had to debate him at every opportunity. This was a case where you wanted him to actually be elevated into the role of a serious candidate.

Bill Schneider: Betsy asked, and I want to pursue, the damage done by the New York primary. I mean, the most remarkable thing about this campaign in covering it was that in New York Clinton won a big state. He became the presumptive nominee coming out of the New York primaries, but he was so battered, he went to New York and he got mugged. Not unusual. He was so bloody and so battered, not by Brown, but by the press corps in New York. [The campaign] came out of that so beaten down that an amazing thing happened. It was just after the New York primary, when Clinton was the presumptive nominee, that instead of his moving up in the polls, Ross Perot suddenly became a factor in the campaign, and it looked like a three-way race.

You started coming in third in the polls right through the middle of June when Perot started getting beaten up by the press. The amazing thing is the New York primaries seemed to do much more damage than good for your campaign.

Frank Greer: The exit polls had 60 percent of the people saying Clinton did not have the honesty and integrity to be President. That was when Stan said, we've got to develop a real strategy to deal with this and position ourselves for the general election. We changed our strategy. We reintroduced Bill Clinton in Pennsylvania with a bio ad, first bio ad we had done since New Hampshire: where he came from and who he was and the struggles he'd gone through in his life. We talked about the hits we'd taken, but nothing like the hits that people of America have taken in Pennsylvania. We came out of Pennsylvania with 60 percent of the people saying he *did* have the honesty and integrity to be President. We completely reversed the trend, but we were, indeed, faced with the challenge of Ross Perot at that point.

Bill Schneider: Betsy?

Betsy Kolbert: Could you talk a little bit more in detail about this whole process of rehabilitating Bill Clinton, coming out of New York, what the strategy was going through California? Also, I'm assuming that you were now looking at a three-way race, and what was your thinking about that?

Stan Greenberg: We did assume that. It was actually James who, I think, first made that assumption after New York. We had decided after Illinois that it was time to focus on the general. Connecticut forced us to then take New York as the battle for our lives, which is the way we treated it. When it was over, James proposed that a number of us pull out of the primaries and begin to focus on and develop a plan for the general. Mickey Kantor approved that and so we ended up, at that point, just pulling back. That was based on the assumption that the general would kick off after California.

In fact, that was the period in which Perot emerged. Perot was very frustrating for us because that's when the spotlight should have been on us, as presumptive favorite, and we should have been getting fairly favorable press. On the day of the California primary, the *New York Times*, in a front page story was talking about a brokered convention. We thought we had to change the environment. We had to change the story. I don't know if you want to go into this now.

Betsy Kolbert: Since we need to wrap up, regarding the last question about the choosing of the vice presidential nominee, how much was the thinking of a three-way race influential in that choice, in the need for the suburban vote at that point?

Stan Greenberg: Well, first of all, there were two processes. One, for selection of the vice presidential nominee, which centered around Warren Christopher and Bill Clinton, of which the political people were very self-consciously not a part. This process went very far without political input. We were asked for our views and there were memos, but the process was very much separated from political calculation. Certainly, the three-way race was an important factor in David's recommendations and my recommendations. Creating a Southern base in a three-way race with Perot was a factor, at least in our recommendations, but there were lots of other reasons as well.

CHAPTER THREE

THE REPUBLICAN PRIMARIES

"If 75 percent of the people in the country think you're on the wrong track and only 40 percent think the President's doing a good job, you're going to have a tough re-election, but that perception never appeared to influence the actions of the White House or the administration."

— Bill Kristol, Chief of Staff to Vice President Quayle

The Discussion

Charley Royer: This afternoon we will discuss the Republican primaries. On your agenda, it says that there are two people from the *Wall Street Journal* here, David Shribman and Jill Abramson. In order to keep this from being a *Wall Street Journal* effort, Dave Shribman has just been named Bureau Chief of the *Boston Globe* for balance. So we're delighted to congratulate him on that move. We'll start with David to set the context, and then we'll get into the Q and A.

David Shribman: Thanks very much and welcome to methadone for campaign junkies. If the Yukon was, as Robert Service said in his famous poem, "The Land That God Forgot," then the Republican primaries were the events that God didn't intend or maybe the events that God, in His infinite wisdom, intended all along. The Republican primaries, I think we'll all agree, exposed some of the weaknesses and vulnerabilities of the incumbent president. They set in motion some forces that I think helped defeat him. And they illuminated some of the themes that were developed as the campaign entered the conventions and the general election.

The Republican primaries of 1992 really had their origins in the Republican primaries of 1980, if not in the Republican struggle of 1964. In 1980, at the end of the Republican primaries — even after

Mr. Bush had won the Michigan primary — there was kind of an uncomfortable marriage, one of convenience, one of necessity perhaps, between Ronald Reagan and George Bush. There it all began for George Bush and, in a way, there it all ended as well. In that effort, George Bush plunged in but he plunged as Shakespeare might have said, "not wisely; but too well." In his effort as the vice-presidential nominee for the Republican party in 1980, he revealed to all of us some of the enormous appeal of George Bush and some of his enormous vulnerabilities as well.

Charley Royer, David Shribman, Jill Abramson

He believed in, if in anything at all, the notion of service, having been bred and raised the child of a Republican senator from Connecticut, who, himself, was the embodiment of the notion of *noblesse oblige*. Mr. Bush had little ideology. He was willing to change positions on important matters — the economy, abortion. His ideology, basically, was service, and he succeeded in politics as long as he served. It was more a sense of stewardship than it was of leadership.

When it came time to display leadership — political leadership, not military leadership of which he had a surfeit and we can be glad of that — he was found wanting. The sense of stewardship was not enough. Bush suddenly seemed to be wearing no armor. In the political world, to the voters at least, he was wearing no clothes.

Pat Buchanan sensed this early, before a lot of the so-called experts did. He sensed it better than other challengers to incumbent Presidents did, on the Republican side at least. Better than Ashbrook, better than

McCloskey.* Buchanan was in the race for himself, as politicians most always are, but he was also in it to focus on issues. Ultimately, he focused the nation's attention on Bush's lack of commitment on issues.

There were other subthemes here. Lee Atwater had died. There was a palace revolt involving Sununu and against Sununu. A very important precursor event happened between September and November of 1991 in Pennsylvania where the Democrats of Carville and Begala showed what they could do, much like the Spanish Civil War gave us an idea of what World War II might be like [the defeat of Thornburgh, Bush's former Attorney General, in the contest for John Heinz's Senate seat].

Then Buchanan plunged in. We saw President Bush reduced to kind of cryptic notions of message — "I care" — and I think it all began to fall apart.

One of the things we should examine is not only how the campaigns approached the New Hampshire primary but how the press approached it, because the reports we were getting at four and five on that February afternoon were substantially different from the way things ended up. We all laid out our pages — not in the *Wall Street Journal,* of course, because we only have one-column headlines. It was a source of great comfort to work there because you knew no one could ever hold up your paper like the *Chicago Tribune* of 1948** because the headlines were too small.

Our pages were laid out with the expectation of a larger Buchanan victory or performance than what we actually got. So I think one of the things we should talk about is the perception-versus-reality continuum, how we all handled New Hampshire, and how our interpretations that we bred and the ripples that came from them changed and shaped the fortunes of George Bush.

I know Jill wants to talk a little about the dual role of the press — observers and participants. We watch you, as politicians, do your job. We don't necessarily criticize you for what you say, although you think we do. We do criticize you on *how* you say it and on how you conduct your campaigns. As critics, we wondered if the Bush campaign was a kind of reluctant participant in all this. I think I'd like to let that lead to how Jill wants to shape some of our following discussions.

Editor's Note: Rep. John Ashbrook (R-OH) and Rep. Paul McCloskey (R-CA) ran against Richard Nixon in the 1972 presidential primary.

**Editor's Note:* In 1948 the *Tribune* announced that Thomas E. Dewey had defeated Harry Truman. The photo of that headline has appeared countless times.

A Reluctant President

"They all started speculating that he was not going to run; but it really was George Bush's clock, which had proved itself to be a Swiss watch in every other campaign. We had no real compulsion to push him into this race before he was ready."

— Mary Matalin, Political Director,
Bush/Quayle Campaign

Jill Abramson: Well, where I'd like to start is back in the fall of '91, where President Bush seemed less than eager, to put it mildly, to begin his campaign. We know that in Bush's head there is always a sharp defining line between governing and campaigning and that he preferred the governing part. He seemed to be displaying such an aversion to beginning the campaign back in the fall of '91 that we wondered whether any serious thought was given, on his part and inside the White House, not to seek a second term.

Mary Matalin: Around that time, they all started speculating that he was not going to run; but it really was George Bush's clock, which had proved itself to be a Swiss watch in every other campaign. We had no real compulsion to push him into this race before he was ready, and he did not want to accelerate the process whereby everything he said would be viewed politically. He knew the minute he crossed that line, he could not govern.

As for the notion that we were not organized, we were organized enough to have a very serious meeting in August of '91 to lay the whole thing out. By that time, we had a 50-state structure, ballot initiatives, ballot referenda, state issues. We knew how to get on the ballot in every state, and we had the matching funds apparatus set up. We had the finance plan. We had everything ready to hit the ground running, except the knowledge that we were going to have a primary. No one could have anticipated in September of '91 what was going to happen in December of '91.

David Shribman: Mary, one of the things we were wondering about was, as you developed your game plan in August of '91, what did you think the campaign would be like and whom did you think you'd be running against? Did you think you'd *have* a primary opponent?

Mary Matalin: Charlie Black, jump in. We thought our biggest vulnerability then was oddly one you left out in your list of vulnerabilities, which is pretty comprehensive. That's the '90 budget deal. That was the worst civil war we were having. We didn't think that was going to lead to a primary so much as just dispirit the effort in the field.

Charlie Black: We were focused almost 100 percent on the economy, why it wasn't getting better, and whether the President should do something in terms of proposals to Congress in the fall of '91. You know, outside advisors were giving their input just like the people who worked in the White House. Maybe we should have known, but we didn't think Pat [Buchanan] was going to run. If somebody brought up that possibility in a meeting, we said, "So what? He'll run in New Hampshire and he'll get 30, 35 percent. Then it's over with."

Mary Matalin, Charlie Black

David Shribman: Why did you think in August of '91 someone running against you could get 35 percent?

Charlie Black: Because New Hampshire was a basket case. The economy was horrible. I'll let Dave Carney speak to this, since it's his home town. You had more negative voter perceptions about the economy or about the President and the party in New Hampshire than in any other place in the country, with the possible exception of California. We also knew that if Pat or anybody else ran a conservative challenge, New Hampshire would be their best state and that we could tap it down in the ensuing primaries. You all tended not to believe, but it proved to be true.

Bill Kristol: Can I just pick up on one interpretation of what you said? I don't think that the President's obvious distaste for launching the campaign quite as early as some might have wanted him to made any difference, and I don't think at the end of the day that the primary challenge made much difference. The Institute of Politics' chronology indicates the campaign season begins with Lee Atwater's collapse on March 5, 1990, and I think that's an appropriate place to begin because that was the collapse of any integration of government — governing, governance — and political guidance at the White House.

A lot of people spent a lot of time trying to make up for that failure over the next 18 months, but by September of '91 we were paying a price, not just for the budget deal, but for the notion that you didn't need a domestic agenda, or the March 6, 1991 speech to Congress, in which the President didn't use his political capital to get out front at all, starting with an aggressive domestic agenda, or to confront the economy, etc. I think a lot of us knew we were vulnerable. Whether or not there had been a primary challenge, we would have remained vulnerable.

If 75 percent of the people in the country think you're on the wrong track and only 40 percent think the President's doing a good job, you're going to have a tough re-election, but that perception never appeared to influence the actions of the White House or the administration. That was the underlying situation we faced in August of '91, in December of '91, and afterwards, in fact.

Charlie Black: Bill's right; but one little amendment. Pat was entitled to run. He proved that by campaigning and running well all the way down to March 18. But it did hurt us, mainly because we were late presenting an economic program to the country. The President should have done it in the fall; those who said it wasn't necessary, not to mention the directors of OMB, prevailed.

We came late with a Bush economic program in the State of the Union. What we needed to do in that first quarter, in order to win the general election, was to re-establish his credibility on the economy, show that he understood the problem, that he had some connection with people's problems, and that he had a plan. We couldn't do it. We presented the plan but it was obscured by the primary coverage and by the horse-race coverage, and by Pat very effectively and articulately pointing out that the President wasn't on top of the economy.

I'm not saying that come September or October, I attributed our loss to Pat Buchanan, but what we needed to be doing in the first quarter was made practically impossible by having to compete with Pat for two months.

Bill Kristol: Just one point. These internal debates are so much more interesting than the outside. Last night someone said that the way the series works is first your opponents attack you, then the press attacks you, and, finally, your own campaign turns on you. We in the Bush administration did it the opposite way. We had the internal debate first so we could set things up for the press and for the opposition. I didn't mean to imply before that somehow we were finished by the fall of '91 and that we couldn't have recouped at a whole bunch of points including, most of all, November of '91 and the State of the Union in January. It's an interesting question, how much the Buchanan challenge distracted us or prevented us from doing what we should have done in terms of an economic agenda and a coherent political economic strategy in January of '92 or March of '92. You were at the campaign, and were preoccupied, and properly so, with worrying about the primary challenge to some degree. I didn't feel that it would have been impossible to have followed up the State of the Union or the March 20 speech more effectively, regardless of what was going on, frankly, in New Hampshire or Georgia.

We had a shot at establishing an aggressive sort of governing agenda that would have served us well in the fall, but the Buchanan challenge was a distraction, and the constant reminders of the budget deal and "read my lips" were distractions. But it needn't have been quite as much of a distraction as you suggest.

Mary Matalin: You can't underestimate the other aspect of "read my lips." It wasn't just the budget deal and tax deal. While that was bad enough, it was credibility. You couldn't get the new stuff through because of the credibility factor. All people could see was "read my lips." Why should we believe this new economic plan, and then another new economic plan on the twentieth? So it was hurtful on many, many levels.

Anger on the Right: The Primary Challenge

"The President made over 450 promises in the 1988 campaign. Just before I left the White House for the campaign, we went back and researched how he did on all those promises. Other than four — one of them being a doozie — we had significant specific action."

— Dave Carney, Director of Public Affairs and National
Field Director, Bush/Quayle Campaign

Bay Buchanan: A couple of things. First of all, we were watching the possibility for about 12 months. In January of '91, Pat and I talked. We watched it and that's when, of course, we ended up in [the Gulf] war. Pat continually said, we will not enter this race against the Commander in Chief when there are troops overseas. We just won't do it. So that was the end of the discussion. That carries right into August. Then a couple of things happened. Pat and I have thought that if Lee Atwater had been alive and healthy, we probably would never have gotten in the race. Because there were several things the President did that pushed us in a very energetic way.

We had the Judge [Clarence] Thomas hearings.* Pat was very public in favor of Judge Thomas. The quota bill came right after that. We felt that that was such an insult. It wasn't needed, it wasn't called for, it wasn't politically wise. It seemed like an affront to the conservatives.

That's when Pat wrote a column about it. I'm sitting there reading my paper, and there was the whole thing laid out, why it's time to challenge the President. I called Pat and said, "You've given me the best reasons why it's time to go."

After we made the decision, though, there were a couple things that we recognized throughout every single day: the President can wake up today and make an announcement that terminates this campaign. You are history.

He introduces a bill that says to Congress you cut taxes, and I'll take the blame. If you don't, you take the blame. Just some action like that, and we would support him, and we would lose our issue. All along we recognized that the President could take action that would eliminate our efforts.

While Pat may have affected the outcome of the general election, you have to remember that in the polls in April, after Pat's run when he was no longer really effective as a candidate, the President was first, Perot was second, and Clinton was third. It's debatable that Pat had an impact on the general election.

Mary Matalin: I just have to answer. I respectfully disagree because what you all did was you ran the Democrats' campaign for them. Bill Clinton barely had to run a "read my lips" commercial. Six-year-olds, two-year-olds running around New Hampshire and all over the country saying, "Read my lips, read my lips, read my lips." You laid the groundwork for the general election. Your effort mattered. The numbers were not reflective going into that period. They were only what they were because Clinton was still unknown, had a very bad primary season, and Perot was a new phenomenon.

Editor's Note: Senate confirmation hearings for Judge Clarence Thomas took place from October 11 through October 13, 1991. He was confirmed as U.S. Supreme Court Justice on October 15, 1991.

Bay Buchanan: I would like to take credit for this ingenious "read my lips" commercial, but everyone in the country had figured that out. That was going to be an effective way to run a campaign. So what we were doing was giving a ten-month wake-up call to the President to say, you have a lot to do out there. You better come home and, buddy, start taking action. If no call had been made and he didn't do anything for those ten months, there would be an excuse here, but he had ten months to take action and he took none.

Charlie Black: Yeah, Jill, let me jump ahead for one minute. I mean, it's impossible to say this one thing cost Bush the election. It was a number of things and most of them were our fault. He's taken a lot of the responsibility, but we all deserve some of it; there were a number of things that, taken together, cost us the election. Pat's candidacy was one of them. He was entitled to run and his people did a good job. In the general election, Pat Buchanan was 100 percent for George Bush; he and Bay did every single thing we asked them to and we appreciate that. There is no criticism in that regard. But when we should have been using the first quarter to be on offense about an economic plan for the country, we were on defense on the economy and a number of issues and slugging it out in a horse race.

Jill Abramson: Charlie, in the first quarter, what was your understanding about the mood of the country and the potential for this huge protest vote in the electorate?

Charlie Black: Well, going back to the '90 election — what you all described as the anti-incumbency factor showed up. It didn't cost a lot of congressmen their seats, but many of them made it with 52 percent of the vote. We were analyzing that anti-incumbent trend as a protest vote, and trying to figure out what impact it might have on Bush.

All through '91, we talked about it a lot. In these meetings, the economic advisors would tell us not to worry because the recession was going to be over the next week, and by the time we have this meeting next week we'll be in recovery. They even had a date. It will be over on May 15, 1991. Oh, great, let's meet on the sixteenth. On the sixteenth, well, gosh, we meant to say June 15. Still waiting. [Laughter]

We knew there was a potential protest vote out there, in our party as well as in the general electorate. Obviously, nobody could have foreseen how it would be housed in a Perot candidacy and the magnitude of it — 20 million votes for an independent candidate in a general election. We knew we had to get the President ahead of the curve on the economy, at least as to convincing people that he understood the problem and that he had a plan. All this debate we had in the second half of '91 about what the plan should be. Whether it was necessary to have a plan that

Congress would pass or not was the sticking point as to why we didn't come out with one. Whatever it was, we stayed behind the curve.

We didn't get ahead of it even though we came up with a good plan and presented it in the State of the Union, gave Congress 60 days, and hit them hard in March — March 20 — and we vetoed their tax increase and so forth. But we never broke through to convince enough people that the President understood the economic problem, cared about them, and had a plan. So, yeah, the protest vote was a two- or three-year phenomenon, in terms of our study of it.

Bill Kristol: We sat in September of '91, at the Biennial Conference of Michigan Republicans; Mary, Charlie, and I were there. You [Bay Buchanan] weren't there, but I know you agreed with us. We all were very worried.

Charlie is much more of an expert on this than I am but we're not idiots. We can see that if the wrong-track number is in the 70's and the President's approval isn't great and his popularity, which is the softest of those numbers, is dropping fast, and the economy is slow or going into a double dip, that you're going to have a tough re-election.

We had seen that the Cold War had taken defense and foreign policy off the table more than the Gulf War had put it back on. The problem is we sat around agreeing with ourselves and tried to influence actual policy. But when you're the President, it's not just a matter of the campaign deciding that this would be a good theme. You have to influence actual governance, actual policymaking, either proposals to Congress or executive actions or personnel.

I think it's fair to say that whatever our views, we never succeeded in convincing those we had to convince to do what was necessary for an incumbent in a re-election context — to convince people that the President himself agreed with most Americans, that the country is on the wrong track, and, therefore, that we had to be on the right side of the wrong track.

We had to blame someone else for the wrong track, which had to be the Democratic Congress. And we had to show that we wanted to act aggressively to change things; you can't just say that occasionally, if you're an incumbent President. You have to do certain things and change certain things in your own administration to show that you are changing the mindset that you've had for a couple of years.

But for whatever reasons, many were honorable, and, really, to the personal credit of the President, he wasn't willing to do some of the things that I think would have turned out to be politically effective.

Bay Buchanan: You know what we found, Jill, in response to your question, was something rather surprising. When we got into the race it was philosophical. There was nothing personal. Pat has, as I do, enormous respect for the President on a personal level. But we got into it strictly because of philosophy, as I spoke about earlier. When we got out there, we were alarmed that much of that protest wasn't just anti-incumbent, "We've got to change Washington." It was pointed towards the President. There was a lot of animosity toward the President. Pat used to continually call me and say, "I can't believe these people are so upset with him, personally."

Jill Abramson: Why did the President sign the civil rights legislation? Having come off the Thomas confirmation battle, why not capitalize by vetoing the civil rights bill, and try to continue mending fences and building a coalition with the right and even some of the religious right groups that had been mobilized? Were you so worried about the backlash already that you felt you had to do something to appease the left?

Charlie Black: No. Let me just tell you a true story. George Bush always wanted a civil rights bill. He is for civil rights going back to his vote for fair housing in the Congress in the 1960s, when he was the only Southern Republican to vote that way. His advisors, who were involved in a technical, legal debate about the thing, convinced him the first time around it was a quota bill, and that it could be made better. So he vetoed it and took whatever heat he was going to take in '90. He came back in '91 and I don't know how much we changed it, enough to satisfy him, but he always, wanted a civil rights bill. Frankly, for the long-term good of the Republican party, it was a good thing for us to get civil rights off the table as a political issue. Both parties should be for civil rights and should be perceived by the voters to be for civil rights.

Bay, with all due respect, there weren't that many grassroots voters upset about the quota bill. They were upset about the economy, tax increases, the tax pledge, ten times as much as they were about the vote.

Bay Buchanan: I agree with you there, but the key is that the activists in the party were very upset with different decisions the President made. He ran against quotas four years ago, so this was another promise broken. It wasn't that we were going to go out there and run on this issue, but it was an offense, it was saying, you guys helped me get here, I ran on your agenda, but see ya later, I'm going in this direction. We felt it imperative that somebody get out there and express our views, as conservatives, be a spokesperson for conservatives saying, this isn't the conservative agenda. That's why we felt we had to move. That was the last straw, and if you had held up two more months, we couldn't have gotten in.

Bill Kristol: Jill, the answer to your question is that there never was the type of meeting that you imagined to have happened where there was a political debate about the consequences of signing the bill. There was never such a meeting before Marlin [Fitzwater, press secretary] went out and pinned the budget deal announcement on the bulletin board in March 1990. The press kept looking for deep motives for some of these decisions. In some ways it's to our credit, I suppose, that there weren't such politically motivated meetings but it meant that one could veer back and forth on policy.

Charlie Black: Well, they all knew the President wanted a civil rights bill, and it wouldn't have surprised most of us a bit, if he had signed that '90 bill ...

Bill Kristol: That's right.

Charlie Black: But Boyden [Gray, Bush's deputy chief of staff] and Sununu thought they could get a better bill and they did, I guess. There was just no political discussion about it. We were all for that, too. Going back to Lee [Atwater] very strongly. He always advised the President, let's get civil rights off the table.

Jill Abramson: Before we leave the first quarter, I want Mary and Rich to give input on this, too. How concerned or aware were you about the problem of having no general to lead the political army? And having the White House and the RNC, in terms of mechanics, not ready to wage war together, and about who was going to lead this battle? It was all so murky. Mary, you're looking at me puzzled.

Mary Matalin: There is one thing about the Republican apparatus. The mechanical part is always ready, in the tradition of [Rich] Bond, our supreme guy who taught us all this in 1980. George Bush is president today because of Rich Bond in Iowa, in 1980. Okay? So we know all that stuff was ready. We're all being so delicate about this but let's just call a spade a spade. There was a political mind which had the political sensitivity of a doorknob in the White House and that was John Sununu. There was no political connection inside the White House. It was not integrated.

Bill Kristol: Tell us what you really think.

James Carville: Don't hold back, honey. Let him have it.

Mary Matalin: It was bad enough when Lee was well. It strained even his Machiavellian talents to work around Sununu. In the nanosecond after Lee got sick, John made his big move. The only guy who could talk to him — that doesn't mean he was always listening — was Charlie. There was this wall, and we didn't even know what kind of information was getting to George Bush. We were ready to the full extent that the apparatus can be ready. I don't really want to do this — put the blame on one person — but I refuse to be delicate about this because I think he created or contributed more than any single person to where we were in the fall and winter of 1991.

Charlie Black: In terms of the apparatus and the mechanics, when Lee was sick, Mary, as *de facto* chairman, kept the party going and kept everything prepared. Then, when Rich took over, we had the best possible guy that we could have to lead the party, from the standpoint of grassroots party apparatus during a presidential year. I don't really think we missed a beat in that regard. Our problems were political, in the sense of decisions and communications capability and not grassroots.

David Shribman: I was wondering if it would be all right for Dave Carney to remark on the Sununu commentary?

Dave Carney: Well, I think it's a deeper structural problem than what Mary pointed out. No one in the country knew about all the accomplishments the President had on the domestic side. The President made over 450 promises in the 1988 campaign. Just before I left the White House for the campaign, we went back and researched how he did on all those promises. Other than four — one of them being a doozie... [Laughter] Buckner only missed one or two balls,* but on over 450 of those promises and commitments we made, we had significant specific action. We either completed them or were underway in doing them. It would stretch the imagination of this entire room here, people stalked the President for four years, to identify those very specific, concrete accomplishments. I think one of the problems was that we did not communicate very well on the domestic side.

On the foreign policy side, there was only one person forming policy. It became self-apparent in that you don't need to worry about how people spin it or how people interpret it or how people ignore it. It's obvious that the President had success there.

On the domestic side, with Congress and the states involved and all these other areas, it was less clear who was in charge and who was responsible for these things. The White House did not take enough credit for the good things that happened. So it was easier for all the candidates, all the wannabe candidates, all the real candidates, to spend, you know, $150 million in a year to trash the President.

Charlie Black: We didn't have any political communications. John Sununu was very smart and did a lot of good. In a lot of ways, he did that job exactly the way George Bush wanted him to do it. But neither George Bush nor John Sununu nor Dick Darman nor anybody else who was there in a position of authority is a political communicator. Some of us on the outside, who were in there once a week for a meeting or something, submitted ideas and sometimes they were taken, sometimes they were not. I mean, we share blame or responsibility because obviously

---

Editor's Note: Bill Buckner, first baseman for the Boston Red Sox, made the error which caused his team to lose a decisive World Series game in 1986.

we weren't effective advisors if we couldn't get them to take our advice, but there was no political communication. That's what Mary referred to last night when we started the campaign and did our first Bush-Quayle major national poll along about the first week of January. Nobody knew what the President's accomplishments were. You ask them open-ended, "What's he done?" "Nothing. The Gulf War, which, by the way, we don't care about anymore."

David Shribman: Well, as enjoyable as hearing people beat up on John Sununu is, we have to move on.

One of the things I'm wondering about is what kinds of vulnerabilities the Bush campaign was feeling during what Jill called the end of the first quarter or as we headed into the new year. For example, President Bush gave this astonishing interview to David Frost, in which he said he would do anything to win. Well, we all quoted that through the next year, as kind of showing the shallowness of the President, but at the time I don't think anybody really thought that it showed any weakness or that it portrayed any vulnerability. As we go into the first part of the year, we see the Buchanan campaign getting organized. David Duke is over there on the horizon, the far-right horizon, and the President begins to campaign. We all are surprised a little bit by the ferocity with which people were reacting to George Bush. Bay Buchanan's remarks about Pat's reaction is kind of reminiscent about our President Kennedy who said, after he was inaugurated, he was stunned to find that things were actually as bad as he said they had been. So, with that, let's go to Jill, who wants to pick up a little bit on the beginning of the semifinals, I guess.

New Hampshire

"We had about a half hour of considering the possibility that we could win the whole thing. But I would say no more than a half hour."

— Bay Buchanan, Campaign Manager, Buchanan for
President

Jill Abramson: Right, and New Hampshire. Bay, when Pat got into it, did he think that he had a shot at winning the New Hampshire primary?

Bay Buchanan: We thought it was a long shot to win the nomination. Winning New Hampshire was never in the cards, but New Hampshire would give us momentum maybe to carry it through Georgia and then possibly an outside chance, in our wildest dreams, to make it through Super Tuesday. Winning New Hampshire for us was just doing well. It was doing better than it was perceived we would do. Pat and I were very familiar with New Hampshire, and Charlie is as well. Ronald Reagan got 49 percent in New Hampshire, but that was perceived as a loss.

What we needed to do was make certain that those expectations were kept as low as possible. So we were up there saying, geez, you know, we're at nine. We hope to get to the teens. One of the Bush people made the mistake of saying "They won't break 30." That's when we said, you know, 30? Please, we're in the 20's. Thirty? Geez, that's so far away. So people started using 30 as the number we had to do. We always said we're in the low 20's at best, but that was a key to us, and we just kept working it. I'll be honest: in our polls we were not over 30. We worked it to death up there with every aspect that we could, including commercials.

In the first six weeks, we didn't have any polls. We didn't want to spend the money that early. What we did was just to watch what the Bush surrogate said and what the President said and we knew what other polls were saying. We knew that they were heavily polling. First they said Pat was a protectionist. Then they didn't say Pat was a protectionist anymore. I said a protectionist wasn't bad, Pat. You're an isolationist now and that must be bad because the surrogate uses it all the time.

So we were tracking our vulnerabilities by reading from what they were saying. Also, every time Bush came up to New Hampshire, we dropped five and he went up five. You know, the President just landed in the state, and we were back to where we started. When you're only at 20, five is a lot of points. We knew that "read our lips" wasn't the key. It was trust that was the key and "read my lips" symbolized the trust issue. It reminded them that we're in this mess because he broke a promise, and not the taxes themselves.

We were able to create an atmosphere so that when the President came in he was that bad guy who raised our taxes and caused this mess. So, in those last two weeks, when he came to New Hampshire and went down in the polls, we picked up. They were wise enough to send Mrs. Bush in. No matter what, Mrs. Bush was just so powerful in the polls. She moved the votes very, very quickly. We were trying to move everything we could, because we knew that if things were tight, he'd come in in the last three days, and that was it for us.

The State of the Union [January '92] was another critical time for us. If he did say those things that Pat had been criticizing him for not saying, we'd be hurt. We lost five points at the State of the Union, and we didn't know if we were going to be able to recover it.

Jill Abramson: What were the Bush people feeling about Buchanan and his best upside potential? We kept hearing the last week that there was worry that Bush was going to be under 50 percent. Was that ever real or not?

Charlie Black: That was spin, pretty much. In the end about 10 percent went to other candidates, but, as far as the two-way head-to-head competition, we wanted to hold Pat under 40. That was our private goal. I guess we would have said we wanted to win by 20 points, which we damn near did.

I guess it would be the subject of a whole other meeting to talk about these exit polls, and what a pleasure it was for me to go on CNN at 8:01 and have Bernie Shaw say: "Well, isn't this great, Bush is going to win New Hampshire by one point." I got back to my room at 11:00. I called CNN; we're 15 points up; can I come back on the show? They hung up on me. But, you know, it turned out about like we thought. Pat was under 40, but it was 53-37. It was a 16-point difference, and a 20-point difference had been our goal.

Nevertheless, the important thing was it was perceived to be closer early in the evening when Buchanan broke whatever the magic number was — some reporters were saying 35, some were saying 30.* It got huge coverage. It did propel them forward with momentum. Again, we were absolutely right that New Hampshire was his best state and his high-water mark, but it took us another month to prove that to you all.

Jill Abramson: Tom Luce, what were you thinking the night of the New Hampshire primary?

Tom Luce: We weren't thinking at all at that point in time. We weren't in existence. The New Hampshire primary was February 18. Perot didn't appear on Larry King until February 20. I'd never dreamed he'd run for president before February 20.

Clay Mulford: Could I follow up on that? Tom called me at home that night and said, "Did you watch Larry King tonight?" I thought this is a test on the intellectual prowess of his law partner. I said, "Of course not." [Laughter] And he said, "Well, you might want to figure out what happened on that show." It was news to everyone.

Jill Abramson: But you'd [Tom Luce] been a Republican candidate yourself. Didn't the results of the New Hampshire primary surprise

---

*Editor's Note: The final results were Buchanan 37 percent, Bush 53 percent, Others 10 percent.

you? My gosh, we really do have a very vulnerable Republican president on our hands?

Tom Luce: I felt the President was vulnerable. I would phrase it a little bit differently about the economy; I don't think it was the economy, in terms of recession, nor the new taxes.

I think the problem was that throughout the campaign most Republican and Independent voters were concerned, not about the recession number or the unemployment number, but because of the fear in their stomach that they will be unemployed next year. They wanted a plan for the economy long term. I just felt like the President was very vulnerable in that regard and I'm sure that's no news to them. If Darman says the numbers go from X to Y, that's not going to quiet the fears of middle-class Americans about what happens to them next year. Is their company the next to be restructured? So I felt the President was vulnerable, but, heck, I was just reading the newspaper like everybody else.

Mary Matalin: Can I make one more point about New Hampshire, just a tactical point about the impact of the press? The only real debate we had on the campaign was when to blow Pat's face off — nothing personal. Some of us wanted to shoot to kill in New Hampshire, but we were overtaken by the forces that did not want to put up with a press story on Bush going negative so early.

James Carville: It didn't bother you all in the general [election] did it?

Mary Matalin: Huh?

James Carville: It didn't bother you all in the general, did it?

Charlie Black: You started it.

Mary Matalin: We were very aware of that.

Charlie Black: Interesting historical footnote: in the debate about going negative on Buchanan in New Hampshire, Teeter was for it and I was against it and I won.

Bay Buchanan: We felt that for the President to go negative that early really would show enormous weakness. We were feeding that story: "Pat, do you know anything else going on down there? Did you hear about a negative commercial?" I said, I hear there is one in the hopper, but I don't think they're going to use it.

Charlie Black: Oh, we had them.

Bay Buchanan: So we kept feeding that, recognizing that they would send the surrogates in to say things, which was expected. But they wouldn't go negative on television. We thought that was our free ride.

We knew if we did well that we were to expect all kinds of bombs coming down, and, of course, they all came down.

Jill Abramson: Were there spots in the can?

Charlie Black: Oh, sure, and we used them two days after New Hampshire because then we had 15 more primaries. We knew that they would stay alive until Super Tuesday and maybe through Illinois. No, it was a major consideration not to show weakness by having to go negative on Pat before Pat ever got a single vote, in New Hampshire or anywhere else. It was debatable. Maybe we should have done it before. I don't know. I'm still glad we didn't, but we were ready and pulled the trigger immediately in Georgia and the other places that were coming up on the calendar.

Bill Kristol: The Vice President thought it was ridiculous to go negative in New Hampshire or even afterwards. He didn't think Buchanan was the problem, he wasn't going to win, and he wasn't going to get over 50 percent in any of these states. I remember after South Dakota, which was — what, a week after New Hampshire — when "Uncommitted" got 30 percent? The Vice-President's comment when he wondered whether some people would start suggesting that we go negative on "Uncommitted" certainly made the point.

Charlie Black: We had enough problems without taking any more risk after Pat got 37 percent in New Hampshire and was catapulted in the news. For a month Pat Buchanan got just as much coverage as George Bush.

Bay Buchanan: Let me ask you, Charlie, was it your decision to send the "Terminator" [Arnold Schwarzenegger] in? We got a great deal of play out of that one.

Charlie Black: I'm not going to finger-point, but I will not take responsibility for that.

Bay Buchanan: That was about the most negative you went.

David Shribman: I think Mr. Bode wants to jump in.

Ken Bode: Can I ask Bill and Charlie and Mary and David a question? At the end of the campaign, there was a great deal of consternation about the fact that the press had not reported the economic situation of the country accurately, that we depicted a much poorer economy than actually existed.

In New Hampshire, where probably there is greater media coverage of politics than any place in the country, at that period of time, you had six Democrats and a Republican challenger running in a state where the economy was in very bad shape. You all referred again and again to the fact that the economy wouldn't turn around, that there was a recession, that the economy was ten times more important than anything else and so forth. How much did that, in your minds, set the tone of economic reporting throughout the campaign? And the President's reaction to it? And his tailoring his message, "I care," and so forth? In 1988 New Hampshire had the lowest unemployment rate in the country, and in 1992 it was just reversed.

Charlie Black: That might have contributed to the tone of the political reporting about the economy, but it's just generally been bad all during the 12 years. Unemployment would go down and your networks would lead off with, inflation reared its ugly head today, or the economy is heating up too much or something.

I think the New Hampshire experience — the fact of having six Democrats advertising and beating up on the President in the free media contributed to the malaise there, in the voters' minds, in addition to what Pat was doing. I don't think it affected the overall national economic coverage that much.

Dave Carney: The coverage for seven or eight weeks was all on the economy and how bad it was: everyone and his brother are unemployed. For the first time in New Hampshire's history, there are more unemployed people than legislators. That was what people watched for six or eight weeks. People had fears about their own economic security. They heard about layoffs over there. They could be next.

I think the other thing about the media coverage in New Hampshire, the biggest disservice to our campaign, was the exit polls. If the exit polls had been right and Pat had had a 16-point victory, it would have been "Buchanan with a spirited effort falls short" or "does okay." They would have taken their hits at it, but it wouldn't have been the frenzy that night and the papers the next morning talking about Buchanan winning by losing by only two points. Some of the headlines were terrible. They went to bed well before anybody figured out there were other candidates on the ballot, and that the President only got so much of the vote, and that a lot of the exit polls didn't account for the 17 other candidates on the ballot. And that hurt. That made a big story.

Ken Bode: Charlie, both you and David have referred to the exit polls, but for the record of this conference, why don't you tell us exactly what happened? Just take a minute and tell us exactly what happened with the exit polls.

Charlie Black: Well, I remember it very clearly because Jim Lake and I landed in Manchester about 5:30, and called the office to Mary or Teeter or whoever was around, I guess it was Teeter, asking, "What are you hearing about the exit polls?" The exit polls said we'll probably win, but it's only going to be by two or three points.

Dave Carney: The reason not to attack Pat earlier was, we're going to win, that's what our polls are showing. Why attack the guy, why make him upset and piss off all his supporters, if you're going to beat him by 10 or 15 points?

Charlie Black: The only way you can spin that is, a win is a win. We finished first, and we made the decision to get out and aggressively do it, which is why I went on your show at 8:00 and so forth. It was probably 10:00, 10:30, before we got enough returns in to see that it was going to be a more comfortable margin.

Now, again, I don't take away from Pat. Thirty-seven percent is a hell of an accomplishment, and it deserved to be a story, but not a story like: "Sitting President Almost Upset in Primary." He wasn't, and I think that just contributed to the drama of the coverage that night and the next day. It catapulted Pat a little higher than he would have catapulted just on 37 percent.

Bay Buchanan: It was without question a terrific asset for us. We were out running about noon when the reporters came to the track and said, "It's 49-51" and we looked at each other. Then I looked at the reporter and said, "Who's ahead?" We were getting carried away at this stage. A 49 was not ever anticipated, but we were hearing numbers like that during the day.

I had this impression that whoever was smiling the most won because people on television aren't really studying the numbers or this and that. So I was thinking Charlie doesn't smile as much as I do. So I would just be there, registering, "This is a great victory for us." My mother finally said after about four primaries, "How can you keep having victory celebrations when you haven't won anything?" I said, "Mom, no reality. Okay? This is all spin here."

But with that talk out there in all the press that we had won by such a great margin, of course, we put something right in the mail. We had anticipated that if people were going to do well at all, we still needed something in the mail. So it hit the next day. They're reading their papers, you know, "Incredible Victory for Buchanan," and a half million dollars came in in the next couple of days. No question about it, it was really to our benefit.

Charlie Black: Which we knew would happen, which is another reason we had to go negative. We couldn't risk …

Bay Buchanan: Oh, you had to go negative.

Charlie Black: … them being out there …

Bay Buchanan: I agree with you entirely.

Charlie Black: … with plenty of money to run until Super Tuesday.

Bay Buchanan: Well, if you hadn't gone negative, we would have been laughing all the way to Super Tuesday.

Charlie Black: That's right.

David Shribman: Bay, as you know, President Reagan used to say that facts are terrible things. When it became apparent to you that it wasn't 51-49, although it was a good performance by you guys, did you have any feeling that there was someplace else you could go and maybe beat this guy? We all know you went to Georgia and did fairly well there. But was there any moment in which you thought you could actually beat the President in a primary?

Bay Buchanan: When we were running on that track — when the reporter told me 49-51 …

David Shribman: I mean, any time after noon?

Bay Buchanan: We had about a half hour of considering the possibility that we could win the whole thing. But I would say no more than a half hour.

David Shribman: And what were you guys doing, exactly, then?

Bay Buchanan: Well, you know there was talk out there that the President might step down. We never spent more than five minutes laughing about that idea. If he does, fine, but we certainly weren't expecting that at any time.

We did feel that there was a possibility, as we went to Georgia, that if we could pick up that momentum, if we had gotten 48 instead of 46 in Georgia, it would have been written that we're doing better, we're going in this direction. Of course, we would have spun it that way. So there was always that hope that something could have turned around and broken in our favor, and you can't run as hard as we did without having that hope. If you had said, are you going to bet on it, I don't think I would have been there with much money.

As I referred to a little bit last night, we had another goal in the South. That was to take David Duke out entirely so that nobody out there could suggest in any way that he was a legitimate spokesperson for the conservative movement. At the same time, we were trying to move policy. We were rather successful at that. We were trying to bring the President home. We were trying to recapture the hearts and souls of the Republican party, which we felt belonged to the Reagan legacy and not in the direction that the President was taking the country.

So it's those things. We wanted to give voice to the millions of Americans that we felt agreed with us but had no one out there to express it for them. That is why we kept staying in it because the people in California were as deserving as those in Georgia to have a person to vote for that they agreed with, whether that person was going to win or lose.

David Shribman: I just have one follow-up. It's something I've always wondered. If we take as a given, and I do, that you didn't think you could win and you take as a given that you wanted to change the party or change the debate, how much of your decision to stay in the race was motivated simply by the fact that you were having a good time?

Bay Buchanan: We once laughed and I said, "Pat, if the President wants to get you out of the race, he should take your Secret Service away from you because then you'll be having a miserable time." I mean, he loved it. He loved every minute of the campaign.

David Shribman: I had that sense having seen him in California about two or three months later, when he was slipping down, when he had more Secret Service guys than supporters. I think you and I talked that day.

Bay Buchanan: Yes.

David Shribman: He was loving this ...

Bay Buchanan: Yes. He also loved New Hampshire where he didn't have Secret Service, don't get me wrong.

David Shribman: Right.

Bay Buchanan: But he liked being a candidate. He enjoyed the repartee with the press. He enjoyed meeting the people. He was out there talking to them continually, asking about their problems and getting the real flavor of what the people in the country were feeling.

David Shribman: But it was more than intersection control, wasn't it, that he liked?

Bay Buchanan: It was a great deal more. At first, he thought it was going to be difficult work. He did not become a candidate thinking "This is going to be great fun, I can't wait to get out there." He said, "Bay, do I have to go out and meet the people and shake hands and go to these functions; I don't know if I can stand it." He had always been on television just talking to millions of people through a camera, and he thought, I can't do it this way. Once he got to New Hampshire and started talking to the people in unemployment lines and factories, he was transformed as a person.

By the last days in New Hampshire, he became a leader of people, expressing their opinions. He really felt it very strongly that some voice had to be given to speak for these people. I think that is why he wanted to stay in — because he thought he was doing good, because he had the letters coming in and the people saying, "Stay in there. We need that voice. We need a leader for this movement." There is no question if it was miserable day after day after day, it would have been a lot harder to say, I should stay in, but he thought he was doing something positive and he very much enjoyed it. There is no question, he had a great time.

Ken Bode: Having said all that, Bay, there is no chance he'd ever do it again, is there?

Bay Buchanan: Well, I would not go that far. He will not make that decision for a couple of years. I would like to see him do it again, and I'll be there.

Let me tell you just one funny story. There was a time we thought Michigan would be good because of the America First theme. Of course, he drove a Mercedes and we knew that that hadn't been overlooked. I had told him to sell the Mercedes so I called him up and said, "Pat, this is the last stop. There is a long shot that we can win Michigan, and I'll tell you how we can win, there's a way to win Michigan." "What's that, Bay?" I said, "I'm bringing your car to Detroit, and you're taking a sledgehammer to it." He said, "I love that car." I said, "We'll buy you a new one."

Charlie Black: Now, wait a minute. Wait a minute. I am obligated to look out for my friend Pat Buchanan. That wasn't his car. That was Shelley's [Buchanan's wife] car.

David Shribman: The voice was the voice of Pat. The car was the car of Shelley.

Orson Swindle: Let me make an observation. Bay is talking about Pat learning to love this. I think it's drifting into something that I thought was a part of what Perot was doing. Is it conceivable that some people in politics do things because they truly believe in what they're doing? Her story about the car just shot my theory to hell, but I think Perot came across as a person who truly believed in what he was doing; and I think Bill Clinton came across as truly believing what he was talking about. I honestly think that one of the great failings of President Bush is that he never conveyed the thought that he truly believed in what he was doing or trying to do. I think that is probably one of the weaknesses he had. I think he's an extraordinarily fine man, but as I mentioned last night, it's like the things he accomplished. If nobody notices them, that's reality. It's a leadership thing. I think leaders have to convey that they truly believe because people don't follow a person very long if they get the feeling he or she doesn't believe.

Bay Buchanan: People said to me that we should get out, and you all assumed the money was going to dry up, we're going to have to cut back. The week after Super Tuesday, when we lost — what, 13 states — a half a million dollars came in. Money came in right up to the convention. So we felt that maybe there are people who are saying to stay in, because they financed us very well throughout the whole campaign.

Jill Abramson: Charlie and Mary, behind the scenes after Super Tuesday, did you approach the Buchanan people and try to get them out of the race? Did anything seriously ever get underway?

Exit Polls

"Week after week we would win, and it would be like losing."

— Mary Matalin, Political Director,
Bush/Quayle Campaign

"Don't Cry for Me, Argentina."

— George Bush, during his first day campaigning in
New Hampshire

Mary Matalin: Before we get to that, I want to add one more comment about the negative impact of the Buchanan primary and that exit poll in particular because it became a persistent problem for us and influenced our activities after that. That was the effect it had on the morale of the troops.

Specifically on that exit poll, Carney has hundreds of people out there, he has a conference call with Teeter, and he had bad numbers. So we had telecast or telegraphed to our entire field organization, this is okay, this is his high-water mark; we're going to come back. It was like a cheerleader call, but it was a very demoralizing message for those troops. And they stayed demoralized for the rest of the primaries.

Week after week we would win, and it would be like losing. People today say, "I can't believe your phone number is listed." They're still looking for me now. I say, "You know why I'm listed? Because, during the campaign, people on the West Coast would call me at home at midnight to tell me how stupid we were, because there weren't enough hours in the course of the workday to say how stupid we were." This went on for that whole primary process, and it really got launched by that goofy exit poll.

Bay Buchanan: You know, we were always five points ahead in the exit poll. We kind of expected it after a while. We said, okay, it says we're at 41; we'll get 36, and we'd get 36. Exit polls were always very fond of us. I think our guys voted earlier.

Charlie Black: It's just a damn tough science, to exit poll in primaries.

Marty Plissner: Wasn't at least part of the problem the traditional leaking of exit polls all around the political community?

Charlie Black: Yeah, that's part of the problem.

Ken Bode: How precise does bootlegged information have to be?

Charlie Black: Let's look past the bootleg stage. Let's go to after the polls are closed and CNN was up. You guys didn't come on until later, but you were giving hourly breaks.

Ken Bode: Oh, yeah, by 8:00 it was more than a two-point margin.

David Shribman: Well, wait a second, aren't we all looking at the same numbers here, Marty?

Marty Plissner: Yeah. Yeah.

David Shribman: You were looking at only two points at ...

Ken Bode: I don't know. I honestly don't know. I just want to clear up one thing. Charlie was going to be the anchor on CNN. It was Bernie [Shaw] that you told, a win is a win. I don't really know what the poll said. I do know that all during the primaries — it's been going on for many years — when each network did its own and now that they have a common exit poll, there is all kinds of bootlegging of information all over the political community all day long. And that's the stuff that Bay and Pat had at noon. Everybody should understand that those are the first waves of the exit polls and that they are enormously unreliable.

Marty Plissner: I must say that when I leak exit poll information, I usually do it with a lot of escape clauses about the unreliability of the first exit poll readings. Unfortunately, nobody pays much attention to these warnings.

Charlie Black: We understand that, and we're just like the Democrats — we're too curious not to call up and ask about it even though we know it might be misleading information. We'd probably be better off if you didn't give it and we could take the day off on election day.

Ken Bode: The polls close at eight o'clock, is that right, in New Hampshire? Marty, at what point would we have had reliable information from the last exit poll wave?

Marty Plissner: By eight o'clock you should have had votes. There were two separate problems. First of all, there was an overall error in Buchanan's favor. That error was especially great in the first returns. On top of that, about 10 percent of the Republican primary vote consisted of write-ins for Democrats, mainly for Tsongas and Clinton. Through an error in the exit poll design, these votes were not included in the Republican estimate. That inflated the estimated percentage for both Republicans.

Mary Matalin: Can I clarify? I wasn't bringing that up so much to trash another pollster as to lay a marker to show where the morale of our troops was, because that was very much underreported. The low morale of our troops resulted in our making certain decisions later on, that you'll see played out at the convention and other places.

I wasn't trying to go revisit this issue as much as to say that in addition to everything else you were seeing on the surface, below the surface it wasn't just the internal fights. The morale of our own troops, starting with that exit poll, was very bad even though Carney told them jokes all day long and had a conference call every day just to tell them jokes. It's a very important underlying fact that will explain later actions we took.

David Shribman: I promise you that before we finish, we'll get the answer to Jill's question. But I want to ask you a quick question and then John Mashek, I know, has a follow-up. Mary, to what extent did the exit poll results you were getting, erroneous or not, change the nature of your get-out-the-vote effort from say two o'clock on?

Mary Matalin: This is Carney's question. Carney is an expert at this.

Dave Carney: We started calling Republican women in certain parts of the state; in fact, in Nashua we called right until 7:30 because polls there don't close until 8:00. We mobilized our phone effort to turn out Republican women. The President could win a higher percentage of women than he could get from Republican men.

David Shribman: So what you're saying, David, is that partial results of the exit polls changed not only the perception afterwards, but the dynamic of the game while it was still being played?

Dave Carney: You know, we've already gone through and ID'd people. The positive pro-Bush people we had already turned out. We just pounded the phones. That's a thing we did all primary long and in the general election. We'd maintain tactical flexibility to do whatever it takes. A small example, in the Connecticut primary, a very similar situation. We thought Buchanan was pretty much put to sleep by then, but he still was doing pretty well.

So we did a lot of calls into Connecticut. The same thing going into certain Congressional districts. On the weekend before the election, we called through on turnout and hit 90,000 answering machines. The more sophisticated the campaigns get, the more sophisticated voters get, not wanting to have to deal with it. Granted it was the weekend and spring — people were out. But 90,000 of our calls went to answering machines.

David Shribman: Which primary was that?

Dave Carney: Connecticut.

John Mashek: Before we leave New Hampshire, could I ask Mary and Charlie about the President's form of campaigning. I believe it was his first day up there and we heard the memorable lines of ...

Mary Matalin: "Don't Cry ..."

John Mashek: "Don't Cry for Me, Argentina" and he called the musical group, "Nitty Gritty Dirt Bag." Did anybody tell him how bad he was, how out of practice, off the beam he was?

Mary Matalin, Charlie Black

Mary Matalin: I found that endearing.

John Mashek: The first day was a disaster.

Mary Matalin: No, I found that totally endearing. I would always sing to him "Don't Cry for Me, Argentina." No, I didn't tell him that. Maybe somebody else did.

Charlie Black: We talked to him afterwards. In a lot of ways, he is a very good candidate once he gets going and decides it's time to campaign. I think he was good in the closing weeks of the general election, but he's got a streak that when he's having a bad day, it's a bad day. You can call it to his attention, but at his age, you can't reform him. So we didn't beat him up about it. We just called to his attention that he didn't have a good day on the first trip to New Hampshire.

Dave Carney: I will tell you this. The local coverage of our trip and the national coverage were two different trips, on two different planets, two different candidates, two different types of reporters.

Charlie Black: Just the President's presence there energized our organization. They were just crying and moaning and complaining that they wanted to get him up there before Christmas and we couldn't do it.

Marc Nuttle: It is important to notice how the Republican primary process helped the Clinton campaign. Jill properly identified this vote as a protest vote. Its foundation was about 25 percent. It was very restless, a more independent party, fewer liberals than conservatives. People were looking for alternatives, either a program or a candidate. The Bush White House could have presented a program. The feeling wasn't just anti-Bush. When they didn't get an economic package, voters began to look elsewhere. The Clinton campaign came from the DLC, and was seen as moderate by this protest vote.

Frank [Greer], it was as early as March or April when some major group — either the NEA or a labor group — endorsed one of your primary opponents. At about that time, there were three independent tracking polls, corporate and special interest groups, in which you could easily detect a five-point shift from this protest vote going to Clinton. He became their alternative now because that group didn't endorse him — I think it was the NEA — and you were disappointed about it, but I'm telling you that it labeled you as moderate and got you this protest vote.

At that point, the Clinton campaign was innocent until proven guilty of all charges that we didn't even know were coming in. When those charges came, the campaign had a foundation. The vote wasn't in your pocket yet, but it was moving your way because of the dynamics of this Republican primary process, this liberal endorsement.

Two things that happened here were kind of unique. The New Hampshire primary makes a front-running incumbent President vulnerable, even though he got the vote, which is unusual, and a leading Democratic liberal group endorses somebody else and that helps the moderate candidate. That played out through the charges and the rest of the primaries. I think that when you get to your general election discussion, it will help in identifying why some of that vote, after the second entry of the Perot campaign, moved to Clinton.

The Empire Strikes Back

*"So we got something going, and lo and
behold, here comes the L.A. riots, [then]
Perot dominating the news."*

— Charles Black, Consultant, Bush/Quayle Campaign

Jill Abramson: I'm going to call half time the period right after Super
Tuesday. Were there ever any behind-the-scenes overtures between
President Bush and his top campaign advisors and the Buchanan peo-
ple to try and crowbar Buchanan out of the race?

Charlie Black: No. Keep in mind, we know each other very well. Pat
and Bay and myself and Jim Lake and some of us have been good personal friends for many years. There is a personal liking and respect
between the President and Pat that, you know, even through the rough
going there, was never broken. We know Pat well enough to know that
he wasn't going to get out until he was ready, and there wasn't anything
we could say to persuade him. It seemed like Bay and I were in a crossfire once or twice a week that whole time, but Bay told me, in a gathering something like this, and said on TV, that they had decided not to go
negative anymore. Pat did pretty good. He wasn't 100 percent, but he
did a pretty good job between March 18 and June of not attacking the
President. You all took him out of the coverage, in terms of daily coverage or treating him as serious contender after March 18 so it didn't matter all that much. We were very confident that he would get out when
he wanted to and that, even if we did talk to him, it wouldn't have any
impact. I kept saying and Mary did and everybody said on the record
over and over that he would be at the convention for the President and
would be campaigning for us in the fall. Once Pat had said that, it was a
lead-pipe cinch that it would happen and it did.

Bay Buchanan: There were some people within our campaign or
friends on the fringes that suggested we discuss this possibility of getting out. Pat was quite tired at the time. He had been out on the road
steadily for months now. So we discussed it and there was talk by some
of the Bush people that if you don't get out, you're not going to speak at
the convention. Anyone who knows Pat or me knows that that wasn't
the right approach. We were not going to back down at that stage
because we felt we had a commitment. So that's when we went public
and said that we're staying in until California. Once we made that public
a statement — again, after Super Tuesday — then that was the decision,

to stay in. But at that time, we did decide not to do anything negative any further. We sent a signal to them: listen, this is no longer a battle against George Bush; it's a battle that we have to fight because we made a commitment to our people, and we're going to stay in.

David Shribman: Once Bay and her brother got out, they wouldn't be able to speak at the convention?

Rich Bond: No. That's not correct. Bay heard what she wanted to hear at the time, and so did Pat. But when asked a question by a reporter, "Will Pat Buchanan speak at the convention," I simply said, "We're not going to have any discussions about any activity from this moment on, until Pat and the President communicate, until Pat and the President get together." It's not my decision to make. The press construed that to be, well, *if* Pat doesn't endorse the President, *if* Pat doesn't get out of the race. There is no record that supports that statement.

David Shribman: Did you feel that the course of the campaign, particularly the general election, was injured by that by-play even though you believe part of it was misinterpreted?

Rich Bond: Well, let me answer it a little differently. I think Pat Buchanan getting in the race, from the period of December 1 to approximately April 1, did us a huge favor. It gave us the opportunity to face up to the inadequacies of our political position and it should have forced us to get the Thornburgh defeat out of our system. I don't think it did, and I'm not — to my colleagues here at the table — pointing any fingers here, but I think this was part of a political breakdown, which continued even after John Sununu was gone, in terms of the political cohesiveness of our operation.

I think after April 1, Pat's continued persistence was a continuing distraction to George Bush and his individual state organizations, particularly in the West, which is where the calendar traveled to, and it was not helpful. At that point — Bay and I can argue about this forever — I think that Pat made a judgment around April 1 that if he could do as well against George Bush up to that point in time as he had done, that George Bush would probably not be re-elected. What Pat did from April on was to position himself to try to put together a national organization, to keep his fund-raising going, to swell his donor lists, to position himself for future reference. I agree with Charlie, Pat was about 90 percent pure. He wasn't deliberately trying to promote the anti-Bush message, but I think he was deliberately trying to promote the pro-Buchanan message, and I don't think that helped us.

Bay Buchanan: I was there with Pat in the decision-making process. In November, we publicly stated we're staying in until California. That was in November. We didn't know what was going to happen in New

Hampshire or Georgia or any of the other states. We had people who were organized in California. We had people calling us saying, "You made a commitment to us, we're out on the limb here for your candidacy, and you're not even going to be in the race." So we felt that it was a very strong commitment that Pat had to keep. It had nothing to do with this organization that he may or may not be building.

In addition to that, there are issues in California that we felt were unique and a critical part of his agenda that we did not express earlier because they weren't pertinent, i.e. immigration. As you know, we spent some radio money on that so it would be raised in a public forum and let the American people, especially Californians, know that this is a very valid issue and concern of theirs that should be addressed by elected officials across the country.

Charlie Black: The fact is, it would have helped us a little bit if he had got out of the race after March 18. But the thing that gets people out of the race is lack of money, and they still had money.

Bay Buchanan: We still do. [Laughter]

Jill Abramson: Charlie, the fact that you were still engaged in the primary process, did that throw off things like getting an effective opposition research going on Clinton and planning for the general election fight that the Democrats talked about this morning? With the Clinton people into that before the primaries were over, was your timetable in the general election fight affected?

Charlie Black: Not really. Just to quickly summarize, we did start late and we kept having these outside intervening events throw us off track. It was perfectly fair for Pat to run but, if we had known he was going to run, we wouldn't have waited until the first week of December to start. So we had to combat Pat down to the middle of March. In the March 20 speech, the President outlined a new economic initiative that actually worked. It was popular. The only time in the whole year the President's job approval went up was in the two weeks after the March 20 speech, after he vetoed the tax bill.

So we got something going, and lo and behold, here come the L.A. riots. It made it impossible for a month to get out any kind of political message that didn't relate to the riots. By the time that's over, here is Mr. Perot dominating the news.

But even though we didn't start until the first week of December, Mary and Dave organized the entire country — a 50-state organization — within a month. It was remarkable. They were ready, and our people out in the field were ready. Mechanically and infrastructure-wise we were fine. It was just in terms of the public presentation of our message that we never could catch up, we were always behind the curve.

Bill Kristol: We had the opportunity to get the Thornburgh thing out of our system, and we didn't. The effect of the Buchanan challenge, if it had caused us to get that out of our system, would have been positive. In itself it was a minor annoyance, causing minor damage. We learned nothing or at least not enough of us learned enough from the Pennsylvania race, which was finished before Pat Buchanan got in the race. You know, all the markings were on the wall way before Pat got in the race. In fact, if I could just go back to pre-Pat entry for one second. If the Gulf War hadn't happened, there would have been more serious, more credible, frankly, conservative challenges to Bush in the primaries, than Buchanan.

People forget that enthusiasm for the President was not high in Republican circles in October of '90. The Gulf War gave him this huge boost that shut down talk of serious conservative primary opponents. More credible possible presidents than Pat Buchanan were thinking of exploring primary challenges, but didn't because they were spooked by the huge surge in the president's popularity for six months or so of '91.

The notion that Pat did a whole lot more than simply reinforce or expose some weaknesses that were there, and that would have been exposed by a competent general election campaign in any case, I think that notion is wrong.

Jill Abramson: Charlie, you were saying that the problem was basically communications and not being able to get the President's message out and a continual chain of distractions. You mentioned the L.A. riots. A moment like that could have been an opportunity for the President, as leader of the country, to get a message out and to speak very directly to the country. Why didn't that happen?

Charlie Black: The President handled the L.A. riots correctly. He and Pat disagreed about how it should be handled. But I don't think it would have been good leadership or good policy to grandstand on it or to handle it differently than he did.

When people perceive that things are on the wrong track and the country is in trouble and you have the worst urban riots in history leading the news every night for a month, it just fuels the wrong-track perception and it is bad for the incumbent. There is no way in the world, I don't give a damn what we propose, that debating urban issues inures to a Republican's benefit. I love Jack Kemp, but no matter what we propose, you're on Democratic turf when you're talking about urban problems.

The Clinton campaign, the day the L.A. riots began, was seized with the terrifying thought that Ross Perot would get in his own plane that afternoon and fly to Los Angeles and that he'd win the election right there. Did you [Perot] guys give any thought to flying to Los Angeles? Why didn't you? Or was this a phantom fear that they had in Little Rock?

Tom Luce: I don't think it was a phantom fear. I think Ross contemplated that, talked about it. Throughout this entire endeavor, Ross seemed to recoil from anything that could be construed as being political. I think he was afraid it was like a virus, and he might catch it and become a politician.

David Shribman: It has no antibodies.

Tom Luce: That's right, and in the end, he decided it would be political and grandstanding, and he wouldn't do it. He said, if he had been President, he would have been on the next plane.

Clay Mulford: He thought that President Bush should have gone right away. I think that he did not go, in part, because he thought he would be undermining the proper role of the President to step in, in a crisis such as that.

David Shribman: How come you guys didn't go, Charlie and Mary?

Charlie Black: Oh, I don't know that it would have served any great purpose to go a couple of days earlier.

Mary Matalin: He was in constant contact with Governor Wilson.

Charlie Black: The fact is they were trying to get things done, and he and [Governor] Wilson and [Mayor] Bradley were talking. They got Ueberroth in the mix early.*

Until those guys were confident that the necessary things were being done on the ground, the President didn't want to go. If all the decisions were being made by us over at the campaign, rather than at the White House, he might have gone a couple of days earlier, but they weren't, and he didn't.

Bill Kristol: There were two different views on the riots in the White House, as Charlie implied. The view that prevailed was the responsible, good government view. We should work with Wilson and Bradley and Ueberroth, do it calmly and solidly, and be very wary of anything that looked like grandstanding.

Second, there was the political view that urban issues are a loser for us, and let's get it off the front pages as fast as possible by just pacifying the situation as well as we can.

The contrary view, held by those of us who thought we were in worse shape than those who had the other view, was that this was an opportunity, that people desperately wanted the President to show leadership

---

Editor's Note: Peter Ueberroth, former Commissioner of Baseball and managing director of the Los Angeles Olympic Organizing Committee (1984), headed "Rebuild L.A."

and a commitment on domestic policy; and that you could combine a sort of Kemp activism with a law-and-order message, which has always been, of course, a very strong message for us and on which we would have credibility.

In fact, if you look at the Vice President's speech, now famous as the "Murphy Brown" speech, three weeks after the riots, he lays out, I think a pretty comprehensive sort of urban strategy, which is part Kemp — economic activism for the inner cities; part law-and-order emphasis — no excuse for rioting; and part the breakdown of the family and what spun off of that, obviously, because of "Murphy Brown."

It just depended on how much you thought we needed to seize any opportunity, at that point, to show leadership, having failed to do so, at least by the common perception, after the State of the Union speech and after March 20.

Charlie Black: Well, I was a leader of a group that wanted to get it out of the news as quickly as possible but I was, also, an advocate of the president coming out for a CCC-style program,* which, frankly, would have been an excellent political move. Most of the people in the campaign agreed with that, but, as [James] Pinkerton pointed out in his *New Republic* article recently, Darman told the President it was communism, and that was the last we heard of that.

David Shribman: Now, Charlie Black has been exceedingly forthright in admitting to spin during the campaign. To what extent, Tom and Sharon, did your people engage in spin, in say May and June, as the Perot phenomenon was gathering force and as AT&T and the shopping networks set new records?

Tom Luce: I'm not sure I can really tell you, in a way that you will find credible. I think that we had this battle for about a year. That is, I think the press kept trying to see us through conventional eyes. I think this is correct, the first press release that went out in the Perot campaign was the hiring of [Edward] Rollins and [Hamilton] Jordan, because Rollins wanted a press release.

Second, until July 16, we never called a single member of the press and planted a story, nor did we return most of your telephone calls. In that time frame it was an extraordinary two or three months.

I know everything sounds glorious now for the Clinton campaign, but those were the days that they were at 20 percent and some people in the party worried about getting federal matching funds.

We had gone from zero to the lead in the national polls, and things were rolling right along. We were in the lead in the national polls, the

---

Editor's Note: The Civilian Conservation Corps, an FDR New Deal innovation which employed young, unemployed people on government projects in the 1930s.

lead in the California poll, the lead in the Texas poll. We had taken no polls, had done no focus groups, and had done no spending.

Ken Bode: Now, Tom, at the same time that you guys weren't spending, I kept hearing of network news presidents and anchors of talk shows and so forth getting phone calls from Ross Perot himself. Is it fair to say that your campaign spun only at the top?

Tom Luce: It is very clear that Ross talked directly to a lot of people, including presidents of television networks, most of whom were calling, just asking him to be on their television show, as opposed to the rival network's television show, so the ratings would go up. That's what most of the conversations were about. Yeah, he was talking to the press all the time. But there just were not a whole lot of strategic conferences. We kept trying to have them. [Laughter]

I looked back in the notes yesterday, and right up until June 20 was our best period. The exit polls were showing that Perot had a real good chance to win California. We were ahead in the Texas polls at that time. We were ahead in the Florida polls. I think those were the high marks. Between February 20 and June 20, because of what was going on in the Democratic party and then the perception of the Republican party, Perot was sailing along and we were engaged internally in trying to put in place an organization and adopt a plan.

Sharon Holman: I will say that — true confessions — I did spin. It happened during the debates, and I had the occasion to both spin and leak on the same occasion, and it was just monumental.

David Shribman: Spin doesn't necessarily rhyme with sin. Well, spin rhymes with sin, but they're not the same thing, I suppose. Sharon, to what extent did the process begin to shape the Perot campaign, even though it didn't want to be shaped?

Sharon Holman: Well, I think we began to look maybe a little bit more traditional. One point I want to make, and I was going to make this tonight, but I think this is a good time to make it. One of the things that Perot had told us over and over again, not just during the campaign, was that we should always think outside the box. That was something that was very, very important to him, not only in this campaign but throughout, that we should never do things just because that's the way they had always been done.

David Shribman: To what extent, Sharon, were you reacting to us the way you did because you were overwhelmed or to what extent was it strategic to keep us at arm's length?

Sharon Holman: Oh, it was not strategic. We were overwhelmed. No question. By the time Jim Squires [media consultant, former editor of the *Chicago Tribune*] arrived, I realized that I probably had the distinction of offending everyone across the board in the media, as far as access and following the rules that one normally plays by. That's simply because we were so short-staffed, and we had no background of knowledge.

Jill Abramson: But Perot seemed to get very much what Clinton got, which is that you could cut us out and go directly to the people. The talk-show route that Perot went is the classic example of that.

Clay Mulford: We certainly didn't need the traditional media. But it was ignored for other reasons as well. Until Rollins came in with some professionals in early June, the staff was devoted entirely to the ballot access drive, legal issues involved there. "Could petitions be used with vice-presidential surrogates?" etc. That's what we were spending our time doing.

David Shribman: Is there anyone here — Sharon, Tom, Clay, Charlie, Mary, Frank, others — who thinks one of the reasons for going to ["The Phil] Donahue [Show"] and that kind of stuff is because the people who ask questions on those shows are easier than the ink-stained wretches who have traditionally asked them?

Charlie Black: I don't think it's true and every time somebody says it, it causes the Donahues and the Larry Kings to get tougher. I don't sense that. I think the more people see of the candidates and the more they hear about the issues and the more they learn, the better it is for the country. So I think it's a great thing that we have all these talk shows.

Our attitude, to speak for Mary and Teeter and our campaign, is, we always called you all back. We tried to spin the hell out of you, because you're going to write a story whether we talk to you or not, and we'd a whole lot rather have our argument entertained by you and get our side of the story out. So no matter how many talk shows there are, we're always going to return your calls.

Bay Buchanan: I agree. Our position was as much free media as we can get, we're going to take it. As tough as the questions were on those Sunday shows, we would never turn them down.

Dave Carney: People watch those shows, one. Two, you get real questions and real answers. People enjoy that. I think they learn more from watching Clinton and Gore on "Donahue" for an hour than they do from a column or a five-minute news program and a 30-second sound bite. Bush started doing these "Ask George Bush" shows in 1979. That's a forum that's always allowed — town meetings, 2,000 people in a high school auditorium, and a candidate answering questions. Vice President Bush did that in 1988. The news media wanted to concentrate on Iran-

Contra. An audience wants to talk about issues all over the map. And the media have to cover the town meeting if that's what the event is.

Betsey Wright: Do people believe that the information that they get from Donahue and King is as important or more important to them than the *Wall Street Journal* because they want the journalists cut out of it? The fact is, that's where folks are getting their information as much as from the news media, and the press go to where folks get their information.

Orson Swindle: I think a step beyond that was in the middle of the second debate where the people asked the questions. I read or heard comments by media people that they didn't particularly like that format. I thought it was the best format because it gave people a chance to relate directly with these individuals. As far as the King show, I don't think it's so much what Larry King said. It's the interplay between the individual who is being asked questions — the few that are asked over the telephone — and a "real person." The opportunity for the American people to see on television President Bush, Bill Clinton, and Ross Perot answering questions from somebody just like them has a value that goes far beyond having someone in the print or television or radio media tell them what the candidate said.

Tom Luce: David, let me come in on one additional point there in terms of these programs. Let me clarify a couple of things. One, we made a policy decision, which we attempted to communicate directly to the press, that we were not going to talk off the record, nor were we going to feed stories about the other candidates. We would respond to inquiries about Perot but not call and say, have you checked XYZ on George Bush.

Mary Matalin: Was that policy after Ed Rollins left town? [Laughter]

Tom Luce: Let me say, we made it clear all along Ed was a different category, in many respects, Mary. Okay? Absent Ed Rollins. And I think we followed that throughout. Number two, I would suggest that the public learns more from what the press considers a softball, open-ended question asked of a candidate than they learn when Sam Donaldson says, "Mr. President, have you stopped beating your wife?"

I would submit the camera will eventually, if you give a person an hour, reveal that person. I don't see anything wrong with a candidate appearing an hour on television, nor do I think a candidate shouldn't answer questions from the press. I don't mean that at all. I think that the public is better served the more media time a candidate gets.

Mary Matalin: There is another dynamic. People were really sick of politics as usual, and, frankly, I think they're a little sick of you guys, who had become part of the process of politics as usual. Sam Donaldson is as much a part of the political scene as all the politicians. These new guys provided what people were looking for in this election, which was a fresh look at the whole process.

Clay Mulford: To follow up on the point that you all were making this morning about the kind of press conference where you assembled questioners from the public that were selected by a pollster, and you were worried that you might get questions on the bimbo eruption — that was our experience, also. We were concerned occasionally when Perot would go on a show or in the second debate, that the quality of the questions would lean over into "What happened to the dog? Who got bit where?" What we found is that the people never asked questions like that. They were interested in very substantive matters. But the media would ask us about that and virtually nothing else. The quality of the questions from the public was really elevated, in our view, over the quality coming from the media.

Bill Kristol: The fact is, candidates have a very easy time answering softball questions from the public, because Bill Clinton gets to look the guy in the eye and give the same speech, with all due respect, he's given 50 times on his health-care agenda or his economic agenda. It's perfectly legitimate to ask where the guy was bit or what have you.

Paul Begala: The toughest question anybody ever asked was Roger Mudd asking Teddy Kennedy, "Why do you want to be president?"

Bay Buchanan: I agree that there is an aspect to those tough questions from the Sam Donaldsons. If your candidate can handle those and really use it to his advantage, he can become credible overnight. The softball ones, everybody likes the guy and everything is pleasant, and they hold their own. But when you go up against the Sam Donaldsons for a half hour and you come off looking good, then that is a terrific statement to your people. They get all the letters. "You did a great job against that guy." It's very, very helpful. We used to call and try to get on. We didn't wait for you guys to call us.

Ken Bode: The question, in part, is how much more information does the public really get from these things? Jill has one opinion on that. Charlie said that people saying that Donahue and Larry King ask softball questions just made them get tougher. If you looked at the last time President Bush was on Larry King, you noticed that Larry King pursued Iran-Contra.

Dave Carney: Well, that's because one of the random calls came in. Some Greek guy called in … [Laughter]

Ken Bode: The polls said that that was a very important issue to people at that point. It was pushed in that Larry King segment for whatever reason. Did we advance the amount of information the public got on Iran-Contra anymore than we would have if you put that on the Brinkley show?

Frank Greer: No.

David Wilhelm: Frank says no. The press had a tougher time.

Rich Bond: It was more believable.

Paul Begala: Where?

Rich Bond: On King. There was a number back in March or April somewhere, 22 percent of the American public said they got their news from Leno and Letterman. Consider the source. It's just become much more believable with Donahue and King, etc., as opposed to the Sunday inside the Beltway or highly sophisticated line of questions.

Mary Matalin: Bay is right, à la 1988 with Bush and Dan Rather. That was a great defining moment for us. But this year the believability goes to that kind of infotainment or entertainment or whatever the hell they're called this time, that feel more like they're real people. News anchors feel like part of the process, and the people believe that their job is to bait the candidates. They don't really think that they're trying to draw something out of them that they want to hear about.

Frank Greer: I totally agree, because I think the Sunday programs especially are so predictable — it's a "gotcha" kind of thing. Can I trap you? Can I put you on the spot? Viewers really resent it. They would much rather have a civilized conversation with real voters or real people asking real questions, even on MTV. The weird thing about it is, you go on "Face the Nation" or "Meet the Press": you know Tim Russert is going to ask you all kinds of little questions about entitlements and the deficit, trying to trip you up.

Betsy Kolbert: There are still more people watching Tim Russert than watching Larry King.

Frank Greer: That's not true, Elizabeth. The numbers moved tremendously when shows involved voters through call-in programs.

Betsy Kolbert: Let's just take the network news. A lot more people watch the network news every night than watch Larry King.

Frank Greer: I think we're comparing two different things here. We're comparing inside-the-Beltway Sunday kind of programming versus Donahue, Larry King, MTV, Arsenio, or whatever it may be. First of all, some people dislike and have a resistance to the style of questioning on those Sunday programs and they get a lot more information out of the longer format program in which it does not appear as if the host or reporter is trying to get you, although, I will say our interview with Donahue was very tough the third time around.

Elizabeth Arnold: But the notion, Frank, that you're reaching more people and that there is more reality — I remember when Clinton went on Larry King. It was a 90-minute program and five questions got through. One of them was Clinton's mother. Okay? It was about Larry King. It wasn't about the American people.

Mary Matalin: I hate this word, it's so abused, but it *empowers* people when they see real people talking to these candidates, that's what this cycle was about. That's what Perot was about. They feel connected to the process because normal schmoes are asking questions of the President of the United States. And the questions are sometimes harder, sometimes easier, often repetitive. It's not really the information. It is the emotional something that goes on between the electorate and the candidate.

Charlie Black: But the more people see the better. I want to have more advertising, not less, because the more people know, the more exposure they get to the issues. It's an adversary process so your opponent is going to say things about you and about your positions. Think about it. McDonald's spends more advertising hamburgers every year than the presidential campaigns put together before Mr. Perot got into the act. It might not be true anymore. What's the most important decision, which hamburger chain you're going to eat at or who's going to be President of the United States?

Turning Point

"The focus on Bush/Perot enabled Clinton to get off his knees. Because the attack turned to us, Clinton was able to go to a neutral corner, get off the front page, heal up...and, I submit, turn his campaign around."

— Tom Luce, Chairman, Perot Petition Committee

David Shribman: I want to shift the direction here a little bit. Tom Luce, on May 17 for the first time the CNN/Time poll shows you guys ahead. What was the reaction inside the Perot campaign? What was Mr.

Perot's reaction? What was your reaction? What was Clay and Sharon's reaction? Was there any moment when you guys said, "Hey, we might actually win this thing"?

Tom Luce: First of all, I did several times feel like — as outlandish as it sounded — that Perot had an opportunity to win the election. If everything broke right and if mistakes were not made, Perot could pull off the improbable and could have been elected president. I still felt like that as of July 16.

I continued the effort I was making to hire professional staff. My first priority, when I came in on April 1, was to try to professionalize the operation. I wanted to run an unconventional campaign but I wanted to run it using professional advice and counsel. I was pushing very hard to hire media consultants, pollsters, Rollins and Jordan, etc. The poll results just intensified the efforts to try to build a professional staff and at the same time to continue the volunteer operation. I knew we weren't going to put in place a field organization like Mary's. But I felt we could use a grassroots organization if we could leave it in place and supplement it at the national level with a sophisticated media campaign staff. Emphasize strategy. We had done no polling. We had no strategic plan about which states we were going to go after. If we could put that in place, I felt we could win. We brought in Rollins and Jordan.

Clay Mulford: Half of it worked out.

Tom Luce: A portion of it worked out, but it just never took. I would like to end the conference by saying that when Rollins and Jordan came in, we were in the lead in the national polls, and I retired.

Clay Mulford: At that first staff meeting when Rollins was there, Tom's introductory remark was, "Let the record show that we're number one when I'm turning this over to you guys." So I guess Ross would want me to ask you, was Rollins a plant?

Rich Bond: We would have warned you, if you had asked us. [Laughter]

Tom Luce: Let me say, it only took 24 hours.

Charley Royer: For the record, Ed Rollins was invited, but he couldn't be here.

Tom Luce: There was in place the possibility of an electoral strategy, which was Texas, Florida, California. The Western states were always strong for Perot. We could have put in place an electoral strategy that could win, but we were, basically, flying blind, without polling. That's what we were really pushing to do.

Jill Abramson: You Bush people, obviously, had very sophisticated polling. How did you evaluate Perot at this point? Formulate your strategy for dealing with his emergence? And in retrospect, how do you think you handled this period of the early Perot boomlet?

Charlie Black: Let me make a couple of comments and then Mary. Regardless of polls, we knew that Mr. Perot would hurt us worse than he would Clinton, in the end. Just common sense told you that he presented a conservative image. He was running an antigovernment, antideficit campaign; the symbols he was sending were conservative symbols. I think that's true. I think he did hurt us worse than Clinton. The exit polls might say that Perot voters would have gone roughly 50/50, but that's after he spent all this money and ran a great campaign, 90 percent of which was directed as negative criticism of Bush.

So we were very concerned about it. We didn't buy this theory that Clinton was going to be third or that we were going to be third or all those kinds of things that were spinning around. But we also wished he were out of the race. When he went ahead, we thought he ought to play by the same rules as everybody else, and decided to criticize him a little bit.

Tom Luce: That seems to me one of the critical strategic calls. In my own mind, June 20 was the high mark of the Perot campaign. June 21, Tom Oliphant had a column in the *Boston Globe* that said the Republicans had just finished some focus groups and were about to turn their guns on Perot. The Woodward story broke in the *Washington Post* that same Sunday, June 21.* Over the next two weeks came President Bush in the Oval Office criticizing Perot. Mrs. Bush, that's when you really roll out the big guns. Dan Quayle, Bob Martinez [former Governor of Florida, drug czar]. I mean, there came a two-week attack, [Representative] Bob Michel, etc. Very effective attack.

Mary Matalin: To me, this is the funniest part of the campaign. You gave us enormous credit but it was spontaneous combustion. Having made that decision, we wanted to do it delicately, surgically.

Charlie Black: We waited a few days to see what the Democrats would do; Clinton hit Perot once, and Ron Brown called him a dictator. Then you all had the discipline to pull back and cut it out.

Tom Luce: Let me finish because I'm not claiming you orchestrated the *Washington Post*, nor am I saying that you engaged in dirty tricks. What I'm saying is, the strategic call — what happened for three weeks was that the campaign turned into a Bush/Perot debate.

Editor's Note: Bob Woodward and John Mintz described efforts of Ross Perot, beginning in 1986, to "find evidence that would demonstrate Bush was what Perot believed him to be—weak, indecisive, and perhaps even corrupt." Perot's allegations ranged from tax questions to Bush's role in Iran-Contra, to investigations about the President's role in the so-called "October Surprise."

Mary Matalin: Yes. That's true.

Charlie Black: That's right.

Tom Luce: The focus on Bush/Perot enabled Clinton to get off his knees. Because the attack turned to us, Clinton was able to go to a neutral corner, get off the front page, heal up, and, I submit, turn his campaign around.

Mary Matalin: And that's why I make the point that we did not intend to launch a full-scale assault, because we were very cognizant that he wasn't on his knees, he was on his belly. We didn't want to let him up. We wanted a surgical strike, get in and get out. This is why we want to make it very clear that we did not send Bob Martinez out there.

Paul Begala: So, just Mrs. Bush couldn't control her temper?

Mary Matalin: As I told the President, there was only one person on the planet whom I was afraid of and it wasn't him. I have no comment on Mrs. Bush.

Paul Begala: But you sent everybody out there.

Frank Greer: Perception is reality, and I've got to tell you that when we were looking at the press, we said this is turning into a real food fight, they are going at each other, and we saw it as an opportunity.

Tom Luce: If it wasn't planned, it was beautiful, a new spokesman each day appeared on the same line for two or three weeks.

Frank Greer: It was a fateful time, because it was the point at which we were launching a new economic plan. We went to the Conference of Mayors, to the National Association of Manufacturers; that whole week that you-all were firing at each other we were out there with a very positive economic plan. And all of a sudden, people in the country said, gee, these guys are really talking about what matters to me, and look at these other two. It was like a classic three-way race.

Mary Matalin: Remember when I was saying earlier about bad morale, I think the reason we had spontaneous combustion is because it was just an act of fighting back. Everybody jumped on the bandwagon. Remember, Bush was not in the campaign mode then, and everybody out there wanted something. They wanted some energy, some fight. So a little spark started a forest fire. Some of the things that looked stupid at the time and still look stupid were the result of this morale thing where people were reacting to any kind of stimulus — it was motion in lieu of progress.

Charlie Black: We knew Clinton would be back. There was no doubt that our opponent was Bill Clinton and not Ross Perot. We also knew that despite coming out of the primaries bloodied up, that all you Democrats would be back. You'd get a message out, you'd run a disciplined campaign, and by the time of your convention — I've got a document somewhere that I'll show you that said after the Democratic convention, you'd be in first place in the three-way race. The turning point in the campaign was that two weeks, including the convention, when you all did the masterful choreography of the Gore selection, the move into New York.

Mary Matalin: I would say that was the turning point.

Charlie Black: The masterful convention, capped by Mr. Perot dropping out on exactly the best possible day for Clinton, and then followed up by the bus tour. That was the turning point in the campaign. You-all went from 25 to 55 in two weeks.

Frank Greer: But that was in three weeks. See, what I'm saying is, that was a key turning point. It was a pivotal point in the campaign. If [Stan] Greenberg was here, he would tell you that we started moving that week and Perot started dropping. Bush stayed about where he was, but then we had a solid week, on the economic plan, putting people first. We were out there campaigning in every corner of the country, getting very positive feedback. The next week we announced Al Gore. Two families stood in back of the mansion. You had that whole imagery. Then we rolled into the convention, a unified party. Out of that, into the bus trip. By the first day of the convention, in our polls, we were already up about 20 points.

Paul Begala: Tom makes a point. Before you started doing that, when Mr. Perot was completely eclipsing us anyway, I was on the road with the Governor, and it was the worst part of the campaign. It was much worse than Gennifer Flowers. Much worse than the draft.

We had this guy out there, who was kicking Brown around the country, which gave us a nice sort of left/right contrast. Made us look more normal and mainstream and everything. It's just what we would have wanted in a vacuum, but we were getting nothing for it. We had 65 percent in all these primaries, and yet we're just being completely ignored by the press and by the voters.

Within a few weeks of the Los Angeles riots, for example, in California we did satellite interviews and sat in a room for maybe two hours. Every TV station in California carried it. We took 43 questions from those stations, and 31 were about Ross Perot or the polls. Fifty-six people had just died in a riot in that state's largest city, and we got two questions about that and one was process — "Do you think the riots will hurt George Bush?" That goes back to Mary's earlier point of why people think reporters are part of the problem, but we were screwed by what was happening.

Once you guys turned your guns on Perot and then Perot had to answer, we were back to our game, which we always thought was Clinton and his ideas and his substance, and getting the economic plan first, the rest of his message second, the convention third. For us that was the whole turning point.

Charlie Black: That was your finest hour, and you did a masterful job, but we had no choice. We could not let Ross Perot stay in first place or for that matter stay anywhere over 20 percent, we figured, and win the race.

Tom Luce: Somebody could have argued, "Look, it's more important to finish off Clinton first. This guy Perot, gee, I don't know if he'll make it. He really is a third-party independent candidate." I'm just interested in the strategic call at that point in time.

Bill Kristol: We couldn't have finished off Clinton. No Democratic candidate has ever gotten less than, what, 39 percent of the votes for President? Bill Clinton wasn't going to get less than 39 percent of the votes for President. He got 43 percent.

Frank Greer: I want to talk about the same period of time from a different perspective. It was, as Paul said, one of the lowest periods because we had finished the California primary. We had finally won, and we were in third place, and, we thought, sinking. I never will forget one meeting where we tried to explain that there was a good thing about the Ross Perot phenomenon. We agreed that it kept the Republicans off balance because they had to concentrate on attacking Perot and not hit us before the Democratic convention.

Murphy Brown: The Quayle Issue

"It was a good argument to make because of where we were in the race, but you did pick the second most popular woman in the country, next to Mrs. Bush. I guess nobody in our campaign watches TV."

— Mary Matalin, Political Director, Bush/
Quayle Campaign

David Shribman: Meanwhile, one of the most important themes of the general election and probably the post-election period was being sounded. On May 19 Quayle gave the poverty of values speech...

Jill Abramson: More commonly known as the "Murphy Brown" speech. When news traveled back that Quayle had launched this attack on "Murphy Brown," what went through your minds? How serious did the discussions get about getting Quayle off the ticket? What's the real story there?

Charlie Black: That's an easy one. There weren't any such discussions. I mean, the President had made it plain from the very beginning that no matter who thought it was a good thing to do politically, which we didn't, by the way, that he wasn't going to entertain any discussion of it. I don't know of anybody that ever went to him and suggested it. I guarantee you I didn't.

Dave Carney: Anybody that knows the President knows that would have been a stupid argument. It never would have made it.

Charlie Black: If you think about it, the biggest political problem Bush has had throughout his career is flip-flop.

Mary Matalin: Furthermore, he had Bush/Quayle on all the bumper stickers.

Charlie Black: I'm going to let Mary respond on the "Murphy Brown" thing because, frankly, she got it, and I didn't. I didn't know the impact. I didn't understand the impact of it when it happened and she did.

Mary Matalin: I think that in many ways and maybe very often during the campaign the Vice President "got it" or articulated it better than we did. He got the issue but he used the wrong vehicle.

I have been cast in this role of being against it. I was not. I understood what the Vice President was doing. It was a good argument to make because of where we were in the race, but you did pick the second most popular woman in the country, next to Mrs. Bush. I guess nobody in our campaign watches TV. By accident, "Murphy Brown" is the one show I watch and "Andy Griffith," believe it or not, and "The Three Stooges." I didn't think it was bad for our base at the time, but it was one more snakebite. As Teeter would say, I'm afraid to pick up my paper in the morning anymore. It was going to be another whirlwind of being off-message. We did not have a plethora of deft spinners. Most of us were like Mack trucks, as is evidenced by our mistranslation to Marlin [Fitzwater], who ended up saying something like, let's make it a pro-life argument here. Well, you know what resulted. I just thought it would throw us off our game, it would aggravate that sector that was already queasy with us over choice, who would otherwise kind of ignore it because it's not a voting issue anyway.

Charlie Black: The family values theme was legitimate and important and served us well, by and large. But in opening ourselves up to being attacked on "Murphy Brown" and letting her get back into it and getting into the fist fight with the VP and all, it was just, as Mary said, the wrong vehicle. We wish, in retrospect, that the VP had used a different example. I must, also, tell you that that speech was available to Bob Teeter and Fred Malek and Mary, in advance. We didn't get it. We didn't ask him not to do it.

Mary Matalin: I didn't read it. But the two days in the entire campaign that my phone lines were jammed with positive calls were "Murphy Brown" day and bimbo eruption day. It's hard to believe that there is a positive effect to this, but it did really inspire the troops. So the positive side for us is that it was speaking directly to those who were remaining demoralized, it was juicing them up, and they felt very positive about it. So it was not without very significant merit to the campaign.

Jill Abramson: Still on the issue of Quayle and the ticket, during the days when the story about Jim Baker's probable return was developing and jumping onto the front pages, our newspaper definitely was getting what we thought was credible evidence from credible sources, within both the campaign and the White House, that at the same time Baker was looking like a done deal to come back, that there really was consideration being given to replacing Quayle. You're now telling us unequivocally that this is not so? We aren't the only people — I mean, the *Wall Street Journal* — indicated this, and I think *Newsweek* in its election issue corroborated this.

Charlie Black: Well, I don't know who had the discussions. I can tell you that inside the campaign we never had in any senior meetings any such discussions. I can further tell you that Teeter, Marlin, Mary — everybody has had the same experience that I did. That for four years every time I was with George Bush and Dan Quayle's name came up, he was totally supportive and defended him. He would specifically say, nobody better come in here and try and tell me that I shouldn't have him on the ticket.

David Shribman: Did you have a sense of security about that, Bill?

Bill Kristol: Despite "Murphy Brown," a couple of people came to me — not authorized people — to suggest that the Vice President consider getting off the ticket. My position and the Vice President's position was that no one keeps that office by divine right. If he and I thought it would help the President and the administration, if someone convinced us that it would, I said that I was open for discussion. I didn't regard it as something that was beyond the bounds of consideration. No one is entitled to these jobs, and we cared about getting the President re-elected. My position was, also, however, that Quayle was pretty low on the list of problems of the Bush administration. There were several extremely senior administration officials I would have put ahead of him.

Jill Abramson: Would somebody else name names?

Bill Kristol: The removal of whom would have benefitted the President more? If there was going to be a huge shakeup I, in fact, thought that might be one instance where one could even consider making the argument that the Vice President offering to step down would actually benefit the President's election.

James Carville: You're beating a coconut here, let's name some names.

Bill Kristol: Your slogan was, "It's the economy, stupid." We had an economic team. The economy wasn't in great shape. The reason our economic message was never credible was that the President never changed any member of the economic team. No one believes you're going to do something different on the economy with the exact same senior advisors.

David Shribman: Were you personally worried, and do you think that the Quayles were personally worried?

Bill Kristol: The Quayles were not worried. There were two days when there was a possibility of a slight snowball which began with the *Wall Street Journal* piece. There was a slight chance of a snowball when the Vice-President said a couple of things on Larry King. First, a perfectly reasonable statement about abortion and his daughter was blown up a little bit; and second, where he said, if I thought it would help the President, I would consider stepping down or something like that. The door was open, I thought, for about 24 to 48 hours for a serious push, but we closed the door pretty quickly on that.

Charlie Black: Let me say two things. I don't doubt that some of the President's friends might at some time have brought it up to him. I don't know about those conversations. But nobody that he picked to run his campaign ever suggested it to him, number one.

Number two, I was there the day that we discussed with him filing the Campaign Committee, which we did in October in order to begin to start fundraising, even though he didn't pick the campaign management until December. Somebody said, "Well, what should we call it? What about Bush-Quayle '92?" I was the one who said, "If you call it that, Mr. President, that will put an end to all of the rumors about dumping the Vice President once and for all, because it wouldn't be Bush-Quayle '92 if you had any intention of doing that." He said, "Great, that will help, let's do it." That's why we named the campaign what we did. So if he entertained it for ten seconds, I don't know about it.

Ann Devroy: Why did the Vice President go to the President twice and offer to get off the ticket, if he didn't seriously think it was a possibility?

Bill Kristol: I don't know if I would quite characterize the conversations that way. I'm not being coy. I just don't know what happened in those conversations. The Vice President didn't tell me much about what happened.

I think there was a period of 48 to 72 hours from, I think it was Wednesday night to Saturday morning of that week when there was a 5 percent chance perhaps that you could get a snowball, sort of spontaneously generated, that could cause serious problems for us.

The second conversation could have gone like this:

I just want you to know, want to say for the record, Mr. President, that if at any time you think my stepping down could help you, I'd be glad to do so. The President might well have said, it's out of the question, Dan, and that would be it.

I decided that Friday morning that because there was a 5 to 10 percent chance, if this conversation had indeed happened, that we should just let people know that it happened. Once we had opened the door by making the offer on Larry King, which is the only answer the Vice President could give, "I would not try to stay on the ticket if I thought it was hurting the President." Once we had opened the door, we had to close it, and I think we pretty well did, with the cooperation of the White House, that weekend.

Charlie Black: But any snowball that started there would have elicited a countervailing snowball from the conservative base of the party against the Vice President stepping down.

Ken Bode: We left a key precinct out of the reporting on the television series "Murphy Brown." It was an important debate, an important event in the campaign. "Family values" was pushed into the debate of the campaign by that speech. We never heard from the Quayle group on exactly how you felt about it, Bill.

Bill Kristol: If I had known it was going to be handled in the way it was handled, and I take some responsibility for that, we probably would have taken that sentence out of the speech. People forget the *Times* and the *Post* led with that speech on the front page the next day and barely referred to "Murphy Brown."

Diane English [producer of "Murphy Brown"] made a statement, and we responded to her. Marlin [Fitzwater] gave contradictory statements the next morning. That turned it into the lead story on the networks as a "White House in disarray" story, not as a "Murphy Brown" story, and it just blew up into a huge thing.

I will take responsibility for launching it. Churchill has this elegant statement — I remember that I thought of it at the time — about the Dardanelles expedition in World War I, a strategically correct one that he lost control over, and it got totally screwed up. He said something to the effect that you shouldn't start something if you can't control it all the way. Even if it was a decent conception and a good speech and a fair point, it spun out of control. I don't know that it hurt us in any serious way, but it did expose disarray to some degree in our camp.

Mary said that it got us off our message. One could also say we didn't have a message at the time, and that the credible publicity it got was because there was nothing else coming out of the White House or the administration. Why did the Vice President's speech to the Commonwealth Club in San Francisco that contained long discussions of criminal justice and economic opportunity and family breakdown statistics, etc., get so much publicity?

Mary Matalin: Nobody on the campaign, I want the record to show, threw you overboard on this. Whoever leaked out of that stupid staff meeting where I said that about "Murphy Brown" being so popular — in fact, anybody that leaks out of a campaign, it's the most treasonable thing you can do. I just hate that. We were not throwing you overboard. We just knew you guys were on the road.

Charlie Black: Marlin got hit before we had time to talk and strategize about it, but, look, it was a good speech; keep in mind the context. Perot was in the race. Our goal at the time was to consolidate the Republican base to win a three-way race with about 40 percent of the votes.

Bill Kristol: There is one thing I want to make clear. The campaign right away understood it in a campaign way, which was consolidation of the base, and, frankly, pushed that line hard. That was never our intention for the speech. The speech was not, in fact, a very political speech. It was the Vice President's decision to respond to Diane English's statement, "Well, gee, if he thinks "Murphy Brown" is so bad, why isn't he for abortion," I believe, that really did turn this into a big thing.

The Vice President made the decision getting off the plane in L.A. that night at ten to go and hit Hollywood, which I happily endorsed. Hollywood doesn't get it. We got in this huge fight with Hollywood. Of course, what made it a huge issue was not "Murphy Brown" per se, but the Vice President following up with the attack on the cultural elite. I think that was, in fact, a promising attack. I don't think the American people are thrilled with what Hollywood puts out. I think, in fact, the Clinton campaign was quite careful not to look too close to the Hollywood elite.

Frank Greer: The American people were still a lot more pissed off at Washington than Hollywood.

Paul Begala: This is a question that at the time I really wanted to ask you guys. The President, if my recollection serves, gave a speech at Notre Dame on the same topic about a week before the Vice President did.

Bill Kristol: Three days before.

Paul Begala: Three days before? Governor Clinton then gave his answer at Cleveland not long thereafter. The Vice President's speech was a lot better speech except for that sentence about "Murphy Brown." The President seemed a lot more timid at Notre Dame than the Vice President was.

Bill Kristol: The White House senior staff were dissatisfied with the speech drafts that the President was getting. It's unfair to blame the speech writers. We had submitted a version of what ended up being the [Quayle] San Francisco speech to the President for the Notre Dame commencement speech. I had been asked by, I think, Sam Skinner [replaced Sununu as White House Chief of Staff] to write up what the speech should look like. So, in fact, what later became the "Murphy Brown" speech was in circulation within the White House as a possible speech at Notre Dame but without the "Murphy Brown" sentence. In the usual way that everything happened in the White House, it got turned into a perfectly pleasant, innocuous speech.

White House Retrospective

"The President would have won re-election against the Democratic Congress. The trouble is he had to run against Governor Clinton."

— Bill Kristol, Chief of Staff to Vice President Quayle

Charlie Black: We had a hell of a hard time with speeches.

Paul Begala: Was it because of the process or because of …

Charlie Black: Yeah.

Paul Begala: I mean, I don't want you to trash your candidate but …

Charlie Black: It was the process …

Bill Kristol: Well, no, it was …

Charlie Black: … and it was partially lack of talent and partially process. You know, we didn't have good speeches. In any given week, you could count on Dan Quayle giving a better speech.

Jill Abramson: Bill, you know how the White House was at a kind of exasperated point. What was it like? Sununu is gone. Skinner is in. What's the problem? How *was* the White House?

Mary Matalin: Skinner inherited, which he realized by April, a structure of very good people, but I always thought of them as whipped puppies. So when you pick up a paper and the dog has been beaten, it cowers. Skinner would raise his voice, and they would think they were going to get another Sununu assault or something.

Charlie Black: I knew she'd figure out how to take this Skinner question and use it to attack Sununu.

Mary Matalin: The phone tree, you know, we had like constant communication. Bill Kristol and I had great communication. We talked the same language and talked in shorthand. Once we hooked up, we could hobble through. The White House was not used to working in that way with each other and they certainly did not work with the campaign in that way. I'm not being critical of them. It's just the culture of the White House.

Dave Carney: It's not the culture as much as it is the structure of the White House after Sununu. Skinner, basically, tried to fix the problem without changing anybody, just slandering people. It became even worse than it was with Sununu. It was difficult to get decisions made.

Rich Bond: David, just one note in Sam's defense. That is the day that Sam was announced as Chief of Staff; he went to a dinner at [Secretary of Commerce] Robert Mosbacher's house and talked about wanting to put his own team in, which he thought he had an agreement on. Including starting with Darman. He assembled a number of people he proposed to put in those jobs and was told he couldn't do it. From that point on, Sam Skinner never owned his own staff in the White House and no wonder that it didn't work.

Dave Carney: Nobody is blaming him. That's just a fact. I'm not blaming Skinner. I'm just saying...

Rich Bond: I didn't say you were. I just wanted to get that on the record.

Charlie Black: Just one other point. We had execution problems with the White House. There were very few people there that had campaign experience, with the exception of Ron Kaufman and Sherry Rollins — who was super, but, hell, she got run out of there because of [her husband] Ed going over the side. So you weren't on the same sheet of music, so it was a problem that related to speeches and a lot of other communication matters. We'll talk more about this tomorrow undoubtedly. But when Baker and his group got there, the execution problems were over, and we got things done.

Jill Abramson: That, in fact, is our last stop today. But Bill, you mentioned, when I was asking you about consideration being given to Quayle leaving the ticket, that he himself might have entertained that notion had it been part of a broader clean sweep.

Bill Kristol, Dave Carney

Bill Kristol: Well, I didn't say he did.

Jill Abramson: Let me just finish. Was there ever any plan or thought to making the Baker return part of a new team, with a bigger, broader sweep? George Bush going on TV and saying, "I'm going to have Colin Powell and Dick Cheney, the team who, with Jim Baker, brought us this great victory in the Persian Gulf, come in and launch a domestic war?" It just seems kind of shocking that something like that didn't happen. That it was just, Jim Baker comes back. There seems something half-hearted about it.

Bill Kristol: Well, Dan Quayle was an advocate for Jim Baker coming back because he thought it would make the White House work better. There was a lot of talk about a clean sweep like that. But it wasn't persuasive to the President, who would have had to have made the sweep.

Jill Abramson: Why? Was the economic team so entrenched that it couldn't happen? Why did that never happen?

Charlie Black: Well, I think it was probably too late by the time Baker came.

Charlie Black: It could have come earlier. The President accepted an inordinate amount of responsibility for the economic decisions — including breaking the tax pledge, the budget summit, and the inaction all through '91.

I've been there when people have come in and criticized [Richard] Darman or [Nicholas] Brady, and he would say, I am the President, I make the decisions, they are just my advisors, don't blame it on them. In this case, it might have been a fatal flaw, to be overly loyal like that.

Bill Kristol: Well, the reason there was no decision made to adopt a brand-new economic team is that the President believed that he may have been analytically right in maintaining the team and the policies. I don't know that he was politically right. He believed that his economic team had probably given him pretty good advice. In fact, as we now see from the numbers, he may not have been wrong about that.

He didn't think you should throw people over the side because there was a perception out there that things weren't working. He was convinced that the odds were pretty good that the economy was going to pick up. So it's not simply that, gee, he didn't want to fire this team. It was that he never bought into the radical critique of the budget deal — either substantively or politically — which is that regardless of its merits, regardless of the causes of the economic slowdown, regardless of what would bring us out of it, the American people demanded some form of government activism.

It certainly didn't have to be big spending. It certainly didn't have to be higher taxes, but you had to project activism. This argument was being made very vigorously by parts of the Cabinet, by parts of the congressional leadership, by parts of the political organization and, to some degree, by the Vice President.

I guess the President, at the end of the day, wanted to go to election day with the hand he was holding. He didn't want to make a fundamental statement, at any point in '92, that, "My second term would be fundamentally different than my first term. My first term I focused on foreign policy. We won the Gulf War. We brought the Cold War to a successful end. We were a little bit slow in adjusting to the realities of domestic and economic policy. In my second term, I'm bringing over" — you can do any version you want — "Dick Cheney, Jim Baker, Colin Powell, 17 new people or whatever and we're going to have a whole new attitude on domestic and economic policy."

I don't know that we could have pulled that off, but there certainly were a lot of people pushing for that basic adjustment. It could have been made as early as mid-'91 or it could have been made late in '92.

The President never believed that that was the right thing to do. Maybe he never believed, also, that it would have worked politically. Therefore, he never went with the bold moves that would have signaled a different second term from the first term. He ended up running for re-election as an incumbent President, on his first term, and it may well be that history will say that his first term was much better than the American electorate thought it was on November 3. But politically it, obviously, didn't work

Charlie Black: Two other factors. We knew that anything he proposed would have a hell of a hard time getting through the Democratic Congress. So, again, you can be critical of Brady and Darman for not having plans or not having new ideas, but when they or anybody else had an idea, it was, well, Congress won't pass it. Second, I believe it's provable that Alan Greenspan held back on the money supply and kept it down and stifled economic growth. You'll never hear the President say this, but I will say it speaking only for myself. Greenspan is as responsible for the recession continuing or for the growth being so anemic in '92 as anyone — the President or Dick Darman or Congress or anybody else. If anybody is interested, I've got a chart I'll show you. [Laughter]

Bill Kristol: Let me make one point about Congress. It's important and it's barely been discussed. I think it's important on the Democratic side, too. The political thinking behind the budget deal was that it takes domestic policy off the table for the next two years, that's three years. You don't have to fight with Congress. We lose fights with Congress. It becomes a fairness fight. With the spending caps and the tax deal, there are basically no domestic issues for the rest of the first term of the administration. Governor Sununu said, in November of '90, he'd be happy if Congress just came in and passed the appropriations bills and went home. We have no need for a domestic agenda. Not because we didn't want to accomplish things, but because people really believed, as a matter of public good, that Congress would make things worse for the country and, therefore, we shouldn't engage with Congress. We, in fact, did succeed politically in neutralizing the Democratic Congress. The Democratic Congress was very unpopular by mid-'92. This would have been great, if we were running against a presidential candidate from the Democratic Congress.

One of the most striking things about the early primaries that I don't think was mentioned much this morning is, of course, that the two incumbent Senators [Harkin and Kerrey], who should have been sort of first-tier candidates, went down in flames. The strongest candidates were the outsiders. Obviously, Democrats tried very hard to portray Bill Clinton as more of an outsider than he really was — barely ever been to Washington, etc. Of course, Perot and Buchanan and Tsongas and the whole outsider theme — it's now well known how strong the outsider sentiment was.

So we had a strategy to deal with the Democratic Congress that I think ignored the fact that someone could get the Democratic Presidential nomination by running against Congress and running against Washington. The President would have won re-election against the Democratic Congress. The trouble is he had to run against Governor Clinton.

CHAPTER FOUR

ROSS PEROT

"The electronic age allowed a Ross Perot to go from zero to a lead in the national polls, without spending a dime on paid television. I submit to you that he could have won the presidency. And you say, 'Well, but, gee, you know, if a frog had wings he could fly.' Ross Perot has demonstrated that it is possible."

— Tom Luce, Chairman, Perot Petition Committee

On Friday evening, December 4, participants and observers gathered for dinner at the Harvard Faculty club to discuss phase one of the presidential campaign of H. Ross Perot. Former IOP Fellow and Perot Petition Committee chairman Tom Luce opened the session and CNN political analyst Ken Bode moderated the evening's discussion

Introduction

Ken Bode: Oftentimes, the truth is most difficult to elicit from the losers. An assistant diving coach at Yale wrote a Ph.D. thesis on the subject, "What do you do after you've left the diving board and know you've screwed up?" The title of the dissertation was "How to Save a Dive." The title of that dissertation applies most appropriately to some portions of this conference. Charlie Black and Mary Matalin and Bill Kristol and David Carney, Bay Buchanan, and all you folks on the Republican side have been really forthcoming, and it's been a terrific conference, and it's always incumbent upon the losers to make it a great meeting, and I want to thank them, especially.

A little news broke out at my table tonight. I knew that the Perot campaign was something that came together rather quickly, that sometimes the mix of personalities was not what you would expect it to be. Anybody who has run into Ed Rollins in the last six months knows that, too. Independent candidacies bring people together from all over the country quickly. However, one of the things I did not know is that Orson Swindle and Tom Luce, two major figures in that campaign, met for the first time here, last night. And that is the headline of this dinner, folks. We have two parts to this session tonight. It all deals with the father of the bride and the leader of the citizen uprising, but the first part is going to be in the hands of the head of the Perot Petition Committee. We're going to go from the time that Ross Perot was on the Larry King show through September 1, which is prior to the time he got back into the race.

Tom Luce, the head of the Perot Petition Committee, is going to speak to us first, and then I'm going to come back here and moderate a discussion which I hope is freewheeling. We will hear from Tom Luce, Sharon Holman and Clay Mulford. Orson Swindle is out of the frame tonight. He's back in business tomorrow because he wasn't in the campaign until later. We'll have a discussion about what happened with Ross Perot's campaign, beginning with Tom Luce's remarks after 15 minutes of which you're free to begin to rattle the glasses and things like that.

Tom Luce: Let me start by saying that I want it clear to this group that I have written a book about my experiences. It has been put out for auction, and, so far, the bidders are *National Enquirer* and Ross Perot. I figure I'll win either way, so keeping that in mind, I'm not sure that I will respond to all of your questions, but I bet I will.

Ross Perot is no John Anderson, nor is he Strom Thurmond. He is, in fact, the person who has gathered the most votes as a third party or independent candidate for president since one Teddy Roosevelt. What I really hope to do tonight — before we get to the "who shot Harry" and "what about Ed" and "Father of the Bride" and all the other questions that I'm sure await me — is to provoke this group to think a little bit about the Perot candidacy and what he did this year, and urge you to separate in your mind your evaluation of Ross Perot the messenger and the Ross Perot movement. Perot's personality is such a large one that there has been an inordinate amount of focus on the messenger, which is certainly understandable. But I think people will miss the full import of what happened unless they separate in their minds the messenger and the message.

Maybe I can do that by sharing with you my experiences in the first phase of the Perot campaign. I came out to help Ross full time around

April 1, but I was involved from February 20* until July 16. Let's start by jumping ahead to the election results, because I think it's important to put it in context. You're aware of the numbers, the almost 20 percent of the vote he got, but there were a lot of other things that were significant in that vote: the fact that he got 20 percent or more of the vote in 31 states, that he finished second in divergent states, such as Utah and Maine. I'm sure you're going to hear Senator Dole talk a lot about Perot because Perot got — what was it? — 27 percent of the vote in Kansas.**

Look at the diversity of the states in which he did well. These results demonstrate that his appeal cut across party lines, cut across geography, cut across demographic lines like maybe no other candidate we've had in modern history. The two parties should think about what it means because if the two parties do not respond in a major way to the Perot movement, electoral politics are going to be transformed in the years to come. Let me share with you at least a little bit about my thesis in that regard.

First of all, let's talk about the volunteer effort in the grassroots movement from February until July, because I know there's a good deal of cynicism and questions about how much was the grass watered and, gee, when he got back in October, what about this and what about that. What I can share with you is my direct knowledge that from February until July there was truly a grassroots movement. Thousands of people called the 800 number. Volunteers self-selected their own organizations in 50 states and, believe me, they organized themselves. I can tell you that as of the time I left, in July, there were only 50 people on the payroll of the campaign staff. Most of that number was totally absorbed in trying to deal with the Byzantine FEC rules that required us to report everything. If a volunteer bought a billboard, we had to account for it. They were totally absorbed in explaining ballot-access rules in 50 states, how to comply with FEC rules, and refereeing intramural fights, but that's really all they did.

There was not a single signature paid for in that time period. As of July 16, when Perot withdrew, he had qualified on the ballot in 24 states, in that time period. There were enough signatures collected for him to qualify in another 16 at that point in time, so except in the state of New York, which was a problem later on, most of the ballot work had been done. It had been done by volunteers who organized their own effort.

A few examples will show you what an unconventional campaign we had. I met the California volunteer chairman for the first time one week

---

Editor's Note: Date of Perot's appearance on "Larry King Live." He said he would run if the volunteers got his name on the ballot in all 50 states.

**Editor's Note:* Kansas vote: 34 percent Clinton; 39 percent Bush; 27 percent Perot.

before the California primary. He reported to me that in the first three weeks they were in existence, they had self-selected their own leadership, opened up 20 offices statewide, and recruited 38,000 volunteers who collected 500,000 signatures in three weeks.

When he came in to see me in Dallas, he said: "I think we're doing real well, and I think in the remaining three weeks we have under California law, we'll collect another 500,000 signatures." He was wrong. They collected a total of 1.5 million signatures, and only one Perot staff person visited California. In two Pacific Northwest states, more than 50 percent of the registered voters signed Perot petitions. In Texas, in five weeks, the volunteers collected 250,000 signatures, which had to be from people who were registered but had not voted in the March primary, and there was no centralized voting list to show the volunteers who had voted in March. So they had to ascertain one, that somebody was a registered voter and, two, that he or she didn't vote in the March primary. They qualified 250,000 signatures, and that was going on all over the country.

Now, the culmination of all that was that from February 20 to June 20, in a three-month time period, Perot went from zero to the lead in the national polls. At that point in time, he had not spent one dime on paid television. The Perot campaign had spent a total of $6 million, as of July 15. Actually, I think it was $6.4 million. By then, the Democrats had spent roughly $25 million, and the Republicans had spent roughly the same amount. Yet Perot went from being a national unknown, a zero, to the lead in several of the polls by the middle of June. Now, folks, that would not have happened if a huge portion of the population did not believe that the two parties were bankrupt.

Let me say, it doesn't give me a great deal of joy and comfort to say that. I've been a lifelong Republican. I ran as a Republican for governor of Texas, but I believe that that sentiment is real.

The critical factor becomes: Does one of the two parties reach out and absorb that movement, just as, let's say, Roosevelt did with the far-left supporters to form the New Deal, or as Nixon did with the silent majority, when he went from 43 percent to the overwhelming victory four years later? That certainly is our history, and that gives me a little bit of comfort that one of the two parties will find a way to reach out and absorb the Perot people and the Perot principles. But if one of the two major parties does not do that, in today's electronic age, I would submit to you that our politics could be transformed, and whether that's bad or good, I don't know, but it'll be very different. There's a revealing historical account of the Kennedy/Khrushchev years by Michael Beschloss [*Crisis Years: Kennedy and Khrushchev 1960 – 1963*] in which he says that when the Berlin Wall went up, neither President Kennedy nor any other representative of the United States government made any response for 12 days, while the government debated what to do. In today's world, CNN would televise it live, and the President of the United States might have 12 hours to develop his or her position.

The electronic age allowed a Ross Perot to go from zero to a lead in the national polls, without spending a dime on paid television. I submit to you that he could have won the presidency. And you say, "Well, but, gee, you know, if a frog had wings he could fly." Ross Perot has demonstrated that it is possible. Earlier today, we referred to the killing fields of the primaries. Someone in the future may also decide that they want to avoid the ordeal and that you don't have to be a billionaire to do that in today's electronic age. I don't want to start any chuckling, but I would submit to you that Rush Limbaugh could decide to run for president of the United States. I would submit to you that Bill Cosby could decide to run for President of the United States. You can make up your own list. The political parties will not be the judge of who can run for president, and the press will not decide who will run for president.

Therefore, the two parties must understand the Perot phenomenon and deal with it, absorb the message. It is there, it is real, it did not go away with the election of Bill Clinton as president, with all due regard to the wonderful campaign that he ran. It will not go away, in my judgment, if Bill Clinton is simply a skillful politician in the conventional mold. It will not go away because there really is a deep alienation and anger with the system. I would draw to your attention a report by the Kettering Foundation produced by the Harwood Group which, in 1991, studied voter attitudes all over the country, trying to "learn why we didn't have higher voter participation." The conclusions of this lengthy study were: People are not voting because they're apathetic. They are not voting because they are angry. They are not voting because they see no connection between the political system and the problems in their lives.They don't believe it matters whether Bill Clinton wins or George Bush wins. They don't think there is any way for themselves to plug into the system.

What you saw in the tremendous outpouring of the volunteers working for Perot in phase one was they saw a way to plug in. They saw a way to be heard, and that feeling is deep and it cuts across economic, geographic, and cultural lines.

The other thing that was very noticeable to me is, in the entire time I worked in phase one of the Perot campaign, I never had a single volunteer ask me if Perot was conservative, liberal, or moderate. As far as they were concerned, those were meaningless terms, a part of the dialogue of the system which they have rejected.

Their basic attitude is, fix the damn problem. That's what I observed and that is going to drive what happens over the next several presidential cycles. I understand what money can do in politics. I ran for governor against Clayton Williams and I understand that Ross Perot had a big advantage in his checkbook. The press decided money made him a credible candidate, but, again, if you study what happened, he didn't use that checkbook in the February-to-July time frame, and that is what we really ought to focus on before we get all wrapped up in what happened in October.

Again let me stress my conclusion, that if the two parties do not respond, we may have a situation like the French had some 20 years ago, with numerous candidates. It was impossible to get 50 percent of the electorate to support somebody. The French government couldn't really function because nobody could get a mandate to lead. That can happen here if the two parties do not respond to what happened. Think about what happened separate and apart from Ross. We can talk about Ross in a minute.

It's going to take some major changes, in my judgment, but I think it's incumbent upon the leadership that's here in this room to think about it and act upon it.

The Discussion

Ken Bode: I want to remind you, since most of us didn't bring our folders along tonight, of the time frame that we're dealing with here tonight. We're focusing on the period from February 20, when Perot went on "Larry King Live" the first time and said he'd spend $50 to $100 million. A month or two after that, he led in the Texas poll. Two days after that appeared, he hired Jim Squires. A month after that, he was ahead in California, in the Mason-Dixon poll, and in Colorado. On May 5, the first negative stories began to appear. Perot the outsider was linked to the Nixon White House, getting special favors and so forth. A week after that, the CNN/Time poll put Perot ahead for the first time nationally, 33 to Bush's 28 to Clinton's 24.

Three days after that, Marlin Fitzwater called him a dangerous monster. A couple of days after that, stories began to appear on his early release from the Navy. Then Marilyn Quayle made her first forays against Ross Perot; she seemed to be the advance guard of the Republican attack forces. In her first comment to the press, she said Perot was trying to buy the election. In her second one she said that he was a snake-oil salesman. A few days after that, Ross Perot hired Ed Rollins and Hamilton Jordan, and a week after that, the *Wall Street Journal* began its stories about his private detectives investigating marital infidelities. A week after that, it was Perot's investigation of the Bush children. The *Los Angeles Times* weighed in with the fact that a naval officer in command of the fleet Perot served in said he was emotionally maladjusted. The *New York Times* revealed that Perot had negotiated with the Reagan administration on various foreign policy things. On July 11, Ross Perot gave the NAACP speech in which he referred to "you people" and "your people."

A few days later, Ed Rollins quit, and on that same day, the *Washington Post* showed that Perot had fallen, and the polls now showed that Clinton was ahead 42, Bush 30, Perot 20. On July 16, Perot was out, and on July 17, the day after he withdrew, Bill Clinton went up 14 points, Bush 3 points. On that day, I had my last conversation with an old friend, Paul Tully.* After Al Gore and Bill Clinton had left town on the bus trip, I ran into Tully, and we talked for a few minutes. I asked him how he felt about everything, and he said this is beyond "yippie." I said "Why?" He said: "Well, because at the present time, 80 percent of the country believes we're on the wrong track. Yesterday, these wrong trackers had three choices; today they only have two choices. So this is the day we win this thing because Ross Perot has gotten out of the race." So he believed that the Perot vote went to Clinton in toto, and that's one of the things we ought to ask Tom Luce and Sharon Holman about.

Withdrawal

"He didn't like the way the campaign was going. He didn't like the political process. He didn't like the professionalism of it. He didn't want to have anybody around that knew what they were doing."

— Clay Mulford, General Counsel, Perot Campaign

Tom Luce: Believe me, Perot's withdrawal had nothing to do with the timing of Bill Clinton's announcement speech. Ross didn't have the foggiest notion that Bill Clinton was making his acceptance speech that night. I met with him on the night of July 14. I saw him struggling with the decision of whether to stay in or get out, and I saw him decide to withdraw. He told me that he felt obligated to announce his decision as

---

*Editor's Note: Paul Tully was a political consultant to the Clinton campaign who died of a heart attack in Little Rock.

soon as possible. I said: "Ross, my weekly press briefing is scheduled for tomorrow at ten o'clock; do you want to take my place at the briefing? That way, you don't even have to call the press to come." He took my place, and that's why the podium was up to his nose when he made the announcement that he was not going to run. [Laughter]

There was no discussion about Bill Clinton, about the timing of the convention. His prepared remarks that day made no mention of a rejuvenated Democratic party. That comment occurred in response to a question from the floor, from the press, and I'm convinced the timing had nothing to do with the Democratic convention. He had decided that he wasn't going to run, and that he owed it to people to tell them right away.

Mary Matalin, Tom Luce

Mary Matalin: No one suggested to Ross Perot the impact that his pulling out in the middle of the convention would have on our candidacy? Because if they didn't, that's very weird, and if they did, then it contradicts what he had said earlier, which was no matter how much he loathed and despised Bush, he didn't want to elect Bill Clinton. I just cannot believe that he made this decision that very day in a vacuum, and catapulted the guy he didn't want to elect President into first place. It seems like such a monumental decision to make in a vacuum, even given the fact that you all were volunteers or whatever. Ham Jordan could not have missed the impact of the decision and the timing of the announcement.

Ken Bode: Was Ham Jordan told about this or did he learn about it from Ross Perot?

Tom Luce: Hamilton was told about it the morning of the sixteenth when Perot had already decided he was going to make the withdrawal announcement. I did not see Ross on that day. Hamilton talked to Ross on the phone, but I don't know what was said between them. There was very little time that morning. Things were rather chaotic, as you might imagine. I don't want to start some sort of semantic quarrel with Ed, but he didn't quit. He was relieved of his duties the day before. I was dealing with that and trying to make sure that Hamilton stayed in. Then that night, I found out Perot was going to withdraw.

Mary Matalin: Not that I want to end this discussion of ceremonious dismissal, but when did Ross Perot ever say or believe that he did not want to elect Bill Clinton president, that if his activities resulted in electing Bill Clinton president, he would back off? Did he ever say that or think that, or were we just deluded because we put a lot of stock in that notion that if he ever thought that he was electing Bill Clinton, that he would temper his ways.

Tom Luce: I never heard Ross say that.

Charlie Black: I have never met Ross Perot, but I do know Tom Luce, and he's an honest man, and what he says goes with me. But, you know, we heard a rumor at the time of the withdrawal that ABC had some big negative piece, that they had, basically, bluffed him out, that the only way he could stop that piece from running on Thursday night was to drop out on Thursday morning. Now, I don't know if anything like that's true, but it's a damn mystery to me how he could miss the point of the particular day he dropped out. Again, I trust you. If you say that, I believe it.

Sharon Holman: It may be my own perspective or my own feelings from that night and having been involved in this, not from February 20, but from March 10 as it gathered momentum, and truly being swept along and emotionally involved in this whole process. Just before Ed Rollins left, there was a true feeling of division, and any time you walked down the hall, doors closed and conversations turned to whispers. You got a feeling that something was amiss, things were not right. It was an uncomfortable time in which this decision came.

My first feeling was one of intense relief, of thank heavens, all this division, all this business, is over. The next morning, when I thought about the volunteers and the turmoil that would result, then I really grappled with it.

Jim King: The Democratic convention had been building a platform for several days before the convention started. The entire nation got reports on what was happening there. Yet by the fourth day of the convention Mr. Perot still didn't know what was going on?

Tom Luce: Oh, come on. That's not what I'm saying. Look ...

Jim King: That's what you did say, sir.

Tom Luce: No, my ...

Jim King: That's what I heard.

Tom Luce: Listen to me, Jim. What I'm really saying is, yes, Ross Perot knew that there was a Democratic convention. He probably knew that Bill Clinton was making his acceptance speech that night. But in my judgment, Ross Perot had no conception, even though he was told, how a message like that would ripple through the political system.

This guy is not a political animal. He didn't understand the furor when he said "you people" in the NAACP speech. "What the hell is the problem with that?" he said. If you're going to understand Ross, you have to understand that he comes from a framework that you are not familiar with. He probably wouldn't have watched the convention four years ago. I don't mean to say he's not knowledgeable of what's happening in the world. He is, but he is not a political junkie.

Jim King: So, what you're suggesting is that he — at that moment in time anyway — didn't fully appreciate the impact of himself and his decision in the context of American politics?

Tom Luce: I don't think Ross understood, for instance, how many stories would follow from his comment about Citibank's loan portfolio.* In his mind, he spoke the truth about the Citibank loan portfolio and didn't realize the ripple effect associated with a comment like that.

Ross Perot communicated in ways different from those of political figures. Part of his appeal was his authenticity and the fact that he came from a framework unlike the political framework — in which everybody in this room operates. Bill Clinton, George Bush, Paul Tsongas, and John Anderson — all products of the political system. You learn a certain vocabulary. You communicate in certain ways. Ross Perot never did and never wanted to do that. You just don't understand.

Jack Germond: Let me bring these things together. You were talking during your presentation about Perot and the numbers, which were impressive as hell. We have two matters here: First, a candidate who

---

Editor's Note: Appearing on a live ABC News broadcast, Ross Perot remarked of the largest American bank (Citibank, by direct implication), that "if you ever take the third world loans that'll never be paid out, it's insolvent." It was later discovered that Mr. Perot had borrowed more than $1 million of the company's stock late in 1991, and again on March 25, 1992, so he could sell it. If the stock were to go down in value, Mr. Perot would benefit, so his remarks were widely seen to be self-serving.

can mobilize the discontent in this country in a very effective way is one thing. The other side of the coin is, can the person who has mobilized all these voters lead effectively? You're telling us now that he paid very little attention — the point Jim King just made — to what was going on in the political system. Corrupt as it may be, we do have two nominating conventions, but they didn't even impact his thinking about when he withdrew. It wasn't just political junkies watching the convention, you know. It was *all* Americans. That suggests to me a real divorce.

Tom Luce: Jack, I don't think so, for this reason. In Ross Perot's mind, the American people — the electorate, the voters — were perfectly capable of deciding for themselves who to vote for, what were important issues, regardless of the timing of Ross Perot's withdrawal. I would submit to you that he acted consistently with that theme in his approach in the campaign. He responded to American voters in a more substantive way, in terms of their ability to deal with the deficit, to deal with an issue. Timing, image, spin, the manipulation of symbols, isn't as important or real to him — or to the American people, for that matter.

Jack Germond: But, Tom, if he's going to be the leader of this country and in touch with the popular culture, doesn't he understand that the fact that if he gets pissed off on Thursday and decides to ...

Tom Luce: No. I didn't say he got pissed off on Thursday. What I said was, he decided on Thursday. I said that he decided to withdraw on Wednesday night. He wasn't angry Wednesday night.

Jack Germond: You don't see a gulf ...

Tom Luce: I absolutely see a gulf in the way politics operates today. I see exactly what you're talking about, Jack, and there is going to be that conflict whenever Perot is on that stage. There is going to be that conflict in the framework of how those actions are evaluated by many people, including a lot of people in this room.

Bay Buchanan: Tom, tell me why I'm wrong. I see the possibility here of something different. We all know the successes and accomplishments of his life; this is not some naive bumpkin who just kind of fell into success politically in the last year.

So there is another possibility here. He has clearly not communicated with anyone in his campaign, much less the press or the people. He has kept to himself entirely. It appears to me, from everything we heard today, that he did think of these things, that he is Machiavellian, that he kept them to himself, and that he understood a lot more than maybe you're giving him credit for. Now, you knew him. I don't know him. Is my interpretation wrong?

Tom Luce: Let me try to put it outside the context of the withdrawal timing because I don't know whether there is anything else I can add to discussion about the withdrawal. Very clearly, there was never a mesh between Perot's concept of what an unconventional campaign meant and mine or Ed Rollins' or Hamilton Jordan's. What I tried to do was bridge the gap between the unconventional and the professional, using my own experience, as limited as it was. I quickly concluded that more than my limited experience was needed, so I brought in two professionals who had been through it and who understood what the hell was going on and what needed to go on. I felt that we could marry the two.

Ed and Hamilton came on roughly 30 days before Ross withdrew — really, less than 30 days. As soon as they came on board, the Republican "non-orchestrated attack" — two-thirds of which was orchestrated, I think — occurred. Ed and Ham were trying to come up with a game plan to recommend to Ross. It was a very chaotic time.

I never succeeded in getting Ross to sign off on the strategy that I thought was winnable. I was pushing very hard to go on television, to define Ross before the Republicans could define him, and all of those things. Perot had it in his mind that that approach was politics. Communicate directly with the American people on television, and they wouldn't care much for all that other stuff anyway. Keep in mind, all the time I'm telling him he can't do it his way, he's going to the lead in the national polls.

Then the attack occurs, and we have nothing in the can, nothing to go on television with. Perot is still trying to get up to speed on all the issues, come to grips with the economic plan, and assimilate Ed and Hamilton. It just never came together in any professional way. I don't know if it could have, with time.

One thing Hamilton said over and over to me: "You know, Luce, Jimmy Carter and I made our mistakes in Iowa." The two of us, alone, with nobody around, driving a Volkswagen. "You and Perot are dropped into the Super Bowl in the fourth quarter, and you're still trying to get your uniforms on."

A certain amount of that was there, and I do think that we never came to grips with a strategy. But I think Ross's strategy was, gee, you just stay on free television, you do an October television blitz. As far as he was concerned, he was going to be able to shape the agenda of the '92 presidential election, "tell it like it was," in his verbiage. If he won, he won. If he didn't, he couldn't have cared less.

He felt like he could control the agenda and he did, with all due respect to Paul Tsongas and Bill Clinton. I don't think Bill Clinton alone could have made the economy the issue. I think Perot took it to a different level. If it had just been Bush and Clinton, it would have been seen as more partisan political finger-pointing. I think Perot impacted the agenda.

Ken Bode: Okay. I'm going to be Carole Simpson from now on.* I'm going to insist that these answers be much shorter. Mr. Luce, got that? I got a whole list of people who want to talk, and I'm going to tell you who you are so you know that I haven't missed you. John Mashek, Frank Greer, Tom Oliphant, Marty Plissner — two of those people are from the *Boston Globe,* but, hell, this is Boston. I know that Orson Swindle wants to talk, but he talked last night and he's going to talk tomorrow. We're going to get to Mr. Swindle, but I'm not going to get to him right away. All right, John Mashek from the *Boston Globe.* One minute responses. Keep the answers crisp and the questions crisp.

John Mashek: Tom, a quick question following Jack's query. We dealt a lot this morning with the character issue, and the fact that President-elect Clinton stood up to it. I'd like to know your reaction to the fact that Ross Perot left the building and you had to face the volunteers, to tearfully tell them that it was all over.

Second, isn't it true that from that night on, when he saw the adverse reaction on television — including his own people outside the headquarters referring to him as the man with no guts, the yellow Ross of Texas and so on — that Perot started planning to re-enter the race, as Ed Rollins correctly predicted, almost to the day that he would get back in the race three months down the track?

Tom Luce: About the character issue, leaving me to tell the volunteers, yes, I think Ross made a mistake, and that was not a good demonstration of character. In all the time I had been with him, he had never done anything like that. I think he was overwhelmed by what happened that Thursday and wasn't thinking clearly.

Second, with respect to his plotting to return, he told me the night before he withdrew, that he was not going to re-enter the race. I even talked to him about the mechanics of how he would get off the ballot. I reject and see no evidence that it was all part of a plot to withdraw from the scene.

I think what happened, John, is that despite my talking to him a great deal Wednesday night about the potential reaction to his decision, he totally underestimated the reaction of the volunteers. From that point forward, he was responding on the fly, if you will, to this pressure and how to best deal with that. I think that he was shocked. As I recall the sequence of events, that was on a Thursday.

---

*Editor's Note: Carole Simpson, ABC News anchor, moderated the second presidential debate.

He flew to New York on Friday and was confronted with Barbara Walters holding up the headline of the *New York Post,* "Perot Is a Quitter" or something. Lambasted that night, and taping a show that afternoon, and then on Larry King that night, he got all that emotional reaction and I'm sure began to say, my God, what have I done, and try to figure out what the hell he was going to do.

Frank Greer: I have not met Tom until today, and I want all of us to realize he's got the toughest job of this whole meeting. It's almost being assumed that he is responsible for the decisions of Ross Perot. I just want us all to realize he's trying to help us understand. Let's not, in the tone of our questions and the way we're presenting these things, hold Tom Luce responsible.

My question is, on that Wednesday night before the Thursday, was he aware that he had slipped into third place, dropped 19 points, partly as a result of the two-thirds orchestrated attack and one-third just out of the blue. In our polls it was almost 20 percent and dropping. After the phenomenon and the excitement of being the front runner and so many people activated, was an embarrassing third place or even lower finish a factor?

The other thing that puzzles me, he must have been aware of the success of the Democratic convention because he talked about the rejuvenated Democratic party, and that was the peg that we kind of hung onto, saying this is almost an endorsement.

Ken Bode: The *Washington Post* poll came out the day before he withdrew, and he was in third place in the *Washington Post* poll.

Tom Luce: He was aware of that. Yes, Hamilton and Ed and I were hammering on him to go on television, to stop the free fall. We were pushing very hard to go on, one, with a biography and, two, release the economic plan. Number three, name a vice-president. I still felt and told him that, yes, he was in a fall but that it was correctable by doing those three things, provided they were done promptly.

He had stopped the bleeding, had gone on television. He had named the VP. He had released the economic plan. It didn't bother me at all that it had a gasoline tax in it. I felt if Perot had done anything differently, he wouldn't be Perot. I mean, he wouldn't be different. I was pushing like hell to get it out and, therefore, the economic plan didn't bother me.

Tom Oliphant: Just to complete the historical record on the subject of conventions — maybe this is a more appropriate question for Sharon or Clay — surely, you must have known what you were doing, and it must have been intentional on your part to make news one month later during the Republican convention, in terms of the announcement about his book, which occurred, if I'm not mistaken, on the day of the President's acceptance speech.*

Sharon Holman: It was controlled by the publisher. That is absolutely the truth.

Clay Mulford: The date was set in the contract for the book, which was an independently negotiated transaction. We were disturbed about how it was going to play, after the fact.

Marty Plissner: I'd like to ask whether at the time he withdrew, you were aware of the concerns he expressed later about disruption of his daughter's wedding?

Tom Luce: Yes. He went over those concerns that night, along with a catalogue of everything else. I'm not going to speculate as to how he weighed them, but he told me that night about that. He told me about the House of Representatives. Everything he has now said, he told me that night as the reasons for his withdrawal.

Linda Wertheimer: Which was determinative?

Tom Luce: It was not clear to me at all. I kept talking about what the situation was, and I don't think that I carried a great deal of weight when it came to those issues; but he went over them with me that night, as part of the catalogue of his reasons.

Clay Mulford: It was a very confusing period. I heard about it late that evening. I was very upset for the volunteer movement — the people I knew in California and other states I had visited. It was a period of great disillusionment with the process. I did not know of those personal reasons until subsequently.

Charlie Black: Did anybody ask a common sense question about why we would want to screw up his daughter's wedding?

Tom Luce: No.

Clay Mulford: This is just an element of a larger problem. He felt he was having his head taken off every morning by the Vice President's wife, for example. He didn't understand that was the process he was in. It was an element; but it was just one element.

Ken Bode: Now, let me ask you something here as a moderator's prerogative: If the campaign had been more professional, do you think the Republicans would have been less willing to unleash Marilyn Quayle?

---

*Editor's Note: The President's acceptance speech was delivered on August 20, 1992.

Tom Luce: I don't think the Republican response was organized. They should have said it's American; we're delighted; it's good for the process; more power to him. That would have been the smartest thing they could have done. But they overreacted and reinforced the idea that we were outside politics instead of saying that we are someone of like kind, in the political process.

Ken Bode: Well, it's possible to argue at this point that Ross Perot's staying in through the whole thing could have helped either Clinton or Bush. So, we can't answer that one, can we?

Bill Nelson: Tom, two weeks ago Ed Rollins was here at the Institute of Politics and the clear impression that was left was that he resigned from the campaign under protest. You have stated the contrary opinion here tonight, that he was dismissed. Would you elucidate for us?

Tom Luce: Well, I have avoided talking about the situation with Ed because I think in fairness, the situation simply didn't take with Ed. Ed bears part of that responsibility. I think Ed leaked the week before he was hired, leaked the first day he was on board, leaked the second day he was on board, and Perot quit meeting with him. Therefore, he was of no use whatsoever. When I say that, I don't say that to degrade Ed or to demean his abilities, which I think are very substantial. Ed and I got along very well.

I think Ed was relieved when I told him Wednesday: "Ed, you know, we're, we're swimming upstream. You're miserable. This isn't working. You're having no impact." I don't want to get into, did he resign under protest, was he fired. I took Ed to lunch and said: "Ed, this isn't working. The campaign is in two armed camps. Perot will not listen to you. It's best if you leave." Ed said: "I'm relieved," and that was it. It was just something that had to be done.

Margaret Carlson: Why on Wednesday, when Perot's dropping on Thursday? Why bother?

Tom Luce: I didn't know he was dropping out, Margaret. I didn't know until Wednesday night.

Margaret Carlson: But didn't Perot know?

Clay Mulford: He wouldn't have cared. We talked about it. We said this is going to look like Ed Rollins drove it down.

Tom Luce: Perot had wanted to fire Ed for two weeks. He couldn't have cared less whether the next day he was going to withdraw or not. I'd been trying to hold that together. And, you know, I just finally reached a point I couldn't do it anymore. I had no idea Perot was going to resign. Let me tell you, I wouldn't have gone through firing Ed if I had known that Ross was going to withdraw the next day.

Ken Bode: So, now we've established that Ross Perot is a gentle soul, who couldn't bring himself to fire Ed Rollins. Betsey Wright of Arkansas could have. Betsey has been dispatched here by the winning Clinton campaign, while Greenberg, Carville, Greer, everybody is gone, except Betsey.

Betsey Wright: Well, my question has been altered considerably since all the questions you took before mine, in your priority setting. My initial question was twofold. It was whether Clay and Sharon also believed that he was oblivious to the timing of the withdrawal.

Clay Mulford, Tom Luce, Sharon Holman

Clay Mulford: Yes. I was serving as general counsel to the campaign, as Tom's lawyer, who had brought me in to it. Tom's first questions were, "How do we withdraw from ballots? Can we get off ballots in the states that we're on?" The answer was that only in a few could we. It was not a planned agenda. We thought about ballot withdrawal a lot, in March: What if we go on the ballots in a few states, don't get on in all 50, and decide not to run? What's our impact? Will we disrupt the process?

The withdrawal came as a combination of factors, most of which related to Perot personally. He was unhappy with the situation. It was not something that he wanted to do. He wanted to go outside the box. We were more traditional. We kept trying to come up with a strategy that would lead us to win. That did not seem to be Perot's objective. But there was no plan to design the withdrawal to help Governor Clinton.

Betsey Wright: It never occurred to me the Perot campaign was trying to help us. It was a tremendous disruption to the acceptance speech, but not the disruption it was to the Bush campaign. Where then did his comments about the Democratic convention come from? Were they truly based on his incredible hatred for George Bush?

Ken Bode: This rejuvenation of the Democratic party? How he rejuvenated it himself at the convention?

Betsey Wright: No, no, this is Ross Perot's insertion of himself into what we were rejuvenating.

Clay Mulford: I'd like to defer this to Tom. I did not know what he was going to say at the time of his withdrawal. We were concerned but underestimated the impact it would have on the people that had seen the candidacy of Ross Perot as a change from the way politics operate. It can't be overstated how strong that sentiment was among our supporters or the public. I think *he* underestimated it, which gave rise to what happened in July and August. He *had* written a withdrawal statement, but the remarks that have now become so prominently etched in people's minds were ad-libbed. I don't know if he measured the likely impact on the Clinton campaign. Tom, do you?

Tom Luce: No.

Joe Schmoe in '96?

"I would submit to you that Rush Limbaugh could decide to run for President of the United States. I would submit to you that Bill Cosby could decide to run for president of the United States. You can make up your own list. The political parties will not be the judge of who can run for president, and the press will not decide who will run."

— Tom Luce, Chairman, Perot Petition Committee

Dave Carney: I admire the intensity of your volunteers, the effort they made, their leadership, their energy. I think any campaign in the country would have been proud to have even one of those state organizations on their side. I think the parties have shown historically that they're not as dumb as people think they are, and that they will respond to a lot of the changes that Perot talked about. It does take something special to generate the kind of media nationally that Jesse Jackson or Ross Perot or Lee Iacocca can get.

I don't think your premise is valid, that any Joe Schmoe who has some good ideas and some energy can be booked on a show and generate four million volunteers without something in his arsenal like $3 billion. I think our party and the Democrats will respond to take care of the problems that Perot talked about — not solving them, but at least — moving in that direction.

Tom Luce: One, I didn't say the two parties were stupid, David, and I didn't mean to offend. I said in a very encouraging way that I hoped that the parties would respond, as they have in the past, to absorb the movement. Number two, I didn't say any Joe Schmoe. What concerns me is, any celebrity may be able to do it. Rush Limbaugh is not Joe Schmoe. You know, people in here might think he's Joe Schmoe, but he's a celebrity. Bill Cosby can get on the Larry King show. There are other celebrities who can get on the Larry King show. Then it's up to them. If they're skillful communicators, the electronic media allows them to have a substantial impact. What I'm trying to say is, there won't be a gatekeeper.

Dave Carney: Pat Buchanan is a great communicator. As a third party or a nonparty person, I don't think he would have been successful. He was able to get three million votes and raise millions of dollars, but he had to do it through the party system. If Rush Limbaugh tried to run for president, people — Democrats — would be out in droves to insure that all the things that he said were out there and people knew more about him. I don't think that Rush, as an independent, could deal with them. It's remarkable for a nonparty-structure person to get on 50 state ballots. Most people in the world don't understand how complicated it is to get the qualifying ballots. Bay is so upset about South Dakota. You have to know the rules, you have to go out and work hard. I don't think that a Rush Limbaugh or a Pat Buchanan or a Ronald Reagan, or any of these other people would be as successful without a party structure.

Jim Connor: How long did it take, from start to finish, to get ballot access? Did you have it done by July 16?

Tom Luce: Twenty-four states by July 16, with enough signatures on hand to qualify in 16 others, which is 40, was the number as of July 16.

Jim Connor: And where were you for electoral votes in there?

Clay Mulford: Let me explain why that doesn't matter. In many states you cannot get on the ballot until a certain date. In Arizona, you can't start until September 9. In New York, we couldn't start until August 11, et cetera.

Jim Connor: All right. There is a season and, if you will, a stepping process to presidential nominations. You have to file by certain times. You have to participate in party caucuses and party primaries. If Perot could bypass this, who else can and does that open the system or devalue the system?

Clay Mulford: I'll leave to Tom the qualitative question about whether it enhances or detracts from the system. As a matter of law, the system is antidemocratic. It's obviously critical to be on the ballot. Ballot access is controlled by the parties in the states. Where the Democratic party fears, as they have in the South, that electors from a state party will not vote with the national Democratic party ticket, there are rules, for example, that are different. It is very difficult to gain ballot access; it's very expensive. John Anderson spent up to $2 million simply on ballot legal issues during 1980. We benefited from his efforts.

Jim Connor: Are we going to find Howard Stern on ballots in 1996?*

Ken Bode: That's a serious question.

Clay Mulford: The interesting intellectual question is, should you have the right to deny Howard Stern access to the ballot? Who is the person charged with the decision of allowing or disallowing Howard Stern ballot access?

Ann Devroy: A lot of people have referred to the primary process as the killing field for candidates. The press thinks of it as the period in which we examine the candidate's qualifications to be president. When Perot got out of that race, as you know, there were a lot of news organizations — including mine, the *Washington Post* — in lots of places, who were seriously looking at him in a way we hadn't when he wasn't going to be president, or had no chance of that. You maintain that there was nothing in his head that said, I can escape the scrutiny these other people had by getting in late, getting out, and then getting in again late. So, you skipped all the killing-field times, that is all the efforts of the press to say we need to introduce this guy to the American people in a way that he won't introduce himself.

Tom Luce: Let me say, in case there is any misunderstanding, the two-party system is very valid, primaries are very valid, in my judgement. I laid out a thesis which David or anybody else in this room can argue with. Today's world is different because of the electronic media.

Editor's Note: Howard Stern, the controversial syndicated radio disk jockey.

Whether I like it or not is beside the point. I would say it's a statement of fact that the primaries are a killing field, and somebody who is ambitious and smart and shrewd will say to himself, why the hell am I going to put myself through that, if I don't have to? I think a lesson from the Perot campaign is, it is possible. Then, I'm calling upon the two major parties to make sure that they adjust, and I think they will.

Joe Grandmaison: Mr. Luce, first of all, it is great that you're attempting to explain this or to justify ...

Tom Luce: I'm not attempting to justify anything.

Joe Grandmaison: Not justify, but just explain. The message this afternoon, as I understood it, was that in the Bush/Quayle campaign, nobody was talking to one another. Now, the message this evening is that Ross Perot was talking only to himself. Do you not find that somewhat frightening, given the responsibilities of someone who might very well be the leader of the free world?

Tom Luce: Oh, I don't know if I find it frightening. I found it very distressing, and it was outside the mode that had been my experience in dealing with Ross in the past. That's one reason why I tried very hard to bring in Hamilton and Ed to make it work.

Whether I found it frightening, I feel — despite Ann's implication to the contrary — that whether or not it was frightening or not was going to be determined by the process. If Ross Perot survived the process, he would have demonstrated his ability to govern, and it wouldn't be frightening because the system itself is a trial by fire. There was a tremendous potential for Ross to have been a unique man, at a unique point in time, who could have survived and been a great leader, or he could have fallen on his face. I took it to be my duty in February or March to try to persuade him not to run. I did everything I could to convince him that he was entering into an arena in which he was not experienced and would ultimately not be productive. I still felt that Ross Perot could perform a useful function to the country in setting the agenda. I thought he had it within his power to do that, and I believe he did have a substantial impact.

I think it's obvious that I don't agree with a lot of things that were done. People in this room need to think about the issues that I have raised, whether they agree or disagree. I think the world has changed, and it is an obligation on all of us to think about how.

Thaleia Schlesinger: Sort of a follow-up on Joe's question. Where were you in the process of identifying and bringing in an individual to be the counterpart to Ross Perot? I think some of the fears that people had about him were exacerbated by the choice of a vice-presidential partner.

Tom Luce: I couldn't agree more. One of the things that had to be done to, to stop the free fall, was to name a first-class person to complete the ticket. That had been my mission for two to three months. I thought it was advantageous to hold off naming one until August, because I felt the longer Ross demonstrated he was viable, it increased the field of potential vice-presidential candidates. It was critical that he demonstrate he could make an outstanding choice. It should be a person who could help persuade, adjust, modify, and push forward the campaign.

Ken Bode: You had a list of vice-presidential candidates in your own mind. Tell us who they were, please?

Tom Luce: Clay, haven't some been named already?

Clay Mulford: Yeah. William French Smith.

Tom Luce: With all due respect to Ed Rollins and Cokie Roberts, I do know who William French Smith is and he was not on the short list. I did know he was dead. Bernadine…

Ken Bode: Bernadine Healy [National Institutes of Health director, 1991-93] was one of the vice-presidential candidates?

Tom Luce: I didn't say she was a candidate. I said she was one of the people that I was very much interested in.

Howard Fineman: What does Bill Clinton have to do to fix the damn problem, and what will Ross Perot be doing to watch over that process, as Clinton tries to fix the damn problem?

Sharon Holman: Well, as far as future plans for Ross Perot and what United We Stand has in mind, we're going to be kicking off a national organization in January. We'll have a national membership drive. The idea is to capture those nineteen million voters and remain united as one voice, be a people's lobby. I think it will be a very effective voice.

CHAPTER FIVE

THE GENERAL ELECTION I

"Look, in the end, the lack of perfor-
mance on the economy was more impor-
tant to the voters than whether you could
trust Bill Clinton. That's the whole race,
if you had to summarize it in one sen-
tence."

— Charlie Black, Consultant, Bush/Quayle Campaign

On Saturday morning, December 5, the participants and observers returned to the Kennedy School of Government to begin the discussion of the general election campaign. The first session was moderated by E.J. Dionne, staff writer, the *Washington Post* with Susan Spencer, White House correspondent, CBS News, serving as questioner.

The Discussion

E.J. Dionne: One of the things we should bear in mind, from what James and Paul wrote the other day,* is that campaign managers really have very little or nothing to do with the campaign, so I'm not quite sure why we're assembled here at all. But we'll ignore their assumption for the sake of this session, and take it forward.

Both sides can ask each other things like, "why in hell did you do that when we knew perfectly well that X was going on," any kind of question you've ever wanted to ask the other side, ask it now. We're going to run through this chronologically so that anybody who has a

---

*Editor's Note: This refers to a *New York Times* Op Ed piece authored by James Carville and Paul Begala that appeared on December 4, 1992.

question should just jump in as we're covering the area that you want to ask about because I'm afraid otherwise we'll lose the question. We have a long list, some items of which are idiosyncratic, and so yours might prove to be less idiosyncratic than ours. This is also the campaign talk-show.

Susan Spencer: I thought you were going to say "idiotic." As E.J. said, we have a lot of ground to cover and we're going to try to be fairly ruthless, so forgive us if we cut you off, but we have to go from before the Democratic convention all the way through the month of September, which is an enormous amount of territory. To get us started, I would like to hear from George and Mary. And let me ask each of you, as you came out of the primaries — it's now the first part of July, before the Democratic convention — what was each of you most worried that the other side would do?

George Stephanopoulos: I think we were worried, first of all, that they would come up with an economic plan, and press on it. And, then, essentially do what I think they ended up doing, which was hit taxes and trust pretty hard. But, basically, come out and make a real strong case for President Bush and be relentless on it.

This was a little later, actually, but one of the things that we thought they did quite well was the Detroit Economic Club speech; that was something, it was an economic plan. We were pretty certain they would run their plan ad for a couple of weeks and just hammer it home. And that would allow the negative attacks on Governor Clinton to work.

Susan Spencer: So, Mary, why didn't you? And what were you most worried about?

E.J. Dionne, Susan Spencer

Mary Matalin: I think what we were most afraid of happening was exactly what did happen, that they would pull together and go forward as a united party. We weren't certain they could do that, given all the negatives and the whining. If you recall, everybody on the Hill and most of the country had a huge lack of confidence in their nominee. Our biggest concern was that their problems would dissipate, that they would have a good convention and pull it together, and get going. We never expected that they would be catapulted into first place, as they were, by the departure of Ross Perot.

E.J. Dionne: Were you thinking of your main opponent as Ross Perot and not Clinton at that point?

Mary Matalin: No, we talked about this yesterday. We always thought Clinton was the guy, but we thought he was pretty much damaged goods.

Charlie Black: Sure, coming out of the primaries. Maybe Fred [Steeper] remembers some of the numbers, but Clinton had huge negatives and he did have a lot of problems. But we had a problem with Mr. Perot being there and looking that strong. We had to do something about that. But we knew, ultimately, Clinton was the opponent.

Susan Spencer: Were you so fixated on Clinton's being damaged goods that you didn't do the kind of thing George was talking about, come out at that point and present an economic program, a reason for people to vote for George Bush?

Charlie Black: No, hell, we tried to come up with an economic program the whole year. We had one in January at the State of the Union and we worked on that for a while, but the primaries with Pat distracted us. March 20, we vetoed the Democratic tax bill, restated the President's plan, and, for about two weeks there, the only time during the whole year, the President's job approval went up. Then we were thrown off track, everything from the L.A. riots to the Perot phenomenon. Over the summer, the White House attempted to put together a new economic plan, but I must candidly say to you that until Jim Baker and Bob Zoellnick* got there and assembled the plan and the ability to articulate it, nothing happened.

Bill Kristol: There was not a functioning White House from the week of the Democratic convention until the week the President met with Secretary Baker in Wyoming and it was clear that there would be a change. I think we lost the election in the period from the Democratic convention until Secretary Baker came on board, the week after the

---

Editor's Note: Zoellnick was Bush's deputy chief of staff.

Republican convention. When you're an incumbent President, as I think several of us said yesterday, the White House is the key decision-making place, not the campaign, at least when your problem is that you don't have an economic plan.

There was nothing in the content of the Detroit Economic Club speech that couldn't have been put out much earlier, but there was no ability to focus attention. Instead, we had a month of stories about when would Baker come, was it possible Quayle would be dumped from the ticket, planning for the Republican convention, etc.

George Stephanopoulos: But you see it happen, you see that pre-Perot period, you have a three-person race, a three-person dynamic. Once you feel that going after Perot will give us the middle and pretty much allow us to do whatever we want for a couple of weeks, why press it?

Charlie Black: We didn't have any choice. With Perot running as strongly as he was, we couldn't win. And we waited a few days to see that you guys hit him once and Ron [Brown] hit him once and then you all got disciplined and backed off. We waited about a week, and it was clear that you all had your discipline in order and weren't going to do it, so we had to rev it up a little bit. We just didn't think we had any choice.

Paul Begala: Why didn't you move Baker over faster? If he was a savior, you don't have to pick Christmas Day, why did you wait until August?

Susan Spencer: Chronologically, we're getting a little bit off because the Baker thing really didn't blossom until after the Democratic convention in terms of this being the story.

E.J. Dionne: I always thought June was a critical month for the Clinton campaign, and it was a combination of the various TV events,[*] Arsenio, MTV, and also Sister Souljah; maybe Stan could talk a little bit about how the Sister Souljah event happened? Tell us what the rationale was.

Stan Greenberg: I think we should put it in context. We came out of the primaries in very difficult shape, I think Mary was right about damaged goods, that is, our negatives were very high. I think the principal advantage that we gained from Perot was his being on the scene in June and our having the space to use that period to rebuild our candidacy.

Editor's Note: On June 3 Governor Clinton chatted and played the saxophone on Arsenio Hall's late-night show. The speech to the Rainbow Coalition, in which he criticized singer Sister Souljah's "racist" remarks, was on June 13. On June 16 he did 90 minutes on MTV, the youth-oriented music channel.

Without Perot, we assumed that, as you had with Dukakis, you would have been on the attack in June and it would have been hard for us to rebuild in that period. So we had some space to work with.

We were fairly patient, I think, with that space; we didn't want to be attacking Perot. We set out first to go directly to people through whatever medium we could find. George organized a good part of that; and Mandy Grunwald [media consultant to the Clinton campaign] had been the architect of the idea of going directly to voters. We were operating at a whole variety of levels.

We had decided that biography was critical, if people really didn't know Bill Clinton, didn't know his life, didn't know his convictions. On the popular-culture talk shows you go directly to people, but more importantly, it was a format in which you could talk about biography, you could talk about your life, which you didn't get the opportunity to do on "Face The Nation." We determined that we would be very clear about what we believed in and find venues in which to state that. Sister Souljah was in that context.

We also determined, in fact we delayed the schedule while doing this, to bring out the scenario in a high-profile way. And our good fortune, I think, was the week that we brought out the plan was the week that Bush and Perot were tangled in fights. So while we were talking positively about where we wanted to take the country, the other candidates were embroiled in a political battle. That was followed by the Gore selection. The whole series of events — I can't single out any one of them as more powerful than the other — collectively set the stage for our movement. Perot was dropping well before he withdrew from the race. The contest had changed in character before that moment, but I think you're right that June was critical for us.

E.J. Dionne: When did the whole Sister Souljah idea come up?

Stan Greenberg: Months before this.

James Carville: It started in Illinois.

Paul Begala: It was not about the regular coalitions, it was not about Jesse Jackson. She had made statements to the *Washington Post,* saying essentially, black people kill black people all the time, why don't we have one week where we all kill white people. And this was two or three days after the Rodney King riots. So the criticism was not of her art, it was of her public statements about a riot. They caught our eye on the road. The Governor was going to speak to a group in Los Angeles called the Show Coalition, so we had a speech prepared there that was going to take on Sister Souljah.

James Carville: No, it really started in the Illinois primary when we went to Macomb County and some people in the campaign said we ought to take on Gus Savage.* It was just one of those things that we never got around to. If we were going to stand up and go to Macomb County and there were Orthodox Jews, we would have to decry racism across the board. So the idea was to endorse Mel Reynolds,** I think that was the name of his [Savage's] opponent. Then we moved to the Show Coalition, which I thought was one of our worst events in the campaign.

Paul Begala: For a variety of reasons, the speech did not come off, so we had the thing on the shelf then. But we kept thinking about Sister Souljah — those comments had been so outrageous. Time passes and I guess it was June and the Rainbow Coalition comes up and we find out that she's on a panel. So then the question is, knowing that she feels strongly about this, knowing that she's been given a forum, do you speak out about it or do you not? So, the Governor did.

E.J. Dionne: Why didn't he mention to Jackson ahead of time that he intended to do this?

Paul Begala: It didn't occur to him.

James Carville: Suppose that Dan Quayle would have had a press conference after the thing with Sister Souljah, and we'd have said nothing. He might say, "You know, it's funny, Bill Clinton goes to Macomb County, takes a bunch of people making $25,000 a year, and gives them a big lecture. Then he goes in front of some Orthodox Jews and gives them a big lecture. Next he goes out to some rich Hollywood women and he gives them a big lecture. Okay? And here he stands at the Rainbow Coalition and he freezes up when somebody had made these kinds of remarks."

Mary Matalin: That's not the question, James. The question is, why didn't you guys clue him in. I can't believe it never occurred to the Governor to mention to Jesse Jackson what he was going to do.

James Carville: Well, if you can't believe it, we can believe it.

Mary Matalin: Did it ever occur to anyone to say, you better give Jesse a heads-up on this.

James Carville: No, because you and I had to go to [*Wall Street Journal's*] Al Hunt's party. [Laughter]

Editor's Note: Rep. Gus Savage of Illinois, seeking his seventh term in the U.S House, lost in the primary on March 17. He claimed there were white and Jewish conspiracies against black people.

**Editor's Note:* Mel Reynolds was the successful Democratic candidate for Congress.

David Wilhelm, George Stephanopoulos, Mark Gearan

David Wilhelm: The Sister Souljah incident was in the context of two other events, one, the appearance before the UAW [United Auto Workers] and another one before AFSCME [American Federation of State, County, and Municipal Employees], in which we also said things that were controversial before those audiences. And, you know, we had been hit by Reverend Jackson earlier in the week.

George Stephanopoulos: Let me say one last thing. Whether or not we should have called ahead of time, it still wouldn't have helped that much. I was in the room and people thought it was interesting at first, even Reverend Jackson didn't appear very upset. Then it just started to bubble up and it kept going. It went on for ten days. Jesse kept bringing it up.

Paul Begala: Reverend Jackson was angered by it over time. At the time it happened, he got up and gave a nice benediction, sort of gave Clinton his blessing, and the Rainbow Coalition gave Clinton a standing ovation. There was a little buzz, but it was not that big, there was no steam coming out of the Rev's ears. As time passed, there was.

Ken Bode: Maybe it was only afterwards that he came to understand it was part of Clinton's counterstrategy, maybe that took a while for it to soak in, and that's what he objected to.

E.J. Dionne: I just wanted to repeat the question we asked at the beginning about what you were worried about, since Betsey's job was to worry about the things you were supposed to be worried about. During that period in June, what were you looking at as a tool, what were the kinds of things you were preparing against?

Betsey Wright: I was very concerned about the Arkansas record. When we get to the discussion of the convention, we'll hear that. The only real failure we had at that convention was being unable to give any sense of Bill having been a great governor. We just couldn't do it, given all our other needs.

The biography thing was very important to me because I was struck at how people didn't know this man and all of a sudden there are all these images absolutely contradictory to the person I knew. One of the most traumatic periods of this whole campaign for Bill was finally moving to the point where he would talk about his personal life. This was something he had refused to do for the previous forty-some odd years, and he resisted the necessity of it. He was not comfortable doing it. For years I had tried to analyze why this was so. Look at his pattern of life. He went to get credentials that kids out of Hot Springs didn't get, a Georgetown degree, a Rhodes Scholarship, Yale Law School, and then attorney general and governor. He wanted to be measured on the success or failure of those things. I think he almost had an inferiority complex about who he was. It really was tough getting Bill to start talking about himself.

When he finally did, I think he got into it in a more canned way, and it was still uncomfortable. We were still debating how to handle the draft situation going into the convention and trying to figure out when to do it. I think all of us have an ability to bury things in our minds; if we really just need to put them away, we will. For Bill, going through all of that meant trying to pull things back out of the old locked box, and it was exceedingly painful.

He had to read letters to and from him during that period of time. I wanted Bill to get to know himself again. I gave him this one letter saying, "This isn't going to be easy, but you have to read this letter." It was from a classmate of his in Hot Springs High School who was in Vietnam in the Marine Corps, telling him, don't come here, and if you come here, don't come in the Marines. It contained pages of description about the emotional feeling of what it's like to kill your first person and to watch your buddies getting killed. I didn't know this kid and I was just choking up over the letter, I'm still choking up about the memory of it. In the envelope with the letter was the guy's obituary — he was killed in action. The letter to Bill was the last letter he ever wrote. Bill looked at me, "don't make me do this," tears in his eyes too, "don't make me do this." All of that is an illustration of the personal, emotional level on which I was interacting with Bill going into the convention.

Susan Spencer: So you're saying that you all decided at this point, this three-month period or whatever, not to have these *mea culpa*, if you will, press conferences, where he would sit there and say, here are the records, ask me anything you want about the draft.

Betsey Wright: We never did that because we never found anything different from what the story had been since 1974.

Susan Spencer: But the story kept dripping on and on and on, particularly if you look — we're way ahead of ourselves — at September.

Betsey Wright: We kept being accused of not telling the whole story. That was not true — nothing that was known to us was not revealed.

George Stephanopoulos: It was faced at a press conference.

Betsey Wright: I did for a time encourage Bill to sit in a David Frost-like setting and have a conversation as a real person about the times and where this got into it. I knew that getting sequences of events jumbled was what happened to every Rhodes Scholar who had been at Oxford with him at that time; these guys were far more confused about when you got your physical and your draft notice than I was. I was a big expert on Selective Service regulations of '69 at that point.

The brightest of people, not limited to Bill Clinton, got all this jumbled over time. What they remembered was the end result. That's where Bill was. He said, "Anything anybody wants to go through, I can explain what it meant."

Charlie Black: As bad as we wanted them to have that press conference, that ought to answer your question.

Frank Greer: One other minor concern during this period of time is that they [the Bush Campaign] also had about five or six million dollars that they had not spent, they had not advertised since Michigan, really. Given the strength of Perot, we thought it was almost a blessing that they weren't going to be able to use that for negative advertising decrying us in June. But they also could have used that period of time, it would have been a wonderful opportunity, to present a positive economic message, as George said, and they had some money resources they needed to spend before their convention. And we thought at some point they might do that in June.

Dave Carney: A question. What was your financial status in the last eight weeks, six weeks, before the convention?

George Stephanopoulos: Not good. In June we had an initial plan to buy four and a half hours of television time. Thank goodness we discovered that we didn't need it, that we didn't have to spend it.

James Carville: Can I say something about the draft story? I believe now that the draft story helped us out after Labor Day because at that time everybody knew everything about it. There was saturation. You couldn't go in a focus group, you couldn't do a poll without knowing that Bill Clinton had files on the draft. We were much more afraid of an ad or an attack on overspending, that because we spend too much, taxes are going to go up, than a draft ad. People basically said, look, I know about that, I don't care, move onto something else. It hurt us in New Hampshire, as we talked yesterday. It hurt us with older women probably as much as anybody else. Whatever damage that was inflicted on us about the draft was done as of Labor Day. It looks like every time the media wanted to write a negative story, they would write it on the draft, and they were being prompted by the Bush people. Because they kept getting sucked into the draft story, they failed to hit us on other things. In retrospect, I really do believe that the story worked in a perverse way to our advantage after Labor Day.

Betsey Wright: So the press could do citizenship stories on top of it?

James Carville: I don't think they'd ever heard it.

Betsey Wright: It was related to the draft story.

James Carville: I don't think it hurt us, Betsey. I'd guarantee you, they would like to go back through that citizenship thing and undo the whole thing right now. That was another thing.

Fred Steeper: We were trying to figure out what line of negative attack to go after Clinton on and the first one that we'd researched in great detail was the Arkansas record. That gave us a lot of trouble because people got confused with the statistics or they said the record sounded so bad that we were making it up, it couldn't be true. We put together a story about the chicken waste, child welfare, and some of the other things that you were worried about.

When we tested ads about draft dodging and not being totally truthful about some of the things in his past, we found they were more credible to people because they already had a third-party endorsement from the press. The problem was, they weren't linking those stories with their vote decisions. So the justification for using the draft stories in September is that we were playing with something that was credible in terms of its being factual and trying to get the voters to link that to a broader assessment of Clinton. Some people in our focus groups said, well, if he would lie about his draft record and lie about some other things, he may lie to us as president of the United States. That's what we were trying to bring out, the conclusion that we were trying to get more people to draw.

Stan Greenberg: There is a very important point of disagreement here in terms of the analysis that was guiding what we were doing and the analysis that was guiding what you were doing. We had concluded that the Arkansas record, particularly in the period after the convention, when he was still new to people, was the area of greatest vulnerability. It was the point of attack people viewed as legitimate, that they wanted to know more about. Indeed our own spots on the Arkansas record produced by Frank [Greer] and Mandy [Grunwald] were the most effective.

I agree with James, the draft was largely discounted. It came in September immediately after you released your economic plan. And you spent the next eight days moving with the draft and right onto the Moscow trip and it buried your economic plan. I think it was an important strategic move.

Fred Steeper: Well, you're arguing that you could only be a 100 percent negative or a 100 percent positive, but most campaigns usually are on a two-track strategy, a negative and positive.

James Carville: On the draft story, and this is a fact, you can look in your book, many more people thought that the President was not being candid about Iran-Contra than thought that Clinton was not being candid about the draft. Okay? The fact that he wasn't being candid about that doesn't drive voting behavior. Thirty-eight percent of the people thought that Clinton was not being truthful on the draft, okay. We had already sustained damage — that story was going to drive voting behavior. What we concluded was, nonperformance on the economy and other things were *more* likely to drive voting behavior.

Charlie Black: Look, in the end, the lack of performance on the economy was more important to the voters than whether you could trust Bill Clinton. That's the whole race, if you had to summarize it in one sentence.

But, nevertheless, we were giving you negatives on trust, draft, all those things. The problem was, that wasn't going to do it for us alone. We also had to convince them he was a taxer, that he had a bad record in Arkansas, and two or three other things.

James Carville: I'll just say, from my vantage point, we would have been worse off, you would have been better off, if after Labor Day say, you didn't mention the draft, you said his spending programs are going to break the country, you told how much he spent and hit him constantly on the spending side and the Arkansas record.

Charlie Black: We did do a hell of a lot more of that than we did the draft stuff.

Fred Steeper: Just to correct the record, we didn't take on the draft foursquare, in terms of paid advertising, until October 11. We started off with Arkansas taxes in terms of our first negative ad.

E.J. Dionne: I want to go back to Frank's [Greer] point. Where did those ads that you spent the $5 million on come from? What was the rationale behind those talking head ads?

Charlie Black: We were trying to solidify our base.

Fred Steeper: We came very close to attacking the Arkansas record the day after your convention ended. And I was at one meeting where that decision was made, because we were having such difficulty coming up with a positive message. It looked like it was easier to attack the Arkansas record.

Susan Spencer: Why didn't you?

Fred Steeper: In retrospect, that was probably a mistake.

Susan Spencer: What was the reason given for not doing that?

Fred Steeper: We always felt our main project or problem was people's perceptions of the President. If we could re-establish his domestic credibility, link him to people's concerns about the economy and other domestic problems, our problem would be solved. The decision was switched to allocate those resources in August to try to refurbish the President's image.

Charlie Black: But also we had to get our base solidified at the time. At the time Fred's talking about, we had two-thirds of the Republicans for Bush and a third weren't. Coming out of that convention, we had to have a solid base. In the end, the ads we used were designed to get behavioral Republicans leaning back toward Bush so we could solidify our base.

Fred Steeper: Another big factor in that decision is Willie Horton. The Republican party and the Bush/Quayle campaign probably got bluffed by the press into thinking that the first negative ad we ran, the press was going to pounce, "There they go again, they're doing the Willie Horton stuff." We were very gun-shy about the timing of the first negative ad — that's why our first negative ad was supposed to be humorous. It was supposed to be more of a light touch, the hillbilly music. So that was a major factor — for us to have had our first paid advertising be negative advertising probably could have boomeranged on us because of the way the press would have covered it.

Bill Kristol: I do think that you should not underestimate that fear. The focus group showed that the Arkansas record was a real vulnerability, and we had good material on it. Going negative on the Arkansas record would have been on substance, on tax-and-spend and other issues, on his record as a governor and not the personal stuff. But there was just huge allergy at top levels throughout about being accused by the press of, quote, "running a negative campaign," and we were bluffed out of doing it and I think it was a mistake.

Susan Spencer: Where did this originate? Was this Bush?

Charlie Black: No, it was all of us. But, look, before we ever ran a damn commercial, four times as many voters said we would run a negative campaign than said Clinton would.

Bill Kristol: So we might as well have done one.

Charlie Black: It was a job you had done on us before.

James Carville: Perot was helping out a little bit.

Charlie Black: I agree with that. The President's credibility was very thin at that point, very thin. I mean, Bill's right in retrospect, sure, I would have done it, I would have done Arkansas record, if we had it to do over. But you had to be very careful that anything that you put out there might backfire.

The Democratic Convention

"But Thursday through Sunday, the big excitement of the Gore selection and the two of them campaigning as a team, then a masterful convention, everything right, I wouldn't want to have to figure out anything that you left out or missed."

— Charlie Black, Consultant, Bush/Quayle Campaign

Stan Greenberg: It's interesting that again, the numbers pointed us in a different direction. We solidified our base at the Democratic convention, but didn't do it by running a convention that was directed at our base. We had a general election broad audience in mind from the beginning. James's point about GOTV [Get Out the Vote] has always been that message is more important than going at the base. The base was excited by the prospect of change and the prospect of a majority Democratic party, and that enabled us to do a convention in which we had a number of tasks.

The most important thing we had as our goal was to introduce Bill Clinton in a personal way with biography, but the other objectives were to show this was a new Democratic party reaching out to Independent voters, that it understood the values of the majority of Americans, that it was an orderly, united party that could govern. And I think on all those goals, it was an extraordinarily successful convention.

James Carville: For the record, a significant thing happened after the New York primary: basically Stan, Mandy, myself, George, though George went down below to be the communications director sometime after that, we killed off the primary process and said, you know, we're just not ready.

And so, by the time the convention had come, we had spent a lot of time, a lot of money, a lot of research on determining what it was that we wanted to do. By mid-June, mid-to-late June, I'd say, we had a pretty good idea of the things that we needed to accomplish, of the nature and depth of our problems and how we wanted to solve them and accomplish our objectives.

Strategically, we knew 85 percent of what we wanted to do by late June. But I think that was a big advantage that we had, that we had spent that much time, and I think Mark [Gearan] was actually the one that okayed the money and the time and made it easy for us to just go ahead with that. But a lot of our campaign just jumped right out of the primary process and really had nothing to do with it after New York.

Mark Gearan: There was a point at which I remember meeting at the Governor's mansion in late June or right after California, six weeks out from the convention, and you did your presentation with Stan. We were in third.

Stan Greenberg: What's important, we had 24 percent of the vote and we were in more difficulty with Democrats than you were before your convention. We made a decision then not to direct our message at Democrats.

James Carville: That's when you were getting a lot of that 38 percent strategy. People said, we can do this thing with 38, Perot is going to be in there. The only people that were saying it were people in the press. No one in the campaign ever said it. It would be some "Democratic consultant" said that they ought to solidify the base and to hell with everything else and do the GOTV. I just wanted to make the point that I think that the campaign freed up the money in time for some of the people to just say, go ahead, rule out the primary process, and get into the general election.

E.J. Dionne: I just want to ask one specific question, maybe of Paul, which is why wasn't Governor Casey [of Pennsylvania] allowed to speak?

Paul Begala: Because he didn't endorse Governor Clinton. Period.

Ron Brown: But Ray Flynn [Mayor of Boston] spoke, he was pro-life. In fact, Clinton talked about abortion.

E.J. Dionne: Did [Jerry] Brown endorse him?

Ron Brown: I'm the only one that knows the answer to that question. There were a couple of basic principles as far as the convention goes, which were set out months before. One was that it was not going to be the usual Democratic celebration of the end of the primary season, but that it would be the kick-off to the general election campaign. We have normally gone into conventions so pleased that the bloodletting is over that we have this love-in that doesn't mean anything and doesn't have anything to do with electing a President. We decided the convention would be totally geared towards the general election campaign, towards promoting our nominee and that everybody who had the microphone would have endorsed our nominee. That was a rule, everybody understood it, from Jesse Jackson to Jerry Brown.

The Jerry Brown situation and the Casey situation were unique. The press reported incorrectly that Casey was denied access to the microphone because he was not pro-choice. He was denied access to the microphone because he had not endorsed Bill Clinton. I believe that Governor Casey knew that. I had made it clear to everybody. And yet it still got played as if it had to do with some ideological split. It had nothing to do with that.

The Jerry Brown situation was also, I think, misinterpreted. Jerry Brown, as any nominee, or as anybody who had sought our party's nomination, had a right to the microphone, not because he was invited to speak, but because he could use the time when his name was to be put into nomination to speak to the convention, which is what he did. In our discussions, I gave him an opportunity to speak at a better time, at a different time, at a time when his message and his appearance could have had greater impact. He could have availed himself of that, had he decided to endorse Bill Clinton. He failed to do that; therefore, he spoke where, under the rules, he had a right to speak, which was during the time that his name was placed in nomination.

E.J. Dionne: But were you also in a box on Casey because Jesse Jackson had endorsed, partly because you laid down this rule and that you had a problem because if you then broke the rule with Casey, you were going to essentially violate the discussions you had with Jackson?

Ron Brown: Those things are interconnected, yes. The rule had to apply to everybody.

James Carville: Do you think that it is an eminently reasonable position for a political party to take, that if you don't endorse the nominee of said party you can't speak at the convention, Mr. Chairman?

Ron Brown: It's something we haven't done in many years.

Bill Schneider: I wanted to ask the question about the convention and the campaign, too. You mentioned that Governor Clinton was cautious, reaching out to a general election audience, not trying to solidify the Democratic base, but that he was not politically correct from a liberal point of view, except in one regard. And I'm curious to know if the focus on gay rights, on the AIDS issue during the campaign, was Governor Clinton's personal commitment. It was admirable, but it was striking in the fact that on that issue alone, he seemed to have a strong personal commitment. A lot was made of it at the convention and during the campaign. It was one of the riskiest issues of all. Where did that come from?

Stan Greenberg: Believe me, it was no part of any strategy out of our research. It was out of Bill Clinton, the person.

Frank Greer: I would also add, it reflected his whole basic inherent opposition to discrimination in any form. And I will tell you that this whole campaign, from day one, came out of a deep-felt opposition to discrimination.

E.J. Dionne: Did this help you in organizing the convention? There had been a lot of talk that there would be disruption, that ACT-UP [AIDS Coalition to Unleash Power] would do a lot of stuff. Did his strong stand on gay rights help you in dealing with ACT-UP and other groups who might have demonstrated?

Betsey Wright: Nothing helped us with that.

Ron Brown: Can I just add to that? There were basically four problems that we faced, and I'm not talking about issue problems, I'm talking about people/political problems going into the convention. One was Jesse. One was Mario. One was Jerry. And one was Doug Wilder, to a certain extent. He still had not endorsed Bill Clinton, although that was less known publicly. We solved three of them: Jesse, Wilder, and Mario. The one we didn't solve, Jerry, really didn't end up hurting us at all. Jerry hurt himself. I think Jerry could have been a star had he decided to endorse Governor Clinton. But we couldn't really reach any accommodation with Brown.

George Stephanopoulos: Really, right up until the last moment, the Chairman was working on it. At the end the Governor tried to talk to him a couple of times, but it was our impression that Jerry Brown couldn't figure out how to get there, how to work through his supporters who had become the most vociferous people on the floor. He was trying, he was looking for a way, he was sending lots of different emissaries, having lots of different discussions, and he just couldn't figure it out.

Ken Bode: There was at this time also a little vice presidential boomlet going on at the convention and it wasn't for Al Gore, it was for Doug Wilder, and it wasn't for Bill Clinton, it was for Ross Perot. We have both Paul Goldman and Tom Luce here. Could you tell us to what extent this was all smoke and mirrors and a charade and to what extent there was anything serious going on there?

Paul Goldman: As far as I know, the first I heard about it was in the *New York Post,* so I assume it came from Ed Rollins.

Tom Luce: Yeah, it did. It came from Ed, and I don't know if Ed was serious, but I know Ed was doing it and I tried to rein it in. I got lots of questions about it, but it was Ed off again, and I don't know whether it was real from Ed's perspective or not.

E.J. Dionne: You didn't like the idea, to be reining it in, or what?

Tom Luce: I just didn't think at that point in time we were going to pick any vice president. Our game plan was to pick one in August, not in July, the week of the convention. Ed brought it up on, I think, the Friday before the Democratic convention.

Susan Spencer: Five days before Ed quit?

Tom Luce: Yeah. He was saying Wilder wanted to know then because of the convention and all that stuff. I don't know whether Wilder was using Ed or Ed was using Wilder. But it went on. It didn't come from Perot and it didn't come from me, although I was aware of it.

Ken Bode: Maybe it was one of those times when there was a two-track strategy going on, kind of what Fred Steeper talked about.

Paul Goldman: You know, I've never spoken to Ed Rollins, but given what I've heard here, you said he leaked from day one and that was when you had problems with him, I assume it came from Ed Rollins.

Tom Luce: I'm convinced it came from Ed Rollins, in case there's any doubt. I just don't know how it was received at Wilder's end. I can't answer that.

Clay Mulford: I think Ed did that on his own. Hamilton was orchestrating the selection of a VP, and Ed was not in that group or in those discussions because of his propensity to leak. So he was operating completely on his own.

Tom Luce: Hamilton was assigned the vice presidential task. I think it was probably meant to be a Rollins/Wilder ticket. [Laughter]

George Stephanopoulos: Before we leave the convention, (maybe you guys covered this last night and if you did, I apologize), would you go through how Ross Perot decided to get out on the last day of our convention.

Dave Carney: We went through that last night.

E.J. Dionne: When did you guys learn of it?

George Stephanopoulos: I remember it clear as a bell. Thursday morning we just heard this buzz and we had picked up something very,

very sketchy two days before that. A close friend, I think, of Perot's had
sent some message to stop attacking him and said, trust us, there's a
real reason for it, but, you know, I didn't think anything of it.

Susan Spencer: Were they from Maine?

Mary Matalin: At this same time, we were all taking bets, we all sat in
Teeter's office and bet — Charlie, who won that thing? I bet he wouldn't
get out.

Charlie Black: I don't remember. It wasn't me.

Mary Matalin: I have a baby question for these guys. How did you
come to write that thumb-sucker of an acceptance speech after 1988?

George Stephanopoulos: President Bush went even longer than we
did.

Mary Matalin: You can ask us about that because that's a good story.

Paul Begala: We had been through a period when Mr. Perot was dominating the news for two months before the convention, when there was
just no spotlight on Bill Clinton, which is why we did all the nontradi-
tional media. We wanted to say a lot in that speech, accomplish a lot of
things in that speech, and we said every damned one of them.
[Laughter]

E.J. Dionne: Did that speech grow?

Paul Begala: There's a possibility. I take responsibility, I was the primary draftsman. There were 21 drafts.

James Carville: There were 21 secondary draftsmen, too.

Paul Begala: It's like, yesterday I was wondering how oatmeal came
out of the White House on family values, when what seemed to be real
clear came out of the Vice President's office. It's the same thing with
speeches. Sometimes you set a strategic goal and you accomplish it
crisply and clearly and easily and sometimes other things get loaded
on.

E.J. Dionne: Who was loading them on?

Paul Begala: I was the speech writer. It was my responsibility.

E.J. Dionne: Before we move onto the event that solidified the
Democratic base — the Republican convention — does anybody have
any other questions?

Paul Begala: Al Gore, I know it's out of chronological order, but that
was key. The strategic turning point was the selection of Gore and I'll let
Mark Gearan talk about it.

Choosing Number Two

"He was, in my opinion, the best: some-
body disciplined on the message, as good a
national candidate as I've ever seen out of
either party. It's extremely rare for a Dem-
ocrat, but he had unbelievable message
discipline."

— James Carville, Strategic Consultant,
Clinton/Gore Campaign

"He was a robot."

— Mark Gearan, Chief of Staff to Al Gore

Mark Gearan: Well, I think, having come from the Clinton side of the campaign, he really kind of started what turned out to be an important surge that, obviously, cooled off the election. What he thinks was very important in this period is when we brought him over to Little Rock for the beginning. We sat down all that afternoon with Stan and Frank and James and George and into the evening and the next day. It was intensive, going through the campaign, and Betsey had a great deal of time with him as well to really go over the campaign, the background, and what we were saying. So, immediately, day one, right out of the box, he was as good as he turned out to be. We did Q's and A's, we did the...

George Stephanopoulos: Tutorials.

Mark Gearan: It was a tutorial of sorts on the Clinton campaign, but we introduced the structure of the campaign at a later point. We spent the next four months explaining the organizational chart.

James Carville: He was, in my opinion, the best: somebody disciplined on the message, as good a national candidate as I've ever seen out of either party. It's extremely rare for a Democrat, but he had unbelievable message discipline.

Mark Gearan: He was a robot.

James Carville: Yes. [Laughter]

Susan Spencer: Going back a little bit, was the Governor troubled about the selection of Gore? I gather this wasn't covered that extensively yet. What were the pros and cons, who were the other people, how did this all work, what led to his being picked in the first place?

Mark Gearan: It was as tightly wrapped an operation as Warren Christopher was able to do.

Susan Spencer: Why don't you unwrap it?

Mark Gearan: My main function was to sneak them all into the Capitol Hilton Hotel under cover of night, renting three different vehicles and using all sorts of ways to get in there. Clinton spent nearly three hours with Gore one evening in Washington. He spent about an hour with each of the other prospects. I was in the other room with [Bruce] Lindsey [political advisor, Clinton/Gore campaign] and there was no question that something very significant was happening.

   The only time they had really spent together before, was when Gore went over to Arkansas to seek his endorsement in the 1988 race. Other than that, they had not spent much time together. But this meeting was critical in their development.

George Stephanopoulos: That's the thing. I mean, you can't really unpack it because it's very analogous to what's happening now. The Governor just talks, he'll ask throwaway questions to people at various times just to get a sense of what they're thinking, but this is his process.

Betsey Wright: The expectation was that Gore was "it" before they talked; I mean the way Bill talked about why he was on the list and all of that was, I thought, just a pro forma thing. After that meeting, it was so clear something had clicked.

E.J. Dionne: What did he say?

Betsey Wright: He talked about how much he learned from him, how smart the guy was, how well he thought everything out. The Governor liked the intellectual stimulation even of the arguments on points where they disagreed. The way Bill referred to him was so contrary to my image of what would have happened in that meeting and what Bill would have selected, it was magic.

Mark Gearan: As Betsey said, at the beginning it was just kind of perfunctory.

Betsey Wright: But, boy, just Bill's reactions, you could tell.

E.J. Dionne: Who else was a serious contender?

Mark Gearan: Senator Graham [Florida].

Susan Spencer: Another Southerner.

Bill Kristol: Another moderate. That's the story, but if you want, I can give you Dan Quayle's reaction when Gore was picked. It was of some interest to us and of course we were watching the Clinton/Gore press conference. Quayle knew Al Gore while in the Senate. He said, "This pick is good." He was looking forward to campaigning against Gore. There *is* a separate vice-presidential campaign. The two of them had debated endlessly in the Senate, and he thought it would be fun to go at it in this round and wasn't particularly intimidated. He believed it was a good choice for him, but a bad one for the President. The Southern stuff I think was always overrated and I assume wasn't that high in your mind.

It seemed to me the choice demonstrated two things: the Democratic party was not going left, and, because Gore supported Desert Storm, the ticket was not suspect on that issue. This was Dan Quayle's contemporaneous quick judgment. The Republican party at the presidential level runs on three issues, three pillars: one of them is foreign policy and defense. This issue had been mostly done away with by the ending of the Cold War, but it was definitively removed by Clinton's taking a pro-Desert Storm VP. As Clinton had been somewhat ambiguous on the war in the Gulf, the selection of Gore appeared to put him on that side of that issue. I don't think it was inevitable that the Gulf War would be a non-issue in the fall, but it became inevitable once Gore was picked. On the cultural issue, the Vice President said at the time, Clinton's response to Sister Souljah pretty much took away a lot of the Republican values text, so we were left with economics, the third pillar, and that was a problem for us.

I think the choice of Gore was very important, not so much because Al Gore is a good campaigner and all, but because of what it signaled about Bill Clinton.

Betsey Wright: Well, I think you're doing what a lot of us did — rationalization after the fact in analyzing the politics of the choice. I think that probably in the history of this country there has never been a less political selection. I think it was a personal selection more than it was the politics of it. The other impact of it had nothing to do with a Desert Storm voting record: the two of them standing there together looked like change.

Mark Gearan: The generational aspect is important, too.

Charlie Black: Yes, that's exactly right. And let me, before you get off the Democratic convention, congratulate these folks for doing the best job in the history of the world with their convention. Normally, you go through a good convention, you dominate the news for four, maybe at the most five, days; they dominated it for two weeks by the timing of the Gore selection, starting that Thursday. Then they followed up with the tour. Coming up to New York dominated the news over the weekend. Again, the first impression was exactly what Betsey said — change, age. Not that many people around the country knew Gore, and people were just getting to know Clinton, so it was an important first impression seeing them there as a team.

But Thursday through Sunday, the big excitement of the Gore selection and the two of them campaigning as a team, then a masterful convention, everything right, I wouldn't want to have to figure out anything that you left out or missed. Then the bus tour, again, genius, to extend the dominance of your coverage and the message and reinforce that impression, you really got a two-week convention out of it. So I don't know who all was in on that, probably all of you, but ...

George Stephanopoulos: The bus tour we did for the sense of history. We knew very clearly the month before the convention; David has this huge map on his wall and he was in his office one day and jumping up and down and he said, "I got it, I got it." And he was running his finger straight across New York and he said, "We're going in buses." And he called James like five minutes later ...

James Carville: And I said it was a terrible idea. [Laughter] "David, you're consumed with the base and just bus stops and everything else, it's just going to send the wrong signal."

Charlie Black: The fact is, in that two-week run, even with Mr. Perot getting out at the exactly right date, the worst conceivable day for us and all of that, the way you did that two-week orchestration of dominance of the coverage, the American people learned ten times as much about Bill Clinton, a hundred times as much about Bill Clinton, as they had heard before. All the bad stuff they knew before didn't matter because you got him up there looking the best he possibly could along with Gore. Even if Perot had not dropped out that week, you still would have been in a pretty comfortable position.

James Carville: How did you pay for that train? Remember we thought about the train or something and it came down to how much it cost.

Charlie Black: Well, we paid a hell of a lot. It was worth it because the best press we ever got in the whole campaign was when we did the train trip.*

David Wilhelm: I would like to say that we knew the bus tour would play exactly that way. I remember a farmer we visited in Utica, Ohio, suggested we go down to the restaurant at the crossroads and maybe 400 people, the local Democrats, could say hello to Bill. When we got to the restaurant, 10,000 people were there.

Even though we didn't fully understand the dynamic at work, a couple of things were clear. In thinking about the electoral college strategy,

---

* *Editor's Note:* On September 26, President Bush began a two-day train trip through Ohio and Michigan attacking Clinton's positions on taxes and auto pollution standards.

the line that I was drawing on the map was the Mississippi River and the Ohio River. It always seemed to me that this region was our key for electoral college strategy, that we could win states along both sides of both rivers.

Bill Schneider: Should have taken a boat trip.

David Wilhelm: We talked about that, actually. But at the time we were thinking about it, the President was at the White House and Ross Perot was in television studios and Bill Clinton's great strength was the energy that he derives from and gives back to average folks. What better way of doing that than the bus trip? It also allowed us to go to key showdown states. I always felt that it was absolutely crucial — coming from Ohio and Illinois, I know those two states — that you lay down a marker early that you are ready to compete with the Republican candidate in the central and southern parts of states like Pennsylvania, Ohio, Illinois, just absolutely crucial. And, as it turned out, we won every single state along the bus trip. So it seems to have succeeded.

Mark Gearan: How did we do in Utica?*

David Wilhelm: Utica, we haven't looked that up. It was two to one for George Bush in 1988, and Wilmington, Ohio, was three to one for George Bush. When we got the kind of crowds that we got in southern and central Ohio and Illinois, we knew that we could compete and it gave us hope for the electoral college strategy moving forward.

Mark Gearan: If I could just add one quick note on the bus trip. The initial plan out of New York was for the Gores to go for a day and a half, then go back to Carthage [Tennessee] to get their life together and take care of their kids and all that stuff. They decided to stay on for the full four days of the trip. Corny as it sounds, a lot of the relationship that Clinton and Gore presently have came as a result of spending hours and hours together on the bus by themselves. The Governor and Hillary and Senator and Mrs. Gore would sit by themselves around a table at the rear of the bus, with a few of us coming in and out, but usually just the four of them. So the amount of time they spent together was extraordinary, and, as a result, their relationship was enhanced. We'll see how that affects the administration, but I believe the bus trip developed a key part of the whole relationship between the candidates.

Bill Kovach: Can we go back to the selection of Gore for just a minute because it keeps coming up. Al Gore did not run for president, he told everyone, because of his personal life, his son's critical injuries in the

---

Editor's Note: In Utica village, Clinton received 39 percent of the vote, Bush, 33 percent, and Perot 19 percent.

accident. I'm curious what you did to convince him to run for vice president and overcome that concern about his personal life?

Mark Gearan: By the time the process had started with him, his son was well on the road to recovery. There was no medical issue involved. The Governor had taken the regional consideration off the chart, so that wasn't an issue. It was Gore's decision.

The Republican Convention

"The lack of coordination and communication at the convention was worse than our dis-coordination in everything ... they were disconnected from us, they were disconnected from Bond, Bond and the campaign were disconnected, we were disconnected from the White House."

— Mary Matalin, Political Director,
Bush/Quayle Campaign

E.J. Dionne: I would like to talk about the organizer of the Republican convention, Bay Buchanan. [Laughter] What were you trying to do? I would like you to relate what happened the week of the platform meetings and your speech and how that related to the tone set by the convention.

Rich Bond: Let me go back even a step before that to pick up where Charlie left off. Heading into the couple of weeks before our convention, we were continuing to be flat. The advertising put on the air didn't catch fire and cut their bounce. They were the heart throbs of the heartland, courtesy of my friend over there in the corner who's laughing, Miss Devroy [Ann Devroy, reporter for the *Washington Post*]. And we had a situation where the new-face/change factor that they exploited so skillfully was not there for us. We were an old story.

As chairman, I've got to shoulder the responsibility for the operation. If I say anything that suggests I'm trying to do less than that, I don't mean to give that impression. It's more fun, as it was in '88, to take credit for success than to be the failed chairman of a broke party.

When you said I was smiling, it was just kind of a wry smile of regret. You all, the Clinton folks, studied very carefully the lessons of 1988. One of the lessons that you will have to study from 1992 is how difficult it can be to run a presidential campaign out of the White House if you just don't have the proper decision-making structure so you renegotiate issue after issue. In terms of our convention, we had a split operation. The President had assigned to one group the overall responsibility for content, timing, and speakers. The campaign had responsibility for platform and some of the other aspects of the campaign, and I got to pay the bills in many cases. That is not to say that I did not have a voice along the way in these questions, because I certainly did, and maybe I didn't speak as forcefully as I wanted to at times, and that's my problem.

There were three things, I think, in the convention that the press was bound to focus on: the Quayle flap leading into the convention, which was kind of a distraction to us; the abortion flap which was never going to go away; and how we were going to handle the Buchanan situation, similar to what Ron [Brown] had to handle, working with the campaign to decide who was going to speak and when.

And as Bay well knows, other than a courtesy call that Bay and I had, I was not exactly on intimate speaking terms with Pat. Their view was they would endorse George Bush during their speech because that would be best for George Bush. I took the exact opposite view. Pat thought he had the right to speak because he had run and I disagreed, saying, "You didn't win a single state. So therefore you don't have a legal right to be there, such as Jerry Brown had a legal right, having qualified for the minimum at the Democratic convention." Pat's third point was that three million people had voted for him and that their voice needed to be heard at the convention. My reply was, and this was a very polite conversation, as Bay would remember, that I didn't really think that was the case, probably about 500,000 voted for Pat and maybe about two and a half million voted to protest against George Bush. I didn't feel that Pat was necessarily going to unify the part of the party that we were having the problems with.

But anyway, be that as it may, the decision had been made and my instructions were to try to be as amenable as possible for everyone's good. And I think we made a mistake when we look at it now, and I can't say that I forcefully jumped up and down and said, this is going to kill us, or anything else. And I think it comes down to what Mary said the other day about being off-message.

The fact of the matter is we had a design that I was very comfortable with at the convention on the first night — with Ronald Reagan focusing on the world. The second night — focusing on the nation with Phil Gramm as a keynoter and Jack Kemp, a person who could very well articulate and touch a very broad spectrum of the electorate and not just Republicans. The third night — focusing on the family dimension led by

Barbara Bush. On the fourth night — coming to the main event which was the President himself, the individual. It was a kind of inverted pyramid right down to Bush.

We then had to put Pat in a spot. It couldn't be the last night because that was Bush and others. It shouldn't be the third night because that was Barbara Bush. The feeling was, well, we really can't deal with it being the second night because that's Kemp and Gramm, which left the first night. So we kind of backed into it which had the effect, with the way the speech was timed and the length of the speech, of stepping on one of our strongest cards out there, which was Ronald Reagan.

And so we ended up putting Pat on the first night, and with the effect of the media seizing upon what they saw as narrow-mindedness or intolerance in the Republican party, which I regret. I don't know to this day, because of this split operation, whether anybody screened Pat's speech. I know that I did not. We probably should have been more forceful in saying, now listen, here's our plan, this is what we want to stick to, this is the theme, but that never happened from my end, and I've got to take a good share of the responsibility for that as well. So that's the lead-in.

E.J. Dionne: I just want to see if I understood what you said. You seem to be saying you would have preferred that Buchanan not speak at all. Is that what you're saying?

Rich Bond: Well, again, as I said directly to Bay, that I had a voice in this process and my voice was not very positive at the time, but that I wasn't out there trying to headhunt per se. I certainly was listening to all the other parts of input at the time that other people were giving about what was the best thing to do for the Republican party and for George Bush. And so I didn't slam my fist down on the table to Bay directly, or to anybody else in the campaign, saying we cannot let this man speak at our convention, he'll be hurtful to us. I just wasn't that thrilled about it, but I didn't prevail and I didn't push as hard as maybe I could have. I think Charlie would say it was a tough call for us at the time. Pat was giving us no reason at the time not to let him speak. He had been faithful to his word of not attacking George Bush. As it came down, it was a close call.

Bill Schneider: Did anyone else jump up and down and get excited? I mean, what happened to all that broken glass he was supposed to be crawling on? It sounds like somebody there, the President, the Vice President might have …

Rich Bond: They were in negotiations with Pat, as Bay knows.

E.J. Dionne: I want to ask one specific question of Bay first and then of Jill and Howard and Charlie. That speech went to the Bush people 24 hours in advance. Is that right? Can you talk about who might have seen it and can you talk about the process the speech went through?

Charlie Black: We weren't going to ask you to change the speech anyway.

Bay Buchanan: What Rich has said here is accurate from his point of view. He was not in the loop except for the initial conversation that we had. We knew that Rich was not in our court as to whether we should speak or not.

This is how it played out: we had said very publicly all along that we were going to endorse the President at the convention, it was the President's convention, he won, it was his right to choose whomever he wanted to speak. We weren't going to make an argument out of that. But in order to push him in the direction of wanting Pat to speak, we also said we were going to have our own convention down the hall with our people, down the street, if they chose not to invite us inside, which we knew would be a great media brouhaha for the President. We had 1,000 people coming to their 20,000, and we recognized that this wasn't great numbers, but that it would be in their best interest to have him speak.

As the weeks went by, we weren't sure they were going to let us, although as Charlie pointed out, Charlie and Jim and I are old friends and we were speaking regularly about it and I knew that they were interested in him speaking and that it would be in their best interest to have him do so. They also knew that Pat would give a speech that was very supportive of the President, so that there would not be any concern as there might have been with Jerry Brown saying something against the nominee of his party.

We agreed there would be a speech and it came down to the timing of it. We recognized that the President had Monday night and that the Vice President or Mrs. Bush was going to be Wednesday night and the Tuesday night was really our option. We wanted a half hour in prime time. And they said, well, the press will possibly cover you if we can move you back to an 8:30 slot. We said, all right, you're trying to help us, but we wanted to come before the keynoter and then if somebody would follow him, you'd have three speeches that night.

Then it came back to us that we were not going to precede the keynote, that we were going to precede Kemp, who would precede the keynote, and I said that would be unacceptable.

Susan Spencer: Bay, who are you negotiating with?

Bay Buchanan: At this stage, it was Charlie [Black] and Jim [Baker]. And it was a very friendly discussion. It was, what do you think about this, what do you think about that, back and forth and back and forth. Nobody was trying to pull any punches or be clever, we were just trying to work out something here.

Then they said, "Come on into town, Bay, we have something we need to talk to you about." So I went into their offices and the offer was, how about Monday night. And I said, "Monday night? What about President Reagan?" And they said, well, it will be the two of you. And I said, "I think I could work this out." [Laughter] So I immediately drove about 100 miles an hour over to my brother's house and I took total credit for negotiating Monday night. I said, they've got this thing worked out so that we will share the hour with the former President. And we were, of course, elated with this arrangement.

There's something I wish to emphasize here. We had very good rapport. They said, what about the speech? This is in a larger meeting, with Pat present. We said, we don't want somebody to start rewriting Pat's speech, we don't want it leaked because we know it will be a juicy piece of information for the press. In order to prevent this from happening, we're not going to give you an advance copy. And they came back and they said, well, we need a copy at least 24 hours in advance, for a couple of reasons, which were very valid. One, we don't want you stepping on lines President Reagan might be saying, and also we want to make certain that the President and members of the White House staff are comfortable with the speech. Although Charlie [Black] and Jim [Baker] were quite confident, there were some other people who might not have been as confident that Pat was going to do what he said he was going to do — for good reason.

So, at that stage, I said, that's very reasonable. Twenty-four hours in advance. We practiced this speech 24 hours in advance, and it was true, some of you know, Pat did not use the speech he was going to give because we did not trust some of the minions at the RNC, afraid that they might put the story out on it. So we used another speech and it was fully read by Craig Fuller and faxed to Bob Teeter so the White House could look at it. Now, I know Bob Teeter read it, but I don't know about anyone else at the White House.

We were given 9:00 to 9:30. It's been indicated, Larry King told it, that Pat was given eight minutes and took 30. We were given 9:00 to 9:30, they called us about 48 hours ahead of time and said, look, Bay, we're afraid things could get backed up, there might be more clapping than we anticipate, we don't want the President moved off from the 9:30 slot, will you be willing to start at maybe five of? We said, that's fine, we're not worried about five minutes here or there for prime time coverage.

And so we were scheduled to start at five minutes of nine, Central Time, which means we would have been off the stage at twenty after which would have given plenty of time for Paul Laxalt [former senator from Nevada] and the President. Paul was going to introduce the President for 9:30. That's basically what happened at the convention.

George Stephanopoulos: The premise here I don't quite get; there's no evidence that Pat Buchanan was off their message going into the week.

Rich Bond: George, what I'm saying is that what we wanted to focus on the first night was the world...

George Stephanopoulos: But forget about the first night ...

Rich Bond: ... and that was the message.

Susan Spencer: But that was before.

George Stephanopoulos: That was before. I mean, that's what I was trying to get to. The Thursday before the convention, you gave a speech about Hillary, and Mrs. Bush took it back. It was clear you guys had decided to stay with the Hillary attacks because you had an opportunity to repudiate them the day you gave the speech, when Mrs. Bush went on television and said, "I don't know why he did that, he shouldn't do it." The next day, you came back to the attacks, and in fact Mrs. Bush changed her tune and it became, okay, they've made a decision, this is one of the things they're going to do that week. I mean, this speech wasn't in isolation. You had Marilyn Quayle on Wednesday night, Phil Gramm's speech, Pat Robertson.

James Carville: Every time the camera went on Pat Robertson, I said, "Freeze it right there."

E.J. Dionne: Let me expand on George's point because there are two related things. In the same speech in which you criticized Hillary Clinton, you also went after the press, and I was curious why that line appeared and then disappeared until the end of the campaign, really. I thought at the time that that was going to be a consistent theme of the campaign. There's the press, there's Hillary, and then there's the whole question of the platform being perceived as well to the right. Indeed there were an awful lot of people from the Christian right on the platform committee who actually put a spin on it that might have been against your best interests. Could you talk about the things that happened the week before, notably your speech?

Rich Bond: Let's go one by one. My job, the week before, was basically to energize the troops. We worked up that speech, for the National Committee, the group that I spoke of before. The idea was to try to put out a whole lot of information about the Arkansas record, which I did, and a whole lot of information about Bill Clinton and the direction he would take a government in if he won. It had been done before by various folks in the party; a lot of it was tongue in cheek, a lot of it was funny in terms of some of the potential Cabinet folks, and it ginned folks up.

Then I took the little quote out of Mrs. Clinton's writings earlier on in the *Harvard Law Review,* an opinion which I personally felt was out of step with the mainstream of America. I'd always had the impression that Hillary was a very forceful person and played a real role in Bill's political life. At the time of the cookies incident,[*] you saw a marked change in how far out front she was in the campaign. I made the assumption that you folks had taken her underground and had decided that she was overexposed or whatever and it wasn't the best thing for you to have her out there playing such a dominant role in the campaign. My view was that she would play a dominant role in a Bill Clinton White House because of her expertise and her interests. It was a legitimate topic — she was an advisor to Bill Clinton, a person who affected his thinking. People needed to be aware of some of her fundamental political or legal views.

Paul Begala: That's not exactly how you put it in the speech, though.

Rich Bond: Well, I think I know the quote as well as Susan could read it. It was "presiding over all this will be Hillary Clinton, that champion of the family who thinks that the kids should have the right to sue their parents and who has likened marriage to slavery." Now, those are both factual statements. I never did talk to Barbara Bush until she came to the convention, I faxed her office the afternoon she criticized me and said, look, let me circle the paragraph that I took this from; that's what I said, and here it is.

Paul Begala: When did you give the speech? I think it was the same speech, wasn't it, in which you said, "We are America and they are not."

Rich Bond: We can go to the transcript if you want. It was the first night of the convention, I was doing an interview with Maria Shriver live, and I said, look, we represent America, these folks don't represent America; we are in the mainstream of America, these folks have not been in the mainstream of America ...

James Carville: Who is not? Am I not in the mainstream?

Paul Begala: I think there's some scapegoating going on in there when the chairman of the party says we're America and they're not, when the chairman of the party attacks Hillary Clinton and now it seems to me you all are blaming Buchanan. He got up and gave a narrow-minded speech ...

E.J. Dionne: I would also like you to talk about the platform, too, and how that thing ...

Editor's Note: On March 16 Hillary Rodham Clinton made the widely quoted remark: "I suppose I could have stayed home and baked cookies and had teas. But what I decided to do was pursue my profession, which I entered before my husband was in public life."

Charlie Black: Let me say several things and then let Mary, Bill, let anybody else speak up. As Ron [Brown] pointed out, you want your convention to relate to the general election. You want to try to send a message out there that kicks off the general election. And, obviously, we attempted to do that. But if you don't have a solid party base at the convention, that's your last chance to accomplish that.

Now we had to do both things because two weeks before that convention, Bush was getting two-thirds of the Republican vote. Perot was out of the race and a number of Republicans were for Clinton or undecided. If we came out of Houston without 90 percent of the Republican vote in a two-way race, we couldn't put it together. So we had that goal in mind as well as the general election message, which the President presented, President Reagan presented, the Vice President, Kemp, Gramm, etc.

Now, I believe that we lost control of the spin of the convention, for which I will accept responsibility. But I also believe that the press did not give us a fair shake in the coverage. We had 128 speakers at that convention, eight or nine major speakers in prime time. The only one that you could claim made a controversial speech was Pat Buchanan. Pat Buchanan made the same damned speech he had been giving all year, geared to those three million people who voted for him, and to the majority at home who were not for George Bush before the convention.

Susan Spencer: You didn't consider Marilyn Quayle's or Pat Robertson's speeches controversial?

Charlie Black: Pat Robertson did not speak in prime time. The four speeches that I am giving you, out of 128, that were controversial, and I wouldn't even consider Pat's a surprise or controversial or anything else. But you could make the case, the press made the case that Buchanan, Robertson, Marilyn Quayle and one other one, what was the other one? Well, the point is, it was four out of 128.

James Carville: You're saying the convention was designed to go at the base of your party, which is essentially right-wing people, I mean, that's the Republican base. But when you went after that group, you sent a signal to everybody else — these are the people that our convention is designed to attract. You can't have it both ways. You moved those people into your camp, but in so doing you offended the other people.

Charlie Black: But that's not all we did, if you think back to the Bush speech, the Reagan speech, the Kemp speech, the Gramm speech ...

James Carville: But people remember the "going right" speeches. If you put Pat Robertson up there and you put William Weld [Governor of Massachusetts] up there, they are going to remember Pat Robertson.

Charlie Black: But the voters didn't see either one of them until the networks played Robertson over and over and Buchanan over and over.

Bay Buchanan, Orson Swindle

Bay Buchanan: In three national polls after the first night — it's not just Pat's speech, obviously the President's speech as well — showed that the Republicans closed it ten points. Three separate polls showed that they were absolutely doing the right thing in bringing people over. What happened after that, and what Charlie's trying to point out, the media went nuts saying that Pat Buchanan's speech was radical and that the whole thing was taken over by this far-right wing, which didn't even exist down there, that I saw. The whole media interpretation of what happened at that convention was false. Take for instance the platform, I must have heard how many times, Buchanan people have taken over the platform. I had one delegate and he was two days late.

Charlie Black: Let's talk about the platform. The platform was not much different, if any different, from the platform that we had in '88, '84, and '80. Now, going into the convention, for years we knew that abortion was going to be a big issue. Obviously there are differences within the party on it. It was something we had to face up to. We did, in my opinion, about as good a job of damage control on that as we possibly could have. We kept it off the convention floor, the pro-choice forces folded the second the convention was gaveled to order on Monday morning, and that issue was off the table.

At the end of the platform committee deliberations, Thursday before the convention, the last act was to pass a "big tent" resolution, which never made your networks. And I still don't understand why. We went ahead over the weekend, there was still tension in the sense that the pro-choice Republicans were still attempting to get enough state majorities to be able to bring the issue to the floor, so it was legitimate to keep talking about and covering abortion until Monday morning. But we never got any credit for the unity resolution, the big tent approach.

E.J. Dionne: Because you wanted to bury abortion you had more Christian right people on that committee than on any of the other committees. There were a lot of changes in the course of that week, notably the one about declaring the tax increase a mistake, which later was changed to, I believe, "recessionary." You also had a lot of little changes that went in the platform all that week pushed by some of Pat Robertson's people. Did they have more power than you anticipated to make all those little changes that helped create the impression that the platform was more right wing than in the past?

Charlie Black: But the fact is that it wasn't. Dave Carney and Mary Matalin knew everybody on that committee and almost all of them got there with the approval and permission of Dave Carney and Mary Matalin. So we knew exactly what to expect out of the whole deal. That's why at the end we could get a unity resolution passed.

But voters out there don't give a damn about whether it said "mistake" or "recessionary," and they don't care about changing a couple of clauses to make it appear more right wing. I'm just telling you, I do not believe we got fair coverage of the platform, the platform process, the big tent resolution at the end and — we'll probably all just disagree on that forever. Really there's nothing different about the '92 platform content from what we had in our last three platforms.

Stan Greenberg: The amount of time that went into thinking through who kicked off prime time on the first night of our convention tells me it was not a casual decision. You had to know the impact of choosing Pat Buchanan as your first prime-time speaker, sharing space with Ronald Reagan.

Fred Steeper: Can I make a comment on that? There was no guarantee the networks were going to cover us from 8:00 to 11:00. The assumption was that they would give us an hour and that we had to fight for any time beyond that hour. It was just assumed that to get more time beyond an hour was a good thing because it would mean greater exposure.

So, part of the consideration with Ronald Reagan was guaranteed coverage. The keynoters were guaranteed coverage. Barbara Bush was guaranteed coverage. The President was guaranteed for the hour he was going to be out. Now how do you suck the networks in to covering more of you? The benefit of Buchanan was the networks would probably cover Buchanan.

I don't want to concede something here that everybody's assuming. As Republicans, we believe that there is a conservative majority in the country. We think we have a lot of data to back that up. We think Marilyn Quayle and Pat Robertson were speaking to what we believe is the conservative majority. And that is just a fundamental difference between the Democrats and the Republicans ...

James Carville: But you risk having Pat Robertson speaking even more.

Bay Buchanan: When Pat was asked to do it, it wasn't in isolation, they didn't just say, okay, come back Sunday before your speech and we'll talk to you. Pat was very interested in knowing what the polls were showing, which of our issues they would want us to take up. We weren't saying to them, "Draft a speech," but we were getting input from them, we had a meeting with about four or five of the top people, including Bob Teeter, specifically saying, what messages do you want Pat to incorporate. They gave us an overall view of how, first of all, we would say good things about the President, then show how the President differed from Clinton, give real reasons why people should come home to the President. Pat took home a mental outline and drafted that speech. It wasn't done in isolation.

James Carville: Bay, no one believes that Pat Buchanan agreed. I mean the point about the coverage, the coverage that the Jackson speech got, when you use a term like Pat used, a religious war. If Jesse had said there's a racial war in this country, then that works for the play over and over; some of it is not just who says it, some of it is what you say.

Mary Matalin: Yeah, but these press guys were all lathered up, pretty hasty to do abortion at the convention. They were convinced we were going to have a floor fight. They were convinced that Randall Terry was going to burn the place down. They wanted to do the abortion story.*

James Carville: You don't think we were convinced that ACT-UP was going to do the same thing?

Mary Matalin: It was not the same level of intensity. Everybody wanted to do this story big; the Republicans are unraveling. They wanted to do a story at your convention; the first good convention in the history of the Democratic party. There was a different press dynamic.

Editor's Note: At the Democratic convention, Randall Terry, founder of Operation Rescue, the militant antiabortion organization, tried to present what was said to be an aborted fetus to Bill Clinton. He was charged with violating a federal injunction specifically barring such an action. On August 26 Terry was sentenced to a jail term of up to six months for violating another restraining order during a protest at a Texas abortion clinic during the Republican National Convention in Houston.

James Carville: Whoa, whoa, that's not true at all.

Mary Matalin: When they didn't get abortion, that laid the foundation, the press said they're intolerant, they hate women, they're taking away their choice, this foundation of intolerance. They didn't get it, so they took the minimal amount, a couple of speeches, and made up the story.

James Carville: The press was reporting that they were trying to find somebody else, that they wouldn't break threshold to get matching funds in 1996.

George Stephanopoulos: No. But the best one was the day of the California primary, the lead story for the *New York Times* is "brokered convention."

James Carville: Brokered convention. A month before our convention, we were facing stories about brokered conventions and, you know, dissident Democrats and who was going to show up at the convention and everything else.

Charlie Black: The fact is you did a good convention, whether it was your doing or the press's. Fred, I don't know how many numbers you have with you, but I think you could verify this. Thursday night after the President's speech, our convention had the desired effect, both in terms of solidifying the base and getting some message out there that was appealing to general election swing voters.

The place we lost control of the spin was really Friday through Tuesday or Wednesday, after the convention. Again, I take responsibility for that. The follow-up coverage was all about what a right-wing convention it was.

Bay Buchanan: This was Newt Gingrich talking about reality.

Charlie Black: Well, he didn't help. And you all remember on Saturday in Georgia and Newt's up there adding Woody Allen to the equation.*

Bill Kristol: Let me just back off these issues and say a couple of things. I mean, I was utterly out of the planning loop on this so I have no stake either way. I think the key point, and this statement has been made so far as James Carville's statement, that people remember certain speeches from the Republican convention, Robertson, Buchanan,

---

Editor's Note: Campaigning with President Bush in Georgia, Representative Gingrich, House minority whip, compared Bill Clinton to Woody Allen, saying Allen was a "perfect model of Bill Clinton Democratic values." Allen was in the midst of the custody fight with Mia Farrow, mother of his three children. Reports were circulating about his affair with Farrow and André Previn's adopted daughter, 20-year-old Soon-Yi Previn.

and maybe Marilyn Quayle. They remember because we did such a poor job — and I disagree with Charlie on this — Thursday night with the President outlining an economic plan that should have stepped on those speeches and governed the coverage over the next weekend.

With all due respect, I don't think the Democratic convention went that great the first three nights. Some of the content was a little bit weird and kind of wacky, including Jesse Jackson's speech. There were statements in there that could have damaged you if you hadn't had a very strong Thursday night that totally obliterated the first three nights from the memory of the American people and allowed you to go off on the Clinton/Gore bus tour and have change and your economic message dominate the next week.

Actually no one remembers the first three nights of any of these conventions. Think of the '88 Republican convention — all you remember is the President's acceptance speech. That totally dominates, it demolishes about 80 percent of what happened in the first three nights, and then you're off to the races.

Sure, there were mistakes made on the first three nights of our convention. I wasn't involved in any of those decisions, but I do think there's too much focus on the mistakes of the first three nights and too little attention on the President's speech. If he had given a slightly jazzier version of the Detroit Economic Club speech he made September 10 on the Thursday night of the convention, it would have given you a very strong message that would carry through the weekend. Whatever damage was done by looking intolerant, etc., on the first three nights or during the platform week would have been very seriously ameliorated.

On the issue of family values, as I said yesterday, it got utterly out of our control. We thought that we could do a pretty good job of holding down the base, frankly. And I think if you look at the Vice President's speech and Bill Bennett's speech nominating the Vice President, there were ways of addressing these issues that would not have caused a firestorm among moderates and liberals and would have been perfectly congenial to our voters. We could have laid the groundwork for a theme that would have been useful during the general election.

We lacked a message and were in such a floundering state at the White House, we grabbed family values. The press jumped on it and people coalesced around it and attempted to make it more of a theme. But it was never an issue that could substitute for an economic message and be the dominant theme at the convention. Focusing on family values gave the press and the Democrats the opportunity to say that the Republican convention was obsessed with family values, gay rights, abortion, etc. I don't think any of us wanted it that way, but in the absence of a strong counter theme, it was easy to sell that argument. Certainly nobody thought it should be the dominant theme coming out of the convention.

So the Thursday night wasn't strong, and the next day the President went to Dallas, and said the Democratic platform didn't have G-O-D in it. Newt introduced the President Saturday with a Woody Allen crack. And so I would say that was really crucial, that Thursday through Saturday.

Susan Spencer: These things just seemed to sort of happen out of nowhere. Who was in charge of any of this?

Bill Kristol: Well, that's a very good question. There were tactical considerations about prime time which were being handled by people competently and professionally. There was very little strategic guidance about the message, and I think there was a bit of disconnect between the White House and the campaign. At this point you literally had a lame-duck White House chief of staff, there was no White House chief of staff for about a 10- or 12-day period, before Jim Baker came aboard, and this was an extremely important time politically. One incident revealed the trouble that can come from the lack of coordination. That was the Kemp/Weber attempt to write something about the budget deal into the platform. A deal was made on that that would have been perfectly adequate. It was reversed at the White House the next morning. This gave the story much more publicity and emphasized the rift between Kemp/Weber and Darman and Brady.* All of it was utterly unnecessary and happened because no one had the authority to make a decision.

Charlie Black: I found that out the hard way. One parenthetical thing before we go to Mary. Just think about this: as big a deal as you all made out of the Bob Casey thing at the Democratic convention, what would you have done if we hadn't let Pat Buchanan speak and Bay and Pat were down the street at the Sheraton raising hell with 1,000 people and all? Then our convention would have been a total disaster.

E.J. Dionne: The moderate, forward-looking Republican party, that's what we would have written about.

Fred Steeper: Just one research finding: the average bounce that Republicans get from their conventions is six points, and that's what we got from the 1992 convention. So if you just look at the numbers, there wasn't anything uniquely good or uniquely bad about this convention: the '92 convention gave us that six-point bounce and cut Clinton's lead

---

Editor's Note: Richard Darman, White House Budget Director, and Nicholas Brady, Treasury Secretary, advised Bush on economic policy and led the attack on Clinton's economic message. Jack Kemp, Secretary of Housing and Urban Development, blamed the Democrat-controlled Congress for Bush's economic problems.

from 23-25 down to 11-12. And that's the best we could hope for from our convention and it was accomplished. There was no boomerang; we did not fall back until a couple weeks after the convention with the brouhaha that you're discussing. We didn't gain any more, but he just held at 11-12. So you don't see a backlash in the data after.

George Stephanopoulos: E.J., let me just say something for a second here. I'm not certain I agree. We had this serendipity on Thursday night where both sides wanted the same headline Friday morning. They gave a speech the center of which was an across-the-board tax cut, which was modified Kemp/Weber. We were prepared to engage on the economy the next day. We were scheduled to go to the Detroit Economic Club the day after and nobody was sure how this was all running, but we were ready to engage on the economy. I think we were in the odd situation on Thursday night of both sides promoting the same part of the speech. I was on the phone all night saying, yeah, let's talk about that tax cut, please, let's talk about an across-the-board tax cut. It gets to be a long-term problem for the Republicans because even when they talked about the economy, they had nothing new or credible to say.

James Carville: We knew we wanted to go right to the most dramatic economic forum we could get the day after their convention. We decided that three weeks before the Republican convention. And understand, too, if we go to the Detroit Economic Club and give a speech about the economy and you go to Dallas to some fundamentalists and say the letters G-O-D are not in our platform, that's going to affect the post-convention press coverage on the thing.

Charlie Black: I do not take the responsibility for Newt. For the rest of it I'll accept responsibility.

E.J. Dionne: Let me throw out a question, maybe to Fred, about Bush's speech, which was long enough to suggest that Paul Begala probably wrote it. [Laughter] And the whole question was why was it so diffuse? What went into that speech, what was the thinking, if one could call it that, behind that particular speech?

Dave Carney: In regard to speeches and other kinds of decisions, there was a structural problem with the White House. We had a long discussion about that yesterday, and it existed until Secretary Baker came on board. I think it was exacerbated by the fact that this was an important speech so more people wanted to have input on it. Big speeches, little speeches, and a whole bunch of things, it was a structural deficit. We had a flawed structure at the White House during the campaign.

Mary Matalin: The lack of coordination and communication at the convention was worse than our dis-coordination in everything. Unlike 1988 when [Fred] Malek and his team were housed with and hourly communicated with the campaign, thereby by osmosis picking up the nuances of an evolving and dynamic enterprise, this convention operation was separate from Bond. If they had been with Bond, they would have picked up the nuances from a good political mind and they would be following the evolution. They had this set thing they were going to do, they were disconnected from us, they were disconnected from Bond, Bond and the campaign were disconnected, we were disconnected from the White House.

Do you want to know how these things happen? You know why we did that Dallas speech? To save money on the plane, we were going to be in Texas, so that was scheduled before the stupid convention.

And here's another thing we did wrong, if we can talk about our mistakes, because we were detached, at least nuance-wise, from the convention. We did not flexibly respond to the departure of Ross Perot. Our convention was set up for a three-way race and our post-convention activities were set up for a three-way race. When Perot pulled out, the Democrats just strategically responded. We didn't react. Moving our convention was like moving a battleship; we didn't adjust to going from a three-way to a two-way race.

Dave Carney: Just one point about the platform. The Republican party really isn't centrally controlled and we don't dictate from First Street on what's going to happen. The state parties have a tremendous amount of influence on who serves on committees and what they are and people who show up and get elected to county caucuses and district conventions. The platform committee members really came to Houston to write a platform, and we had hundreds and hundreds of amendments. They all sat through the committee hearings and they did the whole works. Of course we were concerned about having the platform work for the party and trying to keep the abortion language the same and we were successful doing that. But there wasn't some gigantic Machiavellian strategy that the platform would contain some predetermined doctrine. No one faction had more influence in the platform decision-making process than anyone else.

The number one biggest problem was that the media in this country is totally, absolutely, positively snowed by Ann Stone [Executive Director, Republicans for Choice] and her organization. You all thought that she was somehow going to be a big factor at the convention. She was not a factor at all. She snowed a lot of people but she basically couldn't get six state party delegations to sign a petition to get a floor fight [on the abortion plank]. It was a total, absolute snow job, not just on the media; a lot of people thought she had big clout. She has a direct-mail PR operation, and no organization whatsoever. She set up her trip to the convention for weeks ahead of time. That was the first negative thing that she had done that they had published. The whole build-up to that got tremendous coverage.

Dave Carney, Ron Brown, Ken Bode

E.J. Dionne: I want to ask Bill Kristol a question. What was the think-ing behind the Marilyn Quayle speech? I think that was the fourth speech Charlie was trying to remember that reinforced this theme. Can you talk about where that came from?

Bill Kristol: Well, let me say, I think that speech, standing alone, is defensible. It sailed into a wind that was already blowing with Buchanan and Robertson and caused one sentence in it to be interpreted in ways that might have been damaging.

Susan Spencer: You're talking about woman's essential nature, per-haps?

Bill Kristol: Well, that's an utterly defensible sentence. Reaction to that speech varied all over the place. A lot of conservatives didn't like it, and some nonconservatives did. But I don't believe it would have been a big deal unless the current was already so strong that this was an intol-erant, antiwoman, antihomosexual, etc., convention. I was responsible for the Vice President's speech and Bill Bennett's speech and I'll defend those, maybe more enthusiastically.

Ken Bode: Isn't it a little unusual for the vice president's wife to speak at the convention?

Bill Kristol: That was not our request. That was not Marilyn Quayle's request. She was happy to do anything she was asked to do.

Mary Matalin: The convention operators had this idea of the strategy of the convention, that we would have a sort of family night. And that's how the women, you know, the embodiment of family, got onto the agenda. Once the agenda is set, you're not going to go back to anybody and say, "Get off the agenda."

Bill Kristol: Mary's right. No one had asked us whether we wanted Marilyn to speak or speak before Barbara Bush. Just someone had the idea, oh, gee, Barbara Bush is popular, if she speaks, then Marilyn Quayle should speak and it would be woman's night, etc.

Let me make a point which I think will be helpful, in a more general way. It's my experience in politics that you get a sort of "Nixon going to Red China" problem. Let me take the abortion plank as an issue. I'm pro-life and I'm comfortable with the conservative end of the party. There was a respectable case made that we should have altered that plank a year and a half ahead of time simply to represent a more nuanced and in fact contemporary and true pro-life position, given the realities of 1992. That was ruled out because the President had this historical vulnerability with the right and there was a sense that we just couldn't afford to start playing around with this.

I think this was generally true of the whole run up to the convention. There are Republicans who are not instinctively comfortable with a lot of these issues and who perhaps overreacted in terms of trying to placate parts of "our base." If people had been more confident that we knew how to handle "our base" and could keep them happy, we could have done something with those issues that would have pleased the rest. In the general election campaign, I think the reason that the Vice President was able to move more toward the center on abortion than the President ever had was because there was this fundamental distrust of George Bush from the right that was left over from the 1970s and early 1980s.

Some of the operatives were so intent on "firming up our base," and the way they did that was, frankly, a little simple. There are ways to keep the base perfectly happy and have the votes come home in the end without being quite so dogmatically attached to certain phrases and clauses and individuals. So that's a broader perspective.

Charlie Black: Teeter, Malek, Bond, myself, the leadership of the campaign met with Craig Fuller and the convention staff and gave them guidance and input. But the fact is, it was a full-time job for months to construct a program with 128 speakers. It was not possible for Teeter, me, Mary, or Rich to be involved in every word written and said by each of 128 speakers.

Betsey Wright: Where did you get the number of 128?

Charlie Black: You're right, Betsey, one didn't show up and it was 127 when we did the research.

Paul Begala: One last point. The Republicans did well during most of that time, and the papers responded to Mary Matalin beating up on the press, not as a message to voters, but just working the press. I was gone from the end of our convention to the end of the Republican convention. The anti-family Clintons insisted I take a month off because my wife was having a baby. I came back and the difference was extraordinary: crowds were bigger and much more enthusiastic and much more receptive to Clinton and Gore. That I sort of expected from watching the coverage.

But the reporters, just observing you guys covering us, that worked. I think Mary and Rich convinced you that the reason you wrote good pieces about Clinton was not because he got these spectacular crowds in this summer campaign, but because of some other reason. And they were much tougher on us, at least just person to person, after the convention.

Howard Fineman: I think Bill made a key point when he said the operatives did not feel secure enough in their understanding of the party base to deal with it in a sophisticated way. I wanted to get Charlie's response to that, and also ask you who specifically you're talking about?

Charlie Black: Bill and I talked about this a dozen times over the years. He and I could sit down and rewrite that abortion plank, right to life plank, in 30 minutes, either one of us, make it a hell of a lot better philosophically, politically, and every other way. But the fact is, you can only change it at the convention in the platform committee after it convenes with 2,000 people sitting there breathing down our necks. So the simplest thing was just not to open Pandora's box and to have no change in the language. It was just a tactical decision.

Howard Fineman: But what about this larger point, that the people running the campaign, according to Bill, did not know enough about the makeup of their own party and feel secure enough in dealing with it to handle it skillfully.

Charlie Black: Well, as to platform and those kinds of issues, most of the folks there relied on me, and obviously I don't think I'm unsophisticated. I've got a hell of a lot of experience with the conservative base of the party. Now, again, there's a premise here that I don't agree with — that our convention was some kind of big disaster — and Fred gave you the numbers.

Fred Steeper: The perception that the Republican convention was too right-wing was the twenty-fifth most important concern that people reported to us.

Elizabeth Arnold: As Bill pointed out, there was the failure of the President to eclipse the convention with his own speech. And I'm having a hard time believing that this lack of communication was the reason that that speech didn't work.

Bill Kristol: I know how that speech was written ...

Charlie Black: Well, it wasn't a good speech.

Bill Kristol: I was up at the Vice-President's and we were very busy that week worrying about our side of it. I did go to the Houstonian Hotel once, Sam asked me to come over and it was really speech-writing by committee, unlike the problems Paul might have had. Paul at least was the chief speech writer and Governor Clinton himself presumably spent a lot of time on that speech and was able to give enough of a message through that 54 minutes and it prevailed. We really had four or five co-equals trying to write a speech.

Susan Spencer: Where was Bush in all this?

Charlie Black: He was a player in it. He wanted to do that review of the world that he started out with, which, as you remember, went 17 or 18 minutes. We probably wouldn't have had that long a review of international events, but that was his desire and it was his speech and his campaign, so he did it.

Bill Schneider: I just wanted to highlight something which I think was very revealing about this whole discussion. The Democratic convention was planned when there was a three-way race. And yet, all these Democrats have said to us that they were not planning a convention to play to their base despite the obvious temptation to do that in a three-way race. What came across to the press, and to a lot of others, I assume, was that the Democratic convention was doing exactly what you were doing, trying to go beyond their base — a lot of the speeches used the phrase, "we're all in this together." It appeared to be an open convention, very different from the Democratic past.

Charlie or somebody said, remarkably to me, that their whole convention was planned assuming a three-way race. I remind you, Ross Perot had been out of the race for a month before the Republican convention, it was a two-way race, and yet you people seemed to be obsessed with playing to your base.

Charlie Black: We still didn't have the base intact. It doesn't matter how many people are in the race if you're not getting the votes.

Bill Schneider: Wait a minute. By definition, if you play to your base, you're going to talk a language that says "Us versus Them" and that's going to come across to a lot of people, voters as well as the press, as divisive, harsh, and stigmatizing. In particular, the contrast between the two conventions is what I think made the Republican convention look bad to a lot of people.

James Carville: Everybody sitting at this table knows exactly what it is — both parties have a base. If something happens and that base is basically out of the mainstream, we try to get those folks without really trying too hard to get them, okay.

If it's the far right-wing base of the Republican party, if it's the far left-wing base of the Democratic party, any time that you have an eruption in their party or our party, and you have to go over there and affirmatively get those folks, you hurt yourself with the folks in the middle. It's happened to us in presidential campaigns, it happened to the Republicans this time. That's why a challenge, like a Buchanan challenge, and particularly when it festers, can be so destructive to a party, because the party wants to present itself in its most popular image. They made a decision — it's a rational political decision, I understand it — that after this happened, they had to go recapture these folks that were upset and energized as a result of the Buchanan candidacy. It has happened in our party before. I mean, this is not rocket science. For a long time, I have tried to say, they'll come along, we have got to go beyond that.

How do you energize your base, do you run a GOTV campaign, a broad-base campaign, etc., etc. That's all this is about. It is that simple. Yes, we said, let's make them pay the price for it. There was a whole concerted thing to make them pay a price for picking those votes up, just as if we had done the same thing, you would have been over there at the speed of light saying, look at that, it's the same old Democrats, you know, they're doing boom, boom, boom. That's what happens. I don't think it's much more complicated than that.

TV Strategies: Ad Wars

"I remember our stunned silence when we saw a 60-second spot ... that did not reinforce the notion that this man had an economic plan."

— Stan Greenberg, Polling Consultant,
Clinton/Gore Campaign

E.J. Dionne: We need to cover the debate over debates, we want to cover advertising. I would like to move to the Detroit speech because it seemed to have been designed to rectify some of the problems that the convention had caused, fairly or unfairly. It was a good speech, it had a lot of stuff in it you could run a campaign on, and you got off it awfully fast. I would just be very curious if the Republicans around the table could talk about the process that went into that speech, what you were trying to do, what happened with it, and did it work less well than I thought it did at the time?

Charlie Black: Well, we didn't get off it, we just quit getting covered on it. We spent several million bucks advertising on the same message. We spent almost a million dollars to put a five-minute version of it on television. Then we had two 60-second commercials that followed up on the same subject. Actually the President gave that speech every day. You were out there, did he ever miss a day?

Mary Matalin: Not only did he not miss a day, my job, the sophisticated job I had on the road, was to get him to hold up that book *[Agenda for America]*. That story I told the first night was a true story. I was pasting the front and the back together upside down because he refused to do it. But he gave the speech every day. And what you covered, not to be bashy, because it was partly our fault — we were addicted to always putting in one stupid Clinton line — he was wiggling or whatever the hell it was — and the headlines would be "Bush Goes Negative," "Bush Stays on the Attack." It just never got covered again. He had integrated it, and even when he was ad libbing, it was in every speech, he gave it over and over.

Bill Kristol: The weekend following the speech, the President's people changed his schedule to go to the National Guard convention in Salt Lake City and the press started asking, is Clinton going to go, etc., and we were into the draft thing. Basically the press focus changed to the draft and then to the debate over the debates very quickly after the Detroit speech. I think the press wanted to write about those stories and not about our plan.

Stan Greenberg: There's this constant innocence about the way the press deals with what we do day by day. We were most worried about that speech because we didn't think that ultimately people would re-elect George Bush unless he gave them a reason to believe he had something that he wanted to get done in his second term. The speech was a coherent speech with a coherent strategy. There was some fanfare. There was the million that you spent that night on the five-minute advertising. We were convinced you were going to do an economic-plan spot on television that week in order to reinforce the message. In fact we produced a spot to counter it, based on that assumption. I remember our stunned silence when we saw a 60-second spot which was this computerized-Bush-all-over-the-place spot, domestic Desert Storm, an impressionistic piece that did not reinforce the notion that this man had an economic plan.

The story that week was the draft. And in almost every speech that George Bush gave, he said something about the draft. Now, no matter whatever else you say while there's an unfolding story on the draft, if you put yourself in the middle of that story, that's going to be the news. We had moments in this campaign where we would warn the candidate, "Whatever you do, Bill Clinton, don't say the word Ross Perot, don't say that name, don't let it out of your mouth because no matter what else you say in that speech, you are going to be part of the Ross Perot story." You were in the middle of the draft story that week, and even though you spent a great deal of money, it was not reinforcing the notion that this man had an economic plan for taking this country forward.

Fred Steeper: That was a paid spot we called "What I'm Fighting For." I don't have the script for it here, but it's my recollection that it focused on three or four things that he wanted to accomplish in terms of domestic problems.

Frank Greer: It was amazing. They put a five-minute spot from the Oval Office on Thursday night, I believe, right after the Detroit Economic Club speech. I watched it with a focus group in Rocky Mount, North Carolina, and it was one of the most effective spots of the campaign. He offered a plan or an agenda, I guess we called it, for the future. People really responded to that. Mandy [Grunwald] and I were absolutely convinced — because they had changed their buy, it was going to be 60-second spots for next week — that you were coming on with a plan to reinforce the whole idea of the agenda. The spot you went on with didn't even mention the agenda, didn't even mention a plan.

Fred Steeper: Those spots were produced and cut and ready to go before the speech was given.

Frank Greer: And then, as Stan said, it became a week not about the economic plan or the agenda or whatever you called it, which we thought it was going to be, it became a week about the draft.

E.J. Dionne: Well, let's just follow up on that and include advertising in this. Can Frank talk some about how you put together what you did? On both sides, what stuff did you create that never made the air, what kind of themes did you throw away, that sort of thing? And I would like to ask somebody on the Republican side to talk about what looked to a lot of us like the diffuse nature of the Republican advertising campaign, especially compared with the very sharp focus in '88. Frank, why don't you go and then some Republican?

Frank Greer: George should also jump in here. First of all, as James said, we had done a lot of research, a lot of listening to voters, after the New York primary. From this we had developed a strategy for the general election. One of the things we decided to do was very carefully target 20 states that would be our electoral college majority, with a cushion. We also decided not to go on network television to begin with, but to focus our resources on those 20 states. We were fortunate. We had some states like California and New York that we didn't have to worry about and therefore we had the resources for adequate buys in those 20 states.

Originally we thought about going on the air with a 30-second spot, but Mandy said, "I think we need 60." The other thing that was amazing is, even with the resources you had, we were on the air two weeks early in nine of those 20 states, unanswered, unresponded to, and we went on with a 60-second spot that talked about the new spirit, that captured the sense of the convention and also the bus trip. We were able to define Bill Clinton's record in that two-week period, as well as our economic plan, putting people first, that George had put out. We mentioned things that Stan had already figured out were going to inoculate us, like welfare reform and moving people from welfare to work, which Bill Clinton had done in Arkansas. We did things that not only positioned us on the record, but also on what we wanted to do for the country in terms of the economic plan. And throughout the campaign, because of our careful targeting based on Paul Tully's excellent work, we were able to outspend the Republicans in every one of the targeted states.

Susan Spencer: Mary, why did it take the President's campaign so long to get on the air?

Mary Matalin: We were always debating when we could go negative because we had to get Bush's positives up. That was the point of those talking heads before the convention, which I don't think were effective, because they were without message. The problem is, when you get Madison Avenue guys, they're really creative, but they're not political, they're very slow, and they want to spend a lot of money. So that was a big struggle and they did not come up with an effective product, preconvention. Some of us wanted to go negative on Clinton, but the argument that won was that we have to get the President's positives up before we go negative — a legitimate point.

So that's why we came out after the convention, our spots having failed; they were like a tree falling in a forest, nobody heard them, they didn't do anything. That computer spot was right after the convention.

Fred Steeper: See, Republicans are very frugal with their money. So we decided, in order to save the money and have more towards the end, to wait until September 13 when the TV rates changed.

George Stephanopoulos: I think the period after the convention was a game of chicken. Both parties were trying not to go on the air. We finally went on at the end of August, I think only in about nine states. We had a base of 20, but we went on in about nine.

Fred Steeper: We waited for the rates to go down and that's how it happened.

George Stephanopoulos: Right. Before the rates went down, we were on in nine, and then immediately after we went up to about 20 with some regional. But you have to say the map was working against them. They couldn't afford to play in the states that we could play in, it turned out, because they had so many problems in so many states. They had to go network, which is inherently inefficient. We were able to forego network and instead take the 20 states that had been polled and targeted. We just focused on those states and we put all our media in it.

It turned out it made a huge difference in the nine states we were up in early with a positive economic message, because it gave us a bit of a mattress when the negatives started to hit. And then when we went to 20 states, we could expand on the theme of a different kind of Democrat and really hit hard on the positive parts of the Governor's record in Arkansas which were low tax and welfare reform.

We laid down a base so that when the Republican attacks on those very issues came in, people at least had some other information. They were coming into focus groups and saying, well, he moved 17,000 people from welfare to work.

E.J. Dionne: Is that an accurate description of the Republican problem as you saw it?

Fred Steeper: Yes, we presented our list of targeted states to our media buyer, who said, well, it would be more expensive to spot-buy in these 30 states as opposed to buying network. There was always a cut-off point at which it would be more efficient to buy totally spot, rather than network, but we never hit that point.

James Carville: I don't want anybody to get this impression, like we were sitting over there making wise decisions. We had tremendous strategic advantages when we went into this — big states like Illinois, New York, California that we knew were going to carry and we didn't have to spend any money in. We had a ten-point lead. They had to go and affirmatively kind of get the South Carolinas and the Virginias.

So we've got to be fair to ourselves. I'm not going to say that we didn't know what we were doing, but we were dealt a good hand and played it well. They were dealt a bad hand. I think we all agreed sitting there, that they had to go network. That was part of the reason that we spot-bought, to force them to go network because it got more inefficient.

George Stephanopoulos: We had some relatively nervous days when all the polls started to shift even though CNN changed their poll in the last ten days. But it was our strategy to say, okay, we have a 23-point lead in California, we're going to have to watch that come down. We're going to have to watch the 20-point lead in Illinois come down and just hold on. Try to keep calm. But we knew and we kept warning people that the national number was going to tighten up all the way. We also knew that if we just held onto our 20 states, it would be very nerve-wracking, but we would be okay.

Charlie Black: We made two tactical advertising decisions. One was a non-decision — we had to go network. You didn't have to be a genius, it's just arithmetic. As Fred said, we never reached the point where we could drop below the threshold that the network was more efficient.

Second, we believed, under Fred's advice, that there would be a lot of late decisions this year, which I think was borne out. So we did decide to gut it out and to hold our money and advertise later, which, you know, we got a pretty good surge going at the end until the special prosecutor got in the act. Content wise, our advertising sometimes left a lot to be desired, but tactically, I think we handled it about right.

George Stephanopoulos: That special prosecutor story was a complete red herring.

James Carville: I'm not going to speak for George, but you can't underestimate how valuable Stan Greenberg was to our campaign. If you think about it, a consequence of this is your national number is going to fall. It's one thing to say that. I'm sitting there watching that damn thing fall and I said, what the hell's going on here. We had some trigger-happy people around there. Greenberg kept saying, this is a natural consequence, but needless to say the candidate would call in very concerned when he saw the national number fall. Stan prevented us from doing a lot of dumb things at the end as the numbers started to come down some. He was really a big deal in this thing.

Ron Brown: I think what we might do is distinguish between cycles. When you analyze the media-buy data, what you discover is that this is an exact flip from '88. This time, the overwhelming amount of our TV money was spent on spot television, the overwhelming amount of theirs was spent on network. I think Dukakis in '88 was somewhere over 75 percent on network television, the least effective way to reach targeted audiences.

Part of it was that we had been dealt a good hand, I think, James. Part of it also is we did a lot of work identifying where our targets were and what messages worked with those target audiences. So we were very well prepared for those kinds of buys. And Frank, obviously, did more than reinforce that, he helped put it together.

George Stephanopoulos: To bring the analogy a step farther, it wasn't just in the targeting, it was in the substance of the ads. Every single one of our negative ads was almost exactly the same. Every single one of our negative ads had George Bush talking. And our positive ads all flowed from the same strategy as well. The other side was in trouble. It was a lot like the Dukakis campaign — they were switching ad campaigns every five or six days. And it hurt.

Frank Greer: From our research, we learned that when you had George Bush in the ad speaking in his own words, people did not perceive it as being negative. They thought he was making legitimate points.

In late May, I guess, or June, Mandy and I helped put together a team of some very good Madison Avenue people who played a very significant role. But we always had political coordination with Mandy controlling their efforts. And I think that you perhaps did not have that same kind of political advertising coordination. We had other political advertising firms, too, that were involved in the general election. But with Mandy and also through George and James, there was a strategy-driven paid media effort in which decisions were very carefully made, tested, and rolled out.

Fred Steeper: We did not have that coordination until Sig Rogish [media advisor] came in in late September.

Rather than jumping back and forth, there was one clear thread in our advertising from October 1 on and that was trying to paint the Governor as Governor Doublespeak, as someone who was being disingenuous on a number of issues and somebody that you couldn't trust. It started off with the gray-dot spot and it was followed by a *Time* magazine spot with a headline, and then some man-on-the-street ads. They ran for their seven or eight days. The *Time* magazine ad was not pulled because of a lawsuit threat. It ran its whole schedule. That may not have been the best way to attack Clinton, but it was the decision the campaign drafted, to go after the trust issue. The sequence of four spots starting October 1, right through to the end, kept pushing that theme, to give people reason not to trust, not to vote for Clinton.

George Stephanopoulos: It was too late. You should have taken September to do something, the same thing you were doing for Bush that you did against Clinton. I think you're right, in the last month you were pretty well focused.

Charlie Black: Susan, I know you don't want to get ahead, but give me 30 seconds. Another way of summarizing the whole campaign is that we did a pretty decent job on Governor Clinton negatives. But a prerequisite for winning was to establish some credibility for Bush on the economy, which he did not have the day we started the campaign, and we never got it. So it wouldn't have mattered if we had driven your negatives up another ten points, we probably still wouldn't have won without fulfilling that condition.

The Debate Strategy: Chicken Wars

"The chicken thing, I know it doesn't look very good on TV and intellectually, but the crowds loved it, the President loved it ..."

— Dave Carney, Director of Public Affairs and National
Field Director, Bush/Quayle Campaign

"That's the problem—a six-foot polyester chicken debating the leader of the free world."

— Paul Begala, Senior Strategic Consultant,
Clinton/Gore Campaign

Susan Spencer: Okay, we do want to try to do the debates here, otherwise we'll be hopelessly behind. People keep talking about the hands that were dealt, but did you make a mistake with the hand you had by not going along with the commission's plan and doing the debates rather than having this intervening month of argument?*

Charlie Black: Oh, I don't think so. In the end what we got out of the debates was about what we needed. Our biggest problem with the debates was Mr. Perot's presence, which made it impossible for us to win the debates.

E.J. Dionne: Even before Perot got in, my paper's line from the Clinton personnel during the campaign was, we knew we won the debate on debates when Bush engaged the chicken. When they were running their chicken campaign against you and finally Bush started arguing with a chicken, how did you let that go on so long? You know, why didn't you pull the plug? Related to that, a name has not been mentioned and so I won't mention it, but there is a new chief of staff at this point, and what influence did his arrival on the scene have on this whole discussion?

Charlie Black: There is some wisdom in the idea that agreeing to a debate schedule freezes the race, and we did not want to be frozen

---

*Editor's Note: The '92 debates were being arranged by the Commission on Presidential Debates, a private, nonprofit, nonpartisan group established in 1987 to assure the continuance of presidential debates.

because we were about 15 points down about that time. Second, we wanted more. Before Perot got back in, the ultimate proposal that we made for four debates on the last four Sundays was exactly the right thing for us to propose. We realized we wouldn't get it all. We got as much as we could, but I guess that we probably should have agreed a little bit earlier. We took a horrible beating on the East Lansing thing, which hurt us for the long term in Michigan.* We probably should have settled the whole thing before we let that happen. But it's a matter of a few days and I don't think it would have fundamentally changed the way we approached the debates.

E.J. Dionne: Until you had made the shift, it almost sounded like the campaign was sending the message that they didn't trust Bush in debate and wasn't that an unintended consequence of the way you were doing the debate strategy?

Charlie Black: Well, first of all, voters don't give a damn about any of that stuff, about the debate on debates. It did hurt us in Michigan; we didn't settle it in time to prevent their going in there and grandstanding and raising all that hell in East Lansing. Beyond that, I don't think the debate on debates affected voters a bit.

Stan Greenberg: We talk about measuring people's reactions to the convention. The main thing that people got out of the Republican convention is that George Bush did not go there to address the economy. Every time the President spent his time talking about debates or the draft or family values, voters were hearing, this is not a President concerned with the economy. The main impact, I believe, of the whole debate about debates was an enormous distraction from what you needed to be doing.

George Stephanopoulos: It was an automatic answer for us, any time an attack came, our answer, we didn't even engage a sentence. All we said was, okay, let's go debate.

James Carville: Once you all settled the debate, I said, gee, I got to go back to work. Because every time you would say something, it had what I call the opaque effect. Even though people didn't care, and ultimately the debate is not a voting issue, it blocks out other voting issues

---

Editor's Note: Scheduled for September 22, the debate at Michigan State was cancelled because President Bush rejected the one-moderator format, saying he preferred the panel of reporters arrangement of the 1988 campaign. Clinton went to East Lansing anyway and blasted Bush, saying, "If I had the worst record of any president in 50 years, I wouldn't want to defend it, either." Eventually a debate was held in East Lansing — the final presidential debate on October 19.

because you go there, you give a speech, you say Bill Clinton is a big spender, and we have this plan, and what do you get on the news? "Chicken George." All you get on the news is the Clinton people saying you won't debate. What I call the opaque effect prevents you from getting out other information that may drive voting behavior. That's why I think the issue worked pretty well to our benefit. You were not out there hacking away on us or talking about your economic plan, you were wrapped up in the debate on debates and it was a debate we were winning. Well, there were more things going on at the same time than just that, but I concede I wish we would have ended the debate on debates soon.

Paul Begala: Stan was right, the Governor always treated debates as an economic issue. "If I had that record on the economy, I wouldn't want to debate either." He never made it a macho thing — he's scared of me and that kind of crap — he always tried to take it back to the basic message which is, if I screwed up the economy, I wouldn't want to debate either, and that's the only reason Bush doesn't want to debate, he's a good debater, he just doesn't want to face the economy.

Charlie Black: With all due respect, you all weren't quite as nimble as you usually were when we laid out that four Sundays approach. It took you a couple of days.

Paul Begala: I was going to give you credit for that. That caught us off guard.

Charlie Black: The debate on debates was not a hundred to nothing for your side.

Susan Spencer: And how much impact did those chickens have?

Charlie Black: Oh, I don't know. I think Carney's ducks overshadowed the chickens.

Dave Carney: The chicken thing, I know it doesn't look very good on TV and intellectually, but the crowds loved it, the President loved it when people got up and heckled him. We should pay people to heckle the President.

Paul Begala: That's the problem — a six-foot polyester chicken debating the leader of the free world.

Dave Carney: I will agree, from the people point of view, it's not the best thing, but the dynamics of events, it isn't something that he's going to do. But as Mary said the other night, people would look for the chicken, you know, where the hell's the chicken? It's a great crowd response, it's the dynamic of being on the road that's different.

Mary Matalin: That's an important point because his mindset was very important in the decision-making process. Because we were in this capsule of having fun with the chicken, and Bush, in his mind, always wanted to debate, he wasn't afraid to debate, and the numbers saying that not debating was hurting us were coming in slowly, we let it go a little bit longer than we should have. I would say, "Not debating is hurting us," and he would say, "You have no data for that." In fact, the day that he made that announcement in Clarksville was the very first day we had some significant data that it was cutting against us — I remember calling Steeper from the tarmac. So, his attitude vis-à-vis the chicken was important because he was instrumental in developing the debate strategy.

George Stephanopoulos: Did you delay because you hadn't decided how many debates you wanted or because you didn't know if you wanted to debate?

Fred Steeper: There were several concerns about the debates. Charlie mentioned one, that it was a belief that it would freeze people's decision making, they would wait for the debate schedule. Another concern that entered the decision making was the belief on the part of the campaign that the press was against the campaign; that premise underlay a lot of our thinking. No matter what happened in the debate, the press would interpret it as a Clinton win. We know from past elections and past research on debates, the press's interpretation of what happens in the debate is extremely important. For example, no one knew that Gerald Ford made a mistake when he said that Poland was free of communism in the '76 debate. That all transpired the next day when the press defined it as a blooper.

George Stephanopoulos: The *press* defined it as a blooper?

Fred Steeper: The press pointed out that he had made an egregious error in something he had said. So there was great concern on the media's interpretation. The campaign's perception was that the media was biased against Bush and would, given a kind of a stand-off performance, interpret Clinton as a winner, giving him more of a boost. So that was why the avoidance of a debate — there was a real reluctance.

George Stephanopoulos: It's interesting, because we thought *we* couldn't win the debate because of the press.

Fred Steeper: For most audiences, the pro-Bush people said Bush won, the pro-Clinton people say that Clinton won. It's the next day when the national press said that somebody did an extremely poor job or an extremely good job, that's what affects the swing.

James Carville: We were scared of Bush as a debater; he was not an underestimated candidate in the Clinton camp. We didn't say goody, goody, we're going to go out here and debate this guy. There was a healthy respect. We saw the debates that he had, particularly in the Republican primaries in '88.

George Stephanopoulos: We had serious debates about not debating.

Paul Begala: While all this was going on, we were doing debate prep, going through tapes of old Bush debates. They were very, very strong. We put the best sections of the '88 primary and general election debates on a videotape that Clinton watched.

Stan Greenberg: The other side of this was, we believed there was a mythology that Bill Clinton was a very strong debater based on having been through the primaries. The combination of the belief that we would be strong and that Bush is bumbling, we believed it was very likely the press spin on the debates would be that Bush surprised people and that we would be hurt by that.

Ed Fouhy (standing)

E.J. Dionne: Can I ask Ed [Fouhy, executive producer, Commission on Presidential Debates] what his perception was from where he was sitting, watching this whole thing and being in the middle of it?

Ed Fouhy: We had two perceptions. One was that our strategy, which the co-chairmen, [Paul] Kirk and [Frank] Fahrenkopf had come up with, which we on the staff called a field-of-dreams strategy, wasn't working. [Laughter] We had made a decision on June 11 to go out with a fairly elaborate schedule of debates, part of which was driven by the need to raise the money. And so we had to find four venues that would come up with the $500,000 each to finance it. We found those, we set up a schedule, and it was immediately accepted by the Democrats. We never heard from the Republicans. Whether they did it consciously or not, the Republicans played a terrific mind game that was driving us crazy. The field of dreams had been built and nobody was coming. And by September 29, two of the venues had been cancelled — Michigan State and Louisville, Kentucky. That particular day was a deadline for a lot of logistical considerations; we were going to have to cancel the San Diego debate, which we knew you didn't want to do anyway because of where it was.

That was probably the lowest day that we had, the 29th, because earlier in the day Marlin [Fitzwater] had said, in a rare display of candor, in response to the press question, why aren't you debating?: "At this stage in a campaign, a candidate is driven mainly by his narrow self-interest." I thought, boy, that's the end of our little plan.

Charlie Black: We've been telling you all that for years. The commission had hearings in the first half of '89 and I was designated to testify for the President. I said right then, don't go out there and schedule a bunch of damn debates and just expect the candidates to show up because our philosophy is that once the nominees are chosen, they should talk to each other about what the debate format and system are going to be. Then maybe the commission would be an appropriate sponsor, but do not, I mean, we begged you three years ahead not to do what you did.

Ed Fouhy: It was the money, Charlie. We had to go out and raise the money.

Charlie Black: And I told Fahrenkopf a dozen times.

E.J. Dionne: I want to just turn for a second to Betsey. While all this is going on, Betsey, the press is dredging up all kinds of scurrilous stuff and I'm curious what you were dealing with at that point and what kind of stories you were combating and trying to knock down?

Betsey Wright: I spoke about this yesterday and it's still very difficult for me to do it. It was endless. From the legitimate press point, some analysis of this campaign has got to include the *Los Angeles Times* investment in investigating Bill Clinton. I don't believe that they would think that it was an investment that paid off. Almost nothing that they worked on ever ran as a story, but they put an enormous amount of money and effort into it. The rest of it was tabloids and a bunch of money-grubbing, dishonest people, an industry spawned for lying that spent a lot of money.

What's more important to me right now is to talk about the Arkansas record in the middle of this. Yesterday I mentioned that I'm going to spend the next year of my life trying to do something about the role of tabloid television on politics. And somewhere in this comes time to deal with the value and nondismissive nature of small states, especially ones that struggle.

There were days when I didn't feel that defending the honor of Arkansas against George Bush was any harder than it was defending it against people inside our own campaign. Diane Blair worked with me on the Arkansas record and she was there before I got to the campaign, working on it. Publicly I talked about what it meant for the President to attack a state, for "President Mary" to decide that at least 18 states in the country didn't count. And I took it very personally because I was very proud of the progress that we had made during the 12 years I had worked for Bill Clinton and the seven years I'd spent as his chief of staff.

It seemed like more than an anti-Southern bias went into this on the part of the media, both campaigns, plus the Perot operation. There was a dismissive attitude about the value of such a state and its people. There was an obsession about the disaster of the Arkansas record. I've heard it echoed again here today. Bill Clinton was a good governor. He made and he led incredible progress in the state. In this country we're supposed to care about improvement. There is something really wrong in a United States of America that puts values on states according to their size and wealth. And it was pervasive in this campaign. For me personally, the most difficult thing certainly was inside the Clinton campaign, because I never felt like they gave a damn about Arkansas. There were times when I didn't think Stan Greenberg believed Bill Clinton had ever done one good thing. It was a point of real tension, and one about which I still feel very strongly. We shared a great fear about the Arkansas record in the debate situation, but for different reasons — it never was a link between us.

Dave Carney: Well, I think that if his Democratic opponents in the primary had spent half an hour looking at the statistics of Arkansas to define Bill Clinton a little better, the Arkansas record would have been a tremendous weapon against Bill Clinton.

I come from a small state and I think the statistics as fair or unfair is irrelevant, they've always been used. If you take the Arkansas record and all the various groups and how they've done for 12 years or the Clinton decade, I think people would be appalled. As much improvement as there was, the statistics would not lead people to think he was qualified to lead the country. It has nothing to do with small states. If you came from California with those statistics, you would not be elected president.

I think that if the Democratic opponents had used the Arkansas record more effectively early on, we would have had a better chance.

Betsey Wright: David, with no personal judgment on you, it is impossible for me to believe that an American could say that about a hard-pressed rural state coming out of an agricultural decline, and claim that the statistics indicate failure. Saying that means you don't care about the kinds of Americans who live in those places.

E.J. Dionne: Can I bring Ross Perot into the race? We need to figure out what was going on in Ross Perot's head, if anybody can talk about this. The first question that interests me is, to what extent did Perot have in mind all along that this was what he was going to do? How did it happen that he got back in the race? Then we can also turn to the two campaigns to talk about how they went and kissed his ring before he got in.

Clay Mulford: The press conference when Mr. Perot re-entered the race was on October 1. As far as the meeting with Democrats and Republicans, my response on that was: "Sounds like an interesting idea, but there's no way they'll ever come." But they did.

On October 1 as soon as he announced he was going to re-enter the race, I got on the phone with CBS to try to start buying some air time. We were very concerned that at 7 percent in the polls, we could be marginalized and not get into the debates. We were hearing from the Commission; they wanted to know what our media buys were. The staff attempted to schedule appearances so that we would be visible enough to improve our chances of getting in the debate.

October 1 was a Thursday; over the weekend we had discussions with the Commission and with counsel for the Republican party, and with the Democratic campaign counsel, Tom Donilon. One thing that was not well known in the media is that the agreement, in essence, invited us and invited the commission to participate in the debates. Each of us could take it or leave it.

When I got the draft agreement, which I had difficulty getting, we took that as an official invitation and issued a letter to the commission, letters to Mr. Teeter and Mr. Kantor, saying we accept, we will be participating, let us know what the commission decides. We were afraid the commission would have difficulty developing a calculus that would show how we were different from the Libertarians and the New Alliance Party and so forth. And if we're at 7 percent and we're not making campaign appearances, we're not buying TV time, we're not visible, we could be marginalized and they'd have a difficult time getting us in.

So we issued the acceptance and faxed it out to every media person we could find, trying to get a story going that we had accepted.

George Stephanopoulos: If Ross Perot got up one day and said he wanted to be in the debates, he didn't care what the rules were, he would have been in the debates.

Clay Mulford: Well, we had an alternative that we thought that we could strong-arm it that way, but we didn't know where we would go in the polls. And at 7 percent, if we were going down to 6, to 5 to 4, it would be different from what happened. And we didn't really get much off of 7 until after the debates.

Actually, our understanding, and Ed [Fouhy] may know this better than anybody, was that there was a movement afoot over the weekend to allow us into the first debate and then to re-examine at each debate what our popularity was. But we wanted the commitment up front to be included in all of them.

E.J. Dionne: So we don't get bogged down in the details of the rules of the debates, I wanted to ask Tom Luce, do you think he really dropped out? What is your feeling about what he had in mind when he dropped out in the middle of the Democratic convention?

George Stephanopoulos: Can I make one comment about the debates? Because it has to do with what Fred was saying earlier about the press. We had disagreements, we thought the press was going to give you the debate, and you thought it was going to give us the debate. I think there was no way to know this in advance, but one of the lessons we learned from this campaign is that spin after debate doesn't matter because of the preponderance of polling and focus groups. That no matter what we said, CBS or ABC or NBC was going to go do a poll and that was it. I mean, the spin of the session became waiting for the poll to come back and that was all that mattered. So the press expectations in the future may not matter at all.

Ron Brown: On Perot in or out, I don't know what the commission view was, but I was a part of the negotiation. And there was never any doubt from either of the campaigns about Perot being out. We assumed he was in; the only question was, under what terms.

James Carville: If somebody could have figured out a way we could have kept him out, we would have done it.

Ron Brown: Sure. The terms we agreed upon were that he would be invited as a guest, he wouldn't participate in the rule making, in the scheduling, or in the site selection, but he would be invited to participate in the debates. That decision was made during the negotiations. I don't know what went on after that, but we always assumed that he was a part of the debates.

Perot Strategy: Dallas Wars

"The Republicans were scared that we would
go and they wouldn't go, we were scared that
if we didn't go and they went, all the media
would be there. That's all that happened."

— James Carville, Strategic Consultant,
Clinton/Gore Campaign

E.J. Dionne: What were the two campaigns making of Perot's moves? You said there was about a week and a half where he was sort of moving in, and I know that at some points the Clinton campaign still thought that he might end up endorsing you or doing some nice things for you. I suppose he did in the end anyway, but I wonder what was your perception of what was going on? What were you Republican guys doing, why did Baker meet with him? Just talk about it in that period from both perspectives.

Ron Brown: Well, I could start that because I'll tell you how it all began. Perot and I did "CBS Morning News" together in New York. He was coming out of the studio as I was going in. I had never met him before. We shook hands and talked about how pleased we were to meet each other. I said that I'd just be on for about five minutes, and asked if would he wait for me. And he waited. We went into a little dressing room and we just had a one-on-one conversation.

At the beginning of the conversation I said something like, neither one of us wants to see George Bush re-elected President of the United States and we ought to be spending all of our waking hours trying to prevent that from happening. He said, "You don't understand, I've got to talk to my volunteers." It was the same thing I'd heard him say on television. It made no difference that we were face to face — that was his response: "I'm not driving this, my volunteers are, and this is important to me and I've got to talk to them. By the way, why don't you come on down to meet with my people, we're about to set up a meeting, or why doesn't Mickey [Kantor] come or Bill come?" I mean, that was the basic conversation.

My understanding is that he picked up the phone at CBS and called James Baker, then flew to Washington and met with Baker. And that's how the thing got rolling, as well as I can reconstruct it. I don't think there was anything planned by him, no master strategy. I think it came up in a conversation. He followed up on it, pursued it, and that was the beginning of everybody traipsing down to Dallas to meet with his people.

James Carville: This thing was like a game. If you weren't talking to somebody in the Perot camp, you kind of didn't count. The truth of the matter is, I let the Perot people speak for Perot, but the person I was talking to said, "Hell, I don't have no idea what the son of a bitch is going to do, just do what you got to do; and go on about your business."

Tom Luce: You were talking to the right person. [Laughter]

George Stephanopoulos: There was one person in the campaign who never was snowed at all. Hillary Clinton was warning us from August, to her credit, that he never got out, that he was going to get back in, that we had to take him seriously. I was blind to a lot of it, as a lot of people were, but she, from very early on, saw what he was doing and sounded the alarm quite often.

Orson Swindle: Let me talk about that, from the perspective of not being involved in the first half or first phase of this thing, and being a longtime acquaintance of Mr. Perot in a very different relationship from politics.

I talked to Ross after the grieving session there on July 16 and as one of the few people representing volunteers around the country who knew him, I was totally convinced that he had no intention whatsoever of ever coming back into that race. I was deeply puzzled, and we talked about this last night a little bit, about how he could be so "insensitive" to the Bush campaign to drop out on this significant day. I couldn't help but wonder, why would he *not* be insensitive after they just spent the last three weeks cutting him to ribbons, but that's irrelevant.

But I was astounded that he showed so little sensitivity to the volunteers that he didn't confer with any of them on this decision. I was deeply disturbed by his apparent preoccupation with something that he did not share with me, a very deep personal concern. He did say, "Orson, it has to do with my family and I can't talk to you about it." From everything I could interpret from what I saw and heard, I was convinced he would not run.

We went through that grieving session and got together two weeks later. The group that had been around him and gotten so much attention said, we want to go forward with this thing just in case, we would like to get him on the ballot in all 50 states, we're set up to do it, we want to do it. He said okay. He conceded.

As we got into September, September 18, when we got Arizona, I, as a friend, was deeply concerned again about my friend's credibility. I went to him and said, "Ross, you don't have any alternative but to get back into this race, for three reasons. Number one, your personal credibility, you made a commitment. Number two, there are five and a half million people out there who have sacrificed beyond anything that you can comprehend, Ross." He never fully comprehended. In all fairness to him, I don't think any of us can comprehend the kind of emotional out-pouring and sacrifice that went on because of this unique phenomenon. And then I said, "The third reason I think you got to get back in is because it would be good for the country. These other two candidates are not going to address the issues that you believe are important." I happened to believe they were important, too, and although I didn't agree with everything he proposed, I certainly felt there ought to be a legitimate discussion. I said, for those three reasons, you have to come back in, and I kept pushing and pushing on a very personal basis.

But I don't think, in contrast to what George said about the insight of Hillary Clinton — perhaps in a sense she was clairvoyant and did see it — but I don't think at the time he pulled out, he intended to come back in.

George Stephanopoulos: He spent seven million dollars in August and he spent probably double that in September.

Orson Swindle: That was to accomplish something, to fulfill a commitment.

George Stephanopoulos: But to what end?

Sharon Holman: Basically to support the volunteers, primarily New York. We knew New York was going to be a challenge. They wanted to get on the ballot and they were working hard.

Clay Mulford: Most of that money was for payments made for expenses incurred prior.

Orson Swindle: A lot of that was prior.

Ken Bode: But there's no question that a determined effort went on throughout the month of August to make sure that he was on every ballot.

Orson Swindle: I just said that.

Ken Bode: But you don't do that for any reason?

Orson Swindle: He had a reason. Well, we'll never resolve that because I don't know the inside of his mind, nor do you. But my impression, from a very personal discussion, was a man who was deeply concerned about what he perceived to be a threat to his family, at least that's what I interpreted, and he was not getting back in the race.

Ken Bode: Orson, are you satisfied now that the reason that he got out of the race, that family reason that he told you he couldn't talk about in July, was in fact what we later found out on "60 Minutes" — this intent to disrupt his daughter's wedding?

Orson Swindle: I think it is one of the reasons, and, in my mind, probably the most dominant. I can understand how it would be.

Ken Bode: That he reliably believed that this Republican dirty trick was about to happen?

E.J. Dionne: What was happening on the Republican side with Perot and how did you feel about his getting back in the race?

Susan Spencer: And did either party ever consider stiffing him at this meeting in Dallas?

Charlie Black: No, no, there was no point in that. It was obviously going to be a big covered event, so you might as well go.

We wish he hadn't gotten back in, but we also weren't sure exactly what he was up to, whether he would stay in. We thought there was at least some danger that at some point he would endorse Clinton. He was unpredictable. We just assumed he was going to be in there the rest of the way. But anytime we had the chance, vis-à-vis letting him in the debates or showing up in Dallas and those kinds of things, we tried to be as nice as we could. We didn't know what he was going to do.

Dave Carney: It wasn't that we could do anything to influence Perot or the top leadership. Our goal was to show respect for the Perotistas out there, but we wanted them to vote for us.

Charlie Black: They were going to be watching TV to see if we showed up and if so, what we said and how much attention we gave it and what stature.

Dave Carney: What we didn't want is 50 guys going back saying, Bush people are too good to come see us and the Clinton people came down and they had some good ideas for change. We wanted to at least get in on it, because most of the people in that room would like the things we had to say. They would have an opportunity to hear first hand what our ideas were, what our goals were — less government, that kind of stuff. We went through their book. He had something like 98 or 96 things, you know, 80 of them were right out of our platform and about 16 or so we didn't agree with, mostly tax increases, which a lot of the Perot people did not agree with either.

So, we thought we would at least get a fair shake with the supporters. And we wanted to show respect. We wanted to make sure that the five million volunteers wouldn't be antagonistic to us. It was part of the effort earlier on when we tried to mess up Perot a little bit, you know. We didn't want to put down his supporters, we didn't want to be so heavy-handed. That wasn't our goal because we didn't want the people supporting Perot to be mad at us. It didn't work very well in the spring and we certainly didn't want to have all these people, you know, pissed off at us in October.

Tom Luce: Can I just ask of the two campaigns whether or not there were direct-mail efforts ever directed specifically to the Perot petition signers? The three, four, five million people, was there ever any consideration of that plan, and was it implemented in selected states or nationally?

Dave Carney: We tested your list in Texas and Florida. What we found was totally opposite to whatever he said Perot people were. In Florida, they were more active, they were more likely to be Republicans, they voted in more elections than the average voter and so on. We were going to reach those people with our regular list, so we didn't go to the expense. In Texas, a similar thing, although they weren't primary voters, they were active, they were involved, they were demographically the same kind of people that we were going to reach through regular mailings.

Tom Luce: So you didn't do any specific mail piece?

David Wilhelm: We did not do it, although we did have staff people hired to reach out to your key Perot state leaders after he withdrew. In fact, along the way, we held many press conferences.

Stan Greenberg: It is interesting, I think, that both of these campaigns wanted the same outcome, which was Perot not coming back into the race. We weren't looking for a Perot endorsement. For us, the issue was the definition of a race. We wanted a clear choice versus more of the same. We didn't want to muddy the waters on the economy. Perot entering the race created news on other kinds of stories; we wanted the focus on Bush and Clinton.

Susan Spencer: Was meeting with Perot in Dallas considered a serious opportunity to discourage him from entering the race?

James Carville: No. The Republicans were scared that we would go and they wouldn't go, we were scared that if we didn't go and they went, all the media would be there. That's all that happened. It was not any more complicated than that.

George Stephanopoulos: Also, it was all borne out. You knew, the minute we had a debate prep.

Mary Matalin: And what I need to ask, Orson, were those people in that room real volunteers? We were not received in a friendly way, and the questions quickly deterioriated, except yours, yours were serious. I did not get the sense from sitting up there that those people were real volunteers.

Orson Swindle: Well, first off, let me clear that issue up. Our staff in Dallas to run this national campaign was about 35 people, and pay rates were low. But of the group in Dallas that day, there may have been four people from around the country who were being paid. That was actually a carryover from phase one where, as they were gearing up, Ed and

Ham came in. People were hired to run the state campaigns, and maybe four of them might have been in that room. The rest were literally volunteers, there's no other way to define it; these were people who had given up jobs or were doing this in their spare time.

Dave Carney: Did their state offices get like 7500 bucks a month to operate?

Orson Swindle: After July 31.

Clay Mulford: That was solely because Mr. Perot felt that he had pulled the rug out from under these people. He was surprised by the uproar that occurred after July 16.

Orson Swindle: He was totally overwhelmed.

Clay Mulford: He wanted to give them something to keep going. That was the start of United We Stand, America. You had people like Orson who had come on board two weeks before this and ...

Orson Swindle: I resigned a job two weeks before, after being promised we were in this for the duration and two weeks later, I was sitting there saying what the hell have I done. As for the $7500, after he pulled out, he was very stressed by this thing, emotional, as were the people at the follow-on meetings — they were somewhat nutty. I had never met any of them and I said, "What have I gotten myself into?" He said, come back after a week or two and let's talk about what we can do as a group for the country. He never departed from that approach, much to his credit, and I still to this day think that the thing that drives Ross Perot most of all is his concern for this country and its welfare and the people.

We came back and we said, Ross, we'd like to form an organization that will carry on whether you decide to come back in the race or not; it will be there, if you decide to do it. That's what he provided money for. It had to come under the election umbrella because that was already in place and we were tied to it.

My own view, and I publicly stated it, was, I hope the man comes back in the race, I think it would be good for the country. So for two months I was trying to hold the volunteers together and say, hey, just be calm, let's see what happens, and we'll go forward and try to organize this thing to be an advocacy group that will have a life of its own. In the meantime, Mr. Perot might come back in, and I hope he does. That's pretty much the way it evolved.

Sharon Holman: Well, I want to make the point that one of the factors that we've not taken into account here is that Perot's book* had come

---

*Editor's Note: United We Stand: How We Can Take Back Our Country. New York: Hyperion, 1992.

out, and was running right at number one on the paperback best-seller list.

E.J. Dionne: With a little help from Mr. Perot?

Orson Swindle: His purchases were not registered in the tabulation for best-seller. That idea is absolutely incorrect. It sold on its own. Whoever says that discredits the American people by even suggesting it.

Sharon Holman: He did purchase the books. Those were given to the state coordinators, but Orson is right, the tabulations were only of those books ordered by the various book wholesalers and so on. So it really wasn't helpful to him. But it had a huge impact on where we were and the interest in the economic plan. Plus Arizona turning in and all the volunteers becoming really excited saying, okay, we've done our part, now what about you? That was the point I wanted to make.

Bill Kristol: Just for the record, I think someone said that both camps did not want Perot to get back in. I don't think that was the universal feeling. On our side, at some point after mid-September, I, and the Vice President for that matter, did not believe that Bush/Quayle could actually get 51 percent of the vote, and, therefore, we wanted Perot in.

James Carville: I want to say something about Perot's people. They are serious people. We were down there, we did it because we were scared by what they did. You have to acknowledge that these people put an independent candidate on the ballot in 50 states and ended up with 19 percent of the vote. Perot's people accomplished something important in American political history. We went there for the same reason that the Republicans did — our own self-interest. But given the magnitude of these people's accomplishment, they certainly deserved to hear from presidential candidates.

Clay Mulford: Let me add one final thing, just to answer Bill [Kristol]. It's interesting to hear his remarks. The Democrats' presentation was much more substantive, much more focused on economic issues. The quality of the questions from the volunteers was very high and perhaps surprising to the people that you all sent down; it was a very elevated discussion.

As for the Republicans, we didn't think they had read the book, we didn't think they knew what the issues were, their presentations were very anecdotal. What we got out of it was, well, I guess the Republicans want us to get in and the Democrats want us to stay out.

Mary Matalin: For the record, in that room were a bunch of Kemp lovers and Kemp is an anecdotal speaker.

Orson Swindle: Absolutely wrong, they were not a bunch of Kemp lovers. Let me make a comment here. I'm a long-time supporter of Jack

Kemp and I will be, perhaps, in the future. But I personally walked the damndest tight line I could because I felt if I tended to try to shift that group in one direction, I was going to lose half of them. I felt it was very important that we keep what I call the beauty of it, and that was a very bipartisan, wide spectrum of political philosophies. I'll bet you there weren't three people in there that were avid Kemp supporters, and I know them all.

I made one statement at the end; Bob Teeter got up there and [his remarks were] quite hypocritical, frankly, and it sort of incensed me. I agreed with Bill a year ago, that George Bush was not going to win this election. I think he, as a leader, had lost it, unfortunately, because I happen to think George Bush is a fine man, but the circumstances were such that he could not win.

I told Ross Perot before I committed, I will not be a party to intentionally electing Bill Clinton as President of the United States because I fear he will not be able to deal with his own party leadership in Congress. It would be an open ticket for disaster, I was quoted as saying, and rightly so on that.

But in that meeting at the end, I asked, why in the name of God has the Republican party, the Bush administration, kept Jack Kemp under wraps for three years when he could have made a difference by developing a more populist movement, which our movement was, to keep the Republican administration in office. That's where you got that impression.

James Carville: Orson, do you really think Jack Kemp was under wraps for three years?

Orson Swindle: Essentially, yes. I think Ross brought him out.

Mary Matalin: I just want to state for the record that the campaign, even though we thought the meeting was — scam is not too strong a word — we took it seriously. Phil Gramm was very substantive, very lengthy, very deep, and very thoughtful in his presentation. From our vantage point, sitting on the stage, it looked like whenever Kemp said anything, he got good audience response and sort of followed his nose on it. I don't want you to think that we didn't take it seriously. We did a lot of preparation and read the book inside out, and we were prepared for that specific audience. However, from the outset, our impression that it was a scam, was reinforced. That's all.

Orson Swindle: If it was a scam to help Jack Kemp, then perhaps there's a lesson to be learned there by Republicans. If what he said was well received, that's probably what should have been done for a long time before.

CHAPTER SIX

THE GENERAL ELECTION II: THE DEBATES

"After he watched the performances on Thursday night, Dan Quayle believed the election was unwinnable."

— Bill Kristol, Chief of Staff to Vice President Quayle

The final half-day's discussion was moderated by veteran conference participant David Broder, associate editor and national political correspondent, *Washington Post*, with questioner Elizabeth Arnold, national political correspondent, National Public Radio. The session covered the final four weeks of the campaign.

The Discussion

David Broder: Elizabeth, Charley, and I caucused, and what we are going to try to do in this last time block is first, cover the presidential debates. We thought we would go through the sequence of the three presidential debates and then come back and pick up the vice presidential debate. We'll use that as a vehicle to talk a bit about the role of the vice-presidential candidates generally in the campaign. We hope to do that in 45 minutes.

The second 45 minutes we want to talk about the closing stage, the postdebate stage, of the campaign, what was happening there, and why it was happening. If we can do that also in 45 minutes, then we will have an hour at the end to talk about some of the broader themes and implications of this election, for the Republicans and for the Democrats, who now pick up the responsibility of governing. We also want to take up the question of those 20 million people who voted for Ross Perot, and where they fit into the future of American politics.

Elizabeth Arnold: We heard this morning that the Clinton folks thought that the President was a stellar debater, and the Bush folks basically thought that no matter what they did, and what the President did, the press would say that he had lost. David and I have agreed that there were three noteworthy moments in the first debate, and correct us if you think we are wrong. The first was the Prescott Bush line,* which I understand was intended to be even tougher than it came out. The second was when the President mentioned that Baker would be in charge of domestic policy.

James Carville: It wasn't that big.

Elizabeth Arnold: The third was the appeal of Perot's one-liners. So, if all three camps can talk a little bit about the strategy going in, and then the strategy coming out.

George Stephanopoulos: We kind of knew, from our first practice session, that Perot had a very good chance of winning the first debate. The dynamics made him almost impossible to beat, because whenever we would get engaged in something with Bush, Perot had a choice. He could scold either one or both. He could pile on, or he could just pull out and do some kind of a one-liner, which he had always done, and make himself look apolitical or above politics, or outside of Washington.

Charlie Black: And neither of us was going to take him on.

James Carville: You could see ten minutes into the first practice session. You could see it was a real problem.

Paul Begala: I love it. We had a first practice session early on. We took this very seriously. We asked Tom Donilon to head up our debate prep team. Tom is a big guy in Washington, physically, but also in terms of stature, a guy who we have a lot of respect for, who had done this in prior presidential campaigns. Mike Synar, the congressman from Oklahoma, played Mr. Perot. He had a tough political campaign of his own back home, he spent a lot of time in Muskogee and environs, and he had read all Perot's stuff.

Bob Barnett, a Washington lawyer who had been playing Bush for twelve years, portrayed the President. We took it very, very seriously. There were a lot of briefings, and a lot of time went into it. So, all these characters were ready, and the first time we did a run-through, James is exactly right. Synar, as Perot, just mopped the floor.

Editor's Note: "When Joe McCarthy went around this country attacking people's patriotism, he was wrong," Mr. Clinton said. "And a senator from Connecticut stood up to him named Prescott Bush. Your father was right to stand up to Joe McCarthy. You were wrong to attack my patriotism."

George Stephanopoulos: It was hard to break out of that. Barnett played Bush two ways — either laying back and kind of being grandpa and not going on the attack, and also doing a fairly brutal Bush. Either way, it was problematic for us. The final thing we tried to go for was one of the moments you heard of. We actually had two that we really wanted to have happen, and they both happened in the first ten minutes.

Elizabeth Arnold: The first being?

George Stephanopoulos: "You've had your chance — we've tried it your way for twelve years." And then the Prescott Bush thing — I don't know about that one being tougher. It was word for word, the way we wanted it.

David Broder: Charlie, what happened on your side, and what did you want to do in that first debate? How much of it did you get done?

Charlie Black: I think, as a general rule, we really wanted to use the debates to show some differences. A lot of people didn't understand the differences on the issues between Bush and Clinton. This is a cliché — but to have the President show leadership. People liked Bush personally, but they'd just given up on him as a leader in a lot of cases. We wanted him to be knowledgeable and in command as much as he could. In drawing those differences, you always have to be careful with Bush, because he can't get too negative, or too tough, because then he goes over the line and comes across as shrill. You've seen him do that at some rallies when he gets carried away. So, the coaches, which didn't include us, had a tough job of preparing him to take opportunities to draw differences and take Clinton on, but not to go too far.

Those were the general goals. The news we were going to make out of the first debate, he just muffed. It's no secret, he muffed his line on the Baker thing.

Elizabeth Arnold: You just heard James say he didn't think that was that big.

George Stephanopoulos: The Baker thing was bigger the day after. There was this whole big buzz in the press about how Jim Baker is going to go give the economic speech, and that struck us as the strangest thing we had ever read in our lives. You know, the President is out there hitting Clinton on Vietnam, doing the dirty political work, and *Jim Baker* is going to give the big economic speech.

James Carville: I said: "I don't want to be out there rolling around in dirt with Charlie Black every morning. I'm going to give a speech and let Clinton do that."

Charlie Black: The fact is, and obviously you noticed, that Baker didn't give that speech.

James Carville: It didn't go unnoticed.

Charlie Black: The fact is, the President had a line, and he never got exactly the opening that he wanted, or that he thought was appropriate, to say, "I'm going to have a new economic team. I'm going to work full time with this team beginning right after the election, and Jim Baker will coordinate it, flesh out the program described in the Detroit speech and pre-sell it to Congress." I don't remember the term, "economic security council," but it was something similar. This was a clear signal that Darman and Brady and everybody were going to be gone, there would be new people, and that Baker would be in the next administration. But he never got it out.

George Stephanopoulos: But even if he got it out, let's assume best case, it was a structural problem. It's an admission of failure. Even if it went as perfectly as planned, we have a ready-made attack. If it's such a good idea, why did it take — the Bush line on Carter — why did it take you three and a half years to do it?

Charlie Black: It wasn't supposed to be a home run. It was just supposed to be a little newsmaker, to get us over the hump a little bit, about having absolutely no credibility on the economy. He did a decent job in that debate on some of the Clinton stuff, but he muffed that.

Stan Greenberg: But one of our main concerns was, what was going to happen right at the front of the debate because with Perot going first and the President going last, in the practice debates it became apparent that the President could set the tone — whether he was going to be grandfather or whether he was going to be aggressive. We were determined in the first round to do something that would push the President back and set a tone for the debate, where we would look strong and show leadership. So, we used the opening position to try and set the tone.

James Carville: Clinton is a notoriously slow starter in most debates. We always emphasize, towards the end, we've got to get out and shoot hard, go ahead, and grab it hard. But he almost always would start pretty slow, and I think we saw that in New Hampshire, and in the other primaries. He'd end a lot better than he'd start.

George Stephanopoulos: The other big thing for us going in was that there had been this idea developing in the press, about ten days before the debate, that Clinton couldn't control his temper. We thought that Bush was going to try to rattle him no matter what, provoke some sort of blowup. Clinton spent a lot of time staying focused on the things we wanted to do.

Elizabeth Arnold: What about Perot? Was there any debate prep done at all?

Orson Swindle: I felt inadequately prepared to come in and exchange comments with these two well-oiled political machines, but having heard my Republican friends speak, I feel a little less inadequately prepared.

Charlie Black: We would have been better off just to put him on the plane with Perot and fly in there and start a debate.

Orson Swindle: But back to the "inadequate" phase of it, I have no idea how Perot prepared, other than what he said to you. I would defer to Clay and Sharon. I doubt if they know much more than that. I was totally confident that the man would be superb — he always is. He's quick of mind, and he did exactly what I thought he would do, really well.

Clay Mulford: I was delighted that I could spend 30 or 40 minutes with him the day before the debates. I thought that was an unusual concession on his part to go over a couple of things. I'd prepared a list of issues that might come up. I think he believes that the system would be more productive if there were more head-to-head conversations between candidates and less prep and less theatrics. He was not going to permit any kind of packaging or preparation that he thought would depart from his ideas on the correct structure of a presidential exchange among presidential candidates.

Sharon Holman: Bottom line — against canned answers. We had no choice.

Clay Mulford: No lines were discussed.

Sharon Holman: Let Ross Perot be Ross Perot ... it was very effective.

Clay Mulford: If I had said, "Here's a good line you might want to use," I would have departed right after Ed [Rollins].

Sharon Holman: And none of those lines that you referred to, Elizabeth, were planned in advance. My own thinking is that Mr. Perot is so quick and has such a terrific sense of humor, and that, truthfully, had not come out during the campaign.

Clay Mulford: On the campaign side, you're hitting on one of our objectives, although they weren't communicated to him. There was this perception that he was an oddity, and that people who were supporting him were odd. We just wanted his personality to come through, and I think it did. I think the polling after the debates show that he'd won, and there was a tremendous change in the positives/negatives. That meant to us we'd won. We went from two-thirds negative/one-third positive to an almost overnight inversion, which is a pretty remarkable achievement.

Fred Steeper: I don't think there is any doubt that you won the first debate.

David Broder: What did the first debate cause you to try to do, or try to change, for the next one?

Paul Begala: We were looking forward to the second debate. We couldn't believe that the Bush people agreed to a debate where real people would be questioning them. It was Bill Clinton's idea. When we realized there would be more than two debates, the Governor told Bruce Lindsey to interrupt the negotiating meeting and say that if there were going to be more than two, we wanted at least one of them to be real people asking questions, like at a town hall meeting. When the word came back that the President's folks had agreed to it, we were hooting and hollering. We couldn't believe it.

Fred Steeper: From what I know, or listened to, or watched in rehearsals, I think there was a sense that that format would allow more give and take. The President was prepared to be more aggressive than he was in the first debate. And we did not anticipate, or at least I didn't sense that the campaign anticipated, how much of an iron hand moderator Carole Simpson was going to use.

George Stephanopoulos: It wasn't her. It was the audience.

Fred Steeper: Her interest seemed to be more to get as many questions as possible out of the audience, rather than having the candidates speak. Somehow the audience's interest was more important than the interests of the three campaigns. The President sensed that right at the beginning. You could tell that she didn't want give and take among the candidates. She wanted to maximize questions from the audience. There was a question from the audience, candidate respond, candidate respond, candidate respond, the end, go to the next question. The President was prepared, and prepped, to engage Clinton more one-on-one, be more aggressive.

George Stephanopoulos: He tried that, and the audience stepped on it.

Fred Steeper: He sensed that that would go over poorly with that audience, so he backed off and his responses were wooden.

Dave Carney: She [Carole Simpson] spent almost an hour with the audience beforehand, getting them ready, screening the questions. She asked the audience not to talk about this or that, that's not appropriate. She programmed the audience more than any crowd has ever been. The President has done very well in the town meeting format all over the country. He loves it.

Fred Steeper: Our dress rehearsals for Richmond were much more interesting, much livelier.

Linda Wertheimer, Carole Simpson, Elizabeth Arnold

Dave Carney: She put a very strict damper on that audience.

Ed Fouhy: I'd like to dispute what David Carney just said. Carole Simpson did not ever say, "You're not going to ask that question."

Dave Carney: No, she said, "I'm not going to call on you if you're going to ask that question."

Ed Fouhy: I was in her ear throughout, and I was telling her who to go to next. To suggest that somehow those questions were screened is inappropriate, it's simply not true.

Dave Carney: She spent almost an hour before the …

Ed Fouhy: There *was* an hour beforehand, and I'll tell you why. We didn't know what time the debate was going to be. Do you remember that there was a baseball playoff? We didn't know if it was going to be at seven or at nine. I had to be prepared, as a producer, for a seven o'clock broadcast. So we brought those people to the campus at 3:30, and we had to do something with them. We had not anticipated quite as long a wait, but we were very concerned that they were getting very restless. And also that about 350 had shown up, and we had only about 200 seats.

So we brought them in, partially so that we could have a camera rehearsal. It was a very challenging television production, and no one there had had an opportunity to run it through. I was very concerned that we were going to have some production problems. So we went through a kind of rehearsal for the crew, but what went on between Carole and the people in the audience had nothing to do with what went on during the debate itself.

Dave Carney: Well, it had to do with group dynamics. You have people sitting there for five hours, with the way she talked to them, and the interaction. I'm not complaining, I'm just saying ...

Ed Fouhy: I'm hearing criticism of Carole which is wrong. The choice of Carole Simpson was a joint decision between the Republicans and Democrats. She was mutually agreed to.

Dave Carney: I'm not complaining. I'm stating this set of facts.

Ed Fouhy: She had no idea what I was going to say to her next. I'd say to her, "Go to the woman in the red dress, over your left shoulder." Because of the fact that I could then say to the guy in the truck, "We're going to go over to the woman in the red dress next. Get a camera on her."

Charlie Black: That's instructive to me, because I stood in there and watched her going through that dress rehearsal. I did think there was a definite element there of her having in mind what question to allow these people to ask. If you were making those decisions and not her, that obviates part of the complaint.

Ed Fouhy: Only one question was screened in advance, and I did that. I was concerned that they were going to be too shy at the beginning, so I looked around and said, "Does anybody have an opening question?" A guy down front had one that struck me as being a pretty appropriate question. He was also where we could get a good shot of him, and so he was first. But after that, it was all ad lib.

Mary Matalin: One teeny point on this. And I love Carole, and this was inadvertent on her part, but it goes to group dynamics.

A guy stood up at the beginning and said, "I want to ask a question of Mr. Perot, but I don't want to put George Bush on the spot." And this was not an anti-Bush thing, but the group dynamic of the audience inferred that it was. She said: "We are here to put these guys on the spot. I want you to put the President on the spot." And she meant generically, "put these guys," but the audience laughed, and they took it as "Let's attack Bush." I'm being a little sensitive about this.

James Carville: It was part of a media conspiracy.

Mary Matalin: No, no, come on. I'm not really saying that. There was a group dynamic that allowed that guy with the ponytail to think he could get up there and actually do this thing. We didn't think that you set up the ponytail guy or anything, but that hour of preparation — James, quit making that face. You were not listening to her. [Carole Simpson].

Frank Greer: The second statement from one member of the audience really had to do with whether or not they wanted this to be a

debate about the issues or whether they felt the campaign was too negative. And that really set the tone. I do believe the President would have
been a lot more aggressive.

Paul Begala, Frank Greer, Stan Greenberg, James Carville

Charlie Black: He got two good hits in the first ten minutes, and we
have two participants in a row talking about "Let's not have any more
negative stuff." It definitely changed the tone. It could have been forc-
ing Bush off the attack.

Elizabeth Arnold: Coming out of that, what did you learn from it, and
where did you have to go from that point? Obviously, these guys were
on top of the world talking about how the President didn't get it.

Charlie Black: What we learned is, you're taking a risk any time you
do debates. And when you're experimenting with new formats and all,
they don't always come out your way. The problem is, any debate, when
you're behind, you need to "win" it. And that one was wasted. We did
better in the third one.

Fred Steeper: One small thing we learned. You mentioned the
Prescott Bush thing, but according to the people with the dials [poll-
sters], they did not buy Clinton's explanation of the draft issue and the
trust issue at all, even though he was following his prepared line. Our
focus group people were reacting in a very neutral way, and watching
the Richmond debate they didn't buy his rebuttal at all.

I think if we were successful at anything, it was getting across the
idea that Governor Clinton is not entirely trustworthy, and that any time

in the debates where he tried to defend his trustworthiness, our focus groups did not buy it at all.

George Stephanopoulos: The Prescott Bush thing, in the first debates, was one of the highest lifts he ever had.

Fred Steeper: Not in our group.

Marc Nuttle: I was really struck by how detached Bush was in that debate, after the first couple of minutes. He almost seemed to have given up somewhere in the middle. What kind of mood was he in at the end after that? How did he feel about the whole thing?

Mary Matalin: He was generally cranky about the whole process, and that debate in particular. And then we jumped in his face about looking at his watch, which he really thought was being funny. He thought that Carole was letting Perot go over the allotted time, and that was his sort of body language for "let me in." The various cues that he gave were Bush body language, Bush-speak, to which we attached all these other interpretations. He wasn't detached, he was just signaling, "I'm going to answer the questions, and I'm going to go through this." The whole thing, with Perot being in it, the dynamics of it, was not the kind of a debate he was accustomed to in the presidential and vice-presidential elections. It was just a different animal, and he was going to do his duty and get through it and listen to all of us.

Elizabeth Arnold: Mary, he rose to the occasion in the third debate. Don't you think he did?

Fred Steeper: It's very important to remember: he was ready to rise. He realized his mistakes from the first debate. He was ready to do in Richmond what he did in East Lansing. It was just his sense that it wasn't going to be appropriate, it wasn't going to come off. I think what happened has been misinterpreted. He was prepared to do in Richmond what he did later in the next one.

Stan Greenberg: But I think it misreads the character of that second debate. We're focusing on whether the dial-meter went up.

Fred Steeper: I'm not talking about dials. I'm talking about a sense of what the moderator expected.

Stan Greenberg: But the people were much more important than the moderator.

Charlie Black: That's right. I agree with that.

Stan Greenberg: Bill Clinton, in that second debate, was with the people in that audience, he was relating to those questions. The President wasn't.

Fred Steeper: The President was more prepped to take on Clinton as opposed to interacting with the audience, so we may have misdirected him.

James Carville: During the prep all we said was, "Use the audience. The audience is your friend. We need to go off audience." Clinton does it naturally. He's the best one-on-one politician that I've ever seen. This was his forum. This is the place he wanted to be. We made the mistake in the third debate of underestimating Bush, a thing we said we'd never do. No one said that Bush doesn't have anything, but we just weren't as serious, and we lapsed back. And Bush was a lot better candidate. I'm not saying he was the greatest candidate ever, but he was a lot better candidate than people think he is. He tends to fool you.

George Stephanopoulos: We may still disagree about this, but you said the question of the third debate was, should we have popped Perot back, after he took his shot. I tend to think now we probably should have, but it's an open question. We probably should have hit back.

James Carville: That hurt us. You can't go into a debate saying you're not going to hit back. The audience was the thing in the second debate, but I do think we lapsed into making an error in the third debate. People always underestimate Bush; he's had a pretty accomplished career. While we didn't actually go to sleep, we did kind of nod at the switch a bit.

Mary Matalin: I don't think we even gave a second thought to the format of that, because Bush had been doing "Ask George Bush's" for 14 years. I don't think we focused as much on reminding him that this is a TV kind of thing, and you should act like Geraldo and stuff. We felt he was so comfortable with that format.

George Stephanopoulos: Mary, isn't it a big difference? The "Ask George Bush" things were almost always from Republicans.

Dave Carney: That is not true.

Mary Matalin: That is not true.

James Carville: It took some effort to go find the 5 percent of the voters in this race that were undecided. They came up with an entirely different audience than you get when you do "Ask George Bush" or "Ask Bill Clinton." But for this they went out and aggressively recruited people.

Mary Matalin: We used to do them in New Hampshire. I call them "spit on your shoe" events. He said, "I don't want to see a face in there that I recognize." He's been to New Hampshire so many times and really liked going into hostile audiences.

Dave Carney: We did it in New Hampshire, in the primaries. We specifically got undecided people — only those Republican voters that were undecided. In other places we had organizations do the inviting. In some audiences you always have your Bush supporters, who would be part of the Chamber of Commerce or the school or whatever, but we never, ever, stacked a crowd. Maybe we should have.

Mary Matalin: I think we focused more on continuing to prep him on the Arkansas record, which I don't think he ever got totally confident with. The way in which he was briefed contributed to his lack of confidence in spewing out the Arkansas record. They just threw too much information at him. Left to his own devices, he knows the difference between Republicans and Democrats. He knows the difference between Clinton and himself. He knew what he was running on. He knew his agenda and all that stuff. But throwing a book of Arkansas statistics at him wasn't the right thing to do, and I think that is probably what they continued to do in the briefings.

Clay Mulford: We were involved, and I was concerned about the audience selection process. As you know, we were not parties to the agreement, and there were a lot of holes in the selection criteria. It was up to the Gallup organization to come up with an uncommitted audience, and we were very interested in how that was going to be set up — based on the current polling and so forth. Gallup decided to go first to undecideds, and as James points out, there was concern that someone who was undecided at that point would tend to be undereducated, not as well-informed on public issues, and you wondered about the quality of the questions you'd get.

When they couldn't find enough of a pool from that, they had to go to voters who were only leaning and not committed. We were concerned that we would be too small a percentage of the audience. Ironically, because our support tended to be weaker at that point than the people who were supporting Bush and Clinton, we may have gotten a few more people in the audience than we expected.

Stan Greenberg: Fred and I worked with Gallup on what the criteria would be, and there was a fixed quota on uncertain Perot voters, uncertain Clinton, uncertain Bush, and then straight Undecided. It was a quarter, quarter, quarter, quarter on that. So, there were set criteria. We were concerned because the Richmond media market was, in fact, fairly Republican territory and undecided voters, or voters that we thought would be Bush voters. So, we were happy with a quota across the board, and we did do surveys in the area, to get a sense of the audience.

Our approach to this debate was not to get a point of exchange with George Bush, but to relate to the audience and to understand the audience.

Clay Mulford: I understood that that was your view on the audience selection, and I was comforted by that. But when the process actually began, they moved away from the original plan. We had extended discussions with the head of Gallup over how the audience was going to be set up because I had heard that story from you and another one from the other side. I think that that was the proposal you had on the table, but that was not the way it actually worked out.

The Vice-Presidential Debate

"Who am I and why am I here?"

— Admiral James Stockdale, ret.

David Broder: Let's pick up the vice presidential debate. I'm sorry that Mark Gearan isn't at the table. Bill, how did that fit in, and what was the game plan there?

Bill Kristol: We viewed the quarter base as a package. Since we were behind, the idea of course was to win the debates as a series. We needed to expose serious vulnerabilities in Clinton, on trust and taxes. We hoped the President would open up a little wedge on Sunday night, we would really go at it Tuesday night, and then the President would basically complete it in the more free-form format Thursday night. We thought the kind of questions the audience would ask Thursday night would be affected by the Sunday night and Tuesday night debates also. But we didn't get any momentum out of Sunday night. The President did adequately, but didn't win; Perot dominated, Clinton probably did a little better than the President. So, we had this situation going into Tuesday night of just trying to get momentum from a standing start.

Second, our debate prep, practice debates, also had Stockdale winning the debate easily, on the assumption that he would be a little more facile than he turned out in response. He still had the single best line.*I mean, there was still a huge potential pro-Stockdale constituency. It just turned out he wasn't really able to do it.

We felt we had to go extremely hard, right out of the box, to prevent a repeat of Sunday night, which Perot won, and to get a Quayle/Gore exchange. I had negotiated rules that permitted flat-out straight

---

Editor's Note: "I believe that a woman owns her body and what she does with it is her own business — period."

exchanges. We expected to get that exchange going, to try to force the issues to be taxes and trust, and to keep challenging Gore to defend Clinton on taxes and trust. That was our thinking going into it. But especially after Sunday night, we felt we had to be extremely aggressive, not worry about Gore, but really go after Clinton on the two basic issues.

David Broder: How could you have sent Admiral Stockdale into that debate as unprepared as he seemed to be?

Clay Mulford: Actually, we had people working with him for a long time, for four or five days. They all expected him to do very well. I don't know if it was nervousness — I guess it's kind of a frightening situation to take your initial dip into an ocean that big. I remember I was on a TV show with you, Bill, as well as Gore's chief of staff, that evening, and I thought that next to attending a Perot press conference, it was one of the most painful things I've ever been through. [Laughter] But it was not as damaging to us as we expected it to be, that we feared it would be. Number one, because Admiral Stockdale has a reputation for intellectualism and is regarded highly among his peers. Second, he's a Medal of Honor winner, and it's difficult to attack him without attacking the flag.

What I was more concerned about was that Perot would be criticized for putting him in a position like that, and that didn't happen. I think we got through it. We certainly stepped on the momentum which was really working for us from the first debate. But longer term it turned out the way we hoped it would, which was, people don't vote for a president based on the vice-presidential nominee or the vice-presidential debate.

George Stephanopoulos: They don't, but it really put a wall up in front of you. I don't think there was much of anything real people in the country were talking about the next day except Admiral Stockdale.

Clay Mulford: I think you're right.

George Stephanopoulos: I know that none of us knew what to say after the debate, because we wanted to be respectful. But that's only the filter. Seventy or 80 million people saw the Admiral unable to speak in the debate. James caught it right away. It had a huge impact, and, I think, really slowed you at the time when you were moving quite quickly.

Clay Mulford: What we did in response to that was have him meet with editorial boards around the country, where he was more comfortable than on TV. He's a very impressive gentleman—that came through in the editorial board setting — and he got us some positive publicity.

David Broder: Did the Clinton camp, after that debate, feel that you had to do repair work because Gore had failed so conspicuously to defend Clinton in the debate?

George Stephanopoulos: It's arguable. I know a lot was made of that, and it was smart of you guys to press the way you did afterwards. But turn it around. Let's say, Gore engages. The headline the next day is, "Gore and Quayle Engage on Clinton Character." Who would want that? Instead you had two guys fighting and everyone talking about Admiral Stockdale.

Bill Kristol: We thought that Gore probably made the right decision not to engage. We felt, nonetheless, that we had achieved a bit of an opening for the President on Thursday night by getting that issue out so conspicuously. The fact that you didn't have much of a choice gave us a strategic advantage in that way. Quayle's expectation was so low, once we were able to get in, we hammered on it.

George Stephanopoulos: That's really the problem with Gore. How can he win the expectations game going in? It's almost impossible, and he knew that from June.

David Broder: Did the vice presidential candidates make any difference in this election?

Stan Greenberg: Not poised as a choice between Quayle vs. Gore, which is the way it is normally considered. But the selection of Gore was a reinforcing choice, particularly since we had come out of the last month of the primary process with nothing but bad publicity. Normally we would have gained more and had a more positive press in the period when we were winning primary after primary. It didn't happen. Perot emerged during that period, so people really didn't get to know who Bill Clinton was. We had won with the more liberal segment of the primary electorate. Picking Gore sent a message that this was a young, moderate, Southern, new, presidential candidate. The choice of Al Gore reinforced our strengths. And then came the imagery, which I think we all underestimated, when the two families came out onto the portico of the mansion, that just said, this is a breath of fresh air, this is new. I think it was very important. We found later on in our research, particularly in the South, that it was important to bring Gore into the mix, and we did in our advertising.

James Carville: I would say to the extent you can say something definitively that you can't absolutely prove, we could not have carried Georgia without Gore, nor probably Tennessee, nor arguably Kentucky and Louisiana. Probably Charlie, Mary, and most of the people there would agree. Thirteen electoral votes is a lot for a vice presidential candidate to bring.

George Stephanopoulos: In September to mid-October we ran an ad in North Carolina, Tennessee, Georgia, Louisiana, and a couple of other states, that showed Clinton and Gore together, pictures of the two of them together, and I think the issues focused on were spending, the death penalty, and welfare.

James Carville: I think it helped us enormously in Colorado, New Mexico, and some of those western states.

George Stephanopoulos: As soon as we ran that ad.

James Carville: But to say we couldn't have carried those states without him is arguable. Georgia, I think, is the most you could say with a high degree of certainty.

Fred Steeper: I have a comment on Gore. The first thing we expected was, that given such a heavy loading of Southerners on the ticket, that we'd have to reconfigure our targeting and concede more to the South.

One of the good things coming out of this, when we get to the end discussion, even though we lost some of those Southern states, given the national trends and some rank orders and so forth, we did relatively well in the South, despite the fact that you had two Southerners.

James Carville: Extreme Republican bias.

Fred Steeper: We didn't see any kind of Jimmy Carter effect as in 1976, or even 1980. So, I think the Republican strength from the South actually held up in this election.

James Carville: No question about it.

Fred Steeper: Maybe the bigger effect was on our strategy, by your putting an environmentalist on the ticket. In fact, we had been going after Clinton on his environmental record in Arkansas, which some felt was inconsistent, but the selection of Gore provided you with protection on the environmental issue. At one time I thought for dead certain that we'd be running a chicken waste* commercial sometime in September or October. In fact, some people were looking forward to it. Part of the reason we didn't was because of Gore being on the ticket. Plus, we were also accusing the Clinton/Gore ticket of being environmental extremists, and some thought it might be contradictory.

David Broder: Did the debates make a difference?

Clay Mulford: Yes.

Fred Steeper: A huge difference. It put Perot back in the race.

---

*Editor's Note: This was an environmental issue during Clinton's tenure as governor.

Sharon Holman: Not only that, but speaking of commercials, we had one we wanted to run and for some reason didn't, it was going to be from the debates, the line, "I agree with Ross. I agree with Ross."

Clay Mulford: We made the ad, but we had made an agreement to abide by the debate agreement,* which provided that you could not use the line without the ...

Sharon Holman: The footage.

Clay Mulford: We decided we were not so anxious to play this that we were going to disregard our standards.

David Broder: Does anybody have any crucial points or questions relative to the debates?

Bill Kristol: I think the debates made a huge difference. We were seven or eight points down after the Quayle/Gore debate and 14 down by Sunday after the Thursday night debate. Making up that deficit in three weeks was just too much. After he watched the performances on Thursday night, Dan Quayle believed the election was unwinnable.

Mary Matalin: We stayed even in the first debate. You guys popped us up. Richmond popped us down. And then the last debate popped us back up, if I'm not mistaken.

Fred Steeper: What happened in the debates is that Clinton and Bush both started going down because Perot was going up. The person who benefited from the three debates was Ross Perot. Another point I'd like to make. We were beginning to get through, and we'll probably argue this forever, with the character hit on Clinton. We haven't talked about the Larry King appearance and the Moscow trip, but there was a national conversation going on out there about Clinton's draft dodging, and all the stuff back from the primaries was being rekindled, when the debates changed the topic to Ross Perot. In my mind, if we could do it all over again, we would have had those debates in September. It got in the way of a conversation that the Larry King appearance reawakened,** and it was going in our direction.

Editor's Note: The agreement referred to by Mr. Mulford and Ms. Holman was a 37-page, highly detailed document negotiated between the two campaigns that governed nearly every aspect of the debates. It was signed by Mickey Kantor for the Clinton/Gore campaign and Robert Teeter for the Bush/Quayle campaign. Ross Perot, while not a signatory to the agreement, agreed to abide by it when he became a participant in the debates.

**Editor's Note:* On "Larry King Live" on October 7, Bush claimed that Clinton had met with the Iraqi ambassador in 1986 to discuss grain-credit loans to Iraq. Larry King asked the President if Clinton wanted to arrange loans and Bush replied, "I believe that is the case." Clinton dismissed the allegation as being without substance. He said the meeting was ceremonial.

George Stephanopoulos: We started moving on the Larry King appearance.

Fred Steeper: Moscow was our highest point. In our polls we wanted to keep it going.

Stan Greenberg: We were trying to keep it going.

Orson Swindle: Just an observation about the debates. The impression I got, from talking to a lot of people who asked me about it, the glaring thing — well, Perot I think surprised a lot of people — but the most glaring thing that I saw was a President who had no passion. To me, he reeked passivity throughout all three debates. I thought he did marvelously better in the third one, but it was as if he didn't want to continue and that bothered me greatly; it seemed like he had no fire and no enthusiasm for what was ahead.

Dave Carney: The four days between the Richmond debate and the last debate, we went dark. The point we tried to make during the entire campaign was, the President is dark, we go down. But it wasn't until that moment that we were able to actually show that in those four days there was a tremendous difference, when every day Bill Clinton was doing something, even if it was only jogging.

When we didn't campaign, we were off television, off the screen, it made a big difference. Every day the President should have done something, even if it wasn't a trip. Travel for the President costs the campaign so much, but you only have so many travel days.

The days you're not traveling, when you're in the White House doing the same thing you've been doing for a long time, that isn't really newsworthy. It was the fatal flaw, we should have been doing something to get back in the mix on things. And all we did was give you guys a chance to write, "Didn't do very well." We could have changed the story on Friday, but we showed up in East Lansing, or wherever it was. We were dark. Big mistake. Our tactical mistake.

CHAPTER SEVEN

THE END GAME

"In terms of message, in terms of substance, in terms of a real plan for dealing with the economy, one of the failings of the Bush campaign was that they never offered a plan for the country."

— Frank Greer, Media Consultant,
Clinton/Gore Campaign

The Discussion

David Broder: I think we're going to need to move onto the closing stage of the campaign.

Elizabeth Arnold: Well, Fred already sort of got into something that I wanted to ask you about. Rightly or wrongly, you guys continued the hits on Clinton. I don't know if your greatest fear still was that Bush was going to come out with an economic plan and follow it up at this point. But he moved from accusing Clinton of cutting grain deals with Iraq before the war to Clinton's Moscow trip in 1969. I'm interested. Stan, you said your numbers went up after that?

Stan Greenberg: Both in the focus groups and polling, when the draft issue got extended to the Moscow trip, not only did the Moscow accusations seem way out of line, it also made the draft issue itself seem way out of line. They all seemed to become a package of throwing whatever mud might work, made the President look desperate, and tended to discredit the whole line of attack.

George Stephanopoulos: We were very disciplined in late August to early September about the draft. It's not about the draft, not about Vietnam, it's about changing stories. And the minute you extend into the Moscow trip, into questioning his patriotism, and talking about the other things, it just pops for us.

268

Charley Royer, David Broder, Elizabeth Arnold

James Carville: It's also the law of unintended consequences. When Perot walked up and took the microphone over, I said: "Sherm, come here. You are looking at a man destroying himself. This is an historic moment. He will never survive this. This man is just pulling the grenade, and he's exploding in front of your eyes." Okay? [Laughter]

So, between focus groups Celinda [Lake, of Greenberg-Lake Polling] called and said: "They believed Perot. He said if they looked through Clinton's mother's passport file, they'd mess up my daughter's wedding." I mean, you guys sold that stuff, and then they said: "Okay, you're all doing that." I said: "Oh, no, they can't."

Charlie Black: They believed Perot on "60 Minutes" despite Lesley [Stahl, CBS correspondent] beating the hell out of him.

George Stephanopoulos: They really believed him on "60 Minutes." They believed him a lot on "60 Minutes."

James Carville: When they started out to the press conference, I said: "Kids, this is historic. This man is blowing himself up. Look at this now. Let Uncle James give you a lesson right here." It didn't hurt him at all.

Clay Mulford: It was Tuesday morning. We didn't want him to come over there. It was a big surprise. It was something to watch.

Sharon Holman: There was some discussion and Ross Junior was there and handling it really well. All of a sudden there was a message handed to me saying: "He's in the car. He's on his way over."

Clay Mulford: I'd said, "We've got to shut this down, it's over."

Sharon Holman: He was too late.

Paul Begala: He called in every kid in the headquarters and told them ...

James Carville: I said: "This is history in the making."

Orson Swindle: Did that double-take look real? I have never been so stunned in my life. I exited stage left, sat down in a leather chair, and said: "We just cashed in. This is it." We spent the next five days fighting piranhas, in one-foot-deep water, and we never did anything after that.

James Carville: I thought that and the Stockdale thing, I thought you'd have 5 percent. That's it, man, there's nothing that can stop you.

Clay Mulford: There's more going on out there than you realize.

James Carville: Both Orson and I thought it was over.

Clay Mulford: It was a big surprise to us, because he was saying the night before the worst thing to do is make this a two- or three-day story. We said, "You're right."

Then Don Hewitt ["60 Minutes" producer] said afterwards that he might not have run it without him [Perot]. I wish Mr. Perot had known that. He thought he had to do it to get his side in, the way somebody was discussing on the first day here, why they agreed to be interviewed. He was doing it for the same reason.

Clay Mulford, Sharon Holman, Bill Kristol

Sharon Holman: Yes.

Clay Mulford: He said: "On top of everything else, this is a risk I don't want to take. And I'm not saying it's believable. I'm not saying I can prove it. Just a matter of fact statement." Well, that got portrayed as an accusation, and I think that's what he was trying to answer [at the press conference].

Elizabeth Arnold: Charlie, what was the internal debate over this? You must have had a little bit more control over your candidate than these guys did. What was the internal debate about Moscow?

Charlie Black: Well, Fred can probably pull the numbers out and show you, but we didn't show the Moscow thing hurting us.

Paul Begala: What made you think it would help? My understanding of how the President felt, and he seemed to be genuine, was that he didn't like the idea of somebody going to England and protesting against this country. That's a completely different thing from looking through his passport files and his mother's files, and criticizing him for taking a backpacking trip into Moscow.

Charlie Black: Well, the President did feel strongly about his demonstrating on foreign soil. And over time our position on that gained support. On the trip to Moscow, the point is, Clinton had amnesia. Hell, he said he was over in Moscow for a week, and he couldn't remember anything he did.

Betsey Wright: That's not true.

Charlie Black: Yes, it is true. That is the first thing he said, that he couldn't remember what he did there.

Betsey Wright: *You* said he couldn't remember what he did.

Charlie Black: Well, the second day, he said he remembered spending some time at the university, talking to some students who turned out to be anti-Communist by the way.

Paul Begala: Bush went to Moscow and lived in China. That's a Communist country. What was the point?

Charlie Black: Credibility. The whole point was credibility.

Mary Matalin: The *Arkansas-Democrat Gazette* listed statements he had made throughout his various races about his draft status and his antiwar activities. The first time Frank White [Clinton's opponent in the 1980 gubernatorial race] asked him about his antiwar activities, he said, "I don't know what he's talking about." The next time he said, "I listened to some of the speeches." We kept trying to draw attention to the credibility issue and the ever-evolving stories. We tried different positions. We tried always to come back to, "This guy has got something for everybody, he's got a story for everybody."

But when the President got to those two things, the draft and Moscow, he had some of his own visceral feelings about them; demonstrating on foreign soil was one of them, and serving your country was the other.

Paul Begala: What was wrong with going to Moscow and what was in the passport files? It's different from a demonstration.

Mary Matalin: You're mixing all these things together.

Charlie Black: First of all, and I'm sure I speak for the people from the Bush operation, the only thing we know about the passport files is what we read in David Broder's newspaper, and, believe me, I'm not asking any more about that, because we're not involved in it. Second, Moscow was just part of the pattern of Clinton trying to hide what he had done during those years.

Paul Begala: That's unfair. Come on.

James Carville: This is what you're being asked to believe. By the use of the word "Moscow," and what did he do over there, we weren't, in any way, trying to imply that anything was untold. We were just questioning this man's memory 23 years later.

Fred Steeper: The day before Larry King, our national tracking survey question was: "What have you read, seen, or heard lately about Bill Clinton?" Twenty percent of the voters were saying his economic plan, and 10 percent were giving negatives — "You can't trust the guy. He's a pot-smoking, draft-dodging, womanizer." Two days after the Larry King appearance those two numbers had reversed themselves, and two days after the VP debate, which got them started again, 30 percent were now volunteering that the main thing they were reading, seeing, and hearing about Bill Clinton was that he was a draft-dodging, pot-smoking philanderer, and they didn't like it.

It was changing the conversation away from Clinton's economic plan, which you wanted the conversation to be about, to the subject we wanted the voters to be talking about, which was whether you could trust him as President of the United States. The Moscow part was not important to people. They didn't know what to believe about that. But demonstrating in London, which was somehow connected, they didn't like. Then those stories brought back the draft-dodging reservations, so it rekindled all the stuff that they had heard, and what bothered them about Clinton. So, it served that function.

George Stephanopoulos: You had a strategy. I just don't buy this thing about not knowing what was going on. You did everything you could behind the scenes to create an atmosphere about Moscow, about Vietnam, about anything that was happening in 1969, so that no matter what happened, whenever Clinton came out and talked about it, it would be something that you would be able to characterize as not telling the truth. You would throw out the wildest rumors to everybody in this room about a range of subjects, no matter what, whether it was a leak to *Newsweek* about a bogus investigation of a passport file, or a leak to *Time* from the National Security Council.

James Carville: What about the numbered letters that people saw in meetings? There were numbered letters, and they would collect them, about renouncing his citizenship. "I saw so and so." It was in the meeting, and actually not many reporters in here got calls like that.

Betsey Wright: This citizenship letter is all part of creating an image of an unpatriotic, treasonous, traitorous kind of character. Don't tell me you didn't know some of that stuff that was going on.

Charlie Black: We did not promote that letter, because I didn't believe the letter existed.

Betsey Wright: Oh, come on! That was the highest-placed, best-massaged political rumor, I think, of the century.

Charlie Black: You are wrong.

Betsey Wright: You all worked so dad-gum hard out of the White House, out of the RNC.

Charlie Black: With all due respect, I hope you will talk one-on-one to these reporters here, about how I personally, how our campaign, handled that issue. Because we got an awful lot of calls pumping us about it. "Is there such a letter? Do you know about it? Where is it?" And the answer was: "No. You all go look for it."

James Carville: Did Bob [Teeter] call Elizabeth Tamposi [Assistant Secretary of State] and tell her to go to London to look through the file for a letter?

David Broder: I think we've got the two sides of this.

Charlie Black: David, one last point. Now that they're taking over the government, they can find out what the Bush/Quayle campaign did or knew about the passport file, and you're going to be disappointed, because the President wasn't involved in any way.

Sharon Holman: One other thing I might add, which I believe is a felony. Someone released Ross Perot's naval records.

Clay Mulford: Gave them to the media. And they went through his son's also. People at the Pentagon would call us. But this is the way you guys do it.

Stan Greenberg: At some point George Bush had to show people where he was going to take the country in a second term. This discussion, even on the issues that you're talking about, should also underline that we were maintaining a 20-plus point advantage on the economy during this period. George Bush's job performance was, by our measure, around 30 percent and unchanged. Clinton's lead was not changing. Clinton's advantage on the economy was not changing. Bush's job performance rating was not changing. But the campaign was using critical time to go down this track, which I think was providing you no advantage.

End Game Strategy. Perot.

"We made just chilling, disruptive, massive mistakes along the way, giving the impression that we were all a bunch of amateurs."

— Orson Swindle, National Executive Director,
United We Stand America

David Broder: While tempers cool, let me ask the Perot people to tell us about the strategic thinking that went into two things that he was doing. First of all, the half-hour infomercials, what was going on there? And second, the decision, very late in the campaign, to seemingly switch the target from Bush to Clinton and the Arkansas record?

Clay Mulford: We put together the scroll ads the first week of October. We were concerned about the messenger being perceived as so flawed that the message would not be listened to. So we wanted to stay away from Perot and just do the message. Originally the scroll ads, as we first saw them, didn't even name Perot. Then we did them with "Perot, Bush, or Clinton: The Choice Is Yours." Finally, we decided to go ahead and do it with "Perot" because we were paying for them, so we might as well get some push. Originally we were not going to have a photograph of him, but we had to do that in some markets, to comply with the FCC rules.

The half-hour presentations were Perot's idea. He came to the studio and just prepared some remarks and the flip charts, and gave a speech. We made a film of it, sent it up to be telecast. We edited it through the evening one night, resubmitted it, and they ran the revised version. We just took out a couple of statements we thought could be misinterpreted.

Sharon Holman: If I could jump in for a minute and tell you that that was the first time he had ever used a teleprompter, for the first part of the speech. Most of the remarks with the charts were ad lib.

Clay Mulford: Just based on his familiarity with the things he had been working on for a long time, long before he got interested or involved in politics. We were trying to buy time between the first and second debates to run the solutions tape. We could not buy the time, and we were getting some criticism, if you will remember, in the second debate, about showing problems without solutions. That turned out not to be as big a problem as we thought it might be, and getting that shown on the air solved it.

But going back to when we thought the messenger was not being listened to, we thought we needed to reintroduce him. As we talked about yesterday, there was a terrific amount of interest in him in May and June. Any time he appeared on TV, people were so hungry for information about him, the ratings went through the roof. We missed that opportunity to define him, and instead he was defined by the descriptions from the other sources. Now there was a desire, or a perceived need, to reintroduce him on a personal basis.

The debates did that. The debates took away the negatives from the messenger, so we didn't need to do that. On the campaign side, we wanted to run fewer of those personal messages, half hours, than we ended up running, but we ran fewer than we originally planned, because there was no longer a need.

Elizabeth Arnold: Were you guys surprised at the number of people that were tuning in to the miniseries on the deficit?

Stan Greenberg: Yes.

Clay Mulford: Yes. The CBS counsel, Howard Jaeckel, called me to tell me we outdrew the playoffs. It was just a phenomenal reaction. A significant factor to be evaluated after this, when you all have time to reflect on it, is the appetite out there for substantive discussions. I think you will see more of that in the future, if for no other reason than it has become good politics.

Frank Greer: From the beginning of this campaign, this was a different election. When voters expected something very different, they responded to candidates that had written plans, like Bill Clinton and Paul Tsongas. They responded to straight talk and real, simple, straightforward presentations in the media. And I think that that's one of the reasons they responded to Ross Perot stylistically, as well as substantively. It's one of the reasons I think they responded to Bill Clinton. They wanted to participate in the process. And voters expected much more this year.

Thaleia Schlesinger: They tuned out in the early part; interest was very, very low, but it built up.

Frank Greer: In terms of message, in terms of substance, in terms of a real plan for dealing with the economy, one of the failings of the Bush campaign was that they never offered a plan for the country. And it was one of the great blessings of the Clinton campaign that he thought about the problems facing the country and offered a specific plan.

David Broder: In the decision-making in the Perot campaign, at this point, were you all calculating on how he could win the election, or what were you really doing at that point?

Clay Mulford: It's a good question. I think our foremost objective was to put on the table the issues facing the country as we perceived them. We saw the deficit and some of the economic problems as more a result of the way the political process operated, and not simply problems unto themselves.

So what Mr. Perot wanted to lay out were issues that have to be addressed some time in the future, if they're not going to be addressed immediately. Mainly there is the need for government-business cooperation. Coming from a conservative, or someone who is perceived as a business conservative, that is a very novel, almost a radical, approach, the conventional belief being that those individuals are generally antigovernment. We wanted to get that out. It would also have been nice to win. There would be no better way to shake up Washington than by his arrival. But we think he has altered the political system just by being a powerful force.

David Broder: Why did he whack Bill Clinton at the end?

Clay Mulford: It wasn't so much the timing — it was always in the cards — and he did not want to personally "whack" anybody. And I know it's hard for the Bush people to believe that, but it's true. There was a show on CNN about the Arkansas record, that contained some interesting things. It came to his attention, and he really did decide to do a close analysis of the situation in Arkansas. It was not done as a strategic move to damage Clinton, or to get the "change vote" to Perot, but with a certain earnestness, to examine the record.

Paul Begala: If he found out that Michigan was a badly run state, he would have said so.

Orson Swindle: I have a slightly different perspective. I personally thought we should have been in it to win, and I made the statement early on in the process. I thought that's what we were trying to do, and I still am convinced we had the potential, but a long shot. But in order to do it we couldn't make the mistakes we made. We made just chilling, disruptive, massive mistakes along the way, giving the impression that we were all a bunch of amateurs. I mentioned the other night, if we could have gotten about 20 percent and pushed this snowball over the top of the hill, we might have accomplished the impossible.

As far as the attack on Clinton, I was concerned, and it was evident by some comments I made publicly, that whether he intended to or not, Mr. Perot was giving vibrations against George Bush. But, in another sense, Bush was the incumbent President, and Perot was going to talk about what's wrong with the country, and that's the guy that's responsible for it, so it was natural that the blame was going to fall on Bush, and Mr. Clinton was outside of that.

But, nevertheless, it may have seemed that he put out information that could be seen as critical to Bush, and maybe siding with or favoring Clinton. I asked him about that on a number of occasions. I guess the most concerned I got was when he had a chance, in the debates, when the draft issue came up, Mr. Perot basically said: "Well, that's just a 19-year-old kid, you know."

Because of my personal background, I was particularly offended by Mr. Clinton's past. And, quite frankly, I could give you a dissertation on the Moscow thing, which is irrelevant today. But in my mind I don't like that combination being in the White House. That's a personal thing.

But, more importantly, I got a lot of feedback from around the country, from veterans and from some POWs, whom Mr. Perot has endeared himself to, and who will always be looked upon with great honor and reverence and appreciation. We were concerned that he didn't take the opportunity to say something that was consistent with everything he had done in the last 20 years, vis-à-vis the POWs and their sacrifices. And here's a guy who was getting hell kicked out of him.

I'll tell you one other point. Mr. Clinton started really bragging about his accomplishments in Arkansas, and those accomplishments are, it's well known, challengeable. They are not as they appear to be, by percentage. They are not that great. I think it was important just to set the record straight.

James Carville: I have to tell you, I think you're giving a speech now. In response to your speech, I think somebody else will give a speech, and I'll be glad to hammer them down right now and give my own speech, but I don't think that's what we are here for. Bill Clinton's accomplishments in Arkansas were significant, and I think they have been recognized by fellow governors, the people in Arkansas, and a lot of other people.

Charlie Black: One 20-second point. However much money Mr. Perot spent on television, all of this free media, about 80 percent of that message worked to Clinton's benefit and against Bush's, because it was a critique of the economy, of the deficit, of our position in the world. The charts showed the Reagan/Bush years, when all the deficit came up.

I'm not saying he wasn't honest about it, but there was no way the impact could be balanced.

Clay Mulford: Just to follow up on the same line. There was a perception out there that this was just an effort to defeat Bush, in which we were participating. That was not our objective. By criticizing Clinton as well, it made clear, in our estimation, we were not an advocate of one side or the other, but a legitimate choice.

James Carville: I don't think there's anything wrong. He could buy his half hour. I might dispute what he put on there, but it's sort of a strategic thing.

It doesn't seem to me that on the night before the election, if you're trying to win the election, you say: "Gee, I want to balance this thing out." Most people, the night before an election, are trying to put something on to win.

Stan Greenberg: When he dropped out the first time, Perot voters, pro-change voters, went to Clinton in great majorities. If Perot, coming back in, was serious about winning, why didn't he try to get those voters back?

James Carville: All those voters are gone. When you left those voters in July, they'd been around a revolving door 20 times. I have never seen any evidence that Perot hurt one candidate more than another.

Stan Greenberg: In terms of raw numbers, it was pretty much an even split. I do believe that he affected the environment for the race, at various points, in ways that are hard to measure in polls. I think he hurt us in May, when he was stealing the stage. I think he hurt George Bush in June. I think he hurt Clinton a lot at the end. What people drew from his media was not the specifics, but that he had a plan, he was good on the economy, he was thoughtful. Bill Clinton, as the clear alternative to George Bush on the economy, having a plan and a thoughtful view of the future, lost a lot of that edge with Perot putting so much of his resources behind that message. I think Perot at the end hurt us and muddied the choice somewhat between Clinton and Bush.

Charlie Black: He added greatly to how bad things were, which was our whole problem, that we never could get out from under.

James Carville: In terms of poll numbers, no one can produce a poll number that shows more than a percentage, way within the margin of error, in which his effect was all laid out.

Charlie Black: After $50 million worth …

James Carville: Both of us would have preferred he not get back in. So that shows you how inconclusive it is. When he got back in, the reaction in our camp was the same as yours.

Campaign for President '92

End Game Strategies. Bush and Clinton.

"The numbers literally show the race tightening, and if it had continued over the last four days, we'd have had a damn close race on election day."

— Charlie Black, Consultant, Bush/Quayle Campaign

David Broder: We want to focus, in the last 15 minutes of this section, on what was happening in the Bush and the Clinton campaigns, in the final stages. Dan Quayle and Bill Kristol thought the game was over on the night of the Richmond debate. How widespread was that perception among Republicans? From where you were sitting, did it affect the way in which Bush played out the last couple of weeks of the campaign?

Rich Bond: My job, at that period of time, was to be a reporter more than anything else, to bring back to the President, and to the campaign leadership, how the other campaigns around the country were going, how the ground game operation was going, in conjunction with the Bush campaign and the rest of the ticket, and what political notables were saying about the situation.

I think there was a great deal of despair after the Richmond debate, when folks believed that time was running out and that the opportunity had been lost. A great deal of emphasis was being put on the President's final performance, the East Lansing debate. Our whole operation, and I think we'll get to this later, at least on the ground level, was predicated on getting into the ball game late and riding the wave in. My message to everyone was: "There's a lot of green still left out there, and you've got to stand by and see what happens in the East Lansing debate. If the President turns in a performance in East Lansing similar to what he did in Richmond, we'll have to get enormously lucky to be competitive." So we were feeling a great deal of discouragement, but no one was heading out to the roof at that point.

David Broder: Let me ask the Clinton people. This is the period when, from the outside, we all thought that you all thought that you were going to win, but you were looking for something more than a win, you were looking for a mandate. You were in Wyoming, and other implausible places. What was going on?

Stan Greenberg: Well, we weren't looking for a mandate. I think we banished the word from anybody's discussion. The much-maligned

Western trip was an enormous success, and at the end of it we saw the growth of our support in the West. States like Nevada and Arizona were beginning to look stronger, and we did extend the campaign to those states. In the very last week we added media out there, and Bill Clinton finished the campaign in those states. It wasn't part of a mandate, but part of setting the stage for the Democratic party of the '90s.

We had focused on about 370 electoral college votes. In the end, we lost only one state that we targeted, North Carolina, and we won only one state that we didn't target, Nevada. There were temptations to think about — Florida, Texas — because they were close. But we resisted those. We stayed focused on our 370 electoral votes and poured our resources there.

James Carville: Let me make a point about Wyoming. I think it's important. You know that Bill Clinton has a hard time saying no. Do you know why he went to Wyoming? Because Governor Sullivan asked him if he would go, and he said he would because, he said, the Democrats out there never saw a candidate. That's why we went to Wyoming, and I think it was a good thing.

In this election most things that happened regionally were part of a trend. There was not a reversal of anything in the South. We had some Southern candidates. We carried some Southern states closely. The fact that we carried those states north of the Ohio was something that was set in place in 1988. The real news is in the Western states. Democrats did much, much better than they had historically done in that region. We carried Montana, Colorado, Nevada, and New Mexico, and came within 1,000-2,000 votes in Arizona. It was a totally logically strategic trip, other than the stop in Wyoming.

Mary Matalin: Montana, Colorado, and New Mexico were hard states for us. They were hard states in 1988. We always thought they were competitive, and we were surprised you didn't go in there earlier. Still, to this day though, I can't figure out Nevada.

James Carville: But it was logical on this Western thing.

Charlie Black: It all made sense. The Wyoming thing made sense. It kept Teeter and Steeper and me tied up 24 hours.

James Carville: Don't ask me to explain the Mississippi thing now.

Tom Luce: I would just add, to underscore what James said, that early in the pre-July phase of the Perot effort, a huge amount of the Perot support came from those Northwest states, which were fertile ground for Clinton, because an enormous amount of support was coming in for Perot in all those. That was the change vote, the populist vote. The regional impact was in the West when Perot got out.

Stan Greenberg: Our fear when Perot came back in was that he could take back some of the vote in California and Washington and Oregon, which had been so steady and strong for us. He did not do it in the Pacific Coast states. Our leads held fine.

James Carville: The Wyoming thing is instructive, and I'll tell you why. The Wyoming stop probably did not make strategic sense, but what hurt us was that we stopped there, and the whole emphasis was on that. No one is going to say: "Gee, this man is going to Wyoming. I think I'm going to vote for him." The trip became about a stop at the Cheyenne airport.

Paul Begala: It was the biggest rally in the history of Wyoming, they told us, so they were thrilled.

James Carville: But what happened is, nobody said, "I am not going to vote for Clinton because he went to Cheyenne." No one is. But the things we were trying to say that day, about the economy, whatever our message of the day was, got buried because we went to Wyoming. Therein lies the lesson.

Mary Matalin: Also instructive is that it contributed to this presumptuous attitude that was developing about you guys, this whole mandate thing.

James Carville: At that time our poll numbers were going up.

Elizabeth Arnold: We do want to talk about poll numbers and the perceived surge that you guys talked a lot about Fred, was there a surge? And Frank and Stan, was there a surge?

David Broder: Let's hear the case for the surge.

Fred Steeper: The case for the surge is not based just on our data, which makes it stronger. It's based on everyone's data that was reported, the public polls, plus the private polls that we had in hand. The second point I would make behind this, in terms of the methodology, is that it was not something that we contrived in the last week to make the data look better. We were plotting the national polls for months in the belief that no one national poll was going to be dead on, but the best way to make sense out of the national polls is to look at them all together. You can see if there is any discernible trend, if you do a regression trend line through the polls, once you've ordered them in terms of their field dates.

And for ten months of this year that methodology either showed a line going down for the President or being flat with no gains for the President. It kept giving us bad news, week after week after week, with the one exception of the so-called disastrous Republican convention, which was the only point in time that we had a trend showing that we gained, that we cut the Clinton lead in half with the Republican convention.

After the Republican convention, the methodology showed a steady lead for Clinton from anywhere between 11 and 13 points, all through September, into the debates, and then it did show Perot coming up and both Clinton and the President going down, Clinton a little more, but, still, Clinton maintaining his 11 to 13 point lead over the President. Then this methodology started to generate a different picture a couple of days after the last debate.

Now I mentioned earlier that we always assumed the press was against us. The press did us a great favor, were very magnanimous with us after the last debate. In terms of our own focus groups, the President didn't do that well in the last debate, not as well as it was made out the next day in the press. The press came close to declaring him the winner. At least his performance was much better, and that helped. Bush also seemed to catch fire on the stump during that week. But all that may or may not have worked.

We knew we were within single digits when CNN came up with us being only one point behind. Everybody else's polls were showing margins half as large as they had shown the previous week. And tracking all of those, on the Friday before the election, I was able to leave the strategy group with a trend chart. Someone stole it.

It's going to be hard to see this, but the heavier lines are Bush's results in the different public polls. It lines up here with Clinton. And this is Perot going up during the debates, and then going back down. "60 Minutes" [October 5] hurt him, and he went back down.

But if you project the 14 polls, after the third debate through the Friday before the election, and then project that trend line out to November 3, it's 39-39-10.[*]

David Broder: In the view of the strategists in the Bush campaign, what lay behind those numbers? What was it that you thought was beginning to work at that point?

Charlie Black: Taxes and trust.

Mary Matalin: The one thing Bush did exceedingly well at the debates was to keep saying, "He's going to raise your taxes" about ten thousand times. It was one of those rare instances where he didn't even answer the question. That was his answer to everything, and he stuck to it. And the trust thing.

---

*See Appendix for graphs of projections.

Fred Steeper: We had also started a new TV spot October 22. It was a 60-second spot on the agenda, which was along the lines of, "Here is Bush's program for the future." We had also started the Arkansas record spot, and with what Perot had done in the last debate, Clinton took the Arkansas record hit, which kind of stuck.

Then a very significant thing happened on Tuesday, October 27, the announcement of a 2.7 percent economic growth rate. That caused a little blip in some of our fundamental numbers, as in the question, "Is the country heading in the right direction, or on the wrong track?" There was a 5 or 6 point gain overnight on the country heading in the right direction. Any gain in the right direction in the country went almost totally to the President's benefit. So we got a little bump from the 2.7.

There were a number of things going on, plus the press coverage was more positive. Our press coverage, probably up to the Weinberger memo,* was probably the most positive we had through September and October.

David Broder: Just to let you complete, was the Weinberger indictment the second indictment? Then did that stop as far as you all were concerned?

Fred Steeper: That Friday morning, this is the last one we did. This last vertical line, which you are probably not going to be able to see, is the Friday of the Weinberger memo. There were seven polls done after that, and now the lines divide — exactly on October 30. This is something that anybody can replicate. Just go back to your copies of all the national polls, and just do a standard scatter-spot regression analysis, and see if the trend lines have any statistical significance.

David Broder: What was going on in the Clinton campaign while the Bush people saw this surge?

Stan Greenberg: First of all, the perception of surge. CNN/Gallup Poll played a big part in that story, and in the perception, and it produced anxiety out in the real world. Because it was the reality one had to deal with.

Let me just say something about what I think happened that week, and then talk a little bit about the trends and other data, and the notion of projection. This is a presidential contest, and the parties are much more evenly matched. We never expected this race to end at a 9, 10, or 11 point difference where the polls had it for the most period coming in. We assumed that the race would settle in. We were purposely not on the

---

*An Editor's Note on p. 20 gives information about the Weinberger memo.

air in our top states, so we assumed that not answering the media for long periods, in states like Minnesota and California, would eventually bring our numbers down. We also assumed that the Republican states in the South and in the West would come in faster.

Our polling had us at about a 10-point lead at the weekend, ten days out from the election, and the race began to settle in the first three days of the week, mostly due to Republican consolidation and not to any sizable shift. There was a little shift from us to the Perot voters, and to Bush, but essentially in the early part of the week and flat through the rest of the week.

CNN was showing a monumental collapse in our support midweek. I am speaking based both on our tracking polling, and also on our nightly polling in 30 states. We were dealing with a very large database, and a simulation model that projected the national number on that day, based on the state-by-state numbers, all of which held pretty steady at 7 points. It stayed at 7 right from Wednesday through the weekend.

If you look at all of the polls in that period, excluding our own poll and CNN's, because CNN was using a methodology that wasn't wrong, but different from the one that others were using, the average of the other polls had the race at the 8 to 9 point level on Sunday through Monday. The race was at 8 points, average, in all the polls on Tuesday. CNN had the average at 6 on Wednesday, and 5 on Thursday. On Sunday the polls were at 7 with an average for all of them. So there was a slight up. There was no evidence of a Bush surge pre-weekend. There was some slight evidence of a slight Clinton upward trend over the weekend.

Fred Steeper: We were gaining 9, 8, 7, 6, just keep going, a point a day — 5, 4, 3, 2, 1.

Stan Greenberg: When you're talking about the settling out of a race, there is absolutely no statistical or theoretical reason to assume that it's going to continue in a linear fashion indefinitely. On what basis would you assume that? When Fred extends the line out as the race was closing, he's doing something that's not real.

Fred Steeper: We knew a month before Ross Perot reached 39 percent that he was heading up there, because the poll line, projecting the national polls in May, showed that Ross Perot would get close to 40 percent sometime in June, and he came very near to it.

Stan Greenberg: Here are your numbers in the various polls. Wednesday 36, 37, 35. Thursday 35, 37, 36, 35. On Sunday 36, 37, 36, 35, 36, 36. It is hard to view that as representing a surge for George Bush.

Charlie Black: In our opinion we thought it was moving some, that there was about a 50-50 chance that we'd keep moving, and we'd wind up with a dead heat on election day. We weren't predicting that we were going to win, but that it would be very close. If that had happened in the national numbers and you overlay it state by state, we might have won.

Frank Greer: But, Charlie, did you see an electoral college 270 out of those numbers?

Charlie Black: On Friday morning, when Steeper gave us that analysis, the morning before the Weinberger indictment, we weren't polling in as many states as you all were. We were kind of picking up and tracking from people in a lot of states. But the point is, that day, when I went down state by state, we were within five points in every state that we needed.

Now, I have still sitting on my dresser at home the AP story, dated 2:37 on Friday, about the Weinberger indictment and the memo, which I stuck in my pocket to take home as a souvenir, because I knew then that the race was over.

You don't call it a surge, but we call it a surge. The numbers literally show the race tightening, and if it had continued over the last four days, we'd have had a damn close race on election day.

David Broder: Okay, we've got both sides of that argument.

Stan Greenberg: It's important to consider, if they believe that, that this race was stolen by the special prosecutor on the Friday before the election.

Charlie Black: I didn't use the term "stolen," number one, and you've listened the last day and a half, when I pretty clearly blamed it on the economic decisions made in 1990 and 1991.

Fred Steeper: The important thing about the Weinberger memo is that it dominated the news for Friday and Saturday.

Paul Begala: But, wait, think what that story was blocking out. What I was hearing, what the reporters were telling me, the President was calling Al Gore and Clinton bozos, and saying Millie the dog knows more about foreign policy than they do. He seemed utterly self-absorbed, talking about his polls and "nutty" pollsters, and "I'm doing better." I really thought that the President's message was having a meltdown on the stump, which is why I wasn't worried.

Fred Steeper: Stan's own numbers say that something was working for us in that last poll week. The point we were trying to make about the Weinberger memo is that the President was still behind on Friday, and that his message had to be the dominant message over that weekend for him to keep that trend going. What the Weinberger story did was take our message off center stage and replace it with something that was not only not our message, but was negative on Bush.

Mary Matalin: Another thought we had in the end was that people were beginning to focus on the choice between the candidates. What Bush was talking about were the differences between these two camps, and he really had this litany down, that they are for big spending, big taxing.

James Carville: You call an opponent a bozo, that's going to be on the news.

David Broder: Ladies and gentlemen, that point has been well made. Could we ask one question of the Bush campaign people? This is a conference about management. Did James Baker play any significant role in managing the campaign? [Laughter]

Mary Matalin: Why is that a funny question? Yes, he played an incredible, significant role in managing the process. Pennsylvania Avenue was the black hole. But from the nanosecond those guys walked in there, single-handedly, or five-handedly, things happened from the first week they were there, sans data, sans background, sans nuances. During the preceding election cycle, they had been around the whole world. They barely warmed to the topic, and then they had the hurricane. They had no infrastructure, yet they started moving instantly. Instantly. We got all kinds of decisions. There was no wasted time on several meetings to litigate one point. And Teeter and Charlie and a lot of us who had been involved in wasting our time when we could have been doing other things were freed up. Free at last. And they were doing their job. It was very, very important, not to mention the fact that one of the Baker boys worked himself into a fit of pneumonia to get the *Agenda for American Renewal* done. Margaret Tutwiler [former State Department spokesperson] and Janet Mullins [former secretary of state for legislative affairs] knew that it had to be in a book and that it had to be one page longer than Clinton's, and it had to be out there. There wasn't any kind of a wasted motion, and it was very, very important.

Next, the President had an instant increase in his confidence level, because his pal was there, and he knew the job was going to get done. He didn't have to look over his shoulder. That was very important. And I want to say this to the press, because there was rumbling around this notion that Baker was hiding in the interests of protecting his reputation. For Pete's sake, who did not know that Jim Baker was running this thing at the White House? He made a calculated decision that his being out there would step on the President, because the Clintonistas were ready to say we did pull back on that speech. These guys in the Clinton campaign were poised like cheetahs back there, ready to go with, "Who is the President, Baker or Bush?" And Baker said, "What should I do? I can't get out there because I will raise the 'Bush or Baker' story?"

He was incredibly significant. In addition to all of that, he kept everybody's morale up, saying endlessly: "We can do it. We can do it." In one of those endless series of "asking George Bush," he got a blackboard somewhere. We must have been getting bad numbers on the plane, and he said: "Here is how we are going to do it." He was a phenomenal man. He is a phenomenal man. He made a phenomenal difference in this campaign.

Dave Carney: The whole problem we had in the spring was the lack of decision-making structure. He centralized it. Things were so bad when they got there that the new group focused on the bigger picture, but there were some very small, routine things that they had to fix, too.

Maybe if they had come earlier it would have made a significant difference, but Baker was a tremendous asset. The only reason that it even held close and we put the September speech together, and all these other things, was because of his ability. Everybody knew that he would be making the decisions at the White House, that there were no longer seven or eight power centers at the White House. There was just one.

Mary Matalin: It also prevented you all from writing us off because you thought, "Well, maybe they can put out Baker." And definitely our field organization got a burst of enthusiasm that kept them going.

James Carville: From our vantage point, it was a very rational political decision that Jim Baker made, not to be public. We would have loved for him to get out there. As Mary said, we were poised like cheetahs. I mean, I thought that was a very, very smart thing he did to stay out of sight. He's not going to go out there to get himself clobbered, he's going to be the story. It's a rational political decision that you make at that time, and I was surprised that nobody in the press ever wrote a column saying the thing made total sense. It made total sense to us.

Elizabeth Arnold: Mary, you talked a lot about morale and also a lot about the problem in the lines of communication between the campaign and the White House. Did Baker really make a difference?

Mary Matalin: Instantly, yes. You can't even describe it.

Charlie Black: Execution. When you're an incumbent running for re-election, over half of the execution is at the White House, it's not at the campaign. The candidate's body, the schedule, the press, all of that, the message, the speech writing, all of that is in the White House.

No matter how smart we were in making these recommendations, we could go there and sit down, during the Sam Skinner days, have a meeting, make decisions, and leave, and nothing would happen on the execution a lot of times.

With Baker we sat down for half an hour in the morning, some combination of us, but always Teeter and Malek, with Baker and his gang of four. First of all it was a 20 or 30-minute meeting at the most, because we spoke the same language, we understood each other, everybody knew the candidate, and everybody knew and trusted each other. And when you left, things happened. You never had to ask twice. Our ability to execute, after Baker came on board, went from about a D-minus capability to an A-plus.

Elizabeth Arnold: Will you indulge me and my colleagues on one final question? Weinberger was a problem for you, you guys say that. I remember in Wisconsin Marlin [Fitzwater] at one stop saying, "Well, we lost today because of Weinberger." At the very next stop George Bush voluntarily brought up the Weinberger indictment in his speech, and we were all completely dumbfounded. Was that intentional? Was that Bush on his own?

Charlie Black: I don't remember calling out there and asking him to do it. No.

Elizabeth Arnold: Well, you lost another day. That's what happened.

CHAPTER EIGHT

LESSONS

"I don't think it makes sense to even talk about the Republicans or the Democrats any more. I think the party really is over, much more fundamentally than it was even 20 years ago."

— Bill Kristol, Chief of Staff to Vice President Quayle

The Discussion

David Broder: What we want to try to do now is tap the wisdom around this table, about some of the implications we can draw from what happened this year. Let's start with some of the insurgent campaigns that are represented around the table. What, if anything, do you see, Bay Buchanan, as the implication for the Republican party, or for the next stage of our politics, from what you all were able to do?

Bay Buchanan: Let me address this as a whole, rather than just in regard to the Republican party. One clear statement can be made, that it doesn't matter the size of your battleship, it doesn't matter how many consultants or experts or pollsters or different grassroots organizations you have. They are all secondary.

There are three critical things in any campaign:

It's the candidate;
It's his message; and,
It's the response of the people to the message
and that individual.

If you don't have those three things, the rest does not matter. These people [referring to the Bush/Quayle campaign team] put together a terrific organization, they were well represented in every one of those states. I can tell you firsthand. And they had experienced people, who understood the conservative voters as well as the best of

289

them. They understand how to move it. They had all the people in place, but they didn't have a message, so it doesn't make the least bit of difference.

I think the Perot situation amounts to that same thing. The people want to know what you want to do. They don't care so much whether they agree with you on every single point, but they care that you have a statement, you have a direction, that you believe it very deeply, and that you are willing to stand up for it. Even with all Perot's problems, they didn't want to leave him. They wanted to believe that he was their person.

I think that that is something that every candidate, and every consultant, and anyone involved in this process, should recognize; it's the important thing for the people in the nation. They want to know where you're going to take us, and they want to believe that you're somebody who really believes it.

And a message to the Clinton people: Don't break promises.

David Broder: Our colleague, Tom Edsall, has written a book [*Chain Reaction: The Impact of Race, Rights, and Taxes on American Politics*] focusing on the role of race, crime, and taxes as the driving forces, he argues, of American politics. What happened to those issues this year, and where do we go from here?

Stan Greenberg: I wrote a critique of that book at the beginning of this campaign, and I kid Tom about this at every opportunity. But I remember particularly a depressing conclusion to that book, which basically said that the Democratic party was doomed to be a minority, marginal party for the rest of our time.

The assumption of the book, and the reality of virtually every presidential election since 1968 is, that these elections are fought out on Democratic terrain, exaggerating and widening the fractures within that party, the divisions between white ethnics and black Americans, that plague the Democratic party. In the presidential campaigns, through the use of a range of issues, Republicans play on those divisions, and Democrats have fought among themselves right through the process.

We in the Clinton campaign decided at the beginning that this election was not about that, but that this time it was about the breakup of the *Republican* coalition and the fractures in that coalition. It was possible for us to do it because I think Bill Clinton had brought black and white together in the primary process. He took a message that was about values to both white Americans and to African Americans. He was not someone you could attack on the death penalty or crime with much effect. What that meant was we could play on the problems that were plaguing the Republican coalition. I think this is the first election since 1968 that's been fought out in this way.

The libertarian wing of the Republican party, I think, faced the Christian right in a very exaggerated way, because this was no longer a party that brought growth to the country. The Republicans were having increasing difficulty with the West, in part, I think, because of privacy and libertarian issues.

So, it wasn't just the fact that we had run in a way that made it difficult for them to attack us. We tried to run this race to take away the growth issue, take away the tax issue. Our research showed that we won the tax issue. The Republican party doesn't own the tax issue. They didn't have the economy, they didn't have taxes, they didn't particularly have crime. It's very difficult for them to figure out a way to be a majority party in that context.

Bay Buchanan: Can I respond? You didn't win the tax issue. We handed it to you. It was delivered to you on a plate a couple of years ago, as Charlie referred to.

But there's another thing here. There is a tendency now in this country, and the press has encouraged it, that if you take a strong stance — and similar stances have been taken in years past — that now it's seen as "exclusionist." You can't stand up for anything without being tagged as "exclusionist."

So, people say we've got to say it differently now. We've got to pull our punches a little bit. We've got to be careful. That's the wrong approach. What that says is that the press is right, or your critics are right, or the liberals are right, or whoever it is that is saying it, because you're hesitant now. You backed off.

I think in our convention our mistake was that they hit us hard on it. Charlie was right. It was a good convention, but we backed off. We said: "Okay, we're not going to talk about it any more. We'd better not talk about those things, because we're being hit by it." Immediately that sent a message to the American people, "Well, it must have been a bad convention, because they've indicated it was a bad convention. They've told us, in essence, their response."

I think what you have to do is walk through that criticism. You hear the press say it, and you go right through the storm to the American people. They respond to your message. If they hear you fully and clearly and recognize that you have no malice, all you are doing is saying what you believe, they respond, and the press can say what they want, the people will respond to your message. They may not agree with it, but they'll respond to you on the basis of your message, not what the press tells them.

David Broder: Let me ask Tad and Thaleia a question. Let's assume for the moment that what Stan Greenberg described is what took place, that instead of the battle being fought on the fracture lines in the

Democratic coalition Clinton was able to shift the fight in ways that exposed the fault lines in the Republican coalition. Was there something unique about Clinton that let him do that, or is that something that happened in the Democratic party, or the Republican? Was it there for any Democrat to do?

Tad Devine: Let me tell you how I view this thing, because I think that's the answer to the question. Of all the numbers that came out this year, and all the polling — the right track-wrong track, the President's drop in job approval — the most impressive number that I saw was the CBS poll, sometime in the summer, something to the effect, "Do we need real change here?" An amazing 95 percent of the respondents, 95 percent of the Democrats, 95 percent of the Independents and Republicans, all said, "We need real change."

I think there were two kinds of real change available. One was what we tried to talk about. Senator Kerrey tried to talk about, not very successfully, what he called *fundamental* change. What he meant by that was systemic change — that our system of government and the way we order our politics will be changed fundamentally, that business will be different in Washington and elsewhere.

There is another kind of change, and that is change in the status quo. What happened was that at times in this process, some people started plugging into the more powerful argument, which was fundamental change, systemic change.

Brown got a piece of it, at times. Perot certainly got into it and out of it. When Perot got out of the race, the Clinton campaign, I think very much to their credit, was able to change the argument off systemic change and onto change in the status quo, and they won that argument. People became convinced that, yes, this is what we want, change in the status quo.

That fundamental change, systemic change, is still available. I think this election is a lot like 1968. There is a potential here for an emerging Democratic majority. But the only way we're going to get it in the Democratic party is to do as Nixon did, plug into that other piece that was missing. That other piece is fundamental change, systemic change. That is no more business as usual in Washington. If you get it and you make it happen, I think the Democratic party then will have plugged into a potentially strong political agenda.

Thaleia Schlesinger: I think the basic issue came down to the economy; people were genuinely afraid for their future, for their families future. And that's what I think Paul Tsongas was talking about, when he got in, and it is what Bill Clinton's plan was.

People wanted to know that you have a plan *and* that you have an ideology. From anything I ever heard, people didn't know what George Bush believed in. Therefore, you could go at him, because there wasn't a real George Bush with whom a voter could identify. The Democrats identified the fear that was there. There was a plan. We're going to take the nation forward, there's going to be a change. You put all of that together, and that's what brought the Democrats into a very strong victory.

David Broder: Tom Luce, from your perspective, what questions have been answered, and what questions are still out there after this election?

Tom Luce: I agree with the essence of what Tad says, and I would just add this. If you look at the voters outside of Washington, whatever environment they exist in, their lives have been changed in the last ten years. Every business, every institution, every profession, has undergone radical change to survive. They believe Washington has not changed in that fundamental, systemic way that you are talking about.

As I said last night, the difficult part of their job to add to the 43 percent is to do that when they've produced a tent and the people outside are saying that the tent needs to be changed. It seems to me that they have a much more difficult assignment than Nixon did when he added to the 43 percent, because they're in the tent and the thrust is, it's got to be totally changed.

I don't think the argument any more is between the Democrats and the Republicans, because many people view the parties as virtually the same insofar as the impact on their lives.

Because Perot was a flawed messenger in this sense, James, I would say that when the battle was over changing the status quo, you could win. But if there is a viable alternative out there, where the message and the messenger are good, then they'll choose fundamental change. There are still a lot of people out there that can be moved, and will be moved, in my judgment. The power of the message for systemic change is very strong, as shown in the Perot campaign, with all the flaws of the messenger. I think it's growing and will continue to grow. It's not decreasing. The trick for the Clinton administration is how do you deal with that inside the tent?

James Carville: There is no question that there's a capital-C change going on. The Republicans are declining more than we are, but we are both declining. There is no question about that. It's significant, and I think it's on the verge of being historical. It's something that people, that I, missed in this race. We used to think that political reform was not a particularly good issue for a campaign.

I have a lot of respect for a third-party candidate who gets 19 percent of the vote in this country. Perot may have been a flawed candidate in a lot of ways, but you just cannot discount the fact that he went that far and got that many votes. It would be a mistake for the administration to discount that and just say that it's a phenomenon, and that he had $60 million, etc. There is something going on, and I think that the impact of this political reform, fundraising, etc., is a lot deeper and more prevalent than people like me thought going into the race. That is one thing I am impressed with, as a political issue.

There are votes in this thing, and that is, frankly, what gets my attention, and that of other people like myself. You cannot deny that we're on the verge of an historic change in terms of the party ideal and the parties in this country. You look at any poll and see it. I'm glad that you guys are losing votes faster than we are right now, and that is temporary, believe me. We are both losing people. I also think that this question of political reform is going to be around as an issue in campaigns for some time to come.

George Stephanopoulos: It's definitely true, but it's only true if you get your next step. Political reform will only matter to voters four years from now, if by having political reform, you then have a system that works, and an economy that improves.

James Carville: I think that people invariably will tell you that the system is driven by money and influence, and that there's no equity in it. That bothers them increasingly. Four or eight years ago, I would have said, "Look, I might agree with you, but that's not what people want you to talk about." Now I think if you missed this change, you missed something that is really swirling around there. It used to be, when I came up, the Republicans had sort of a natural advantage on this, because the Democrats would call it big-boss parties. At worst for us it's a standstill. We might be a little better on it right now than you. It's not really on the subject, but I wonder if the Congress people have realized that?

Stan Greenberg, Mary Matalin, James Carville, David Wilhelm

Tom Luce: The remarkable change now is that there is a large group of people who are what I call the radical centrists. Maybe you used to call them moderates. They are not moderates, they are radical in their desire for change. They are in the center when it comes to tolerance, when it comes to race, when it comes to a lot of issues that you use to label people moderate. They are centrist, but they are radical in their outlook on how many defects and how many termites there are in the system. They put a pox on both parties in that regard, on Congress, and on the President. They view them as all the same.

George Stephanopoulos: That's funny. The first time the *Philadelphia Inquirer* endorsed Clinton, they titled the editorial "Radical Moderate."

Tom Luce: I would say, George, I understand exactly what you are saying. I think that's what he did successfully and will continue to do for four years inside the tent; it's going to be a very difficult task.

George Stephanopoulos: And after Illinois came in, when he became an incumbent, that was when we were in trouble, because we had lost the mantle we had had all the way through New Hampshire and coming into New Hampshire. A lot of people forget, or a lot of people in Washington forget, that that first ad in New Hampshire had a strong pay-raise component. And it was pretty tough.

James Carville: I tell you, the best ad I've seen in the last two years was Wofford's thing about free health care [during his Senate race]: they get this until they do this and do that. That thing hit like a ton of bricks, because it was about political reform and health care. It was tying them together.

David Broder: Bill Kristol, how well or how badly are the Republicans positioned to deal with this situation?

Bill Kristol: I guess I'd answer it this way. James has pointed it out, and he's absolutely right. There's a little bit of a correction to Tad's formulation, in which you wind up with an emerging Democratic majority. I don't think it makes sense to even talk about the Republicans or the Democrats any more. I think the party really is over, much more fundamentally than it was even 20 years ago.

Bill Clinton ran away from the Democratic Congress, and probably got into some trouble to the extent he had to come back a little bit to his own party in the general election. I have come to the view that this was a watershed election, that it was the end of the 1968 to 1992 cycle, if you want to think in a big way, as 1968 was the end of the 1932-1964 cycle. You had a kind of emerging Republican majority, but only at the presidential level. So you had in effect a partial and an incomplete realignment over those years, with a somewhat stable set of campaigns.

Our campaign has been criticized. We ran what would have been a reasonably proficient campaign for that cycle, but it turned out that we were in the first year of a new historic cycle. Now, what that cycle will look like, God only knows. None of us is a prophet.

I would just mention a couple of things. I do not think people in general, in either party, have really thought through how dramatic the changes are. What is holding the party system together? Almost nothing. The party idea is decreasing. Only the campaign finance laws are really holding it together. It's too hard to raise money a thousand dollars at a time unless you're personally wealthy.

But we are going to have campaign finance reform. We're also going to have term limits covering a third of the members of Congress, if the state actions are constitutional. A combination of those two, if Congress either constitutionalizes term limits or the court finds them constitutional, that combined with campaign finance reform, depending on what kind of reform it is, could just totally change the character and internal dynamics of Congress, just to begin with that.

What happens to seniority? You know, the deference to the senior committee chairman, if someone serves no more than twelve years. I don't know how it changes it, but it seems to me it will change it. You've got primaries all over the place, with everyone forced to go up or out. Then, depending on how campaign finances change, you can have Independents running at different levels. We do have two Independent governors [Lowell Weicker, Connecticut, and Walter Hickel, Alaska], and I think the potential is there for more.

I think if you look at each of the branches of government, at each of the levels of government, you can make the argument that we really are at the end of an era. How the Republican party reacts to that is a hard question to answer. But in both parties it seems to me that there is a danger of saying, "We had a poor economy, didn't run an adequate campaign, or the White House was in disarray, and we lost, but we can come back. Let them have the problem of running the government for four years, and we can come back. We didn't do badly in the congressional and Senate races, etc."

The Democrats' danger is obviously that they get in and get sucked into the swamp of Washington, make the Senate finance chairman the secretary of the treasury and the former deputy secretary of state head of the transition, have a very respectable administration, and have it all spin out of control within two years. I am not sure either party is ready to face the situation.

David Broder: You may be the last Republican National Chairman who ever sits at this table, from the way this conversation is going. Is there anything that you see taking place in party structure, either on your side or on the Democratic side, that is likely to change the scenario that's been laid out here?

Rich Bond: First, David, to go back to something that they said, because you disagreed with Bill's assertion earlier that we have to say things a little differently. And, Bay, if I understood you correctly, you felt that that was pulling a punch, and not being true to your soul on it.

So let me follow, and say that I don't want to personalize this to either you or Pat, but as a broader impression of a problem that the party ended up with at the end of this election. That is, if hard-core conservatives think that you can't be in the Republican party if you're gay, and there is no home for that in the Republican party, that's wrong.

If you feel, not you personally, or Pat, but if Phyllis Schlafly feels, for instance, that the next party chairman cannot be pro-choice, and that if you are pro-choice, you can't be in a position of party leadership, you can't be a respected party spokesman, you can't be a candidate, you can't be a decision-maker, that's wrong.

If the Governor of Mississippi wants to assert that we should not recognize the role of the Judeo-Christian heritage in America, that's wrong.

I think what we have to do, especially since there will be a new RNC chairman in about two months, is to look very carefully. I think we have the great commonality of wanting to be thoughtful conservatives. We honestly see government differently from the way Betsey does, the way that James and George, and the rest do. It's an honest disagreement, and it can be an honest, civilized disagreement on things like foreign policy or the economy. And yet we ended up this election with the image and a reputation for being narrow-minded, or for being intolerant.

I don't think, coming full circle to what Bill was saying, that if there is to be a viable Republican party, notwithstanding what Ross Perot or others may do in the future, we can go in that direction. I want to agree with Bill, to say we can express positions and principles, but if we step over the line to be judgmental of other people in a way that is hostile to their very being, I think we've made a fundamental mistake.

So what I would like to see is a great deal more thought and care in our communication of principles and positions. I happen to be a Catholic, so I happen to be pro-life, but I am not going to close the door on anybody, to be chairman of the party or to be a candidate for office in the party, or to be an official of the party, or to be a member of the White House staff, just because they believe differently from me on that issue.

Now, I think Phyllis Schlafly and I may have a great debate and a great argument over that issue, and I think that is a fundamental problem that we as a party need to come to grips with, before we can ever be successful. If we don't overcome these obstacles internally, then they will have to screw it up in the next two years with their personnel, with their first 100 days, with their agenda, with their handling of the economy, to hand us a big victory in the 1994 mid-term elections, similar to what Jimmy Carter did in his first term in 1978. His mistakes positioned us just perfectly, to go back with Ronald Reagan, the way we did in 1980.

Bay Buchanan: When I suggested pulling punches, what I'm saying is, we have a desire now not to offend anyone, to make a statement that somehow loosens up what we really believe, in an effort that people will say then, "It's okay now." Take abortion, we're pro-life. If you want to change the wording, to make everybody happy, you can't. You can't do that. You're either pro-life or you're not pro-life. I mean, it's very simple. When you make an effort to please the press or please pro-choice friends, it's a clear signal that you're walking away from a belief. You either walk away from it or you stick with it. You can't do the middle.

And it doesn't matter what the issue is. Just because they hit us if we say we don't believe gays should be in the military, that's a very legitimate discussion. People will disagree with us. It doesn't mean that we're exclusionist, it means this is a very serious belief and a conviction that we have.

Disagree with us, call us names, do what you want, it's our belief. But the parties shouldn't mush it all up and be the party of mush, because we have more than one already in Washington. So, let's stand up for something, and if we lose, we lose. But let's stand up for something. That's the only way you attract, if you believe.

Rich Bond: Standing up for something.

Bay Buchanan: One second. That is exactly relative. The whole purpose of life for the people in this room is to win, but the purpose in life for the people in this country is to believe in something and have a direction, and they want their party to have those things. The purpose of the party isn't simply to have more R's in the column, it's to have a direction for the nation, so that when we do elect our president he is taking us somewhere. If the people then say "We don't want to go there," fine, but we are taking them somewhere. What happened in the last four years is we elected a person who we thought was taking us somewhere, and nobody seemed to know, after four years, where the heck we were going. And all we worried about was winning. We needed to redefine ourselves.

Rich Bond: That's a fine principled statement, especially in terms of your latter comments about the fact that you felt the President strayed off his compass, which was a compass that you thought you shared with him previously. But if standing up for principles means closing a door in somebody's face, that's wrong.

I seem to be picking on Phyllis Schlafly, whom I do have many disagreements with, coming off of that convention, particularly where she was perfectly happy on abortion, and then turned around and said that Bush is going to lose the election because he betrayed us on taxes. Well, thank you, Phyllis. Phyllis's love for her son was a mother's love, and that meant that the door to her home was still open to that child, and we have got to understand as human beings that we cannot take positions on one level and talk about it, and then on the other level just totally discard people on a judgmental basis.* I'm not saying that you did it, or Pat did it, we'll let you decide what you've done or said. The point is, we cannot build a party to come back and govern again if we totally run people off the reservation.

Bay Buchanan: No. But what you're suggesting is what we should go out and reach around and say: "Everybody, this is a party for everyone."
    You missed a step. The first step is to say, "This is where we are taking the nation. These are our principles. We're going to state them. You might not like them, but this is where we are going together. It gives us direction. We wish everybody would help us. You may disagree, just as our pro-choice friends in our party, who offer a great deal to our party, disagree with our pro-life status. Fine. Join us. Help us on those things you think are the most critical. It could indeed be the limited-government aspects of our party."

Rich Bond: That's right.

Bay Buchanan: But do not first say, "Everybody come on in. We're not excluding anybody."

Rich Bond: That's not what happened. If we can say we stand for certain things, but if you don't agree with these certain things, that's still okay. Come and agree with us on the things we can agree on.

Bay Buchanan: I don't have any problem with that.

Elizabeth Arnold: We're going to be hearing a lot about this, I have a feeling, in the next few years. But there are some loose ends we want to cover, and I think, quite fittingly, this is a loose end, and it's interesting that it is a loose end. We haven't talked about Hillary at all. What do you think the limits of Hillary's role in the administration should be?

Bay Buchanan: In the administration? I'm certain that Hillary is a very intelligent and knowledgeable, accomplished woman. I think there should be no limits whatsoever. But she has to choose whether to take on a policy role or the honored position of being First Lady, which is far less controversial, where you don't take strong policy positions but help causes and address issues in a very powerful way. She could take on something like abused women, abused children, that everyone would

---

Editor's Note: The September 6, 1992 issue of *QW*, a gay magazine, identified Phyllis Schlafly's son John as gay. On September 18 he said he was homosexual and that the magazine was trying to embarrass his mother, who publicly opposes such things such as same-sex marriage, which many gays support. John Schlafly said the Republican party was not biased against homosexuals and that he endorsed his mother's views on abortion and other issues.

agree with. But if she chooses to move ahead on agendas that are very firmly defined and controversial, she will bring upon herself a great deal of criticism, which would be warranted. It would be very difficult for a President, who is going to have to take very difficult positions, also to have his wife under attack.

Barbara Bush is someone who is very much loved by the whole country, and she ends up as a real asset in an administration where the President is the one who has to take the criticism.

Elizabeth Arnold: James, you look like you're angry.

James Carville: No, I'm not angry, but I thought we were here to discuss what happened in the campaign, and now we've got Hillary's role in the White House. We have a saying that says, "If you see a turtle on a fence post, you can pretty much assume somebody put it there." She's great. She's the one that helped me come up with the campaign. I think she's wonderful.

And that's another rule in this world. The person that has the last word with somebody before they go to bed at night, and the first one when they get up in the morning, go ahead and take that person seriously. From my vantage point, I hope she has a lot of influence. She's a smart, bright woman, and that's the whole thing.

I want to go back to something that was said. I think when these words occur in these campaigns — this whole thing about exclusion and the way that the Republican party is viewed — when you say things, people pick them up.

I certainly would never vote for somebody who stands up there and says: "This is a Christian nation," and then Carroll Campbell says: "Are you a Christian?" I'm going to tell you, if someone would have addressed six million Cajuns, and said it was an Anglo-Saxon nation, and then added, "no, it's a Gaelic Anglo-Saxon nation," that would have sent a message to me.*

I think Rich, and a lot of Republicans, understood. And if you say something about gays, and it turns out that your son is gay, people are

---

*Editor's Note: At the closing news conference of a Republican governors' meeting, Gov. Kirk Fordice of Mississippi and Gov. Carroll Campbell got into a discussion on the role of religion in U.S. politics. Fordice said, "The United States of America is a Christian nation, which does not mean ... to infer... religious intolerance ...The less we emphasize the Christian religion, the further we fall into the abyss of poor character and chaos in the United States." Governor Campbell broke in with, "The value base of this country comes from the Judeo-Christian heritage we have ... I just wanted to add the 'Judeo' part." Fordice responded, "If I had wanted to do that, I would have done it." Rich Bond called Governor Fordice's statement contrary to the party's platform and "wrong."

going to notice that, and they're going to report that. And that's going to send a signal.

Words don't come up in vacuums, and events don't come up in vacuums. I think that the reaction to what Governor Fordice was — I don't know. The staff in our office could argue that, about whether it's a Christian nation or a Judeo-Christian nation. From what I learned, it's a bunch of crooks that came to Georgia. [Laughter]

What I'm saying is, you just can't discount words and their meaning when you use them. People hear something different ways, based on their own experience, and the experiences of other people. That's my point.

David Broder: I want to try, at the risk of getting my head handed to me, to see if there is a way of linking what we've been talking about in the campaign to what now lies ahead in terms of government. I'd ask maybe Carney and Kristol to say, from where you sit, having been in the White House, what demands does this kind of political environment put on a new president, in terms of the way in which he operates? Can he adapt to the kind of political climate, and the kind of voters, that we've seen this year?

Dave Carney: Two things. One is, I think, in today's climate, both with the media and with the opposition in 1996, that every word the president utters is on the record, is available. There is constant scrutiny of the performance, and there will not be a honeymoon in the way the media and the opposition respond to the first appointments and to the implementation of campaign promises.

What Ron Brown gave to the nominee was a party united and under control — be good, behave, be quiet, and let's get somebody elected, and let's see what it's like to be back in the White House.

People don't have to rely on Washington insiders to interpret what he does. You can see it live. They saw him in the campaign, and they'll see him in performance. You know, Clinton is a good politician. But what happens when he starts to make decisions on who his cabinet members are going to be?

There's an incumbent who's been in Washington since 1948, and he's been involved in every fiscal decision made, the budget, all the pay raises, all of that.* Every tax increase he's been in charge of. Does he symbolize the dynamic new change that we're going to bring in the White House? All those kinds of decisions have to be outlined, and it's going to be very tough to walk that line that Ron Brown gave to the nominee, whoever the nominee was going to be. Now they're going to want to see

---

*Editor's Note: Lloyd Bentsen was elected to Congress in 1948 at age 27 where he served six years. He returned to Washington in 1970 as a U.S. Senator from Texas.

delivery. That's internal pressure, and the whole country is going to watch it unravel. People underestimate how difficult it is to be in the White House — to do a good job of governing *and* to be political. It's very, very tough to do both.

Mary Matalin: It is possible. Ron Reagan did it. Jim Baker did it for Ronald Reagan, and then Jim Baker pulled the levers on the 1984 campaign. It takes much of what they did in the campaign, but in a different way. Not a campaign way. It takes discipline, focus, and you cannot disconnect government from politics. It's an easy concept, very hard implementation.

Mary Matalin, Charlie Black

Bill Kristol: It's a big question. I do think the Reagan model of always being anti-Washington somehow changed. Of course, when he became President, it was a helpful model, and of course, that's easier said than done.

I think the Democratic Congress is the biggest problem in the new Democratic administration. On the one hand they need desperately to get things passed, and they do need to show genuine progress in addressing the issues that they highlighted successfully during the campaign.

On the other hand, they have to work with the most unpopular institution in America, I suppose, to get the stuff done. Let's see Bill Clinton wanting to get legislation through the Democratic Congress and also having a very visible fight with the Democratic Congress, vetoing some pork-barrel spending or insisting on the line-item veto, whatever. Doing both of those at once I think is a challenge, but it's not undoable.

With the political challenges and the decline of the parties, everything is so volatile. You need more control in the White House than perhaps you once did.

I think Bill Clinton should take his top seven people and make them his chief of staff, deputy chief of staff and top five assistants to the President, for economic policy, domestic policy, national security policy, and political affairs, and make sure they control the administration.

We did a terrible job in the Bush administration in the disciplining of the Cabinet. I just think the White House needs to control things much more directly. The White House needs to be on top of everything that gets into the evening news level of attention. We permitted all kinds of Cabinet fights to go on, and I think we paid a huge price for that down the road.

One funny point. In places like the Kennedy School they mention this a lot. There is great lamenting about the fast turnover of political appointees. The idea is you cannot have a consistent policy unless you keep people in office longer.

Well, the Bush administration, I am certain, had the longest tenure for its political appointees of any administration in modern times, from the top down to the lower — look at the Cabinet, look at the top economic team. The stability was extraordinary, but I think we probably paid a price for that. I'm not saying that they were bad, but the energy does go, people get tired, and they have a huge stake in defending their decisions of two years ago or three years ago. Like any corporation in this day and age, you need to mix things up, shake things up a little more than would be the inclination, in this case, of a president who thought people should stay in the job until there was a very manifest reason why they should leave. The main thing one has to resist, I suppose, is sitting back and assuming that things are going okay.

David Broder: George, would you like to respond, in terms of what makes sense out of what you've just heard?

George Stephanopoulos: First of all, I agree that you do need control in the White House. I think that that's not necessarily new. Reagan did it in 1980. They came in and they had very, very sound discipline. They had a legislative strategy. They had strong control over what was going to get on the news every night, and what was going to be on the agenda of the Congress.

I think it is just common sense that you can't try to solve every problem that comes across your plate. You've got to pick what you want to do. Whether or not there was a mandate, people clearly elected Bill

Clinton to do something about the economy, and you can't avoid making that your number one priority and pushing away everything that moves away from that. You cannot separate politics from government at all. There were some stories, even this week, about the endless campaign. There is no way around it.

Right now we have 24-hour news cycles, and I think that was one of the other things in the campaign. You saw it. There is no one cycle a day, no two cycles a day. CNN assures that you are forced to react at any time, and that's going to happen throughout the time of the presidency, and it probably will get worse if you get up to 500 channels on television. You have to pay attention to the signals you're sending out all the time.

The toughest part of this is discipline. And I think that is going to be the hardest thing we have to grapple with. You have to have discipline, to decide what we want to do, to build a consensus to do it, and then to stick by it once it's done.

David Broder: Thank you very much.

CAMPAIGN CALENDAR HIGHLIGHTS

1990

March 5 — Republican National Chairman Lee Atwater collapsed and was hospitalized.

October 5 — In a late night session, 104 House Republicans joined 147 Democrats to reject the budget compromise in which President Bush had agreed to a tax increase, thus breaking his famous "no new taxes" pledge.

1991

January 16 — Allied forces launched a ferocious air attack against Iraq. President Bush addressed the nation, confirming that "Operation Desert Shield" had become "Operation Desert Storm."

February 23 — Allied forces began the invasion of Kuwait (and parts of southern Iraq).

February 27 — President Bush announced that Allied forces would suspend military operations in the Gulf War at midnight. "Kuwait is liberated," he said. "Iraq's army is defeated."

March 3 — The Gallup Organization reported that a new poll it had just conducted showed President Bush with a job approval rating of 89%. This was said to be a record for any president.

March 29 — Republican National Chairman Lee Atwater died at a Washington hospital.

April 30 — Former Massachusetts Senator Paul Tsongas announced his candidacy for the Democratic presidential nomination.

May 23 — Former Democratic presidential nominee George McGovern, speaking at the National Press Club, said he would not run for President in 1992.

July 17 — In a two-page letter which he sent to his House colleagues, House Majority Leader Richard Gephardt (D-MO) said he would not run for President in 1992.

August 15 — Governor Clinton said that he would form a committee to explore running for president in 1992. He said he would decide by Labor Day whether or not to run and that he would resign as chairman of the Democratic Leadership Council (DLC).

August 21 — Tennessee Senator Albert Gore, in a written statement released from his home in Carthage, said he would not run for president in 1992.

September 3 — Former California Governor (1975–1983) Jerry Brown said he would drop his campaign for the U.S. Senate, and would instead form a committee to explore running for president in 1992. He said that if he did run for president he would accept no contribution of more than $100.

September 13   Virginia Governor Douglas Wilder announced in a Richmond speech that he would seek the 1992 Democratic presidential nomination.

September 15   Iowa Senator Tom Harkin announced that he would seek the 1992 Democratic presidential nomination.

September 30   In a speech at the state capitol in Lincoln, Nebraska Senator Bob Kerrey announced that he would seek the Democratic presidential nomination.

October 3   Governor Clinton, in a speech at the state capitol in Little Rock, announced that he would seek the 1992 Democratic presidential nomination.

October 6   NPR and Newsday reported allegations that Supreme Court Justice nominee Clarence Thomas had sexually harassed a woman who worked for him at two federal agencies. The allegations were made by Professor Anita Hill, who teaches at the University of Oklahoma Law School.

October 11   President Bush filed papers with the FEC, forming the re-election committee, the "Bush-Quayle '92 Primary Committee." Filing of the papers allows the campaign to conduct fund-raising activities.

                The Senate Judiciary Committee began a set of hearings into allegations that Supreme Court Justice nominee Clarence Thomas had sexually harassed women in his office. The committee heard testimony from Judge Thomas and his accuser, Anita Hill.

October 15   By a narrow vote of 52 to 48, the Senate confirmed the nomination of Clarence Thomas to be a justice of the Supreme Court.

November 2   The Reverend Jesse Jackson announced that he would not seek the 1992 Democratic presidential nomination. He asked his supporters to withhold their support from other candidates.

December 4   David Duke, a former leader of the Ku Klux Klan, announced his intention to seek the 1992 Republican presidential nomination. Mr. Duke spoke at a news conference in the National Press Building.

December 10   Patrick Buchanan announced that he would seek the 1992 Republican presidential nomination. Buchanan attacked President Bush for breaking his "no new taxes" promise, and called for an "America First" policy.

December 15   At the state party convention, Florida Democrats cast the following straw votes for presidential candidates:

                | Clinton | 950 | 54% |
                | Harkin | 549 | 31% |
                | Kerrey | 181 | 10% |
                | Others | | 5% |

December 20   New York Governor Mario Cuomo announced that he would not seek the 1992 Democratic presidential nomination. Mr. Cuomo said he could not run because he needed to continue work on the state budget deficit.

December 28   It was reported that Nebraska restaurants and health clubs owned (in part) by Senator Bob Kerrey, who has been making national health care a main campaign theme, do not provide health insurance for most employees.

1992

January 1	Economic Indicators as of January 1, 1992

DJIA	(Dec. 31)	3168.83
Annual GDP Growth Rate	(3Q 1991)	1.8%
Annual Unemployment Rate	(Nov. 1991)	6.8%
Annual Inflation Rate	(Nov. 1991)	3.0%

January 8   Governor Douglas Wilder announced that he was quitting the race for the 1992 Democratic presidential nomination. He blamed his decision on the need to spend time on his duties as governor. Analysts suggested Governor Clinton was the candidate most likely to gain from Governor Wilder's decision.

During a visit to Japan, President Bush became ill at a dinner given by the Japanese Prime Minister. He was seen collapsing, then being assisted by his doctors, by Secret Service agents, and by the Japanese Prime Minister.

January 15   Campaigning in New Hampshire, President Bush said that the economy was in "free fall." He acknowledged he had been slow to admit the economy was not recovering from the recession as quickly as he thought it would. This was the President's first trip to New Hampshire as part of his effort to stave off a challenge from Patrick Buchanan.

January 17   Several tabloid newspapers reported that Governor Clinton stood accused of having had affairs with five women. The charges were contained in papers filed in a lawsuit by a fired former Arkansas state employee, Larry Nichols. Mr. Clinton denounced the reports as an "absolute total lie."

January 23   Gennifer Flowers, who worked for the Arkansas state government, said she had a long-running affair with Governor Clinton. Ms. Flowers also said she had audio tapes of phone conversations with him. The charges were printed in the "supermarket tabloid" *The Star*. Clinton, campaigning in New Hampshire, said: "The allegations in today's *Star* are not true. I have nothing to add to what I've said in the past."

January 26   The Clintons appeared on a special edition of "60 Minutes" following the Super Bowl broadcast.

January 27   At a New York City news conference, Gennifer Flowers played portions of her audio tapes of her phone conversations with Governor Clinton. The tapes did not explicitly confirm her claims re an affair, but were fairly intimate. The tapes contained an attack on Governor Cuomo, for which Clinton subsequently apologized.

January 29   In his annual State of the Union message to a joint session of Congress President Bush revealed his set of proposals to deal with national economic problems.

February 1   Rich Bond, a long-time political aide to President Bush, was elected to replace Clayton Yeutter as Republican National Chairman.

Economic Indicators as of February 1, 1992   vs. Jan. 1

DJIA	(Jan. 31)	3223.39	+54.56
Annual GDP Growth Rate	(4Q 1991)	0.3%	
Annual Unemployment Rate	(Dec. 1991)	7.1%	+0.3%
Annual Inflation Rate	(Dec. 1991)	3.1%	+0.1%

February 6	The *Wall Street Journal* quoted a former draft board official and a former ROTC recruiter as saying that Clinton had manipulated the draft process. Clinton, who opposed the Vietnam War, denied improperly avoiding military service in 1968-69. Clinton never served in the military.
February 10	Iowa Senator Tom Harkin won the largely uncontested Iowa precinct caucuses. Uncommitted finished second, and Nebraska Senator Bob Kerrey finished fifth.
February 12	President Bush announced that he was a candidate for re-election. Mr. Bush did not mention challenger Pat Buchanan in his speech.
	The Clinton campaign released the text of a letter (dated 3 Dec. 1969) which Clinton wrote to Col. Eugene Holmes, then head of the University of Arkansas ROTC. In the letter, Clinton thanked Holmes for "saving me from the draft."
	Following a speech to the Institute of Politics at Harvard University, Governor Cuomo said in answer to a question: "In my own state, they're saying lousy things about me. If they want to say nice things about me in New Hampshire, I'm going to encourage them."
February 14	The Associated Press reported: "Senator Wendell Ford (D-KY) said today that Lloyd Bentsen had told him he would be willing to enter the Democratic presidential race if party leaders asked him to do so."
February 18	Former Senator Tsongas won the New Hampshire primary with about one-third of the total vote. Governor Clinton, calling himself the "Comeback Kid," finished second with 25%. The other Democratic contenders fared poorly at the polls.
	President Bush won the New Hampshire primary with a bare majority of the votes cast. Pat Buchanan ran a strong second, garnering the support of over a third of Republican primary voters.
February 20	Appearing on the CNN "call-in" program "Larry King Live," Texas billionaire Ross Perot said he would run for president as an Independent if "grass roots" supporters got his name on the ballot in all 50 states. Perot said he had a plan for reducing the federal budget deficit "without breaking a sweat."
February 23	Paul Tsongas won the Maine caucuses, barely defeating Jerry Brown in the town-by-town tallies. Tsongas garnered 30% of the delegates elected, Brown 29%. Uncommitted finished third. Bill Clinton finished fourth.
February 25	Senator Bob Kerrey won the South Dakota Democratic presidential primary, with 40% of the vote. Iowa Senator Tom Harkin finished second with 25%. Governor Clinton finished third with 19%.
	President Bush won the South Dakota Republican presidential primary tonight with 69% of the vote. Pat Buchanan was not on the ballot. "Uncommitted" received 31% of the votes cast.
March 1	Economic Indicators as of March 1, 1992 vs. Jan. 1

			vs. Jan. 1
DJIA	(Feb. 28)	3267.67	+98.84
Annual GDP Growth Rate	(4Q 1991)	0.8%	
Annual Unemployment Rate	(Jan. 1992)	7.1%	+0.3%
Annual Inflation Rate	(Jan. 1992)	2.6%	-0.1%

March 3	Bush Job Rating: Horse Race:

Bush Job Rating:

Approve	41%
Disapprove	53%

Horse Race:

Bush	44%
Unnamed Dem	48%

It was particularly notable that Bush was (nominally) trailing even an unnamed Democrat, for the first time.

Governor Clinton won the Georgia Democratic presidential primary, capturing an impressive 57% of the votes cast. Paul Tsongas finished a distant second. Elsewhere, Jerry Brown won the Colorado Democratic presidential primary. Paul Tsongas won the Maryland and Utah Democratic presidential primaries. Senator Tom Harkin won the Idaho caucus vote.

President Bush crushed Pat Buchanan in the Colorado, Georgia, and Maryland Republican presidential primaries, winning all three states by margins of about 2-1.

March 5   At a Senate Office Building news conference in Washington, Senator Kerrey announced the end of his presidential campaign.

March 7   Governor Clinton continued his sweep of Southern primary states, crushing Paul Tsongas in the South Carolina primary by a huge margin (63% - 19%). Elsewhere, Tsongas won the Arizona primary, and Clinton won the Wyoming caucuses.

President Bush rolled over weakening challenger Pat Buchanan in the South Carolina Republican presidential primary. Mr. Bush captured 67% of the votes cast. Mr. Buchanan received about a quarter of the total vote. David Duke won 7%.

March 9   Senator Tom Harkin ended his bid for the 1992 Democratic presidential nomination

March 10   Governor Clinton crushed his opposition in key Super Tuesday balloting, winning the Florida, Louisiana, Mississippi, Oklahoma, Tennessee, and Texas primaries, all by wide margins. President Bush also buried his opponents, Pat Buchanan and David Duke, in every state primary ballot.

March 17   Governor Clinton won the Illinois and Michigan primaries with majority votes. Clinton pointed to the Midwestern states vote as proof of his national appeal. President Bush's steamroller continued along, crushing Pat Buchanan in both Illinois and Michigan by wide margins.

Speaking at the National Press Club in Washington, Ross Perot said he would be willing to spend millions of dollars of his own money on his presidential campaign, and that donations would not be accepted. He outlined a plan to "take out the trash" of the Federal government.

March 19   Former Senator Paul Tsongas "suspended" his campaign for the Democratic presidential nomination. He had won four primaries and five caucus states, prior to dropping out of the race.

March 20   Ross Perot was quoted as saying he was prepared to spend between $50 million and $100 million of his own money on a run for the presidency.

March 24   Former California Governor Jerry Brown defeated Governor Bill Clinton by the barest of margins in the Connecticut Democratic presidential primary. Mr. Brown received 37% of the votes cast, Mr. Clinton 36%.

310   *Campaign for President '92*

March 29	The *New York Times* reported that Telco said Perot's phone banks in Texas had received more than one million phone calls over the past three weeks.
April 1	On the syndicated Phil Donahue show, Governor Clinton was questioned about allegations of marital infidelity and draft evasion. Clinton said, "I don't think it's an example of bad character to admit you're not perfect."

<table>
<tr><td colspan="4">Economic Indicators as of April 1, 1992</td><td>vs. Jan. 1</td></tr>
<tr><td>DJIA</td><td>(Mar. 31)</td><td></td><td>3235.47</td><td>+66.64</td></tr>
<tr><td>Annual GDP Growth Rate</td><td>(Mar. 31)</td><td></td><td>0.4%</td><td></td></tr>
<tr><td>Annual Unemployment Rate</td><td>(Feb. 1992)</td><td></td><td>7.3%</td><td>+0.5%</td></tr>
<tr><td>Annual Inflation Rate</td><td>(Feb. 1992)</td><td></td><td>2.8%</td><td>-0.2%</td></tr>
</table>

April 3	After various news organizations were apparently made aware of its existence, Governor Clinton issued a statement admitting that in the spring of 1969, while studying at Oxford, he received a draft induction notice. He said he had not mentioned it earlier because he regarded it as a routine administrative matter.
April 7	Governor Clinton won the New York primary by a comfortable margin over Jerry Brown and Paul Tsongas. Mr. Tsongas, an inactive candidate, finished second in the voting.
April 9	Paul Tsongas said he would not re-enter the race for the Democratic presidential nomination. The matter had arisen because Tsongas had continued to receive substantial numbers of votes in recent primaries, despite his having pulled out of the contest.
April 21	The Texas Poll released data from a poll of 674 likely general election voters in Texas, interviewed April 9-18. Mr. Perot led with 35%, President Bush received 30%, and Governor Clinton trailed with 20%.
April 22	David Duke announced he was ending his bid for the GOP presidential nomination. He said he would not run as an Independent presidential candidate in the fall.
April 27	The *New York Daily News* published an interview with Jesse Jackson in which he was quoted as saying: "If I am rejected this time, I am prepared to react." Later in the day Jackson issued a written statement which included this: "Let me be clear. At no time did I threaten the candidate or the party over the vice-presidency or anything else."
April 28	Governor Clinton and President Bush posted big wins in their respective parties' Pennsylvania presidential primaries. Clinton received 57% of the Democratic vote. Mr. Bush received 77% of the Republican vote.
April 29	Racial rioting began in Los Angeles, following a jury verdict acquitting several L.A. policemen accused of brutality against Rodney King.
May 1	

<table>
<tr><td colspan="4">Economic Indicators as of May 1, 1992</td><td>vs. Jan. 1</td></tr>
<tr><td>DJIA</td><td>(Apr. 30)</td><td></td><td>3359.12</td><td>+109.29</td></tr>
<tr><td>Annual GDP Growth Rate</td><td>(1Q 1992)</td><td></td><td>2.0%</td><td></td></tr>
<tr><td>Annual Unemployment Rate</td><td>(March 1992)</td><td></td><td>7.3%</td><td>+0.5%</td></tr>
<tr><td>Annual Inflation Rate</td><td>(March 1992)</td><td></td><td>3.2%</td><td>+0.2%</td></tr>
</table>

May 4   As a result of state conventions over the weekend in Maine and Wyoming, President Bush attained the simple majority of the 2209 GOP national convention delegates necessary for renomination.

May 13   The California Poll (Mervin Field) published data from a poll of 1107 California registered voters conducted May 6-9. The poll showed Ross Perot leading President Bush and Governor Clinton by 37% - 31% (Bu) - 25% (Cl).

May 17   Results from a *Time* magazine/CNN survey of 917 registered voters, conducted May 13-14 (by Yankelovich Clancy Shulman), showed Perot (33%) leading President Bush (28%) and Governor Clinton (24%).

May 19   Speaking in San Francisco, Vice-President Quayle charged that the lack of family values caused the L.A. riots. He also attacked the television program, "Murphy Brown."

May 20   In an interview with CNN, former President Ford said the possibility that the Perot candidacy would push the presidential election into the House worried him, because he thought it would cause a "constitutional crisis." He said the House might deadlock, and added: "It's a scary scenario."

May 22   The *Los Angeles Times* quoted the White House Press Secretary Marlin Fitzwater as saying Ross Perot was a "monster." Mr. Fitzwater was also quoted as saying that he thought Mr. Perot was "dangerous."

May 23   Associated Press reported that in 1955, after serving two years, Ross Perot wrote to Republican representative Wright Patman: "I have found the Navy to be a fairly Godless organization ... I constantly hear the Lord's name taken in vain at all levels ... " Perot also complained of moral squalor and philandering. His request for early release was denied, because Navy officials decided "no hardship exists."

May 28   Attacking Ross Perot, Marilyn Quayle said: "I think it's pretty sad when someone can capture the imagination of the country with money and no policy. He [Perot] doesn't stand for anything and that is worrisome to me, that you can in essence buy an election without standing for anything."

June 2   Governor Clinton defeated former Gov. Jerry Brown in the California Democratic presidential primary. Mr. Clinton received 47% of the votes cast, Mr. Brown, 40%, of the vote.

June 3   Former Carter White House chief of staff Hamilton Jordan and former Reagan campaign manager Ed Rollins announced that they had been hired to be co-managers of the Perot presidential campaign.

June 4   Marilyn Quayle said of Ross Perot, "He reminds me of the rainmaker, the fellow that went around with his cart and his pony and sold snake oil medicine, or he said he'd make rain on your farm, and he hoodwinked people and got to their souls and made them believe, and yet there was nothing there ... I think he's selling a bill of goods."

June 11   News agencies reported that the Clinton campaign had run out of cash, and was not able to pay its staff. Campaign workers were being asked to forgo their paychecks until the campaign was able to raise more money. The Democratic National Committee paid $400,000 for a nationally televised program (on NBC) because the Clinton campaign did not have the money.

Despite the strong (if recent) support of President Bush, the House voted against a balanced budget amendment to the Constitution. Governor Clinton opposed the amendment.

June 12   The *Wall Street Journal* (Rogers and Abramson) reported that Ross Perot often used private detectives to gather information about his employees and competitors. The long story said the surveillance frequently focused on marital infidelity.

Vice-President Quayle attacked Perot, saying, "It would be a serious mistake to replace a genuine statesman with a temperamental tycoon who has contempt for the Constitution of the United States." The latter was (apparently) a reference to charges that Perot once proposed fencing (or sealing) off a section of Dallas and conducting house-to-house searches looking for drug offenders. Perot denied having made this proposal.

Speaking to a meeting of the Rainbow Coalition, Governor Clinton attacked a black rap singer, "Sister Souljah," for having used racially inflammatory language in an interview with the *Washington Post.* She was quoted as saying, "Why not have a week and kill white people?"

June 18   The *New York Times* reported more details about the money troubles of the Clinton campaign, which was not paying its staff. It also owed an Arkansas bank $2.7 million. A Clinton fund-raiser blamed Ross Perot for the financial difficulties, saying his candidacy gave contributors an "excuse" not to donate funds until "people know what it means."

June 21   Governor Clinton spelled out a detailed plan for the economy. It (1) abandoned his proposal, made during the primary season, for a flat 10% "middle-class tax cut," proposing instead a system of tax credits; (2) included tax increases for the rich (top 2%) and foreign corporations; (3) offered $150 billion deficit cuts in existing programs and military outlays; and (4) suggested hiring veterans to rebuild infrastructure.

The *Washington Post* reported that Ross Perot had a falling out with then-Vice-President Bush in 1986 over the so-called MIAs. Then, said the *Post,* in the following year Perot launched a series of investigations in pursuit of information that might uncover improper conduct by Bush. The investigations were fruitless.

At a news conference in Annapolis, Perot said: "There has been a ninety-day effort to redefine my personality by a group called Opposition Research of the Republican party. They're generally known as the dirty tricks crowd." Later, on "Larry King Live," Perot said he had evidence to support the charge, but declined to disclose it.

June 25   Speaking in an interview with Barbara Walters broadcast on ABC, Bush said of his decision to agree to increased taxes: "That was a mistake, because it undermined to some degree my credibility with the American people."

June 29 The U.S. Supreme Court upheld most of the Pennsylvania abortion restriction law, but also explicitly renewed its support for *Roe vs. Wade*. President Bush reacted in a written statement in which he said he was "pleased" by the decision, adding that he believes the Pennsylvania law is in keeping with his support for "family values." Governor Clinton said, "The constitutional right to choose is hanging by a thread."

July 1 Economic Indicators as of July 1, 1992   vs. Jan. 1

DJIA   3318.52 +149.69
Annual GDP Growth Rate   (1Q 1992)   2.4%
Annual Unemployment Rate   (May. 1992)   7.5%   +0.7%
Annual Inflation Rate   (May 1992)   3.0%   same

July 2 The unemployment rate for June was 7.8%, the highest rate since 1984. During June 117,000 jobs were lost from the economy.

July 9 At a rally in Little Rock, Governor Clinton announced that Senator Albert Gore (D-TN) was his pick for the Democratic vice-presidential nomination. Gore immediately accepted.

July 11 Speaking at a national NAACP convention in Nashville, Ross Perot was accused (by a 21-year-old college student in the audience) of insensitivity. In discussing the U.S. economy Perot said "you" and "your people" were the ones hurt first and worst by bad economic times. NAACP leader Benjamin Hooks sought to play down the incident; Perot later said he meant no offense.

July 13 The Democratic National Convention opened.

July 15 Ed Rollins announced he was leaving the Perot presidential campaign. He said there were "irreconcilable differences" between him and Perot over campaign strategy.

Ross Perot announced he was withdrawing from the race.

The Democratic National Convention nominated Governor Clinton as its presidential candidate. The roll call vote was as follows:

Clinton   3372   Tsongas   209
Brown   596   Others   80

Governor Clinton accepted his party's presidential nomination with a 54-minute speech in which he pledged to put the government back on the side of the American middle class.

July 17 Governor and Mrs. Clinton and Senator and Mrs. Gore left New York City in a bus caravan that would visit eight states.

Appearing on "Larry King Live," Ross Perot encouraged his supporters to continue efforts to put his name on state ballots, although he repeated he would not be a candidate.

July 19 A Gallup Poll, from interviews with 755 registered voters conducted July 17-18, showed Governor Clinton leading President Bush by 56% to 34% nationally.

July 22 It was reported that Secretary of State James Baker would leave his post to return to the White House as President Bush's senior policy advisor and head of the re-election campaign.

July 26 President Bush said that Vice-President Quayle's position on the Republican ticket was "very certain." Quayle said on "Larry King

Live" that if he thought he was in any way damaging the President he would leave the ticket. But he added that he was in fact helping the President.

Published details of Ross Perot's plan for cutting the federal budget deficit said it would raise gasoline taxes, increase taxes on Social Security benefits, double federal tobacco taxes, cut Medicare spending, impose 10% cuts on federal "discretionary" spending, increase the top income tax bracket (to 33%), and cut more defense spending than proposed by President Bush.

July 28   The so-called Consumer Confidence Index fell to 61.0 from 72.6 in June, a drop of 16%, which erased nearly all of the gain since February when the index stood at 47.3.

August 1   Economic Indicators as of August 1, 1992   vs. Jan. 1

DJIA	(July 31)	3393.78	+224.95
Annual GDP Growth Rate	(1Q 1992)	1.4%	
Annual Unemployment Rate	(June 1992)	7.8%	+1.0%
Annual Inflation Rate	(June 1992)	2.8%	-0.2%

August 11   In Houston at a GOP National Committee gathering, Chairman Rich Bond attacked Hillary Clinton for being anti-family. Governor Clinton said: "I feel sorry for them. It's pitiful."

August 17   Pat Buchanan and former President Ronald Reagan addressed the opening session of the Republican National Convention. Mr. Buchanan's speech created an enormous stir in the broadcast booths and in the "media village."

August 19   President Bush and Vice-President Quayle were renominated by the Republican National Convention. Texas put them over the top.

August 20   President Bush accepted his party's nomination with a long speech in which he apologized for breaking his "no new taxes" pledge and refused to apologize for the time and attention he had given to issues of national security. He said of Governor Clinton's multiple positions on Operation Desert Storm: "He bit his nails. We bit the bullet."

September 1   Economic Indicators as of September 1, 1992   vs. Jan. 1

DJIA	(August 31)	3257.35	+88.52
Annual GDP Growth Rate	(2Q 1992)	1.4%	
Annual Unemployment Rate	(July 1992)	7.7%	+0.9%
Annual Inflation Rate	(July 1992)	3.2%	+0.2%

President Bush traveled to Florida and Louisiana, going to the areas most affected by Hurricane Andrew.

Campaigning in Macon, Georgia, Governor Clinton told a group of senior citizens: "Of the $294 billion in budget cuts over the next five years Mr. Bush proposes, more than 127 billion come from Medicare." The Bush campaign accused Clinton of "fear-mongering."

September 3   Governor Clinton accepted endorsement from AFL-CIO and blasted President Bush for coddling the "rich" with tax breaks and hitting everyone else with (proposed) spending cuts.

Bush campaign chairman Bob Teeter said the campaign will not agree to the debate format and dates proposed by a group seeking to sponsor the events.

September 4	The Sierra Club announced its endorsement of the Clinton-Gore ticket. Mr. Clinton and Mr. Gore attended the media event at Pinnacle Mountain State Park, Arkansas.
	The Labor Department released data showing a slight drop in the unemployment rate (to 7.6%). The data also showed that in August the U.S. economy lost 167,000 jobs. Apparently as a result of the job-loss report, the Federal Reserve Board lowered its "Federal Funds Rate" to 3.0% (from 3.25%)
September 7	Asked about his evasion of the draft, Governor Clinton said reporters should instead be looking into Mr. Bush's record on Iran-Contra.
September 9	Concerning welfare reform, Governor Clinton said: "First, people who can work ought to go to work and no one should be able to stay on welfare forever. And second, no one who does work and who has children in the home should live in poverty as too many are today." He outlined a $6 billion plan of job training, child care, and education.
	President Bush said this about his position on taxes: "I found out the hard way, I went along with one Democratic tax increase, and I'm not going to do it again. Ever. Ever." Later, Marlin Fitzwater said this should not be construed as a pledge not to raise taxes.
September 10	Addressing the Detroit Economic Club, President Bush again spoke of his plan for the economy. He called for $130 billion in spending cuts, which he said would make possible a cut of 1% in tax rates. Bush also talked about his plan in paid television (five-minute) spots on ABC, CBS, and NBC.
September 11	Governor Clinton said he wants every young person to have the chance to go to college, saying the government should give them loans to that end. The students could repay the loans, he said, "by going back home and serving their communities ... , by going home and working for two years in a peace corps here in America to rebuild America." Mr. Clinton also chided Pat Buchanan and the Republican party for trying to divide the country on religious and "family" issues.
September 15	Both President Bush and Governor Clinton addressed a convention of the National Guard Association in Salt Lake City. Mr. Bush spoke movingly of military service. Mr. Clinton said he was ready, willing, and able to be the commander-in-chief of America's armed forces.
September 16	Having received no acceptance from the Bush camp, the debate commission canceled the presidential debate it had promised to conduct next Tuesday in East Lansing, Michigan. Clinton spokeswoman Dee Dee Myers said: "I think it's tragic."
September 17	In an affidavit released in Little Rock, Colonel Eugene Holmes asserted that Clinton lied to him in 1969. The Colonel said he now remembers a conversation with Clinton during which Clinton deceived him "both in concealing his anti-military activities overseas and his counterfeit intentions for later military service."
September 18	Perot supporters turned in petitions seeking to place his name on the Arizona ballot. He already had been certified to be on the ballots in 48 states and certification is pending in New York, where

petitions had previously been filed. Perot (on the "McNeil-Lehrer NewsHour") continued to speak ambiguously in public about his plans.

September 19   In Little Rock, former Joint Chiefs of Staff Chairman, Admiral William Crowe, told reporters: "My discussions and contacts with Governor Clinton have led me to believe that he is the most qualified man to set us on a successful course for the future."

Desert Storm commander Norman Schwartzkopf criticized Governor Clinton, telling *Newsweek:* "How does a person who admits that he deliberately did not agree with the war, and therefore did not want to go to that war, how does he handle it when he has to send other people to war?"

September 20   President Bush hosted a White House gathering of G-7 economic officials who had been meeting in Washington to discuss the European currency crisis. He made a public speech to them in the East Room, during which he said that he would seek to prevent the U.S. presidential campaign from interfering with world economic relationships.

The Clinton campaign began running a so-called negative television spot. The spot uses sound bites of Bush at various times in the past three years saying the economy was in good shape/getting better and juxtaposes them with data re problems in the economy.

September 21   President Bush addressed the U.N. General Assembly, talking about (among other things) the enhanced role of the U.N. peacekeeping forces in the world and the potential future U.S. contribution to those forces.

Speaking about Clinton and the draft on the Rush Limbaugh radio talk show, Mr. Bush said: "The fundamental difficulty is that he [Clinton] has not told the full truth, the whole truth, nothing but the truth ... I think that Governor Clinton ought to level with what happened on this."

Governor Clinton traveled to Chicago to receive the endorsement of a group called "Business Leaders for Change." It was said to be made up of 400 CEOs.

September 22   President Bush, campaigning in states bordering Arkansas, assailed Governor Clinton's record in state government, saying he had failed to control taxes and spending while serving as Arkansas chief executive. Mr. Clinton, campaigning in Michigan, defended his record.

Asked if it was possible he might return to the presidential race, Ross Perot told CBS News "We'll know in a few days,"

While campaigning in Tennessee, President Bush vetoed the "Family Leave" bill, saying it would hurt economic growth.

September 23   The Bush campaign began running a so-called "negative" television spot about Bill Clinton. The ad attacked Clinton for raising taxes while governor and said his plans for economic stimulus would inevitably lead to higher taxes.

September 24   Speaking to employees of a drug company in New Jersey, Governor Clinton gave details of his current health care proposal — basically a plan to require employers to provide health care insurance for employees. The government would provide coverage for the unemployed. It would also set medical spending limits, impose drug price controls and prohibit insurance companies from refusing coverage due to pre-existing conditions.

September 25   A former Reagan National Security Council aide, Howard Teicher, told reporters that he told George Bush in early 1986 that the U.S. was trading arms to Iran in exchange for the release of hostages. President Bush brushed aside Mr. Teicher's allegation.

September 26   President Bush blasted Clinton's plan to increase taxes. Said Bush: "To capture all the revenue that he wants to raise, to pay for all these promises, Bill Clinton will have to go after the middle class. I am not going to let him do that, and neither are you."

September 28   Aides to President Bush and Governor Clinton presented their respective parties' economic plans to the assembled state coordinators of the Ross Perot organization. At the end of the presentation, Ross Perot said he wanted the "volunteers" of the Perot organization to let him know by Thursday whether or not he should re-enter the race for the presidency.

September 29   President proposed that he and Clinton debate on four consecutive Sunday evenings: October 11, 18, and 25 and November 1 (and that there be two vice-presidential debates as well). Bush also said: "If Ross Perot decides to enter the race, I'd be pleased to see him included in these debates."

Senator Gore stated that Bush wanted the American people to see him as the hero who put out a raging fire, but that he was the one who set the fire. "He not only struck the match, he poured gasoline on the flames."

The Consumer Confidence Index (produced by the Conference Board) declined again in September, to 56.4.

September 30   As expected, the House failed to override President Bush's veto of the "Family Leave" bill. The override vote fell short by 27 votes.

October 1   Economic Indicators as of October, 1992   vs. Jan. 1

DJIA	(Sept. 30)	3271.66	+102.83
Annual GDP Growth Rate	(2Q 1992)	1.5%	
Annual Unemployment Rate	(Aug. 1992)	7.6%	+0.8%
Annual Inflation Rate	(Aug. 1992)	3.1%	+0.1%

Ross Perot announced he would become an active candidate for president. Saying he was responding to the wishes of his volunteer supporters, Perot read a statement, which included the following: "My decision in July hurt you. I apologize. I thought I was doing the right thing. I made a mistake. I take full responsibility for it."

October 2   The national unemployment rate declined from 7.6% to 7.5%, according the Bureau of Labor Statistics.

October 3   The Bush and Clinton camps, which on Thursday announced they had reached an agreement on presidential and vice-presidential debates, released the details of that agreement. The plan called for three presidential debates and one vice-presidential debate in various formats.

October 4   Governor Clinton said he approved the NAFTA (North American Free Trade Agreement) accord but said side agreements with

Mexico and Canada will be needed. About them he said: "I'm convinced that I will do it right. I am equally convinced that Mr. Bush won't."

October 6   Ross Perot addressed the nation on CBS-TV via a 30-minute paid commercial. He spoke about the Federal budget, using a pointer and various graphs. The program got a 12.2 Nielsen rating, making it second in its time period.

October 7   President Bush spoke at a ceremony in San Antonio during which NAFTA was initialed by representatives of the U.S., Canada, and Mexico. Mr. Bush spoke of his strong belief in free trade and open markets.

The Perot campaign began running three 60-second TV ads. The spots all used scrolling text, with an announcer voice/over, and were all focused on the economy.

The Clinton campaign began running a "positive" spot saying that Clinton and Gore represented a "new generation of Democrats."

President Bush — saying he was speaking from the heart — commented about Clinton's activities in the 1960s: "I'm just saying, level with the American people on the draft, on whether he went to Moscow, how many demonstrations he led against his own country from … foreign soil. Level. Tell us the truth, and let the voters then decide who to trust."

October 8   Governor Clinton dismissed President Bush's remarks on "Larry King Live," saying he "felt really sad" for Bush that his campaign had "descended to that level." Bush meanwhile renewed his attack on Clinton's patriotism.

October 11   The Bush campaign began running a television spot directly attacking Clinton on the draft.

President Bush, Governor Clinton, and Ross Perot took part in a 90-minute debate from the campus of Washington University in St. Louis. During the course of the debate, Mr. Bush said that if he were re-elected, James Baker would remain in the White House to coordinate a series of new domestic programs.

October 13   Vice-President Quayle, Senator Al Gore and Admiral James Stockdale, the Perot ticket candidate for vice president, participated in a debate in Atlanta. Quayle and Gore engaged in many spirited exchanges; Mr. Stockdale appeared confused and hesitant.

October 14   It was reported today that the U.S. embassies in London and Oslo had been ordered to search their records for any information about Bill Clinton while he was a student in England. The searches were said to be in response to Freedom-of-Information-Act requests from some news organizations.

October 15   The second debate among Bush, Clinton, and Perot was conducted this evening in Richmond, Virginia. The three candidates answered questions from various members of the 209-person audience, who were allegedly "Undecided" voters. The debate was uneventful, although commentators believed Clinton was very effective and that Bush was disinterested.

October 16 — Ross Perot bought another half hour of television time on NBC to outline his proposals for dealing with the national debt. His previous program spelled out the problems as he saw them. This broadcast featured his proposed "solutions" and achieved a 9.0 rating, according to Nielsen Research.

October 17 — The Ross Perot campaign aired two half-hour programs on ABC — an interview with Perot about his life and times and a repeat of the program aired October 16. The program(s) had an 8.0 rating.

October 19 — The third of the three debates between Bush, Clinton, and Perot was held on the campus of Michigan State University. Post-debate analysis was mixed. The broadcast had 44.6 rating, slightly higher than the second debate.

October 25 — In television and print interviews, Ross Perot said one reason for his withdrawal from the race in July was reports he had received that the GOP planned to use a fake picture of one of his daughters to smear her, and also planned to disrupt her wedding ceremony (in August). These charges were flatly denied by numerous Bush campaign representatives and dismissed by others as "crazy."

The New Yorker, which recently acquired a new editor, published a story alleging that in July 1986, George Bush had a conversation with CIA Director William Casey and, as a result, became involved in a complicated scheme with Iraq to help free hostages in Iran. White House spokesman Marlin Fitzwater trashed the report, calling the story "baloney."

October 26 — The Perot campaign began airing six new 60-second spots and three new 30-second spots. All of them continued to focus on national problems, particularly the U.S. economy and related matters.

October 27 — The latest U.S. GDP (Gross Domestic Product) figures were released, showing that in the third-quarter growth was at an annual rate of 2.7%. This was a substantial increase over the second-quarter GDP data. Bush said the figures proved the economy was on the mend, and whacked Clinton for attacking the state of the economy.

October 30 — CNN reported the latest tracking poll numbers from the Gallup Organization. President Bush (40%) and Governor Clinton (41%) were statistically tied in the polling. Ross Perot trailed with 14%.

New counts were added to the Iran-Contra indictment of former defense secretary Caspar Weinberger. In connection with the new indictment, the text of a Weinberger memo was released (apparently for political reasons). The memo appeared to indicate that (then) Vice-President Bush was more informed about details of the arms deal with Iran than he had said he was. Asked for comment, Governor Clinton accused President Bush of lying about his role in the Iran-Contra matter.

October 31– November 2 — President Bush, Governor Clinton, and Ross Perot campaigned in key states across the country in a last dash before election day. President Bush was hounded by questions about his role in the Iran-Contra affair. Governor Clinton all but lost the use of his vocal cords. Ross Perot said: " ... we're going to win all 50 states and drive nuts.

November 1	Economic Indicators as of November 1, 1992		vs. Jan. 1	
	DJIA	(Oct. 30)	3226.28	+57.45
	Annual GDP Growth Rate	(3Q 1992)	2.7%	
	Annual Unemployment Rate	(Sept. 1992)	7.5%	+0.7%
	Annual Inflation Rate	(Sept. 1992)	3.0%	+0.0%

November 2   Governor Clinton and Ross Perot blanketed the airwaves with lengthy paid television broadcasts aimed at winning over late-deciding voters. President Bush chose not to air an election-eve broadcast, although his campaign continued to run 30-second commercials in national and spot advertising markets.

National popular vote result (with rounded percentages), for the three major candidates, with a nominal 100% of the precincts reporting:

Clinton	43,728,375	43%	370 Electors
Bush	38,167,416	37%	168 Electors
Perot	19,237,247	19%	0 Electors
Others	773,170	1%	0 Electors
Total Vote	101,906,208	100%	538 Electors

Ross Perot conceded defeat at his election-night headquarters in Dallas at 10:30 (PM Eastern Time). He said Bill Clinton had won and extended his congratulations to Mr. Clinton.

President Bush conceded defeat at his election-night headquarters in Houston, Texas. Mr. Bush said he planned to get "very active in the grandchild business."

Bill Clinton and Al Gore addressed a large crowd of supporters assembled in front of the old state house in downtown Little Rock, Arkansas. Mr. Clinton spoke for seven minutes. Among other points, Clinton praised President Bush for "his lifetime of service to his country."

APPENDIX

Text of Clinton's Letter to ROTC Director.
Provided by the Clinton for President Campaign.

This is the text of the letter that Arkansas Gov. Bill Clinton wrote to Col. Eugene Holmes, director of the ROTC program at the University of Arkansas, on Dec. 3, 1969:

I am sorry to be so long in writing. I know I promised to let you hear from me at least once a month, and from now on you will but I have had to have some time to think about this first letter. Almost daily since my return to England I have thought about writing, about what I want to and ought to say.

First, I want to thank you, not just for saving me from the draft, but for being so kind and decent to me last summer, when I was as low as I have ever been. One thing which made the bond we struck in good faith somewhat palatable to me was my high regard for you personally. In retrospect, it seems that the admiration might not have been mutual had you known a little more about me, about my political beliefs and activities. At least you might have thought me more fit for the draft than for ROTC.

Let me try to explain. As you know, I worked for two years in a very minor position on the Senate Foreign Relations Committee. I did it for the experience and the salary but also for the opportunity, however small, of working every day against a war I opposed and despised with a depth of feeling I had reserved solely for racism in America before Vietnam. I did not take the matter lightly but studied it carefully, and there was a time when not many people had more information about Vietnam at hand than I did.

I have written and spoken and marched against the war. One of the national organizers of the Vietnam Moratorium is a close friend of mine. After I left Arkansas last summer, I went to Washington to work in the national headquarters of the Moratorium, then to England to organize the Americans here for demonstrations Oct. 15 and Nov. 16.

Interlocked with the war is the draft issue, which I did not begin to consider separately until early 1968. For a law seminar at Georgetown I wrote a paper on the legal arguments for and against allowing, within the Selective Service System, the classification of selective conscientious objection, for those opposed to participation in a particular way, not simply to "participation in war in any form."

From my work I came to believe that the draft system itself is illegitimate. No government really rooted in limited, parliamentary democracy should have the power to make its citizens fight and kill and die in a war they may oppose, a war which even possibly may be wrong, a war which, in any case, does not involve immediately the peace and freedom of the nation. The draft was justified in World War II because the life of the people collectively was at stake. Individuals had to fight, if the nation was to survive, for the lives of their countrymen and their way of life. Vietnam is no such case. Nor was Korea an example where, in my opinion, certain military action was justified but the draft was not, for the reasons stated above.

Because of my opposition to the draft and the war, I am in great sympathy with those who are not willing to fight, kill, and maybe die for their country (i.e. the particular policy of a particular government) right or wrong. Two of my friends at Oxford are conscientious objectors. I wrote a letter of recommendation for one of them to his Mississippi draft board, a letter which I am more proud of than anything else I wrote at Oxford last year. One of my roommates is a draft resister who is possibly under indictment and may never be able to go home again. He is one of the bravest, best men I know. His country needs men like him more than they know. That he is considered a criminal is an obscenity.

The decision not to be a resister and the related subsequent decisions were the most difficult of my life. I decided to accept the draft in spite of my beliefs for one reason: to maintain my political viability within the system. For years I have worked to prepare myself for a political life characterized by both practical political ability and concern for rapid social progress. It is a life I still feel compelled to try to lead. I do not think our system of government is by definition corrupt, however dangerous and inadequate it has been in recent years. (The society may be corrupt, but that is not the same thing, and if that is true we are all finished anyway.)

When the draft came, despite political convictions, I was having a hard time facing the prospect of fighting a war I had been fighting against, and that is why I contacted you. ROTC was the one way left in which I could possibly, but not positively, avoid both Vietnam and resistance. Going on with my education, even coming back to England, played no part in my decision to join ROTC. I am back here, and would have been at Arkansas Law School because there is nothing else I can do. In fact, I would like to have been able to take a year out perhaps to teach in a small college or work on some community action project and in the process to decide whether to attend law school or graduate school and how to begin putting what I have learned to use.

But the particulars of my personal life are not nearly as important to me as the principles involved. After I signed the ROTC letter of intent I began to wonder whether the compromise I had made with myself was not more objectionable than the draft would have been, because I had no interest in the ROTC program in itself and all I seemed to have done was to protect myself from physical harm. Also, I began to think I had deceived you, not by lies (there were none) but by failing to tell you all the things I'm writing now. I doubt that I had the mental coherence to articulate them then.

At that time, after we had made our agreement and you had sent my I-D deferment to my draft board, the anguish and loss of my self-respect and self-confidence really set in. I hardly slept for weeks and kept going by eating compulsively and reading until exhaustion brought sleep. Finally, on Sept. 12 I stayed up all night writing a letter to the chairman of my draft board, saying basically what is in the preceding paragraph, thanking him for trying to help in a case where he really couldn't, and stating that I couldn't do the ROTC after all and would he please draft me as soon as possible.

I never mailed the letter, but I did carry it on me every day until I got on the plane to return to England. I didn't mail the letter because I didn't see, in the end, how my going in the army and maybe going to Vietnam would achieve anything except a feeling that I had punished myself and gotten what I deserved. So I came back to England to try to make something of this second year of my Rhodes scholarship.

And that is where I am now, writing to you because you have been good to me and have a right to know what I think and feel. I am writing too in the hope that my telling this one story will help you to understand more clearly how so many fine people have come to find themselves still loving their country but loathing the military, to which you and other good men have devoted years, lifetimes, of the best service you could give. To many of us, it is no longer clear what is service and what is disservice, or if it is clear, the conclusion is likely to be illegal. Forgive the length of his letter. There was much to say. There is still a lot to be said, but it can wait. Please say hello to Col. Jones for me.

> Merry Christmas.
>
> Sincerely,
> *Bill Clinton*

National Three-Way Trial Heats with Likely Voters
October 30, 1992

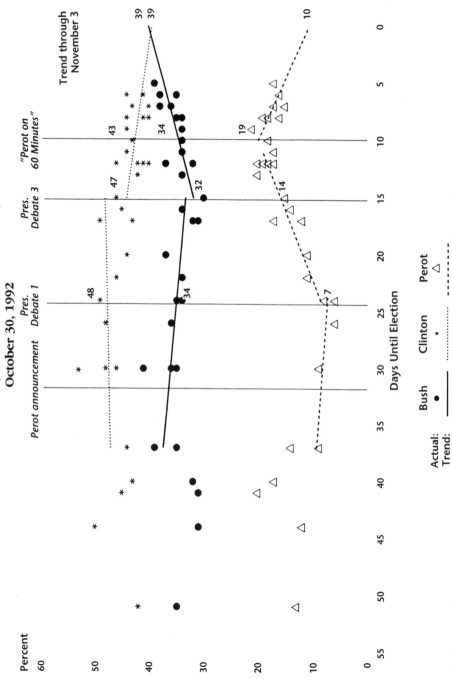

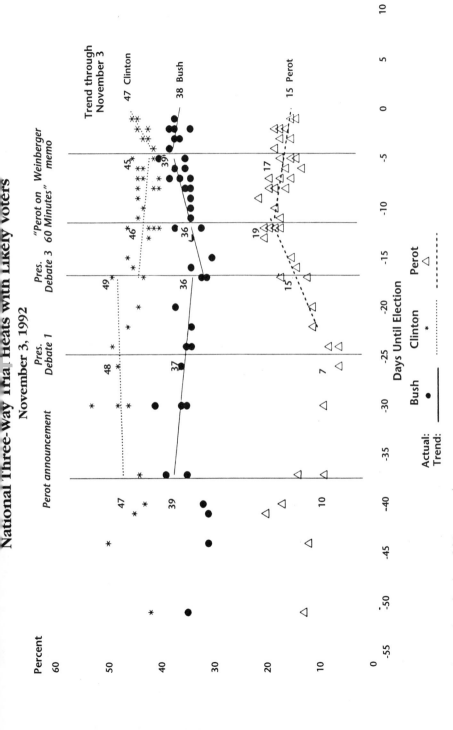

National Three-Way Trial Heats with Likely Voters
November 3, 1992

Trends are of results since GOP convention

Vote for President
November 3, 1992, General Election*

State	Total	Clinton (DEM)	Bush (REP)	Perot (IND)	Other	Plurality Total	Party	DEM	REP	IND	Other	Rank DEM	Rank REP	Rank IND	Total	DEM	REP	IND	DEM	REP
Alabama	1,688,060	690,080	804,283	183,109	10,588	114,203	R	40.9	47.6	10.8	0.6	29	3	47	1.6	1.5	2.1	0.9	46.2	53
Alaska	258,506	78,294	102,000	73,481	4,731	23,706	R	30.3	39.5	28.4	1.8	48	21	2	0.2	0.2	0.3	0.4	43.4	56
Arizona	1,486,975	543,050	572,086	353,741	18,098	29,036	R	36.5	38.5	23.8	1.2	43	23	11	1.4	1.2	1.5	1.8	48.7	51
Arkansas	950,653	505,823	337,324	99,132	8,374	168,499	D	53.2	35.5	10.4	0.9	2	35	48	0.9	1.1	0.9	0.5	60.0	40
California	11,131,721	5,121,325	3,630,574	2,296,006	83,816	1,490,751	D	46.0	32.6	20.6	0.8	12	43	27	10.7	11.4	9.3	11.6	58.5	41
Colorado	1,569,180	629,681	562,850	366,010	10,639	66,831	D	40.1	35.9	23.3	0.7	33	32	14	1.5	1.4	1.4	1.9	52.8	47
Connecticut	1,616,332	682,318	578,313	348,771	6,930	104,005	D	42.2	35.8	21.6	0.4	27	33	24	1.5	1.5	1.5	1.8	54.1	45
Delaware	289,735	126,054	102,313	59,213	2,155	23,741	D	43.5	35.3	20.4	0.7	19	37	28	0.3	0.3	0.3	0.3	55.2	44
Florida	5,314,392	2,072,698	2,173,310	1,053,067	15,317	100,612	R	39.0	40.9	19.8	0.3	35	16	29	5.1	4.6	5.6	5.3	48.8	51
Georgia	2,321,125	1,008,966	995,252	309,657	7,250	13,714	D	43.5	42.9	13.3	0.3	20	9	44	2.2	2.2	2.5	1.6	50.3	49
Hawaii	372,842	179,310	136,822	53,003	3,707	42,488	D	48.1	36.7	14.2	1.0	7	29	39	0.4	0.4	0.3	0.3	56.7	43
Idaho	482,142	137,013	202,645	130,395	12,089	65,632	R	28.4	42.0	27.0	2.5	50	13	4	0.5	0.3	0.5	0.7	40.3	58
Illinois	5,050,157	2,453,350	1,734,096	840,515	22,196	719,254	D	48.6	34.3	16.6	0.4	5	40	34	4.8	5.5	4.4	4.3	58.6	41
Indiana	2,305,871	848,420	989,375	455,934	12,142	140,955	R	36.8	42.9	19.8	0.5	42	10	30	2.2	1.9	2.5	2.3	46.2	53
Iowa	1,354,607	586,353	504,891	253,468	9,895	81,462	D	43.3	37.3	18.7	0.7	23	26	32	1.3	1.3	1.3	1.3	53.7	46
Kansas	1,157,335	390,434	449,951	312,358	4,592	59,517	R	33.7	38.9	27.0	0.4	46	22	5	1.1	0.9	1.2	1.6	46.5	53
Kentucky	1,492,900	665,104	617,178	203,944	6,674	47,926	D	44.6	41.3	13.7	0.4	16	14	41	1.4	1.5	1.6	1.0	51.9	48
Louisiana	1,790,017	815,971	733,386	211,478	29,182	82,585	D	45.6	41.0	11.8	1.6	14	15	45	1.7	1.8	1.9	1.1	52.7	47
Maine	679,499	263,420	206,504	206,820	2,755	56,600	D	38.8	30.4	30.4	0.4	37	47	1	0.7	0.6	0.5	1.0	56.1	44
Maryland	1,985,046	988,571	707,094	281,414	7,967	281,477	D	49.8	35.6	14.2	0.4	3	34	40	1.9	2.2	1.8	1.4	58.3	42
Massachusetts	2,773,700	1,318,662	805,049	630,731	19,258	513,613	D	47.5	29.0	22.7	0.7	8	49	19	2.7	2.9	2.1	3.2	62.1	38
Michigan	4,274,673	1,871,182	1,554,940	824,813	23,738	316,242	D	43.8	36.4	19.3	0.6	18	30	31	4.1	4.2	4.0	4.2	54.6	45
Minnesota	2,347,948	1,020,997	747,841	562,506	16,604	273,156	D	43.5	31.9	24.0	0.7	21	46	10	2.2	2.3	1.9	2.8	57.7	42
Mississippi	981,793	400,258	487,793	85,626	8,116	87,535	R	40.8	49.7	8.7	0.8	30	1	50	0.9	0.9	1.2	0.4	45.1	54
Missouri	2,391,565	1,053,873	811,159	518,741	7,792	242,714	D	44.1	33.9	21.7	0.3	17	41	23	2.3	2.3	2.1	2.6	56.5	44
Montana	410,611	154,507	144,207	107,225	4,672	10,300	D	37.6	35.1	26.1	1.1	38	38	7	0.4	0.3	0.4	0.5	51.7	48
Nebraska	737,546	216,864	343,678	174,104	2,900	126,814	R	29.4	46.6	23.6	0.4	49	4	13	0.7	0.5	0.9	0.9	38.7	61
Nevada	506,318	189,148	175,828	132,580	8,762	13,320	D	37.4	34.7	26.2	1.7	39	39	6	0.5	0.4	0.4	0.7	51.8	48
New Hampshire	537,943	209,040	202,484	121,337	5,082	6,556	D	38.9	37.6	22.6	0.9	36	25	20	0.5	0.5	0.5	0.6	50.8	49
New Jersey	3,343,594	1,436,206	1,356,865	521,829	28,694	79,341	D	43.0	40.6	15.6	0.9	24	8	38	3.2	3.3	3.3	2.6	51.4	4
New Mexico	569,986	261,617	212,824	91,895	3,650	48,793	D	45.9	37.3	16.1	0.6	13	27	35	0.5	0.6	0.5	0.5	55.1	4
New York¹	6,926,925	3,444,450	2,346,649	1,090,721	45,105	1,097,801	D	49.7	33.9	15.7	0.7	4	42	37	6.6	7.7	6.0	5.5	59.5	4
North Carolina	2,611,850	1,114,042	1,134,661	357,864	5,283	20,619	R	42.7	43.4	13.7	0.2	25	7	42	2.5	2.5	2.9	1.8	49.5	5
North Dakota	308,133	99,168	136,244	71,084	1,637	37,076	R	32.2	44.2	23.1	0.5	47	6	16	0.3	0.2	0.3	0.5	42.2	5
Ohio	4,939,967	1,984,942	1,894,310	1,036,426	24,289	90,632	D	40.2	38.3	21.0	0.5	32	24	26	4.7	4.4	4.8	5.2	51.2	4
Oklahoma	1,390,359	473,066	592,929	319,878	4,486	119,863	R	34.0	42.6	23.0	0.3	44	11	17	1.3	1.1	1.5	1.6	44.4	5
Oregon	1,462,643	621,314	475,757	354,091	11,481	145,557	D	42.5	32.5	24.2	0.8	26	44	9	1.4	1.4	1.2	1.8	56.6	4
Pennsylvania	4,959,810	2,239,164	1,791,841	902,667	26,138	447,323	D	45.1	36.1	18.2	0.5	15	33	33	4.7	5.0	4.6	4.6	55.5	4
Rhode Island	453,471	213,299	131,601	105,045	3,526	81,698	D	47.0	29.0	23.2	0.8	10	50	15	0.4	0.5	0.3	0.5	61.8	3
South Carolina	1,202,527	479,514	577,507	138,872	6,634	97,993	R	39.9	48.0	11.5	0.6	34	2	46	1.2	1.1	1.5	1.1	45.4	5
South Dakota	336,254	124,888	136,718	73,295	1,353	11,830	R	37.1	40.7	21.8	0.4	40	17	22	0.3	0.3	0.3	0.4	47.7	5
Tennessee	1,982,638	933,521	841,300	199,968	7,849	92,221	D	47.1	42.4	10.1	0.4	9	12	49	1.9	2.1	2.2	1.2	52.6	4
Texas	6,154,018	2,281,815	2,496,071	1,354,781	21,351	214,256	R	37.1	40.6	22.0	0.3	41	19	21	5.9	5.1	6.4	6.9	47.8	5
Utah	743,999	183,429	322,632	203,400	34,538	119,232	R	24.7	43.4	27.3	4.6	51	8	3	0.7	0.4	0.8	1.0	36.2	6
Vermont	289,701	133,592	88,122	65,991	1,996	45,470	D	46.1	30.4	22.8	0.7	11	48	18	0.3	0.3	0.2	0.3	60.3	3
Virginia	2,558,665	1,038,650	1,150,517	348,639	20,859	111,867	R	40.6	45.0	13.6	0.8	31	5	43	2.5	2.3	2.9	1.8	47.4	5
Washington	2,288,230	993,037	731,234	541,780	22,179	261,803	D	43.4	32.0	23.7	1.0	22	45	12	2.2	2.2	1.9	2.7	57.6	4
West Virginia	683,762	331,001	241,974	108,829	1,958	89,027	D	48.4	35.4	15.9	0.3	6	36	36	0.7	0.7	0.6	0.6	57.8	4
Wisconsin	2,531,114	1,041,066	930,855	544,479	14,714	110,211	D	41.1	36.8	21.5	0.6	28	28	25	2.4	2.3	2.4	2.8	52.8	4
Wyoming	200,617	68,160	79,347	51,263	1,847	11,187	R	34.0	39.6	25.6	0.9	45	20	8	0.2	0.2	0.2	0.3	46.2	5
District of Columbia	227,572	192,619	20,698	9,681	4,574	171,921	D	84.6	9.1	4.3	2.0	1	51	51	0.2	0.4	<.1	<.1	90.3	
UNITED STATES	104,425,027	44,909,326	39,103,882	19,741,657	670,162	5,805,444	D	43.0	37.4	18.9	0.6				100.0	100.0	100.0	100.0	53.5	4

¹Democratic vote also includes ballots cast for Clinton-Gore as nominees of the Liberal party; Republican vote also includes ballots for Bush-Quayle as nominees of (the con-)servative and Right to Life parties.

Vote for Presidential Preference:
Republican Primary Election 1992*

State	Total	Bush	Bu-chanan	Uncom-mitted	Others	Bush	Bu-chanan	Uncom-mitted	Other	Bush	Bu-chanan	Uncom-mitted	Other	Total	Bush	Bu-chanan	Uncom-mitted	Other
	Top candidates					Top four candidates (state vote) — Percent of total vote				Rank¹				Percent contribution to national vote¹				
Alabama	165,121	122,703	12,588	29,830	-	74.3	7.6	18.1	-	13	35	4	-	1.3	1.3	0.4	17.1	-
Alaska	-	-	-	-	-	-	-	-	-	-	-	-	-	-	-	-	-	-
Arizona	-	-	-	-	-	-	-	-	-	-	-	-	-	-	-	-	-	-
Arkansas	54,883	45,590	6,551	2,742	-	83.1	11.9	5.0	-	3	31	7	-	0.4	0.5	0.2	1.6	-
California	2,156,261	1,587,369	568,892	-	-	73.6	26.4	-	-	14	10	-	-	17.0	17.3	19.6	-	-
Colorado	195,690	132,100	58,753	-	4,837	67.5	30.0	-	2.5	24	5	-	21	1.5	1.4	2.0	-	1.2
Connecticut	99,473	66,356	21,815	9,008	2,294	66.7	21.9	9.1	2.3	29	18	5	23	0.8	0.7	0.8	5.2	0.6
Delaware	-	-	-	-	-	-	-	-	-	-	-	-	-	-	-	-	-	-
Florida	893,463	608,077	285,386	-	-	68.1	31.9	-	-	23	3	-	-	7.0	6.6	9.8	-	-
Georgia	453,990	291,905	162,085	-	-	64.3	35.7	-	-	31	2	-	-	3.6	3.2	5.6	-	-
Hawaii	-	-	-	-	-	-	-	-	-	-	-	-	-	-	-	-	-	-
Idaho	115,502	73,297	15,167	-	27,038	63.5	13.1	-	23.4	34	30	-	1	0.9	0.8	0.5	-	6.7
Illinois	831,140	634,588	186,915	-	9,637	76.4	22.5	-	1.2	10	16	-	24	6.6	6.9	6.4	-	2.4
Indiana	467,615	374,666	92,949	-	-	80.1	19.9	-	-	8	19	-	-	3.7	4.1	3.2	-	-
Iowa	-	-	-	-	-	-	-	-	-	-	-	-	-	-	-	-	-	-
Kansas	213,196	132,131	31,494	-	49,571	62.0	14.8	-	23.3	37	27	-	2	1.7	1.4	1.1	-	12.3
Kentucky	101,119	75,371	-	25,748	-	74.5	-	25.5	-	12	-	3	-	0.8	0.8	-	14.7	-
Louisiana	135,109	83,744	36,525	-	14,840	62.0	27.0	-	11.0	36	8	-	8	1.1	0.9	1.3	-	3.7
Maine	-	-	-	-	-	-	-	-	-	-	-	-	-	-	-	-	-	-
Maryland	240,021	168,374	71,647	-	-	70.1	29.9	-	-	19	6	-	-	1.9	1.8	2.5	-	-
Massachusetts²	269,701	176,868	74,797	-	18,036	65.6	27.7	-	6.7	30	7	-	13	2.1	1.9	2.6	-	4.5
Michigan	449,133	301,948	112,122	23,809	11,254	67.2	25.0	5.3	2.5	25	12	6	20	3.5	3.3	3.9	13.6	2.8
Minnesota	132,756	84,841	32,094	4,098	11,723	63.9	24.2	3.1	8.8	32	13	9	11	1.0	0.9	1.1	2.3	2.9
Mississippi	154,708	111,794	25,891	-	17,023	72.3	16.7	-	11.0	16	23	-	7	1.2	1.2	0.9	-	4.2
Missouri	-	-	-	-	-	-	-	-	-	-	-	-	-	-	-	-	-	-
Montana	90,975	65,176	10,701	-	15,098	71.6	11.8	-	16.6	17	32	-	5	0.7	0.7	0.4	-	3.7
Nebraska	192,098	156,346	25,847	-	9,905	81.4	13.5	-	5.2	5	29	-	15	1.5	1.7	0.9	-	2.5
Nevada	-	-	-	-	-	-	-	-	-	-	-	-	-	-	-	-	-	-
New Hampshire	174,167	92,233	65,087	-	16,847	53.0	37.4	-	9.7	38	1	-	10	1.4	1.0	2.2	-	4.2
New Jersey	286,967	240,535	46,432	-	-	83.8	16.2	-	-	1	26	-	-	2.3	2.6	1.6	-	-
New Mexico	86,967	55,522	7,871	23,574	-	63.8	9.1	27.1	-	33	34	2	-	0.7	0.6	0.3	13.5	-
New York	-	-	-	-	-	-	-	-	-	-	-	-	-	-	-	-	-	-
North Carolina	283,571	200,387	55,420	-	27,764	70.7	19.5	-	9.8	18	20	-	9	2.2	2.2	1.9	-	6.9
North Dakota	49,428	39,863	-	-	9,565	80.6	-	-	19.4	6	-	-	4	0.4	0.4	-	-	2.4
Ohio	860,453	716,766	143,687	-	-	83.3	16.7	-	-	2	24	-	-	6.8	7.8	5.0	-	-
Oklahoma	217,721	151,612	57,933	-	8,176	69.6	26.6	-	3.8	21	9	-	17	1.7	1.6	2.0	-	2.0
Oregon	304,159	203,957	57,730	-	42,472	67.1	19.0	-	14.0	26	21	-	6	2.4	2.2	2.0	-	10.5
Pennsylvania	1,008,777	774,865	233,912	-	-	76.8	23.2	-	-	9	15	-	-	8.0	8.4	8.1	-	-
Rhode Island	15,636	9,853	4,967	444	372	63.0	31.8	2.8	2.4	35	4	10	22	0.1	0.1	0.2	0.3	<.1
South Carolina	148,840	99,558	38,247	-	11,035	66.9	25.7	-	7.4	28	11	-	12	1.2	1.1	1.3	-	2.7
South Dakota	44,671	30,964	-	13,707	-	69.3	-	30.7	-	22	-	1	-	0.4	0.3	-	7.8	-
Tennessee	245,653	178,219	54,548	5,022	7,827	72.5	22.2	2.0	3.2	15	17	11	18	1.9	1.9	1.9	2.9	1.9
Texas	797,146	556,280	190,572	27,936	22,358	69.8	23.9	3.5	2.8	20	14	8	19	6.3	6.0	6.6	16.0	5.5
Utah	-	-	-	-	-	-	-	-	-	-	-	-	-	-	-	-	-	-
Vermont	-	-	-	-	-	-	-	-	-	-	-	-	-	-	-	-	-	-
Virginia	-	-	-	-	-	-	-	-	-	-	-	-	-	-	-	-	-	-
Washington	129,655	86,839	13,273	-	29,543	67.0	10.2	-	22.8	27	33	-	3	1.0	0.9	0.5	-	7.3
West Virginia	124,157	99,994	18,067	-	6,096	80.5	14.6	-	4.9	7	28	-	16	1.0	1.1	0.6	-	1.5
Wisconsin	482,248	364,507	78,516	8,725	30,500	75.6	16.3	1.8	6.3	11	25	12	14	3.8	4.0	2.7	5.0	7.6
Wyoming	-	-	-	-	-	-	-	-	-	-	-	-	-	-	-	-	-	-
District of Columbia	5,235	4,265	970	-	-	81.5	18.5	-	-	4	22	-	-	<.1	<.1	<.1	-	-
UNITED STATES	12,677,405	9,199,463	2,899,488	174,643	403,811	72.6	22.9	1.4	3.2					100.0	100.0	100.0	100.0	100.0

¹Limited to the 37 states and the District of Columbia that held Republican presidential primaries. ²Does not include corrected vote for the Massachusetts category "all others", which would increase the vote for other candidates to 18,037 and the state total vote to 269,702.

*Copyright 1993 by Election Data Services, Inc., *The Election Data Book: A Statistical Portrait of Voting in America.* Reprinted with permission.

Vote for Presidential Preference:
Democratic Primary Election 1992*

| State | Top candidates | | | | | | | | | Top three candidates(national vote) | | | | | | | | | |
| | | | | | | | | | | Percent of total vote | | | Rank¹ | | | Percent contribution to national vote¹ | | | |
	Total	Clinton	Brown	Tsongas	Uncom-mitted	Kerrey	Harkin	LaRouche	Others	Clinton	Brown	Tsongas	Clinton	Brown	Tsongas	Total	Clinton	Brown	Tsongas
Alabama	450,899	307,621	30,626	-	90,863	-	-	6,542	15,247	68.2	6.8	-	6	35	-	2.2	2.9	0.8	-
Alaska	-	-	-	-	-	-	-	-	-	-	-	-	-	-	-	-	-	-	-
Arizona	-	-	-	-	-	-	-	-	-	-	-	-	-	-	-	-	-	-	-
Arkansas	502,617	342,017	55,234	-	90,710	-	-	14,656	-	68.0	11.0	-	7	25	-	2.5	3.3	1.4	-
California	2,863,419	1,359,112	1,150,460	212,522	-	33,935	-	21,971	85,419	47.5	40.2	7.4	24	1	30	14.1	13.0	28.3	5.8
Colorado	239,643	64,470	69,073	61,360	-	29,572	5,866	328	8,974	26.9	28.8	25.6	34	6	8	1.2	0.6	1.7	1.7
Connecticut	173,119	61,698	64,472	33,811	5,430	1,169	1,919	896	3,724	35.6	37.2	19.5	31	2	12	0.9	0.6	1.6	0.9
Delaware	-	-	-	-	-	-	-	-	-	-	-	-	-	-	-	-	-	-	-
Florida	1,123,857	570,566	139,569	388,124	-	12,011	13,587	-	-	50.8	12.4	34.5	21	23	4	5.6	5.4	3.4	10.6
Georgia	454,631	259,907	36,808	109,148	17,256	22,033	9,479	-	-	57.2	8.1	24.0	15	31	9	2.2	2.5	0.9	3.0
Hawaii	-	-	-	-	-	-	-	-	-	-	-	-	-	-	-	-	-	-	-
Idaho	55,124	27,004	9,212	-	-	-	-	2,011	16,897	49.0	16.7	-	23	19	-	0.3	0.3	0.2	-
Illinois	1,504,130	776,829	220,346	387,891	67,612	10,916	30,710	6,599	3,227	51.6	14.6	25.8	19	20	7	7.4	7.4	5.4	10.6
Indiana	476,850	301,905	102,377	58,215	-	14,353	-	-	-	63.3	21.5	12.2	12	11	20	2.4	2.9	2.5	1.6
Iowa	-	-	-	-	-	-	-	-	-	-	-	-	-	-	-	-	-	-	-
Kansas	160,251	82,145	20,811	24,413	-	2,215	940	631	29,096	51.3	13.0	15.2	20	22	17	0.8	0.8	0.5	0.7
Kentucky	370,578	207,804	30,709	18,097	103,590	3,242	7,136	-	-	56.1	8.3	4.9	17	28	34	1.8	2.0	0.8	0.5
Louisiana	384,397	267,002	25,480	42,508	-	2,984	4,033	3,082	39,308	69.5	6.6	11.1	5	36	22	1.9	2.5	0.6	1.2
Maine	-	-	-	-	-	-	-	-	-	-	-	-	-	-	-	-	-	-	-
Maryland	567,224	189,906	46,480	230,490	36,155	27,035	32,899	4,259	-	33.5	8.2	40.6	32	29	3	2.8	1.8	1.1	6.3
Massachusetts²	792,885	86,817	115,746	526,297	-	5,409	3,764	2,167	52,685	10.9	14.6	66.4	39	21	1	3.9	0.8	2.8	14.4
Michigan	585,972	297,280	151,400	97,017	27,836	3,219	6,265	2,049	906	50.7	25.8	16.6	22	8	16	2.9	2.8	3.7	2.7
Minnesota	204,170	63,584	62,474	43,588	11,366	1,191	4,077	532	17,358	31.1	30.6	21.3	33	5	11	1.0	0.6	1.5	1.2
Mississippi	191,357	139,893	18,396	15,538	11,796	1,660	2,509	1,394	171	73.1	9.6	8.1	3	27	29	0.9	1.3	0.5	0.4
Missouri	-	-	-	-	-	-	-	-	-	-	-	-	-	-	-	-	-	-	-
Montana	117,471	54,989	21,704	12,614	-	-	-	-	28,164	46.8	18.5	10.7	25	16	23	0.6	0.5	0.5	0.3
Nebraska	150,587	68,562	31,673	10,707	24,714	-	4,239	1,148	9,544	45.5	21.0	7.1	26	12	31	0.7	0.7	0.8	0.3
Nevada	-	-	-	-	-	-	-	-	-	-	-	-	-	-	-	-	-	-	-
New Hampshire	167,800	41,522	13,654	55,638	-	18,575	17,057	-	21,354	24.7	8.1	33.2	35	30	5	0.8	0.4	0.3	1.5
New Jersey	392,744	256,337	79,877	45,191	-	-	-	7,799	3,540	65.3	20.3	11.5	10	13	21	1.9	2.4	2.0	1.2
New Mexico	181,537	95,933	30,705	11,409	35,269	-	3,233	2,415	2,573	52.8	16.9	6.3	18	17	33	0.9	0.9	0.8	0.3
New York	1,007,726	412,349	264,278	288,330	-	11,147	11,535	-	20,087	40.9	26.2	28.6	29	7	6	5.0	3.9	6.5	7.9
North Carolina	691,875	443,498	71,984	57,589	-	6,216	5,891	-	106,697	64.1	10.4	8.3	11	26	28	3.4	4.2	1.8	1.6
North Dakota	32,786	4,760	-	-	-	-	-	7,003	21,023	14.5	-	-	38	-	-	0.2	<.1	-	-
Ohio	1,042,335	638,347	197,449	110,773	-	22,976	25,395	17,412	29,983	61.2	18.9	10.6	14	14	24	5.2	6.1	4.8	3.0
Oklahoma	416,129	293,266	69,624	-	-	13,252	14,015	6,474	19,498	70.5	16.7	-	4	18	-	2.1	2.8	1.7	-
Oregon	354,332	159,802	110,494	37,139	-	-	-	3,096	43,801	45.1	31.2	10.5	27	4	25	1.8	1.5	2.7	1.0
Pennsylvania	1,265,495	715,031	325,543	161,572	-	20,802	21,013	21,534	-	56.5	25.7	12.8	16	9	19	6.3	6.8	8.0	4.4
Rhode Island	50,709	10,762	9,541	26,825	703	469	319	300	1,790	21.2	18.8	52.9	36	15	2	0.3	0.1	0.2	0.7
South Carolina	116,414	73,221	6,961	21,338	3,640	566	7,657	204	2,827	62.9	6.0	18.3	13	37	15	0.6	0.7	0.2	0.6
South Dakota	59,503	11,375	2,300	5,729	-	23,892	15,023	441	743	19.1	3.9	9.6	37	38	27	0.3	0.1	<.1	0.3
Tennessee	318,482	214,485	25,560	61,717	12,551	1,638	2,099	-	432	67.3	8.0	19.4	8	32	13	1.6	2.0	0.6	1.1
Texas	1,482,975	972,151	118,923	285,191	-	20,298	19,617	12,220	54,575	65.6	8.0	19.2	9	33	14	7.3	9.3	2.9	7.0
Utah	-	-	-	-	-	-	-	-	-	-	-	-	-	-	-	-	-	-	-
Vermont	-	-	-	-	-	-	-	-	-	-	-	-	-	-	-	-	-	-	-
Virginia	-	-	-	-	-	-	-	-	-	-	-	-	-	-	-	-	-	-	-
Washington	147,981	62,171	34,111	18,981	-	1,489	1,858	1,060	28,311	42.0	23.1	12.8	28	10	18	0.7	0.6	0.8	0.4
West Virginia	306,866	227,815	36,505	21,271	-	3,152	2,774	3,141	12,208	74.2	11.9	6.9	1	24	32	1.5	2.2	0.9	0.
Wisconsin	772,596	287,356	266,207	168,619	15,487	3,044	5,395	3,120	23,368	37.2	34.5	21.8	30	3	10	3.8	2.7	6.5	4.
Wyoming	-	-	-	-	-	-	-	-	-	-	-	-	-	-	-	-	-	-	-
District of Columbia	61,904	45,716	4,444	6,452	5,292	-	-	-	-	73.8	7.2	10.4	2	34	26	0.3	0.4	0.1	0.
UNITED STATES	20,239,370	10,495,008	4,071,210	3,656,104	560,270	318,460	280,304	154,484	703,530	51.9	20.1	18.1				100.0	100.0	100.0	100.

¹Limited to the 38 states and the District of Columbia that held Democratic presidential primaries. ²Does not include corrected vote for the Massachusetts categories "no preference" and "all others", which would increase the vote for other candidates to 53,915 and the state total vote to 794,115.

INDEX

Index